RAGE AND
CARNAGE *in* THE
NAME OF GOD

RELIGIOUS CULTURES OF AFRICAN AND AFRICAN DIASPORA PEOPLE

Series editors: Jacob K. Olupona, Harvard University   Dianne M. Stewart, Emory University
and Terrence L. Johnson, Georgetown University

The book series examines the religious, cultural, and political expressions of African, African American, and African Caribbean traditions. Through transnational, cross-cultural, and multi-disciplinary approaches to the study of religion, the series investigates the epistemic boundaries of continental and diasporic religious practices and thought and explores the diverse and distinct ways African-derived religions inform culture and politics. The series aims to establish a forum for imagining the centrality of Black religions in the formation of the "New World."

RAGE AND CARNAGE *in* THE NAME OF GOD

RELIGIOUS VIOLENCE IN NIGERIA

Abiodun Alao

Duke University Press   *Durham and London*   2022

Typeset in Portrait by Westchester Publishing Services

Library of Congress Cataloging-in-Publication Data
Names: Alao, Abiodun, author.
Title: Rage and carnage in the name of God : religious violence in Nigeria /
Abiodun Alao.
Other titles: Religious cultures of African and African diaspora people.
Description: Durham : Duke University Press, 2022. | Series: Religious
cultures of African and African diaspora people | Includes bibliographical
references and index.
Identifiers: LCCN 2021049658 (print) | LCCN 2021049659 (ebook)
ISBN 9781478015536 (hardcover)
ISBN 9781478018162 (paperback)
ISBN 9781478022770 (ebook)
Subjects: LCSH: Religion and politics—Nigeria. | Violence—Nigeria—
Religious aspects. | Intergroup relations—Nigeria. | Religion and culture—
Nigeria. | Nigeria—History—1960– | BISAC: HISTORY / Africa / West |
RELIGION / Christianity / General Classification: LCC BL65.P7 A44 2022
(print) | LCC BL65.P7 (ebook) | DDC 201/.7209669—dc23/eng/2022118
LC record available at https://lccn.loc.gov/2021049658
LC ebook record available at https://lccn.loc.gov/2021049659

Cover art: Background courtesy istockphoto.com/modify260 and map
courtesy shutterstock.com/windwheel.

Another one to the memories of
Nathaniel Ojo and Abigail Mojoyinola

The wonderful people who gave me life
Gbogbo ibikíbi tí ẹ bá wà, ilẹ̀ ire o
(May whichever grounds on which you are resting be blessed)

Contents

Scholarship is more of a collaborative enterprise than we tend to admit when we put just a single name on the cover page of any book, and this book, like most others, is a collective effort displaying the name of a single individual. Although I have long been interested in religious violence in Nigeria, having experienced the early parts of the 1980 Maitatsine religious riots in Kano and having lost a first cousin in one of the city's numerous religious conflicts, my first sustained academic interest in the subject came in 2007 when, along with Professors Funmi Olonisakin and James Gow, I worked on an Economic and Social Research Council grant awarded to King's College London on religious radicalization and political violence in West Africa. However, this book owes more to another grant, this one from the Carnegie Corporation of New York to the African Leadership Centre at King's College London's School of Global Affairs to research peace, society, and the state in Africa. My first debts are to these institutions for these awards.

My list of individual appreciations is long. To start with, I am grateful to my colleagues at the African Leadership Centre. The friendship within the team is much more than superficial camaraderie. It is as genuine as it is all-encompassing. First to be mentioned at the Centre, of course, is Professor Funmi Olonisakin. After more than thirty years together at King's College London, Funmi and I have become a "professional item." Together, we passed through the flames of hardship, and emerged purified! I thank the other members of the team: Drs. Eka Ikpe, Olawale Ismail, Barney Walsh, David Mwambari, Olaf Batchman, Sarah Nyeri, and Sonja Theron. Similarly to be recognized at the Centre are Shuvai Nyoni, Adeoti Dipeolu, Nayanka Perdigao, Telema Georgewill, Fola Aina, Damilola Adegoke, Kingsley Chukwu, Sylvanus Wekesa, Ademijulo Obafemi-Olopade, Alfred Muteru, and Jacob Kamau.

Also important to be acknowledged at King's College London are the lifelong career opportunities offered by Professor (Sir) Lawrence Freedman. Indeed, if there be any (as I guess there may be a few) who rejoice at what I have been able to achieve in my career, it is to God and Sir Lawrence that their gratitude is due. I also want to mention the friendship and support of Professor Jack Spence, Dr. Barrie Paskin, and professors Keith Hoggart, Frans Berkhout, James Gow, and Mats Berdal. Thanks too to Professor James Mayall, Emeritus Sir Patrick Sahee Professor of International Relations at Cambridge, for his friendship over the decades.

My very deep gratitude also goes to the following people: Professors Jacob Olupona, the doyen of religious studies in Nigeria; Simeon Ilesanmi, whose knowledge on the philosophical underpinnings of religion in Nigeria is unrivaled; Wale Adebanwi, whose exceptional brilliance made me take a second look at issues; and Olufemi Taiwo, whose originality of thought has made a tremendous impact on me over the decades. Professors Toyin Falola, Olufemi Vaughan, Mathews Ojo, Ebenezer Obadare, the late Abdul Raufu Mustapha, and Dr. Hassan Kukah should also be acknowledged as their works on the politics of religion in Nigeria served as my Rosetta Stone. Many thanks too to my adopted "son," Abdulbasit Kassim of Rice University, who freely placed at my disposal his extensive knowledge of Boko Haram, and to Dr. Ini Dele Adedeji, who, at the last minute, volunteered to read the entire manuscript. I am also grateful to professors Niyi Osundare, Kyari Muhammed, A. G. Adebayo, Adigun Agbaje, Tade Aina, Chris Alden, Hakeem Danmole, Sola Akinrinade, Ibrahim Rashid, Bayo Olukoshi, Alade Fawole, Ademola Popoola, Dele Layiwola, Adebayo Oyebade, Solomon Akinboye, Abdullahi Zuru, Kasali Adegoke, Ayodeji Omotayo, Ibrahim Jawondo, Amadu Sesay, Seyi Ojo, Tony Olusanya, Tayo Adesina, Wahab Egbewole, Ademola Abass, the late Layi Abegunrin, and Akin Alao. My gratitude also goes to Drs. Akin Oyetade, Temilade Abimbola, Obiyemi Obiseye, Akin Iwilade, Joseph Aihie, Awino Okech, Kunle Ojeleye, Comfort Ero, Ranti Lawumi, Tunde Afolabi, the late Thomas Jaye, Kehinde Bolaji, Penda Diallo, Fatima Akilu, Remi Oyewumi, and Jide Akanji. Also, former Nigerian Chief of Defence Staff Lt. General Martin Agwai (Rtd.), Rear Admiral Bolanle Ati-John (Rtd.), Rear Admiral Babs Egbedina (Rtd.), Adewale Ajadi, Ambassador Martin Uhomoibhi, Yisa Abdulkareem Oke (YKO), Idiat Babalola, Debo Olawuyi, and Dr. Sunkanmi Shadare were very helpful. I thank them.

My association with the Nigerian Defence Academy as a visiting professor was extremely useful. I am grateful to the former commandant, Major General Inua Idris (Rtd.), for the opportunity to be attached to the academy and for the several hours of debate and discussion on Nigeria's security. I also benefited from discussions with many serving officers of the Nigerian Defense Force. As would be expected, the sensitive positions most of them occupy caution against mentioning them by name. I cannot thank them enough for sharing with me their insights and experiences. Thanks too to colleagues on the governing councils of Osun State University Oshogbo and the Federal University of Petroleum Resources, Effurun.

The editors of the Duke University Press series Religious Cultures of African and African Diaspora People, professors Jacob Olupona, Terrence Johnson, and Dianne Stewart, have affectionately and generously guided this book through the publishing process. I am very grateful to them. Equally, I want to thank the commissioning editor of the series, Miriam Angress, for all her support in seeing this book through production and for tolerating my overbearing emails. Many thanks, Miriam!

Five families hosted me during my numerous research trips to Nigeria, those of Dotun and Jumoke Adeniyi, Suleiman Baba and Zainab Ali, Danlami Abubakar and Mariam Sule, Mallam Yusuf Olaolu Ali, Senior Advocate of Nigeria (SAN), and Labo Popoola. These families provided friendship and comfort such that the only unhappy moments of my stays with them were the departures. Really, l don't know what I did to deserve friends like them, but whatever it was, I am glad I did it. I also want to thank them for the numerous discussions we had on the politics of religion in Nigeria. Mallam Yusuf Ali should again be specially thanked for granting me undisturbed access to his extremely rich library.

Thanks more than I can ever say to many family members and friends, including Professor and Mrs. J. O. Fawole, Professor M. O. Fawole, Bayo and Made Bello, Demola and Ronke Salau, Bishop Paul and Pastor Joyce Fadeyi, Eniola Fagbure, Doyin and Wemimi Sheyindemi, Laja and Bimbo Mustapha, Isiaka and Tinu Oyebamiji, Deola and Bunmi Magbadelo, Atta Barkindo, Bode and Laide Esan, Remi and Funmi Adeseun, "Ogbeni" Rauf Aregbesola, Christie Adejoh, Kayode and Bisi Fayemi, Olufemi and Ngozi Edun, Oyewole and Jibike Oyewumi, Yemi Aderemi, Segun Obafemi, Abiodun Onadipe, Ozonnia Ojielo, Remi and Remi Ajibewa, Wumi Morohundiya, Engineer Tunde and Mrs. Grace Ponnle, Ademola Aladekomo, Jide and Rowena Fawole, Kayode and Lucy Fawole, Bisi Fawole, Wale and Doyin Afolabi, Akin and Funmi Onifade, Olaloye Badamosi, Dr. Banjo and Dr. (Mrs.) Adeola Adeleke, Bode Adesida, Segun Adeniyi of *This Day* newspaper, Yinka and Kibby Oduwaiye, Dale and Funke Ojutiku, Kale and Kudi Belgore, Wale Fagbohungbe, Kenny and Augusta Alowoesin, Wale Afolabi, Dewumi and Kemi Oyemade, Sam and Wumi Omokan, Jumai Ndalugi, Gboyega Akinsanmi, and Brodericks Arigbodi.

My siblings continue to make the word *family* ever so meaningful. I am extremely grateful to Olufemi, Kayode, Funmi, Folasade, and Olusayo. The greatest gratitude, however, goes to my immediate family. My children, Fiyinfolu and Ajibola, continue to be sources of inexpressible delight. That we now share academic interests has also meant that we discussed aspects of the book, sometimes fruitfully disagreeing. I am particularly happy that they are maintaining the family tradition of independent thought. My wife, Ronke, has remained my central source of support and the engine room for the entire family. It is impossible to thank her enough. As I have said several times: in the lottery of life, when it comes to marriage, I hit the jackpot. Thanks more than I can ever say, Ronke.

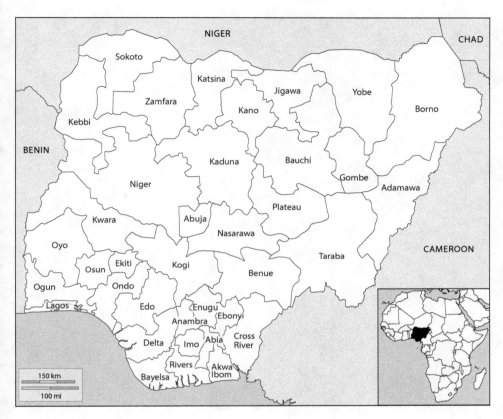

Map of Nigeria's states.

Introduction. OF NIGERIA, RELIGION, AND VIOLENCE

There are certain important points to note on . . . Nigeria's evolution. First, the entities that today constitute the Nigerian state were brought together by force of arms. . . . [Second,] several of these conquests and mergers of territories were not executed by the British government but by a profit-making enterprise, the Royal Niger Company. Finally, the use of the term "amalgamation" . . . underscores the fact that the integration of the peoples and cultures within the merged territories was not the overriding objective of the colonialists. —TUNDE BAKARE, "Negotiating the New Nigeria"

Of all the animosities which have existed among mankind, those which are caused by a difference of sentiments in religion appear to be the most inveterate and distressing, and ought most to be deprecated. —GEORGE WASHINGTON, letter to Edward Newenham, October 20, 1792

When Nigerians interpret events in their country, especially the ones connected to religion, the nation's history is a central part of their reflections. They ask themselves and each other what should have happened in the past, and what could have been different. The process that led to the creation of Nigeria began in 1900, when Britain withdrew the charter of the Royal Niger Company and the area that later became Nigeria came under the direct supervision of the Colonial Office in London. Up to this time, three separate entities existed: the colony of Lagos, the Southern Protectorate, and the Northern Protectorate. In 1906, the colony of Lagos merged with the Southern Protectorate and in 1914, the Northern and Southern Protectorates amalgamated to form the new entity called Nigeria. Those who ponder the *ifs* of history wonder how things would have turned out if the amalgamation had not taken place and both entities had subsequently won independence as separate countries. Indeed, the country owes most of its paradoxical characteristics to the circumstances of its composition.

Although battered and bruised, postindependence Nigeria remains upright and unbeaten. With a population of about 200 million people, it is the world's seventh most populous country and the nation with the largest population of Black people; it is the twelfth largest producer of oil and one of the largest producers of natural gas; it has one of the world's largest columbite reserves and the second largest bitumen deposits; it also has one of the world's largest deposits of iron; two of the world's major rivers pass through its territory; it has a broad array of vegetation that can be cultivated into agricultural products for domestic use and exports; it has some of the earliest known evidence of human existence, dating back to 9000 BC; its population includes some of the world's most energetic youths. Given all of this abundance, there are expectations that Nigeria should surpass countries that have basic human and natural endowments. Indeed, the country faces such expectations from three sources: from its huge citizenry, most of whom believe that their country has everything that it takes to give them a better quality of life; from other Africans, who think that Nigeria's population and endowment should translate into continental leadership; and from Black people all over the world who want to see Nigeria as a Black nation rise to global prominence. The country has, however, not met any of these expectations, due in part to the acrimony that has characterized relations between its component units.

Of all the issues that have been at the center of controversy in Nigeria, religion is one of the most prominent. A British Broadcasting Corporation survey carried out in January 2004 depicted the country as the world's "most religious nation," with over 90 percent of those sampled saying that they "believed in God," "prayed regularly," and were ready to "die for their religious belief."[1] Religion seems to be particularly contentious in Nigeria. For example, the number of Nigerian citizens who have died as a result of religious violence in the last four decades is higher than that of all other African countries combined. The country's religious challenges have brought it to global attention, as when the militant group Jamā 'at Ahl al-Sunna li-Da'wa wa-l-Jihād (widely known as Boko Haram) kidnapped the so-called Chibok girls in April 2014. Furthermore, Nigerian citizens abroad have been involved in religious radicalization, as in the cases of Umar Farouk Abdulmutallab, who attempted to bomb an American airline in December 2009, and of Michael Adebolajo and Michael Adebowale in the London murder of Fusilier Lee Rigby in May 2013. Indeed, by 2018, Nigeria was the third worst-hit country on the Global Terrorism Index—after Iraq and Afghanistan.[2] By the end of 2020, the situation had become even more worrisome, with religious violence becoming connected to other ethnopolitical violence of such anarchic proportions that many were concerned about the continued existence of the Nigerian state itself.

Globally, one of the most disturbing features of the last decade is the extent to which religious violence created security challenges that stunted development, destroyed advances in the international search for good governance, and threatened harmonious relations within and among states. In the course of the past decade, virtually all the continents of the world recorded cases of extreme violence motivated by the expression of religious beliefs. Several distinctive features make this category of violence particularly worrisome: the borderless aspects of its theaters, the facelessness of many of its actors, the indiscriminate range of its victims, its spectacular and devastating methods, and the relative inability of most affected countries to cope with its aftermath and consequences. As is discussed later in this chapter, most of this violence is linked to radicalization, a term whose vast literature has often confused and complicated its meaning.

Although recent religious violence has been inextricably interconnected, with radical international religious organizations having sympathizers across the world, there are still geographical specificities to its causes and manifestations. In Africa, these manifestations frequently bring together variables that may, on the surface, appear unconnected. Indeed, issues such as ethnicity, political governance, developments in other nations, and socioeconomic factors have complicated the relation between religion and violence.

But before going into detailed discussions on religion and violence in Nigeria, there is the need for some background discussion, including working definitions of both religion and violence and how the linkage between the two currently manifests. There is also the need to identify and discuss the origin and meaning of key issues that have been at the center of global controversies over religion and violence. These are particularly important because of the ways such issues pervade discussions throughout this book.

Very few subjects are as difficult to define as religion, and as Milton Yinger has noted, every definition is satisfactory only to its author.[3] At the same time, religion remains one of the most important and most controversial identity issues in the world, a major factor that affects relationships and interpretations of actions and/or inactions. While this introductory chapter does not explore the many aspects of religion or go into profound epistemological questions, it does identify some key aspects germane to this book.[4] Religion can be defined most simply as a position rooted in personal conviction. Yinger notes, "Where one finds awareness of and interest in the continuing, recurrent, permanent problems of human existence—the human condition itself, as contrasted with specific problems; where one finds rites and shared beliefs relevant to that awareness, which define the strategy of an ultimate victory; and where one has groups organized to heighten that awareness and to teach and maintain those rites and beliefs—there one has religion."[5] Huntington also defined it in a shorter way as "the central force that motivates and mobilizes people."[6] Also, Pargament defines it as "a process, the search for significance in ways related to the sacred."[7]

Broadly, religion has core aspects, and scholars like Stanley Eitzen and Maxine Baca Zinn have identified three of these: (1) a social construction, "created by the people and as part of a culture"; (2) an "integrated set of ideas by which a group attempts to explain the meaning of life and death"; and (3) a "normative system defining immorality and sin as well as morality and righteousness."[8]

Central to most religions are three things: ritual, prayer, and orthodoxy. While ritual and prayer are largely geared toward the ultimate beneficiary of the adulation, orthodoxy shapes the attitudes and behaviors of those practicing a religion. What also seems characteristic of religion is the idea of benefits from sacrifices that people make in the pursuit of the religion. Most people who take part in religion have the expectation of reward for their belief, either in life or after. Among others, merely looking forward to the meeting of their earthly needs in an afterlife has made many people hold onto their religious faith, but it also, quite ironically, has made them vulnerable to manipulation and amenable to violence.

The question of violence has also attracted its own body of scholars.[9] Studies here fall into four categories: its causes and effects; its targets (e.g., women, children, ethnic group, etc.); broader thematic lenses, like society, politics, and religion; and type (whether physical, sexual, emotional, psychological, spiritual, or cultural). Again, avoiding profound philosophical postulations, this book focuses on violence as a behavior, usually unlawful, in which a person uses physical force to hurt, damage, intimidate, or kill.

The calculated use of violence in the name of religion is not a new phenomenon; its roots go deep in history.[10] The Sicarii, a group of militant Jewish zealots, waged terrorism against the Roman occupation between 66 and 70 AD.[11] This group operated in broad daylight and targeted Roman priests.[12] They also frequently went to public places with hidden daggers to strike down persons considered friendly to Rome. Like modern-day radical groups, they sometimes released their captives after the payment of ransom. Suicide activities were also part of the group's strategies. Indeed, it is believed that many of its members preferred to commit suicide rather than allow themselves to be captured by the Romans. Another early violent religious group was the Assassin sect, a radical Shi'ite Ismaili group during the eleventh century. (We get the modern English word *assassin* from them.) The group directed their activities against Sunni rule, and their practice, too, was to commit murder in public places as a way of intimidating the population. Sometimes they only threatened enemies into submission.[13] Further historical evidence of violence in the name of religion is the wars between Christian Crusaders and Muslims that occurred between 1095 and 1281, and the Spanish Inquisition of the fifteenth century, countering apostasy, witchcraft, heresy, and other practices considered crimes against the Catholic Church.[14] Sanctioned by the Pope at the behest of the Spanish monarchy, the Inquisition burned thousands at the stake and expelled Jews and Muslims who refused to be baptized from Spain.

In its current form, the roots of recent violence in the name of religion can be traced to the end of World War I, when the Western colonial powers agreed to establish several new states and to redefine the borders of old ones, without taking into consideration the ethnoracial, religious, and geopolitical realities of the respective regions. While this balkanization did not immediately result in extreme political behaviors, it laid seeds that would germinate in Central Europe and the Middle East. The relative peace continued until World War II, after which several other groups emerged across the world to challenge these new boundaries. Religion thus became intermingled with politics and nationalist sentiments. These groups soon found political means ineffective and turned to militancy.

But while all the major religions have been associated with one form of debate or another, the Islamic religion has been the one most associated with recent controversies in global politics. This is because, according to Simon Mayall, Islam is much more than a religion but also a complete sociopolitical system, leading to the concept of "Political Islam," which in this context is broadly defined as the intermix of Islamic religion with the process of political governance.[15] The exact origin of the idea of political Islam in sub-Saharan Africa is somewhat difficult to ascertain. Some consider the first case to be the 1804 jihad of Usman dan Fodio.[16] But a variant of political Islam began to appear in most of the former colonial territories not long after independence. Indeed, by the late 1960s, Sudan, Somalia, and Eritrea had recorded traces of

Islamic revivalist movements.[17] It was, however, not until the late 1980s, when the National Islamic Front successfully engineered a military takeover of power in Sudan, that a new dawn began in political Islamism. The takeover coincided with an Islamic revival in western regions of Ethiopia, and more importantly the emergence of Islamic jihad groups in Eritrea. At this point, Somali Islamic fundamentalist movements were in their infancy, but they blossomed in subsequent years.[18] Islamic radicalization in sub-Saharan Africa was a product of increasing interconnectivity among radical groups in the region and between the groups and wider global networks, and it also catalyzed further networks.

To understand the phenomenon of political Islam, there are a few important things to note because of the ways it has become connected to violence. The first of these is how Islam sees the state.[19] Although it needs to be acknowledged that there are debates across many varieties of Islam, Islam's orthodox understanding of the state is profoundly different from the Westphalian principle of state sovereignty, in that the Islamic idea puts the whole concept of sovereignty within Allah—the Supreme Being—at whose pleasure all human beings exist and in whose name governance should be undertaken. Consequently, Islam sees an elected or appointed leader as God's representative.[20] The main duty of government is to enable individual Muslims to lead a good life that glorifies the name of Allah, and this can only come through their strict adherence to the Qur'an and its stipulated law, the Sharia. This law is believed to be divinely established and consequently not subject to change or human interpretations, unlike secular laws.[21] The Qur'an 3:103 enjoins unity among Muslims. While Islamic religion recognizes *ikhtilāf*, which denotes dissension of views, it preaches that this should be done without violence.

A central and contested concept in political Islam is *jihad*, a term with a variety of different interpretations, and one that evokes strong reactions.[22] In its origin, the term has its roots in the word *jhd*, which in Arabic means "to strive" or "exert oneself"—in short, to struggle. There is a recent tendency to interpret *jihad* dramatically, in a strict radical "dualism, as the permanent Manichean struggle between the forces of good who seek to restore a true moral order for the salvation of mankind (often assumed to be the jihadists) and the camp of the cosmic foes who are determined to impose a secular governance in the world based on western norms and values, as opposed to the desired Pan-Islamic caliphate advocated by the jihadists."[23] In his book *Terror in the Mind of God: The Global Rise of Religious Violence*, Mark Juergensmeyer describes how al-Qaeda and its affiliates frame their violent struggle against perceived Western imperialism as a "transcendental or sacramental act with the imprimatur of the divine or with a moral, sacred and religiously-sanctioned validation—in short, as cosmic war."[24]

In fact, the word *jihad* has four connotations in Islam. The first is the jihad of the heart. This struggle is with the self, an interior effort aimed primarily at self-purification. The objective here is to live according to the Sharia, to strive to do what is right and to reform individual bad habits. In short, Muslims must personally strive for interior perfection. The second is the jihad of the tongue, or preaching, which is understood as a gesture of peace to the unbeliever by inviting him or her to join the faith. The third is the jihad of the hand, otherwise interpreted as charity.[25] It is only if these first three have been found ineffectual in changing the world that the *ummah*, which refers to the community of believers, can resort to the use of the fourth—the jihad of the sword. Even so, the permissible mode is defensive (*jihad al-dafa'a*): jihad is the external defense of Islam from non-Muslim aggression.[26] It is not an offensive exercise.

Islam is, however, as much at war with itself as it is against other religions or ideologies. There are, indeed, present-day Muslims who use jihad as a justification both for attacking the West and for attacking Muslim governments and other members of the Islamic faith. The roots of this phenomenon go back to the historical foundations of Islam, even if the revival is modern and the resonance decidedly contemporary.

Radical Islamic groups have shifted from defensive to offensive strategies: "transitional jihadi groups have elevated offensive military campaign[s] to impose radical Islam on everyone as the sixth pillar of Islam." Their objective is to propagate violent war against two categories of people: the infidel and the heretic. The origin of this was the Prophet Muhammad's Medina period (AD 622–32). The definition of what constitutes an infidel or heretic is problematic. Under the broadest definition, both concepts include anyone who acts against the Sharia. Moreover, these jihadi groups have interpreted jihad as *fard ayn* (individual obligation), rather than *fard kifaya* (collective duty).[27]

The concept of jihad seemed to enter a new phase during the 1980s and 1990s, when it was mixed with nationalist and separatist sentiments, as it manifested in countries like Bosnia and Chechnya. The jihadi-Salafist radical philosophy saw governance according to anything other than God's laws as a violation of God's absolute sovereignty. This phase brought the Islamic religion to global attention, and from the mid-1990s Osama bin Laden extended his brand of jihadism to the United States and the West. In Nigeria, Boko Haram took this position.

A phenomenon that has also attracted considerable attention in all discussions about radicalization is suicide operation. As noted earlier, this practice is not new, as it dates to the period of the Assassins that operated between 1090 and 1275. Indeed, the Islamic religion has a special celebration for individuals who die in the process of protecting the *ummah*.[28] In the Islamic religion, suicide missions can be acts of martyrdom. However, Brahimi has noted that there is still a distinction between suicide and martyrdom. Quoting the Egyptian Islamic scholar Sheikh Youssef al-Qaradawi, Olomojobi points out the distinction: "Suicide is an act or instance of killing oneself intentionally out of despair and finding no outlet except putting an end to one's life. On the other hand, martyrdom is a heroic act of choosing to suffer death in the cause of Allah, and that is why it is considered by most Muslim scholars as one of the greatest forms of Jihad."[29] Some radicals have quoted the Qur'an to justify suicide operations. For example, Qur'an 2:216 notes, "Fighting is prescribed for you, and ye dislike it. But it is possible that ye dislike a thing which is good for you and that ye love a thing which is bad for you. But Allah knoweth and ye know not." But many Muslims also argue that only a complete misrepresentation of this injunction will interpret it to mean the adoption of violence and that the supreme injunction of peaceful coexistence is at the center of the Islamic religion.[30]

Islam's position on the just war theory (*jus ad bellum*) is distinctive: it justifies and even requires followers to prosecute some wars to preserve the Islamic faith (Qur'an 8:60, 73). Those who lose their lives in such a process are guaranteed a blissful life in eternity. Indeed, the Prophet Muhammad admonished Muslims not to think of those who have died while killing in God's way as dead. Rather, they are alive with God, well provided for, happy with what God has given them of his favor; rejoicing that for those they have left behind who have yet to join them, there is no fear, nor will they grieve; rejoicing in God's blessing and favor, and that God will not let the reward of the believers be lost. The Qur'an also encourages those who are reluctant to fight for the Lord to join in. From this, it can be concluded that the Qur'an ordains just war for legitimate purposes.

An aspect of physical violence in Islam that has attracted considerable controversy is the one that stipulates stoning to death (*rajm*) as the punishment for adultery (*zinā*). Even some Muslims have argued that it runs contrary to the provision in the Qur'an 24:2–3 that stipulates flogging one hundred times (*jald*) for the same offense. A scholar of Islamic religion, Yasir Quadri, has tried to clarify the contradiction here when he notes that "stoning to death is not contained in the Qur'an; it is however contained in hadith which reported that the Prophet of Islam applied it."[31] According to Quadri, "the first culprits who were sentenced to death by stoning by the Prophet were not Muslims but a Jew and a Jewess. He applied a Jewish law to the Jews (Leviticus 20:10 and Deuteronomy 22:22). He also applied the same law to two Muslims (Mā'iz ibn Malik al-Aslamī and a Ghamidiyyah woman), apparently before the revelation of Qur'an 24:2-3, which appears to have been revealed to abrogate the punishment of adulterous Muslims by *Rajm*."[32]

Generally, the association between violence and religion has brought a number of political issues to the forefront. Issues like election and harmonious intergroup relations are factors in religion across the world. The practice of elections, central to political governance, appears in the central writings of Christianity and Islam. Christianity recognizes the practice; for example, in the book of Deuteronomy, 1:9-17, the people of Israel were instructed to choose among themselves those who would rule over them. Apart from this, the Bible also recorded several instances of the freedom of choice—the essence of an election—being given to the people of Israel. Election continues as a Christian practice today. Catholic bishops elect the pope, the head of the Catholic Church, and Anglican Church bishops also elect their head, the archbishop. In the Christian view, generally, taking part in a secular election is a civic duty, a demonstration of good citizenship, and emphasized by their religion. Similarly, while Islamic scholars posit that neither the Qur'an nor Hadith makes a categorical statement concerning elections (and neither uses the word), some argue that Islam has room for the related idea of representation. For example, H. A. AbdulSalam points out that the political system in Islam operates in three dimensions: *tawhid* (belief in God), *risalah* (messengership), and *khilafar* (vice regency).[33] According to him, *khilafar* also means representation, and anyone who occupies this position is expected to represent and lead according to the word of God.[34] The Qur'an also encourages mutual consultations in political matters and governance through *shura*, which means consultation, and the Hadith notes that leadership is to be chosen by consensus after due cognizance has been taken of the leadership and spiritual capabilities of all the people. The Hadith dictates that the best among the people in terms of knowledge and fear of God are selected as the leaders. The Prophet, however, further instructed that anyone who puts himself or herself forward for leadership should not be appointed. Further evidence that elections are not un-Islamic can be seen in the regular elections in predominantly Muslim states, including Egypt, Iran, and Pakistan.

Similarly, both the Bible and the Qur'an encourage the crucial practice of harmonious intergroup relations, focusing on reconciliation after a conflict. In the Bible's 2 Corinthians 5:18-19, it is written, "All this is from God, who through Christ reconciled us to himself and gave us the ministry of reconciliation; that is, in Christ God was reconciling the world to himself, not counting their trespasses against them, and entrusting to us the message of reconciliation." Also, Romans 5:10 reads, "For if while we were enemies we were reconciled to God by the death of his Son, much more, now that we are reconciled, shall we be saved by his life." Finally, Matthew 18:15 notes, "If your brother sins against you, go and tell him his fault, between you and him alone. If he listens to you, you have gained your brother." The Qur'an also underlines the importance of reconciliation. In Ash-Shura 42:40, it notes, "The Recompense for an evil is an evil like thereof; but whoever forgives and makes reconciliation, his reward is with Allah." Also, in Al-Hujuraat 49:9, it states, "And if two parties or groups among the believers fall to fighting, then make peace between them both. But if one of them outrages against the other, then fight you (all) against the one which outrages till it complies with the Command of Allah. Then if it complies, make reconciliation between them justly, and be equitable. Verily! Allah loves those who are equitable." Finally, Al-Hujuraat 49:10 declares, "The believers are nothing else than brothers [in Islamic religion]. So, make reconciliation between your brothers, and fear Allah, that you may receive mercy." Thus, both the Bible and the Qur'an teach reconciliation after a disagreement.

In the last decade, however, violence connected to religion has heightened, and this has been linked to radicalization, or the adoption of radical views by various religious groups across the world. Radicalization has become a trendy term and, like most words that have fallen into that category, it has become vulnerable to distortion. Its interchangeability, rightly or wrongly, with other terms like extremism, fundamentalism, and terrorism has added further layers of controversy and confusion to its conceptualization. Radicalization, in all its ramifications, has been studied rigorously by scholars, such that any detailed discussion in this chapter will not serve any additional purpose.[35]

In the context of this book, a radical group is one that professes a belief system that rejects the status quo and actively aspires to an idealized past or envisioned future, embedded in the paradox of past as future and change as a return to the past. Such a group calls for its adherents to use violent and unconventional means to realize that change. Its nostalgic view of aspects of the past and expectant view of the future signal a group's rejection of the present. Radicalization, then, is the process of transforming the mental and emotional motivations of a person or group to shift from peaceful to violent behavior.

Broken down further, six aspects of this definition are particularly important. First, radicalization is a process (with identifiable phases) and not an event, its dynamics formed by the complex interaction of multiple events, actors, relationships, beliefs, and institutions. Second, it emphasizes and aims for profound change: the transformation of socioeconomic situations, cultural and political values, institutional practices, and belief systems—whether of an individual, a group, or a society. Third, its unconventional means include behaviors, attitudes, values, and moral standards that are not only alternatives to the status quo but are often opposed to it. Fourth, it operates at multiple levels—individual, group, and societal—and the distinctions between them often blur. Fifth, it spans different spheres of life, including the religious, political, social, economic, and cultural. Finally, it is underlined by fundamental principles, worldviews, and understandings about human and societal existence. But what the discussion above on religion and violence has implied is that the manifestation of both depends on the society where they occur.

Following these background considerations on religion and violence, the discussion can now go back to Nigeria. In this country, religion has become interwoven with the politics of the nation's ethnopolitical divide and its fluid socioeconomic structure; indeed, religion underpins Nigerian politics, governance, and intergroup relations. The global and the local intersect in the politics of religious violence. The complexity of the country's history, across its sixty years of existence, makes it profoundly difficult to understand: it has had fifteen different leaders; five military coups (each of which resulted in a change of government) and an unknown number of unsuccessful, suspected, and alleged coups; a bitter civil war; an annulled election; an interim administration; a brutal dictatorship; and several cases of violent ethnonationalist agitation. Efforts to describe Nigeria in all its variety frequently result in paradox, with one historian even pointing out that anyone who claims to understand the country is "either deluded or is a liar."[36] In short, the country exhibits major contradictions between what is expected and what has so far been achieved.

Three issues have influenced the history of religious conflicts in Nigeria: ethnicity, politics, and economics. Although the connections of each of these with religion are shown in subsequent chapters of this book, their distinct characteristics as features of the Nigerian state should be briefly noted here.

Matters of ethnicity in Nigeria have centered largely on access to power and state resources and on how different groups interpret actions or inactions in the country's zero-sum politics. The root of ethnic disputes in postindependence Nigeria, as in most other African countries, is colonialism, which forced disparate ethnic groups together into nation-states.

Most of the conflicts ignited by ethnicity in postindependence Nigeria can be brought under three headings: the rivalry between the three dominant ethnic groups in the country; the agitations and complaints of the numerous minority groups directed against these dominant groups; and the controversies and competitions among the various minority populations. The perception of Nigerian political elites of the role of ethnicity in politics and intergroup relations is another issue, with long-term implications for the country. Since independence, many political leaders have had a very narrow understanding of national unity. For example, in a 1952 speech at the Northern House of Assembly, Abubakar Tafawa Balewa, who eight years later was to become the country's first prime minister, noted that "the Southern people who are swarming into this region daily in large numbers are really intruders. We don't want them, and they are not welcome. . . . The fact that we are all Africans might have misguided the British government. We here in the North, take it that 'Nigerian Unity' is not for us."[37] Although statements like this by regional leaders across the ethnic spectrum are divisive, it seems likely that their positions were colored by other factors beyond raw ethnic differences. Economic fears, political anxieties, and inadequate empirical information about each other could be argued to have been the primary factors responsible, rather than a deeply held hatred.

Nigeria's complex politics has many dimensions, one of these being military involvement in politics and its consequences. The military intervened in politics in 1966 and ruled the country for two periods, for an initial thirteen years (until 1979) and later for another fifteen years (from 1984 to 1999). Many analysts have concluded that these military interventions inhibited the nation's development. They further stunted Nigeria's political evolution, already imperfect, militarized its society, and distorted its social fabric. But what seems to have had the most significant consequence was the country's brutal civil war between 1967 and 1970. While forms of acrimony had characterized ethnic relations since the struggle for independence, they were fairly well managed until the military's assassination of political leaders during its first coup in January 1966 started the process that led to the civil war.[38] The war ended in 1970, but has remained a major reference point in public discourse and a force shaping the affairs of the country.[39]

The question of political leadership is also critical to religion. In the zero-sum relationships among the various ethnic groups in Nigeria, which group will produce the leader is often a contentious issue. Ethnic groups have argued that leadership of the country has been dominated by another ethnic group. To ensure broad acceptability and representation, political parties have taken ethnic configurations into account when selecting leaders and election candidates. Concepts such as zoning have become part of Nigeria's political vocabulary.[40] Another factor that is important in the leadership controversy has to do with the caliber of leaders that have ruled Nigeria. This has many ramifications, and many Nigerians believe that most of the leaders saddled with running the country found themselves in charge contrary to their own desires or leadership ability.

The role of economics in understanding controversies in Nigeria is also complex. Most Nigerians think that the country's economy has been badly managed, given the frequent allegations of corruption leveled against those who have held political office. Much of the population also believes that those who have held economic management positions have been either incompetent, dishonest, or both. Thus, when governments call on the populace to accept belt-tightening economic measures, the general response has been that citizens are being made to pay the price of the leadership deficits of their ruling elites. The issue of corruption is, however, the most profound. While corruption in Nigeria has many facets, its manifestation in public office holders has attracted the most interest.[41] Indeed, of the thirty-six governors who assumed office after the 1999 election, fifteen were facing corruption charges in various courts by the first quarter of 2020, while two were serving jail terms for corruption.[42] What most people find curious about corruption in Nigeria is the huge dichotomy between official denunciations of the act and the absence of official identification and punishment of perpetrators. Governments, both civilian and military, have come to power with promises to stop corruption, with some even creating special institutions for that purpose, but they have rarely followed through on their pledges.

The controversies surrounding economics in Nigeria are also connected to the politics of managing its natural resource endowments. While all of Nigeria's natural resources have been at the center of long-standing debates in the country, oil has been one of the most contentious. The high profits to be made from it, the environmental consequences of exploring for it, the international scope of its distribution and politics, and its role in Nigeria's ethnopolitical and socioeconomic affairs have made the resource particularly contentious. A central point of dispute is who should control the country's oil: the communities who bear the environmental consequences of its extraction, or the central government, which has the constitutional power to distribute natural resources throughout the nation. The question of who defines national interest itself has been extremely controversial. People from oil-producing communities sometimes complain that what is advertised as being in the national interest is nothing more than the selfish desire of an ethnic oligarchy. The country's ethnic configuration, which defines the ethnic group in possession of the oil as a minority, has further complicated the link between ethnicity, resource control, and politics. The other national resource in contention is land, which has not only economic but spiritual, political, and social importance, because it is valued as the place of birth; the burial place of the ancestors that the Creator has designated should be passed down to successive generations; and the final resting place for every child born on its surface. The government has always tried to ensure its control of land; the 1978 Land Use Act entrusts all land in the country to the state governor. To summarize, there are multiple layers of inherent lack of trust between the nation's various components, and virtually every segment of society is engaged in a complex web of zero-sum relationships and competition with at least one other segment: there is conflict between the majority groups and the minorities; youths and adults; politicians and the citizenry; military and civilians; elites and masses; employers and employees; and so on. While it may be argued that all of these conflicts are also present in other countries, the ramifications are especially complex in Nigeria because of its weak political systems and structures, which are unable to withstand multiple contradictions, and its enormous population. All these issues have affected the politics of the country's religious outlook.

Religious controversies in Nigeria have prompted some brilliant studies, and in the last decade or so this body of scholarship has increased astronomically because of the activities of the radical group Boko Haram. Many of the recent books on religious violence in Nigeria have focused on this group, making a significant contribution to the literature on national and global radicalization. But this book is not, primarily, about Boko Haram, even though it does discuss the subject substantially. I have decided to avoid concentrating on a phenomenon-specific subject or quasi-ethnographic cases, and instead look at broader themes: how religion has been associated with violence in postindependence Nigeria and how this has affected the nation's socioeconomic and ethnopolitical relations. It starts with a handful of basic questions: Is religion's susceptibility to violence in Nigeria internal to (each) religion or due to external forces—or both? Are its social and ethnopolitical relations conditioned by religion or vice versa? If religion conditions political relations, does that mean that the violence of Nigerian religion is permanent? Some of these questions are discussed in the chapters ahead as they relate to Nigeria.

I advance five main arguments in this book. First is that religious violence in postindependence Nigeria has arisen largely because of the numerous contradictions—social, economic, and historical—that underscored the establishment of the Nigerian state. Second, contrary to what is often assumed, no religion in Nigeria has a monopoly on violence, and all three main sectors in the country—Islam, Christianity, and traditional religions—have engaged in violence and threatened to use it, although the scale of their actions has been different. Third, various elites have exploited the unrest in order to further advance their self-interest. Fourth, the causes of religious violence in Nigeria are largely internal, and even when external factors account for violence, local issues often affect how it plays out. Fifth, and last, is that recent cases of religious violence in Nigeria have benefited from some of the consequences of globalization.

Anyone writing a book on religion and violence in Nigeria should confess some diffidence, given the many challenges of the task. No single book on the subject could ever capture all the ramifications of the phenomenon, and this book does not make such a claim. Despite all of my efforts to prevent oversights, some things will almost certainly have escaped my attention. In addition, writing on the topic is fraught with many difficulties, especially because one can always find reasons to include or exclude any occurrence from the broad discussion—including possibly key issues of natural resource management, chieftaincy matters, ethnicity, elections, and even commercial relations—depending on time, place, and circumstance. Similar occurrences in different social and political contexts could be categorized as religious violence (or not). Thus, deciding what to include (or not), and finding explanations for these distinctions, has been one of the profound challenges I faced as I wrote this book. Indeed, these issues are often interwoven in ways that make delineations almost impossible. Also, the boundaries between and among religions in Nigeria are extremely fluid and blurred across time and practices, to the extent that it is sometimes difficult to compartmentalize each religion in Nigeria. Finally, events in Nigeria, especially along the lines of religion and violence, change rapidly, and sometimes quite profoundly, thereby making the work of researchers trying to catch up with developments intensely difficult. Any book on religion and violence in Nigeria is thus always a work in progress.

A brief note on the methodology that I adopted seems appropriate in this introduction. The book is based on the library-historical method, long-term observation as a student of Nigerian politics and society, and interviews with some actors around the country. I consulted libraries across Nigeria, the United Kingdom, and the United States. All interviews complied with the research ethics standards of King's College London.

I need to include a major disclaimer at the outset of this book: none of Nigeria's three main religious divisions—Christianity, Islam, and traditional religions—is inherently violent or violence prone, and this book does not presuppose that. Rather, all religions, like identities, are subject to intense instrumentalization (and manipulation) in the pursuit of particular interests by individuals and groups. The way actors instrumentalize religions is one of the themes that thread through this book.

The book has eight substantive chapters. The first discusses Nigeria's key religions and the historical politics of their emergence and development, laying out the sociopolitical and historical background of the roles that religion and religious violence have played. It addresses the defining features of Christianity, Islam, and traditional religions, and tracks how they arrived in the territory that later became Nigeria. It also looks at the effects of colonization, ending with independence and how it affected the role of religion in the affairs of the new country.

Chapter 2 discusses the political violence of Islamic radicalization in Nigeria, tracing its history, phases, contexts, manifestations, and socioeconomic and security ramifications, and investigates the efficacy of mechanisms aimed at addressing it. It explores the Maitatsine riots and the activities of other violent groups. Finally, it discusses patterns and methods of recruitment, the membership makeup of radical groups, and their reactions to the activities of other religions. It also looks at intra-Islamic religious differences, radicalization in tertiary institutions, and the role of the media.

Chapter 3 examines Christianity's association with violence in Nigeria, seeking to document all the known cases when Christians used violence, and the cause of each instance, asking to what extent they were reactions to Islamic radicalization. It discusses a radical Christian group that was formed specifically to challenge Boko Haram militarily and compares the position of this group with those groups of mainstream Christians who did not turn to violence. The chapter also explores some isolated cases of violence carried out in the name of Christianity against hapless segments of the population, especially children. This chapter also discusses radical Christian clergy who openly called for their congregants to violently defend the Christian faith against attacks from other religions.

The objective of chapter 4 is to complete the circle by discussing the link between Nigeria's traditional religions and violence. Among other topics, the chapter looks at the underlying motivations of worshippers of traditional religions when they engage in violence. It also looks at links between the worship practices of traditional religions and violence among their practitioners and with adherents of other faiths. There is also a discussion of some of the violent clashes that have involved traditional religions, especially their patterns of manifestation and the processes of resolution.

Chapter 5 describes the new radicalization and political violence in Nigeria. It looks specifically at the activities of Boko Haram. The chapter first considers the origin of the group and how it transmuted into a major national threat. It also considers the doctrinal issues surrounding the group's formation, its connection with national politics, and the activities that have brought it global attention. In addition, the chapter discusses bickering within the organization and how this has affected members' attitude toward violence. Boko Haram's sources of funding, its recruitment strategy, and its targets are highlighted, as is the Nigerian state's attitude about the group's insurgency activities. Finally, the chapter looks at the broader cross-national activities of the group, especially incursions into neighboring states and the counterreactions this has attracted from those states.

Chapter 6 discusses religion, religious violence, national politics, and the intricacies of intergroup relations. The chapter analyzes how successive administrations have addressed the key religious controversies they confronted, and how the religious predilections of individual political leaders have been reflected (or are believed to have manifested) in their management of state affairs. Also discussed is how religious violence is connected to agropastoralist issues in some parts of the country. The chapter also touches on controversies around the alleged attempt to Islamicize Nigeria.

The seventh chapter discusses the economic ramifications of religious violence in Nigeria. In counting the economic costs, the chapter assesses various ways that the national economy has been affected by insurgencies, including the consequences of violence for farming, trading, and commercial activities. The chapter also looks at the economic consequences of the government's fight against religious violence, especially the allegations and denials of graft by top military officers when they procured arms to fight insurgent groups. There is also a consideration of how economic disempowerment has fueled religious violence, ensuring a cyclical relationship between these realities.

Chapter 8 goes global, looking at how Nigeria's religious violence links to international radicalization. The chapter first explores global involvement in Nigeria's religious controversies immediately after independence. It then discusses how external forces—in particular, events in the Middle East, including the rise of Ayatollah Khomeini in Iran—have been affected by religious politics and religious conflict in Nigeria. More profoundly, the chapter investigates the various links between Boko Haram and global Islamic radicalization and the nature and extent of the support the movement is receiving from this source.

The book's conclusion asks why religion remains one of the most contentious identity issues in Nigeria and how its link with ethnopolitical violence has helped define intergroup relations in the country. It also discusses how religion and violence play into the equation of the #EndSARS protests that pervaded the country between October and November 2020.

1. RELIGION AND
NIGERIAN SOCIETY

The Political conquest of the South was a religious obligation that the Northern People's Congress owe the world of Islam, the Qur'an has to be dipped into the Atlantic Ocean before the Jihad could stop. —MUHAMMED RIBADU, Minister, Nigeria's First Republic, *Weekly Trust*, March 22, 2014

Nigeria belongs to Jesus. We shall not bow to any intimidation from any quarters; if you bow, you will burn. Arise and shine, for the glory of the Lord is risen. —BENSON ANDREW IDAHOSA, one of Nigeria's early Pentecostal pastors, *You Are God's Battle Axe*

The objective of this chapter is to discuss the establishment of the dominant religions, Islam and Christianity, in Nigeria, and the interconnections among them and the traditional religions that people were already practicing. The chapter also looks at the key aspects of this relationship that were subsequently to underline conflict. The central argument the chapter advances is that the seeds of later acrimony between their adherents lie in the history of their establishment. The chapter also argues that the occasional cases of intrareligious violence that were to become prominent after independence were also rooted in the historical evolution of the country.

Some key questions should preface any discussion on traditional religion, including: What is traditional about a religion? What are the markers of that traditionality (versus modernity)? How changeable or unchangeable is that traditional religion? African traditional religions would seem to be constructed around certain cultural mythologies, history, and in most cases the instrument and exercise of power in indigenous Africa. It is impossible to date the beginnings of traditional religions in the area that was to become Nigeria. As is the case with indigenous religions across the world, they presumably originated in the desire of societies to explain the unknown and contextualize the incomprehensible. Each community had its own traditional religion; most of them grew out of the history of their respective societies or legends peculiar to that history. Belief in an omniscient and omnipotent Supreme Being is the pillar around which all other beliefs of this region's traditional religions are built. This being is kind to those who follow required dictates but is also capable of giving punishment as may be deemed necessary. Another feature of traditional religion in Nigeria, however, is polytheism, a commitment to multiple deities. Also distinctive is the practice of perpetual communing with the ancestors, a constant link with those who, having lived a good life, are believed to be in places where they can intercede on behalf of their descendants still on earth. Some non-African observers erroneously interpret this practice as ancestor worship.[1]

The practice of sacrifice, which has also often been misconstrued, is another characteristic of traditional religions here. As is standard practice in religions across the world, sacrifices are specifically made for appeasement or are targeted toward a request. While no doubt there were cases of human sacrifice in some traditional religions in precolonial Nigeria, it was by no means a dominant practice; and again, this was not peculiar to African traditional religions.[2] More practically, traditional religions regulate human conduct. This thus makes religion society-centered, well captured in the famous phrase of an expert on African traditional religion, John Mbiti: "I am because we are; and since we are, therefore I am."[3]

Another expert on African traditional religions, Jacob Olupona, describes traditional religions here as "less of faith traditions and more of lived traditions," with rituals, ceremonies, and lived practices being more important than doctrine.[4] Concerns for health and wealth are central, he notes, and people developed institutions for healing, commerce, and the general well-being of their practitioners and adherents of other religions as well.[5] Women play a key role, and there are many goddesses.[6] Indeed, the traditional approach of indigenous African religions to gender is one of complementarity, in which male and female forces operate in harmony.[7] Finally, Olupona notes, oral traditions form the core of Nigeria's indigenous religions and are intricately interwoven into arts, political and social structure, and material culture.[8] The oral nature of these traditions allows for a great deal of adaptability and variation within and between indigenous Nigerian religions. At the same time, specific forms of oral literature, such as the Ifa tradition among the Yoruba, are important sources for understanding the tenets and worldview of these religions; in a sense, they are analogs to scriptures such as the Bible or the Qur'an.[9]

Brief examples of how these features have manifested in key societies across the country may help illuminate them. In pre-Islamic northern Nigeria, there was the Bori religion, which involves animism, magic, and spirit possession. Many spirits have specific powers; Aminu Bala notes that "each spirit has its name, receives appropriate sacrifice, and is believed to control sickness."[10] The Bori religion gives considerable primacy to women. The royal priestess of the religion is Inna, or "mother of us all," and she leads the other members of the religion in spiritual rituals. She also cleanses society from evil forces and protects it as well, and she is active in healing. This religion is still practiced today in some Hausa areas such as Kooni and Dogondutchi, presently the south of the Republic of Niger. Other traditional deities in Hausaland before Islam were Uwandowa, goddess of hunting, and Uwargona, goddess of agriculture.

Iboland's traditional religion is based on the belief that there is one creator, Chukwu, a shortened form of Chi-Ukwu, implying Great Being, or Chineke, the Being That Creates. The Ibos believe that Chukwu is the greatest of all spirits. The incomprehensibility and indescribability of Chukwu is central to the Ibos' belief, and there is no shrine containing a carved or painted image of Chukwu anywhere in Igboland. Chukwu can be approached through numerous other deities and spirits in the form of natural objects, most commonly through the god of thunder (Amadioha). The ancestors, the Ndiichie, also play major roles in Igbo traditional religion, and their souls are invoked during prayers through the pouring of libations. Next in the layer of Ibo traditional religion are the Arusis or elemental beings; that is, the four basic elements of land, water, fire, and wind each have elemental gods and goddesses who oversee everything that concerns them.[11] And the Ibos believe that every human born into the earth is given a Chi, or personal god, which accompanies the person all through life.

Yoruba traditional religion holds that human lives are predestined, specifically that before coming into the world, human beings choose the totality of their lives—or their Àyànmó (destiny). Once they come into the world, however, their choices are forgotten. Àyànmó actually has two forms: Àkúnlèyàn, the life freely chosen by the individual; and Àkúnlègbà, the life that the Supreme Being allocates to individuals. All this is captured in the Yoruba proverb "Àkún-lèyàn làdáyébá," meaning "we consciously implored the supreme deity for our chosen destinies before our arrival on earth." The Yoruba recognize a Supreme Being, Olódùmarè, whom they approach through intercessors called Òrìshà.[12] One thing that makes Yoruba traditional religion unique is its use of divination to communicate with the heavenly realm. Specially trained intercessors— either Babaláwo (Father of Secrets) for men or Ìyáláwo (Mother of Secrets) for women—undergo an intense period of training to learn the techniques to help clients seek help or advice from the heavenly realm. Finally, the town of Ile-Ife is held to be the place of creation.[13] Before the formal establishment of the Nigerian state in 1960 and before the arrival of Islam and Christianity, these traditional religions united various societies and ensured societal harmony.[14] While of course there were occasional tensions, structures were also in place to curtail excesses, manage demands, and regulate expectations.

In concluding this discussion on traditional religions in Nigeria, it needs to be pointed out that discussing the religions can embed and hide important conceptual challenges and slippages. It can even oversimplify complex phenomena. It is strongly intertwined with other identities and practices, including ethnicity, culture, and politics. It is thus narrow to see traditional religion as a religion-only reality. In most cases, it is many realities rolled into one.

Islam and Nigerian Society: Emergence and Growth

The first foreign religion to come into the territories that later became Nigeria was Islam. It came in two phases, with the Kanem Bornu Empire, on the northeast shore of Lake Chad, the first part of latter-day Nigeria to convert. The exact date of this first phase is difficult to ascertain: while most sources have dated it to around the twelfth century, some scholars put the date significantly earlier. For example, S. A. Balogun, quoting Abdullahi Smith, argues that a Muslim party led by Uqba b. Naffi had raided areas of Kawar on the caravan route to Kanem as far back as around 666 AD.[15] But we know that by the eleventh century, there was a small Muslim community in the empire. Islam made a lot of advances during the reign of Dunama Dabalemi (1221–59).[16] By the twelfth century, thanks to the activities of scholars and traders from North Africa, the religion had become more entrenched.[17] During this first phase, Islam was mainly a religion of the elite.[18]

Apart from Borno, other parts of modern-day northern Nigeria to encounter Islam very early were Kano and Katsina, and, much later, Kebbi. In Kano, it is believed that Islamization of the ruling house came with the arrival of the first Wangarawa, possibly in the late fourteenth century.[19] As John Hunwick noted, "by the early fifteenth century, one of the rulers (of Kano) Sarki Umah (1410-21) is portrayed as giving up his throne out of piety."[20] Further impetus to convert to Islam also came in the middle of the century with the arrival of Fulani preachers. Again, not much is known about the spread of Islam in other parts of what later became known as northern Nigeria, except that from the mid-sixteenth century, during the reign of Muhammed Kanta, the sultan of Kebbi was Muslim. It is also possible that his predecessor, Kuta Kanta, was a Muslim. By the time of Muhammed Rumfa (1463-99), the ruling family in Kano was also evidently Muslim. On its part, Islam would seem to have come to Katsina much later. The individual considered to be the first Muslim ruler was Muhammed Korau, who was believed to have reigned from about 1540 to 1593. His two predecessors, Ibrahim Sura (c. 1493-98) and Ali (c. 1498-1524) were also believed to have pursued Islamic policies. Ibn Yasin, a Sufi sheikh, by 1400 had spread Islam to some parts of Kano and other Hausa towns. Indeed, as Joseph Kenny has noted, some Hausa kings had accepted Islam by the sixteenth century.[21]

Although Islam was established in the area later known as northern Nigeria during this period, the extent of its wide acceptance is still contentious. There are grounds for believing that traditional religious practices were still practiced in conjunction with Islam. For example, some accounts stated that Islam had been consolidated in Kano under Yayi, as the Sarkin, but the Kano Chronicle described his son and second successor, Sarkin Kano Kanajeji (1390-1410), as a "Pagan."[22]

Although political upheavals dominated the affairs of the Kanem Bornu Empire subsequently, which slowed the spread of Islam, things were stable enough by the era of Idris Alooma (1570-1602) to allow the further propagation of the religion. As an expert on northern Nigeria, Rowland Adeleye, has noted, by the seventeenth century, Islam had not only "invaded" Kanem Bornu but had made important incursions into the ranks of the general population in Hausaland, with places like Birni Gazargamo, Kano, and Katsina at the forefront.[23] Adeleye also posits that the various settlements that grew around famous religious followers became strong outposts of Islamic leanings, as in Hausaland and Borno. It was also at this point that Islamic scholars began to establish Islamic education across Hausaland and Borno.[24] In fact, by the eighteenth century, the leaders of Islam in most of northern Nigeria had shifted from kings to religious figures.[25] Indigenous religions still had a considerable number of adherents in what was to become northern Nigeria, and it was this remnant that was to be affected by the second phase of Islamization.

That second and perhaps more decisive phase came with the 1804 jihad (religious revolution) of Usman dan Fodio that swept most Hausa rulers off their thrones and established Fulani hegemony in most of present-day northern Nigeria.[26] About fourteen of dan Fodio's generals later established emirates in Katsina, Kano, Zaria, Adamawa, Gombe, Bauchi, Ilorin, Nupe, Kazaure, Hadeija, Daura, Misau, Katagum, and (temporarily) Bornu. Within years, the Islamic religion was dominant, its converts having established themselves through trade, social contacts, and war. Key Hausa towns attracted Muslim scholars. According to Lawal Malumfashi, Fulani scholars had arrived in Bornu by the seventeenth and eighteenth centuries.[27] He also notes that places like Katsina and Kano had attracted scholars from North Africa such as Shaykh 'Abd al-Karim al-Maghili and Ayda Ahmad al Tazakhiti.[28] With them also came Islamic architecture and art.

It is not known precisely when Islam came to southwest Nigeria, and centuries of contact preceded the establishment of the religion there. Adebanji Akintoye posits the possibility of some forms of contact between Yoruba and Islam possibly as far back as the fourteenth century, noting that the Yoruba word for Muslim (Imale) originated from the people's association of the Islamic religion with itinerary traders from Mali, with whom the Yoruba have been in contact since the fourteenth century.[29] Also, another Yoruba historian, Adeagbo Akinjogbin, claims that Islam had come to the ancient Yoruba kingdom of Oyo by the fourteenth century through trans-Saharan trade.[30] It is, however, certain that, though some forms of contact may be traced to these dates, Islam had not established any foothold in southwest Nigeria at the time it got to the north around the fourteenth century. Historians believe that the first mosque was built in Oyo-Ile in 1550, and that Islam was practiced in Old Oyo during the reign of Alaafin Ajiboyede (1560–70).[31] This was traced to the activities of one *mallam*, also called Baba-Kewu, who apparently came from the Nupe ethnic group. Certainly, by the sixteenth century, Islam was no longer an unknown religion in Yorubaland, as attested by documentary evidence of references to Yoruba Muslims. Indeed, a Hausa scholar, Abdullaah Muhammad b. Massanih, in a book titled *Shifa Ruba fee Tahrir fuqaha*, talked about "the learned men of Yoruba," explaining to them the Islamic method of determining sunset. Yoruba towns that are believed to have had early contact with the religion include Iwo in 1655, Iseyin in 1760, and Saki in 1790, while people in Ibadan, Abeokuta, Ijebu-Ode, Ikirun, and Ede all knew about Islam before the 1804 Fulani jihad.[32] The Scottish voyager Hugh Clapperton recorded the presence of Hausa Muslims during his travels in Yorubaland between Badagry and Oyo Ile between 1825 and 1826.[33] Islam came to Lagos in the eighteenth century, where the first mosque was built in 1774. However, although initial contacts were made during this period, this never translated to any serious Islamization of the Yoruba, and the adherents of Islamic religion remained in a significant minority. Although scholars such as Samuel Johnson put Islam's establishment in Yorubaland as an eighteenth-century occurrence, this is clearly incorrect.

Important but often neglected in the spread of Islam in Yorubaland was the influence of returnee Muslims, Muslims who returned after the slave trade had stolen them from their homes. While most of the slaves that returned were Christians, some were Muslims. According to the historians Gbadamosi and Ajayi they had varied backgrounds. Some had become Muslims before they were captured, while others fell under the influence of Hausa-Fulani slaves while in captivity.[34] Apart from increasing the number of Muslims, they also raised the status of Islam in southwest Nigeria, comparing effectively with their Christian counterparts; some had learned masonry, carpentry, and tailoring, and others had acquired considerable financial fortune.[35]

A major phase in the link between the Yoruba and Islam was the 1804 jihad of Usman dan Fodio. During this phase, the Islamic teacher Shaykh al-Aalim, popularly known as Shehu Alimi, came from the present-day Republic of Niger and won followers across Oyo, Iseyin, Ogbomoso, and other Yoruba towns. His influence later became a source of concern to the Alaafin (king), who expelled him from the Oyo Empire. The governor of Ilorin, Afonja, later sought Alimi's assistance to escape the Alaafin's control himself. Alimi helped Afonja, but then took over Ilorin. Ilorin was to play an important role in the percolation of Islam into Yorubaland. Kanuri migrants under Mallam Abdullaah Tahir, nicknamed Solagberu, had settled in Okesuna (literally translated as the hill rock of Sunnah), and it was from here that Solagberu traveled extensively across northern parts of Yorubaland spreading the Islamic religion. After Alimi's arrival, the propagation of Islam throughout Yorubaland heightened. Islamic scholars of Fulani origin also brought Islam with them into Yorubaland, including Shaykh B. Sanni, Shaykh Maliki, Shaykh Ismail, and others. Some scholars of Malian origin, including Shaykh Yusuf, joined Shehu Alimi at Kobayi. The third group of Islamic scholars who migrated to Ilorin after the arrival of Alimi were of Sudanese origin; they formed the core of Islamic scholars at Agbaji. Other prominent Muslim scholars established Qur'anic institutions in Ilorin. One was a Fulani known as Shehu Muhammad Ahmad b. el-Gore (known today as Belgore), whose understanding of Islam's branches of knowledge, such as Tafsir, Hadith, and Fiqh, was widely acknowledged. Another was Shehu Muhammad Ameen Salisu, who toured Yorubaland extensively preaching Islam, but made Ilorin his permanent base.[36]

Islam in Yorubaland, however, was not without a measure of syncretism with local religions. This, according to Muhib Opeloye, took different forms. One was believers' tendency to simply add Islam to the indigenous religion, thereby becoming loyal to both. Another was to practice Islam while participating in another religion at times, such as when one identifies as Muslim but at times of personal crisis patronizes the witch doctor or uses fetishes, magic, charms, and divination.[37] This attitude finds expression in the popular Yoruba saying "Bó ti wu ni làá sè mòle ẹni," meaning, "One practices one's Islam as one likes."

Meanwhile, the establishment and spread of Islam in what later became eastern Nigeria is still shrouded in controversy. Some scholars date it to the last decade of the nineteenth century, pointing to evidence of close interactions between Hausa-Fulani and Nupe Muslim traders with Igbos living around Nsukka. It is, however, doubtful whether this led to any form of sustained spreading of Islam. It appears that the northerners the Igbos met were more interested in trade than in Islam. Indeed, Hausas' presence, to which the spread of Islam to the area was closely linked, "was rare or non-existent in Iboland before 1900, despite the closeness of northern Igboland to northcentral and northern Nigeria."[38] The part of Iboland first exposed to the religion was Nsukka, strategically located as a trading post with Hausa-Fulani and Nupe Muslim traders. With the capture of the town by the Igala in the late eighteenth century came an acceleration of Islamic influences. Other issues—the impact of Nupe scholars and constant intermarriage—also led to the development of the Islamic religion in the town.[39] From the discussion in this section, it can be seen that Islam came to communities across Nigeria at different times and that the manifestations were different, tendencies that were to be affected by colonialism.

Islam and Colonialism

Having looked at the origin and early development of Islam in the area later known as Nigeria, there is a need for a brief discussion on the impact of British colonial rule on religion. The British did not interfere much with the Muslim religion in the north but made sure to accommodate both British interests and the concerns of the Fulani ruling class.[40]

However, the extent to which the British favored Islam is now a subject of debate. Many Muslims have traced the antecedents of some radical Islamic views to British colonial control of the country. Three issues have come out here. First, many Muslims in the country believe that one of the main motives of British colonialism was to stop the spread of Islam, and that Britain remained hostile to the religion.[41] This view is quite controversial. Some scholars believe that there is not much truth in this assertion. For example, Toyin Falola has argued that British rule was not hostile to Islam and that the colonial government was "ambivalent in their attitude to Islam, but consistent in a belief that irrational treatment of Muslims would stand in the way of colonial objectives."[42] Not many Muslims in Nigeria, however, share this view. Indeed, during a focus group discussion undertaken in the process of writing this book in Abuja, one of the participants who runs an Islamic school was emphatic that the main motive of British imperialism was to stop the advancement of Islam, which he argued was spreading down to the coast where Britain had significant economic interests.

Second, some Muslims believe that the colonial educational system impeded the development of the Islamic religion. Muslims were allegedly kept from establishing schools for Muslim children, so Muslims had to go to Christian schools. In many focus group discussions held across the country for this book, many Muslims were bitter about this: many claimed that they were almost forcefully converted to Christianity. A politician and former state commissioner who took part in one of the discussions said that he felt that the educational systems of the period made conscious attempts to subtly convert Muslims to Christianity.[43] Many Muslims claim that British colonial rule deliberately pursued an educational policy that was anti-Islam, especially through its refusal to recognize the coherent and progressive Islamic educational system in northern Nigeria that was in existence before colonialism. The nonrecognition of this system, they argued, gave the Christians an advantage that ultimately resulted in a disparity in educational standards between the north and the south.[44]

Finally, some see the whole picture through the prism of the divide-and-rule strategy of British colonial policy. In this view, any division along religious lines was part of the wider attempt by the British to divide the country along ethnic lines.[45] Britain allegedly pursued a policy of never allowing Nigerians to freely interrelate with one another and, consequently, Nigerians failed to fully understand and appreciate their different cultural, religious, and social backgrounds before winning independence. Those who hold this view also argue that the amalgamation of the Southern and Northern protectorates was just a policy on paper and that many important political departments in the colonial office remained so separated that the administrative officers were hardly ever cross-transferred. Indeed, a colonial officer, Sir Theodore Adams, warned as late as 1941, almost thirty years after the amalgamation, that the people in the north regarded themselves as belonging to a separate country and that enforced cooperation with the south could lead to demands for what he called a separate independent existence along the line of religion that he likened to Pakistan, which, on the grounds of religion, had separated from India.[46]

A scholar on Islam, Muhammad S. Umar, argues along the same lines that the British had anti-Islam tendencies, though he also notes visible signs of support for Islam.[47] In his opinion, the British strategy in northern Nigeria involved a four-legged approach of appropriation, containment, surveillance, and outright antagonism, depending on the time and the interest to be pursued.[48] In applying these variables, he argued, the British were gradually modifying the geopolitics of the erstwhile Sokoto Caliphate, Sharia law and courts, and Qur'anic schools; appropriating Muslim taxes; undertaking socioeconomic activities like slave manumission and self-redemption; stifling Islamic practices, as in the case of Mahdiyya and Tijaniyya; and strictly surveilling some perceived anticolonial scholars all over colonial northern Nigeria and beyond into Saudi Arabia, Egypt, and Sudan where Islamic scholars of Nigeria resided.[49] Controversies over the attitude of the British colonial office are likely to continue to attract scholars. But while this continues, ethnicity too became an issue among Islamic sects.

Islamic Sects and Ethnicity

It is also appropriate to look at the origin of the main Islamic sects in Nigeria and the relationships between them in the period before independence and shortly afterward, and particularly to investigate the antecedents of postindependence tensions between some of them. In the period after independence, there were two main Islamic orders in Nigeria, the Qadriyya and the Tijaniyya. The former got into West Africa during the fifteenth century, while the Tijaniyya sect was founded by Ahmad al-Tijani in Fez, Morocco, and reached Nigeria in the 1820s, coming into the country through Kano. Even at these early stages, ethnicity and politics had become a factor in the relationship between the two groups. The Qadriyya was firmly linked to the Fulani leadership in Sokoto, even though it was to spread to other places. For its part, the Tijaniyya was more rooted in Kano, and it was said that the doctrine symbolized the independence of Kano from Sokoto where the Qadriyya held sway.

Considerable attention came to the Tijaniyya/Qadriyya relationship and the Kano/Sokoto rivalry when in 1937 the emir of Kano, Abdullahi Bayero, openly identified himself as Tijaniyya.

Although both had similarities in their doctrines, including the acceptance that a savior (Mahdi) would come at the end of time to ensure the triumph of Islam over other religions, there were still major doctrinal differences between them.[50] For example, riots broke out in Sokoto in 1949, when the sultan, who also doubled as the Sarkin Musulumi, ordered the destruction of several Tijaniyya mosques. Riots were to recur in 1956.[51] The period immediately after independence in 1960 was to witness more tension in the relationship between the two groups, and here again politics and ethnicity were to play prominent roles. Throughout the First Republic (1960–66), when Ahmadu Bello (the Sadauna of Sokoto) was the premier of northern Nigeria, the Tijaniyya had a difficult period when they had to operate almost like an underground movement. This is further discussed in chapter 6.

There is a need to look at the causes of doctrinal differences between the Qadriyya and the Tijaniyya. First, the Qadriyya opposed the ritual and doctrine of the Tijaniyya, like the crossing of arms during prayer; the Sardauna (the head of Nigeria's Muslim community) decreed that all prayer leaders should pray with their arms at their sides. Second, the Qadriyya objected to what they saw as the Tijaniyya tendency to venerate Ahmad-al-Tijani over and above the Prophet Muhammad, in part by calling him the "Seal of the Saints." To the Qadriyya, Muhammad was the last of the prophets. There were also disagreements over the treatment of women, with the Tijaniyyas being more relaxed in general and also somewhat opposed to the hijab (women's head covering). Smaller sects like the Mahdiyya and the Ahmadiyya found more adherents in Kano than in most other parts of northern Nigeria. The Mahdiyya believed that Mohammad Ahmad b. Sayyid Abdullahi was the proclaimed Mahdi. Meanwhile, the Ahmadiyya movement was established in northern India in the late nineteenth century by Ghulam Ahmad, who claimed to be the Mahdi and a reappearance of the Prophet Muhammad. When it is considered that Tijaniyya also had its early roots in Kano, it may be concluded that Kano, at least at the time immediately after independence, was receptive to innovative Islamic doctrines.

Also, important to note is the ethnic dimension of Islam in the country. Right from the beginning, the Hausa/Fulani north differed on Islam from the Yoruba southwest. Joseph Kenny captures this reality succinctly: "while Northern Islam has been firmly reformist and separatist with regards to anything non-Islamic, Yoruba Muslims have been accommodating, so that in one family you can find both Muslims and Christians and some involvement in the traditional religion."[52] The Yoruba have always had a relaxed attitude toward religion, freely mixing Islam with other religious practices; this is why traditional Yoruba chieftaincy titles penetrated Muslim positions in mosques, a tendency that is also prevalent among Yoruba Christians. It is also important, however, to acknowledge that some see the whole situation under a social framework, that is, not as a case of religious purity but as a case of liberal Yoruba versus conservative Hausa. For our purposes, the strictness of Hausa/Fulani Muslims means that they owe greater allegiance to their religion than to their ethnicity or even the Nigerian state. For many of them, they are first Muslims, then Hausa/Fulani, and finally Nigerians. Many Yoruba Muslims find this loyalty arrangement somewhat difficult to countenance. On their part, they see themselves first as Yoruba, then as Christian or Muslim, and last as Nigerians.[53]

Christianity and Nigerian Society: Emergence and Growth

Like Islam, Christianity came to the territory that later became Nigeria in two phases. First, the crusading zeal that drove the Portuguese incursion into the West African coast in the fifteenth century brought Christianity. As it was largely an extension of the general trade in gold, ivory, pepper, and slaves, Christian priests traveled with merchant traders. They sought "either to check the advance of Islam—at the time the hereditary foe of Christendom," historian Kenneth Dike noted in a 1957 lecture, "or to extend the Christian message to unknown lands."[54] Missionary activities during this time were, however, quite minimal, as the focus was more on trade. But in the sixteenth century, Portuguese traders took an interest in spreading the Christian religion. The places of initial missionary interest were Benin and Warri; records show that the Oba of Benin, Oba Esigie (1504–50), sent an embassy to King Manuel of Portugal in 1514, and in the following year, Christian priests arrived in Benin. Records of the famous Benin historian Jacob Egharevba show that under Esigie, churches were built in Benin, and prominent citizens, including the Oba's son, were baptized. This trend was continued by Esigie's successor, Orhoghua.

Not much success attended this effort. Dike pointed to the character and organization of the slave trade: "under the chaotic and unsettled conditions in which the slaves were captured and sold, the spread of the Christian message proved impossible."[55] Moreover, Dike noted that, with very few exceptions, the early European missionaries worked in territories in which Africans were sovereign. Consequently, African governments supported the indigenous faith against that of the trading Europeans. The third factor was the high mortality among the missionaries as they encountered diseases new to them, such as malaria.[56]

The second phase was in the nineteenth century. In 1842, Badagry became the first place of settlement of Christian missionaries; the Methodist mission led the phase with the arrival of Thomas Birch Freeman.[57] Not much success, however, attended their efforts either, as the town's association with the slave trade gave the white men a negative reputation. Freeman later moved to Abeokuta, where he was followed by Henry Townsend of the Anglican Church in December 1842. Both were welcomed by Sodeke, the king, and they were subsequently followed by missionaries of Baptist and Catholic denominations. There were, however, other reasons why the Egba accepted Christianity: they thought that the conversion would bring the white missionaries to their side in their bitter rivalry with their Lagos, Ibadan, and Ijebu neighbors. Abeokuta was thus the first Christian town in Yorubaland—a claim to Christianity that the Egba people relish with pride and delight to date, hence the popular song:

Òwu ló Ni Jésu
Òwu ló Ni Jésu
Tótoró nì'gbàgbó tí koko bẹrẹ
Òwu ló Ni Jésu

Owu (people) own Jesus
Owu (people) own Jesus
Totoro was where Christianity originated
Owu (people) own Jesus

Things changed with the abolition of slavery in 1833 and the subsequent freedom of former slaves who had accepted Christianity. The early evangelization included freed slaves who arrived from Sierra Leone and began to retrace their way back to Nigeria via Lagos, Badagry, and Abeokuta. They also had opportunities to acquire education offered by the Church Missionary Society (CMS). Over time, a good number of former slaves converted to Christianity. One of these was Samuel Ajayi Crowther, captured at age twelve by Fulani slave raiders and sold to Portuguese slave traders. He later regained his freedom and went on to become the first African to be ordained a bishop by the CMS in addition to his consecration as bishop of the Niger territory in 1864.[58]

From the 1850s, Christian missions spread into other parts of Yorubaland. While there were occasional tensions between the new Christians and the adherents of Yoruba traditional religions, things never really got completely out of hand and a measure of tolerance existed. The arrival of Christianity altered the outlook of the southern parts of Nigeria. Christian missionaries forbade or at least discouraged many traditional practices: polygamy, blood pacts, oath swearing, oracles, vows, divination, and secret societies. But as with Islam, people did not stop practicing their traditional religions. It was indeed common for a measure of harmony to be reached between Christianity and traditional religion. This song, commonly sung among the Yoruba, reflects this harmony:

Áwa ó So'ro ilé ilé wa o
Áwa ó So'ro ilé ilé wa o
Ìgbàgbò kò pé, o yee
Ìgbàgbò kò pé ka wa so'so
Áwa ó So'ro ilé ilé wa o

We are going to worship our ancestral deities
We are going to worship our ancestral deities
Christianity does not imply
Christianity does not imply that we should not worship our ancestral
   deities
We are going to worship the deities of our ancestors

This cross-allegiance between Christianity and traditional religion continues among the Yoruba, even if it is now somewhat less common.

Christianity in the area that was later to become northern Nigeria has been present much longer than it is often assumed. In a seminal work, historian Emmanuel Ayandele noted a record of not less than 100,000 Christian adherents in the kingdom of Korofa as far back as 1708, and that the Roman Catholic Church had built a hospital in the kingdom.[59] He also pointed out that there was an attempt to introduce Christianity into Borno with the arrival in the area of one Father Carlo de Genova. Although Ayandele reported that the initial efforts were feeble, missionary efforts in northern Nigeria continued, especially in the mid-nineteenth century, when the objective was primarily to counter what was seen as the "false doctrine of the imposter from Mecca."[60] Generally, it would appear that efforts to bring the Christian religion to the area later known as northern Nigeria were largely uncoordinated, with different religious groups coming into the region to seek converts.

The advancement of Christianity in the region also owed a lot to the activities of Ajayi Crowther and William Balfour Baikie, who led a mission into the region in 1857. Their encounter with Hausa Muslims gave them a passion for the people. When he thus became the head of the Niger Mission in 1871, Crowther was able to actualize his desire to Christianize the area. With considerable effort and persuasion, he won the confidence of the emir of Bida, who allowed him to open mission stations in two strategic caravan posts, Kippo and Shonga, in 1875 and 1876 respectively.[61] Furthermore, recommendation letters were sent by the emir to the emirs of Nassarawa and Yola introducing Crowther's initiative. The emir also sent his son along with Crowther to undertake Western education. A further invitation came later in 1893 from Kontagora, Nassarawa, and other places, but this approach to the rulers did not win converts. In 1890, Graham Brooke led a team of twelve missionaries known as the Sudan Party to Lokoja with a different strategy: immersion in Hausa customs. This too failed. In 1899, Bishop Tigwell came to the region and succeeded in converting many people, and after considerable challenges he was able to build a mission house and dispensary in Girku, near Zaria.

In 1881, a Wesleyan mission focused on Nupe through the activities of Allakura Sharpe, an ex-slave of Kanuri origin. He had previously pleaded for the mission to extend missionary activities to Hausa, Tapa, Kanuri, and Fulani communities.[62] Ayandele noted that in 1881, the American Board of Commissions for Foreign Missions expressed the wish to introduce Christianity in Yola District and in 1899, the Foreign Board of London considered sending missions to Kano or Katsina. In Ayandele's opinion, the board's special interest in Hausa land during this period could be attributed to the "idyllic picture of the racial characteristic of the Hausa people painted by many expatriates [that] in intelligence, physiognomy, material culture and literary achievements," the Hausas were superior to the southerners.[63] The Roman Catholics opened a mission station in Lokoja in 1884, with three priests spreading their faith. But one of the fathers died in 1885. Father Andrew Dornan was subsequently sent to replace the deceased. After some years, the Roman Catholic mission headquarters was removed from Lokoja to Asaba by Father Carlo Zappa.

Interest erupted again in 1906 when the missionaries of the Cambridge University Missionary Party collaborated with the CMS to work in the Bauchi Highlands. Shortly afterward, the Sudan United Mission, which had been founded in Edinburgh, Scotland, in 1904, also came to Wukari in the Bauchi district, where they were joined by American Quakers in Lokoja and Wukari in 1905. In July 1910, all the missions held a conference to plan how to evangelize northern Nigeria. As Gbadamosi and Ajayi have noted, their achievements in terms of converts were small: "up till 1910, there were only 45 Churches and 650 pupils in mission schools in the northern part of Nigeria. By contrast, there were 116 Churches in Ijebu Ode district alone and over 4,000 children in schools in Abeokuta [alone]."[64]

In Eastern Nigeria, much of the development of Christianity can be linked to an Irish Catholic priest, John Shanahan. He brought Catholicism to Oghuli, where he built a primary school, conducted baptism classes, and learned the Ibo language. Shanahan had founded a holy order, the Sisters of Our Lady of the Holy Rosary, in Ireland in 1920. The sisters were trained to offer service to the Catholic Missions of the Holy Ghost Fathers in the eastern parts of Nigeria. Father Shanahan also converted many Ibos to Catholicism. By 1924, the Catholic Church in Nigeria was staffed by Ibos. In 1933, Shanahan consecrated a new cathedral that was built by the Church in Nigeria. Table 1.1 lists the dates of establishment of some Christian denominations in Nigeria.

Southerners' access to Western education was to have an impact on religion. Indeed, the advantages of this access were factors in the politics of religion in postindependence Nigeria. Over time, the educated southern civil servants were sent to the north during the colonial period, creating fears among northerners that their region would be dominated by rival ethnic groups.

In the early 1930s, a new phase began in which Nigerian Christians set out to indigenize the religion. Some of the resulting churches included Cherubim and Seraphim Church, Church of the Lord (Aladura), Christ Apostolic Church (CAC), and Celestial Church of Christ under the leadership of Moses Orimolade, Josiah Olunowo Oshitelu, Joseph Ayo Babalola, and Samuel Oshoffa, respectively. According to a scholar on the subject, Rotimi Omotoye, "these churches combined the fundamental elements of Christianity and African culture, in a way that advertised their Christian intentions without undermining their African credentials."[65] He also notes that the churches "emphasized some features which are relevant and valued by the African people, such as, prophecy, healing, prayer, vision, dream and the use of sacred objects."[66] These churches grew phenomenally in the nooks and crannies of Yorubaland and beyond. One, the CAC under the late Joseph Ayo Babalola, began what may be considered the first revivalist mission in Nigeria and for a long time was the dominant "firebrand" Christian denomination in Nigeria. Many key individuals who were later to occupy prominent positions in advancing Pentecostal Christianity had their roots in this church. Another major actor in Christian evangelization in Nigeria just about the time of Ayo Babalola was John Elton, an English missionary who came to Nigeria with his family in 1937 and remained there until his death in January 1987. Pa Elton, as he was affectionately called, served as a mentor to many who were later to be household names in Nigerian Pentecostalism, including Benson Idahosa, Enoch Adeboye, David Oyedepo, and Wale Oke.[67]

By the late 1960s and early 1970s, the concept of Christian Pentecostalism had entered the equation. Although Pentecostals believe in the Holy Bible,

TABLE 1.1 Early Christian Denominations in Nigeria and
Year of Establishment

Denomination	Year of Establishment
Wesleyan Methodist	1842
Scottish Presbyterian	1842
Church Missionary Society	1844
Southern Baptist Foreign Mission	1850
Roman Catholic Mission	1861
Sudan Interior Mission	1893
Sudan United Mission	1904
United Missionary Society	1905
Seventh-Day Adventist	1914
Assembly of God	1939
Qua Iboe Mission	1952

Source: Ajayi, *Christian Missions in Nigeria*, 257.

their point of departure is speaking in tongues. Pentecostals argue that the promise made by Jesus Christ on the day of Pentecost (Acts 2:4) was an essential element of the Christian faith: that the Holy Spirit would descend, and Christians would be able to speak in an unknown tongue. The roots of Pentecostalism in Nigeria are much longer than is often assumed. Two groups, the Student Christian Movement (SCM) and the Scripture Union, served as antecedents to Pentecostalism in Nigeria. The Scripture Union was established in England in 1867 and had come to Nigeria by 1884.[68] The SCM was also established in Britain in the early twentieth century and expanded to West Africa in the 1930s through West African students who had studied in Britain. In particular, two Nigerians, Akanu Ibiam and Theophilus Ejiwumi, brought the movement to Nigeria, according to Matthews Ojo.[69] Ibiam, who had studied medicine at St Andrews University in Scotland, had returned to Nigeria in 1935, while Ejiwumi had studied at University College London and had returned to Nigeria in 1940 to take up a job at the Yaba High College, where he established the SCM.[70] From there it spread to the University of Ibadan and subsequently to other institutions. In the early 1970s, the Scripture Union spread widely, with groups of youths across tertiary institutions expressing radical Christian views. These groups were dominant in academic institutions across the southern parts of the country. At the beginning, Pentecostalism was predominant in the south, but as time went on, it made inroads in the north; many radical Christian churches started to establish branches in areas largely populated by

Muslims. Prominent among Pentecostal churches today are the Deeper Christian Life Ministry, the Redeemed Christian Church of God, the Living Faith Church (also known as the Winners' Chapel), Rhema Church, New Testament Church, Church of God Mission, Latter Rain Assembly, Christ Chapel International, Sword of the Spirits, Christ Embassy Church, and Synagogue, Church of All Nations.

Pentecostal Christianity met and still meets subtle objections—doctrinal and procedural—from mainline churches. On the doctrinal level, conventional churches find Pentecostal practices like speaking in tongues and falling under the anointing alien to Christianity. While not necessarily saying that there might not be biblical injunctions to back up such practices, mainline churches have doubts that the ways these practices are used by Pentecostal Christians are the ways they manifested in the Bible. Mainline Christians thus consider aspects of Pentecostal practices youthful activities that are more in line with social exuberance and as such have no place in conventional churches. On the procedural aspect, conventional churches find it inappropriate that Pentecostal churches appoint pastors who have not undergone formal training in seminaries or Bible colleges, only claiming to have been called by God. Also, by extension, mainline churches worry that the absence of hierarchies and procedures makes Pentecostal churches vulnerable to abuse and manipulation by leaders. But mainstream churches also saw that Pentecostal churches were not slowing down and that they were losing their own youthful members to the Pentecostal fold. So mainline churches are introducing elements of Pentecostalism into their services.

There is, however, subtle infighting among Christian churches of Pentecostal flavors, with largely doctrinal roots, even if it has become somewhat personal. The issue here is that some Pentecostal pastors doubt the Pentecostal credentials of others. In this case, pastors may claim that others were not called by God and as such are not fit to be categorized as Pentecostal. Other Pentecostal pastors recognize that individual callings might be different, but criticize others for doing things they consider unscriptural. Two issues are at the center of controversy here. The first is the allegation that some are practicing Pentecostalism in ways that bring in elements of occultism. The second cause is that others are exploiting the vulnerability of their congregation for financial benefit. These are discussed at some length in chapter 3.

Some features are common to many Pentecostal Christian churches, two of which are worth mentioning here. The first is that many of the churches are run as family affairs, with the founder's wife (and in some cases, children) also deeply involved in the management of the church. In many cases, wives wield significant influence, and they are addressed by various honorifics. Often, they are showered with gifts and flattered with encomiums. A second feature is the attitude toward material wealth. A survey of Pentecostal Christianity in Nigeria finds considerable flamboyance, with many church leaders spreading the gospel of Christ with what some consider unimaginable extravagance; some even have private jets.

There is a need to look at what may be described as the professional dimension of Christian evangelization, which takes the form of Christian professionals coming together to form associations. Of all the groups under the banner of religion, perhaps the best known is the Nigeria branch of the Full Gospel Businessmen's Fellowship International. The primary aim of this group is to advance the Christian religion through the establishment of honest business principles. Although most members are businessmen, it is also open to those who may not be in business but belong to other professions that give them social and financial clout. The past decade has also witnessed increased radicalization on university campuses, where lecturers with radical Christian views have become important power political actors on university campuses. They organize weekly meetings, and many of them have become associate pastors in Pentecostal churches.[71] Now that an overview of the birth, development, and a few features and peculiarities of Christianity and Islam has been provided, this chapter briefly discusses the preindependence relationship between adherents of the main religions.

Relationship between the Religions during Colonial Rule

Those who observed traditional religions did not protest the arrival of Christianity and Islam; the relationship between the three religions was at first largely cordial. There was inevitably some rivalry between Christianity and Islam, as both sought converts and members. Early on, Christianity was on the defensive, as Islam had an upper hand both in the northern part of the country and at least initially among the Yoruba.

A new Christian offensive was launched around 1876, when the Reverend James Johnson came up with a strategy that he thought would hijack the initiative from the Muslims. As part of the strategy, local Christian ministers were admonished to reach out to Muslims, to learn to write Christian tracts in Arabic and Yoruban languages and get them circulated among the Muslim population. While some of them taught themselves Arabic, others hired teachers. Prominent Christian clergymen, including Reverends M. S. Cole, T. A. J. Ogunbiyi, and M. T. Euler-Ajayi, became knowledgeable in Arabic and produced tracts in the language. There were also ongoing healthy debates and sustained dialogues between leaders of both religions, which continued until independence.

Of all the Christian strategies, perhaps the most prominent were the efforts by Christian clergy to indoctrinate Muslim children attending Christian schools. Reverend Johnson was unequivocal about this: "our desire is to get as much as we can get of our religion in Mohammedan scholars before they leave school."[72] The idea of using schools as a tool for evangelization was particularly favored by Ajayi Crowther. The Muslims saw through this strategy and in some places refused to accept Christian missionary education. For example, in places like Iwo and Iseyin, both in the southwest, Muslim leaders persuaded their chiefs to frustrate the establishment of Christian mission schools.[73]

The Muslims soon saw the fruitlessness of their antagonism toward Western education. Those who sought more gainful and prestigious employment with the government or commercial houses had to have Western education. But at this stage too, the colonial government saw the need to disengage Western education from the Christian faith and in 1898 organized the building of the Government Muslim School in Epe, Lagos, and Badagry.[74] Some Muslims attended these schools; others went to Christian schools, and some of the latter ultimately converted to Christianity. Overall, although people engaged in heated debates and intense rivalry, they did so with a measure of cooperation and toleration. There was hardly any record of the violence that was to be the hallmark of the postindependence period.

Religion and the Nigerian State: Politics and Intrigues of Diversity

With independence, how did religion mix with politics and identity? How did the country's constitution see the place of religion in politics and the role of the state? These are crucial questions, as the constitution has been intentionally or unwittingly used to encourage violence.

The current Nigerian constitution is at best confusing on the nature of this relationship, and the source of this confusion is worth recording because of its relevance to religion and violence in the country. The antecedents can be traced to the mid-1970s: during the debate for the promulgation of the 1979 constitution, some Muslim members of the Constituent Assembly called for the new constitution to incorporate Sharia law. Specifically, the Sharia court that was demanded at this stage was to deal with issues such as the sharing of an inheritance among members of a family, settling marital disputes, settling other issues of relationships among relatives, settling the custody of children, and other similar civil matters. This demand polarized the country, especially as most of those making the case for adopting Sharia were from northern Nigeria, where the Muslim population was dominant. The problem could not be resolved until the military overthrew the Second Republic in 1983. Then in 1985 the military government of General Ibrahim Babangida brought Nigeria into the Organization of the Islamic Conference. This is discussed in detail in chapter 6; for now, it is enough to say that it confused the secularity of the country.

As Simeon Ilesanmi has noted, Nigeria's constitutional provision on religion is far more complex than often acknowledged.[75] First, there is the nonadoption clause (section 10) and second is the exercise of free expression clause in section 39. The former asserts that "the Government of the Federation or of a State shall not adopt any religion as State Religion," while the latter guarantees freedom of expression in the country. These are separate from the extensive portions of the constitution devoted to the administration of Sharia and Sharia courts. The task of interpreting these provisions has sparked considerable debate among legal scholars. Complicating this task is that the words *secular* or *secularity* do not appear anywhere in the constitution. It is an inference that some interpreters have drawn from different provisions of the constitution, and there is no consensus on any interpretation.[76] Broadly speaking, it is common for Christians, southerners, and nonreligious people to give precedence to the nonadoption clause and use it as a basis for inferring secularity, while their northern counterparts rely on the exercise of free expression clause. Neither side has said much about the nondiscrimination clause and the extent to which this might impose the duty of neutrality toward religion on the state and the government. Thus, jurisprudence on religion in Nigeria is relatively inchoate and of little guidance for balanced democratic deliberation.[77]

The reality of the Nigerian situation is that the government has, through different methods, eroded all of these rights. Governments set up institutions that control religious affairs and rites, including pilgrimages. Then elites hijacked the process, and intense rivalries emerged between Christians and Muslims. In the northern parts of the country, for example, Muslim and Christian elites formed rival political parties—respectively, the Jamaatu Nasril Islam and the Northern Christian Association (NCA)—to advance the causes of their respective religions. In 1964, the NCA changed its name to Christian Association of Nigeria, "covering all Christians in Nigeria as a way of providing a platform for a national association capable of providing avenues for common interest, enlistment of strong bargaining power, generating more resources, and establishing a uniting bloc."[78] As will be shown later, these two associations have, over the years, wielded power to protect and defend their members and reduce internal divisions. However, while both were formed to spread their respective religions and ensure harmony within their respective folds, both have expended more energy countering each other in what gradually became a zero-sum game.

Scholars and Their Interpretations of Religion and Society in Nigeria

The topic of the link between religion and Nigerian society has secured its array of prominent scholars, each focusing on different aspects of the complexity.[79] While it is, of course, impossible to discuss all the major studies on the subject, the central arguments of a few key ones should be noted. In *Religion, Politics, and Power in Northern Nigeria*, published in 1993, Matthew Kukah looks at the Islamization policies of Ahmadu Bello, the premier of northern Nigeria in the early 1960s, then traces their evolution through successive regimes. Kukah names four stages of Islamization: the emergence of Hausa/Fulani hegemony up to the assassination of Ahmadu Bello in 1966; Gowon's regime (1966–75) and the run-up to the establishment of civilian rule in 1979; Sheu Shagari's civilian rule (1979–83); and the military regime of Ibrahim Babangida.[80] Kukah explores the extent to which the Hausa/Fulani elite advanced the Islamization of the country during each of these administrations. He details the role played by the media, especially the northern-based New Nigeria and the Federal Radio Corporation in Kaduna. In discussing elites, the book looks at the importance of cohesiveness, sometimes cutting across ethnic divides, which the Hausa/Fulani oligarchy has used to advance the Islamization agenda.

Simeon Ilesanmi, in *Religious Pluralism and the Nigerian State*, published in 1997, argues that religion is the most important problem confronting Nigeria but that the crisis between religion and the Nigerian state is still a relatively modern problem. Specifically, Ilesanmi indicts colonialism for broadening pluralism and also blames the elites for de-emphasizing and marginalizing religion. He contends that scholarship on the subject has not adequately considered the pluralistic context and the idealistic pretensions of the state that inhibit the possibility of forging enduring civic amity among Nigeria's diverse groups. Ilesanmi addresses two main questions relating to the link between religion and society: (1) what political framework can foster a "just relationship" between the Nigerian state and religious groups; and (2) within what political and religious attitudes the various religious groups can realize both their freedom and constrictions. In addressing these questions, Ilesanmi argues against seeing religious pluralism as inherently problematic. Indeed, to him, religion should be a unifying, rather than a divisive, factor: "not an evil to be overcome, rather, it is to be celebrated."[81] Four public philosophies in Nigeria have set the tone of the discourse on religion since the 1970s, he says: civil religion, that is, references to religious idioms in public issues; attempts to generate respect for the rule of law; definition of the purpose of government; and the cultivation of a dialogic and tolerant political attitude.[82] Ilesanmi also expresses views about elites, who, he says, undermine credible discourse through their "shallowness and recklessness."[83]

Toyin Falola's 1998 book *Violence in Nigeria: The Crisis of Religious Politics and Secular Ideologies* is one of the earliest pieces of academic scholarship to look at religion in Nigeria from the perspective of conflict, interrogating its causes and consequences, and reviewing the options for conflict resolution. Falola argues that the multiethnic, multireligious, and multicultural nature of Nigerian society has rendered the country particularly vulnerable to religious crises; the Nigerian elites have also played a role in fomenting religious conflict in their desperate desire to acquire power. Specifically, Falola provides a study of the various religious crises in Nigeria between independence and the time of publication, especially the Maitatsine riot of 1980, and identifies and discusses the impact of ethnicity, poverty, religious pluralism, and partisan politics. The book traces the history of religious violence in Nigeria to the nineteenth-century Islamic wars that brought Islam to northern Nigeria, and the impact of colonialism, which brought Christianity in the nineteenth and twentieth centuries. In Falola's view, Christian-Muslim violence in Nigeria is rooted largely in the tendency of the two sides to see one another "as rivals fighting for the control of converts and the state."[84]

Olufemi Vaughan, in *Religion and the Making of Nigeria*, published in 2016, examines how Christian, Muslim, and indigenous religious structures have provided the essential social and ideological frameworks for the construction of contemporary Nigeria. Tracing historical accounts, Vaughan looks at Nigeria's social, religious, and political history from the early nineteenth century to the present. During the nineteenth century, the historic Sokoto Jihad in today's northern Nigeria and the Christian missionary movement in what is now the southwestern part of the country provided the frameworks for ethnoreligious divisions in colonial society. Following Nigeria's independence in 1960, Christian-Muslim tensions became manifest in regional and religious conflicts over the expansion of Sharia, fierce competition among political elites for state power, and the rise of Boko Haram. These are not simply conflicts over religious beliefs, ethnicity, and regionalism; they represent structural imbalances founded on the religious divisions forged under colonial rule.[85]

Perhaps the latest book that offers a comprehensive discussion of politics and religion in Nigeria is Ebenezer Obadare's *Pentecostal Republic: Religion and the Struggle for State Power in Nigeria*, and it offers an analytical discussion of how religious politics manifested in the period following Nigeria's return to civilian rule in 1999. In the book, published in 2018, Obadare makes two complementary arguments: that the return to civil rule in 1999 coincided with the triumph of Christianity over its historical rival, Islam, as a political force in the country; and that this political triumph happened in tandem with Pentecostalism's creeping domination, not just of Christianity, but of popular culture, politics, and the entire democratic process.

From this literature, we can see that religion has come to the center of controversies in Nigeria in different ways. The first is that people disagree profoundly about how much religion should influence the state. For some ethnic groups, religion and politics are the same, so that religious laws are inseparable from governance; for others, religion is completely separable from governance. How to address this dichotomy has remained a source of major controversy in Nigeria. The second factor that makes religion a subject of controversy in Nigeria is tension between the three main religions, especially between Islam and Christianity. Third, political and even religious elites have exploited religion to serve their selfish interests. Finally, external political and religious events have permeated national sociopolitical and religious life in Nigeria.

Conclusion

In most societies, religion remains a major identity issue and undoubtedly one of the most emotional. When it is mixed with ethnicity, as it is in many African countries, the divisive tendencies can become more profoundly challenging. The arrival of Islam and Christianity in Africa introduced competitions that were to affect inter- and intragroup relations, especially because of the zero-sum nature of the race for converts. Among the other factors that have further complicated the situation for African countries are the issues created by the vicissitudes of colonialism, which brought disparate groups together to form nation-states. All this caused complications on which the religious rivalries could feed, thus fueling disharmony. In this chapter, I have argued that long before colonialism, religion had been a major issue in the territory that was later to become Nigeria. To establish this, I have discussed the contents of traditional religions and have traced the history of Islam and Christianity across ethnic communities in precolonial Nigeria. I have contended that the processes through which Islam and Christianity came to the territory were difficult and involved competition, and that these processes sowed the seeds of rivalry in the country. Indeed, the formal evolution of the state only further reinforced religious divisions, just as elites of various sectors found it a subject to exploit to attain personal and class ambitions. Equally, I also contend that the ways religion has percolated into regular activities, like politics and inter-group relations, and perceptions have all made it more complicated in Nigeria. Finally, aspects of the country's history are some of the root causes of disaffec-tion: the perception by Muslims that British colonialism gave Christianity an advantage over Islam, which has been at the center of some of the disagree-ments between the two religions; and the constitution itself is contradictory about the role of religion in state affairs. While similar things may have hap-pened in other African countries, the consequences have been more profound in Nigeria because of the extent of its diversity and the complications of its body politic. How Islam, the first foreign religion to come into Nigeria, is as-sociated with violence in the country is the subject of discussion in chapter 2.

2. ISLAM AND VIOLENCE IN NIGERIA

Allah is our target, the Prophet is our example, the Qur'ān is our canon, jihād is our way, and dying for the cause of God is our noble wish. —Creed of the Jamā'at Tajdīd al-Islām (Society for Renewal of Islam in Nigeria), adopted from the Creed of the Muslim Brotherhood

This society that we are living together needs sacrifice. Those who sacrifice, their compliment is not just in this world (only); their name will not just be known in this world, in the hereafter; paradise is their reward from almighty Allah. Paradise is the reward of your sacrifice; meanwhile, your life sacrifice is the dooms day flattery. As we all know, the life in this world is not eternal. —SHEIKH EL-ZAKZAKY

Clashes among Islamic sects and between the sects and the government were occasional occurrences during the colonial era and into independence.[1] In postindependence Nigeria, however, clashes between sects, the government, and adherents of other religions became common. This chapter discusses the various ways that Islam has been associated with violence in Nigeria, exploring the patterns of this violence and their consequences for intergroup relations.

Like mainstream Muslims, most Nigerian Muslims who have taken to violence maintain the five pillars of Islam: Shahadah (profession of faith), As-Salat (prayer), Zakat (gifts), Saun (fasting), and Hajj (holy pilgrimage). But some radical groups have modified them and have thus espoused versions of Islam at variance with mainstream Muslims. Some also strongly believe that governmental policies, legacies of colonialism, and the activities of other religions make it difficult for them to live according to these pillars. Others also believe that Islam ought to be practiced exactly the way it was during the time of Prophet Muhammad, and anything preventing that should be violently opposed.[2] Furthermore, radical Islamic groups think that there is a mutually reinforcing link between global development (as it relates to Muslims) and the role of Muslims in Nigeria. Disagreements among different Islamic sects have also been a key cause of violence, at least as important as the rivalry with Christianity.

The key issues that have linked Islamic religion to violence in the country have been largely internal. Islam's connection to violence in postindependence Nigeria seems to have come in three hardly distinguishable phases. The first was around the early 1970s, when the late Mohammed Marwa, widely known as Maitatsine, began espousing his radical doctrine that would result in violence in 1980. The second started around the mid-1980s and lasted till the 1990s, or the period immediately preceding the emergence of Boko Haram. A string of external issues, like the successful revolution of the Iranian people against their shah, combined with a number of domestic issues, like the introduction of the Sharia law, which sparked an awakening of Islamist tendencies across northern Nigeria. The third phase has witnessed the activities of Boko Haram, which are discussed in chapter 5.

Maitatsine: Origin of Islam's Association with Violence in Postindependence Nigeria

The first major violence attributable to Islam was the Maitatsine riots, led by Mohammed Marwa, which engulfed key northern Nigerian cities between 1980 and 1985.[3] Marwa, a native of Marwa village in northern Cameroon, had migrated to Kano in the early 1940s and attained prominence as an Islamic scholar with a remarkable following. The riots introduced many of the tactics that were to become prevalent in Nigeria's later religious violence: mobilization of poor communities against urban Muslims, the justification of violence against non-Muslims, identification with global Islamic movements, and the incorporation of global jihadist tactics into local operations. The group's version of Islamic fundamentalism—its doctrine, activities, manifestation of violence, and governmental reactions—also set a pattern that was to dominate religious violence in Nigeria. And the internal and external dimensions of extremism visible here were to surface again later.

Aspects of Marwa's teaching were initially not violent, including warnings against ostentatious living and accumulating wealth. Like Mohammed Yusuf, who was to lead the Boko Haram group more than three decades later, Marwa also believed that Western education is not compatible with Islam, and his critiques of social problems (corruption, poverty, and unemployment) drew followers among largely uneducated and unemployed members of society. He was also known for his charisma and oratory. But other aspects of Marwa's doctrine were more unusual. He saw himself as the real Prophet. There were reports that after his death, copies of the Qur'an found in his house had the name of the Prophet replaced by his own.[4] His followers preached that he was their true prophet, and they called on others to desist from mentioning the name of Prophet Muhammad.[5] Indeed, one of his leading lieutenants had a Hausa inscription around his neck that reflects this:

> Idan aka yanyanke ni guda kuma in mutu, zan sake dawowa. Babu wani mutumin kirki kamar Muhammadu Allah (Annabi Muhammad). . . . Idan na mutu, kiyayya ta kare, wauta ta kare, arna da karshen rashin yarda. . . . Tun daga halittar mutum babu kafiri kamar Annabi bakinsa Isa.

> If I were cut into pieces and I die, I will come back again. There is no worthless person like Muhammadu Allah (Prophet Muhammad). . . . If I die, animosity ends, madness ends, paganism and unbelieving end. . . . Since the creation of man there was no infidel like Prophet Annabi Isa [Jesus].[6]

Although Marwa recognized the authority of the Qur'an, he believed that he was the only person who could interpret it. He also said that all the Hadiths and Sunnah were wrong. His followers were instructed never to face the Ka'aba while praying, and to never use the common phrase "Allahu Akbar" (God is great) during prayer. With views like these, confrontation with the state and mainstream Muslims was inevitable.

His shift into violence was also similar to that of subsequent Islamic radicalization, especially of Boko Haram. In the early 1960s, he targeted the Kano establishment, especially the emir, Sanusi, for attacks. In 1962, the emir released a royal indictment of Marwa, with an Islamic judge sentencing him to a ninety-day jail term and then deporting him back to Cameroon. His home country was, however, unwilling to accept him, and sent him back to Nigeria, where he stayed in Gongola State. The opportunity for him to return to Kano came with Sanusi's abdication in 1963. Now he and his group intensified their militarism and established mosques that rhetorically attacked established Muslim orders. They found a ready audience in the marginal and poverty-stricken sections of the population, whose rejection by the more established urban groups fostered their religious opposition.

The first real eruption of the Maitatsine riot was in December 1980. Because of his use of incendiary language, the police had dispatched units to stop Marwa's outdoor preaching. Marwa's supporters fought them fiercely, soon supported by reinforcements from other parts of northern Nigeria. Even professionals in the Nigerian army recognized their bravery and fearlessness in what was a militarily hopeless enterprise.[7] The police arrested thousands, and by the time the first phase of the unrest ended toward the end of December 1980, 4,177 people were dead.[8] Marwa himself was injured and later died.

Handling those arrested after the riots was difficult for the government: they did not have facilities to house them all. In the end, the government decided to deport the foreigners among them while pardoning those who were Nigerians on Independence Day, October 1, 1982. This clemency was later seen as misguided. Three weeks after the amnesty, on October 26, another uprising broke out in Bulumkutu, near Maiduguri, resulting in the deaths of 3,350 people; three days later, there was another uprising in Kaduna. In both cases, Maitatsine followers were clamoring for the removal of all governmental structures that contradicted their own version of Islam.

The sect later moved to Yola, where it organized its military operation into three sectors: defense, led by Musa Makanaki, from Gombe; an assault group led by Bagobiri, from Yawuri, Sokoto State; and an ambush group led by Danbarno, believed to be from Borno.[9] Here again, the objective was to ensure that all societal structures at variance with their own version of Islam were removed. It took the combined operation of the army and the air force to bring down this round of the rebellion, with an estimated death toll of between seven hundred and one thousand people.[10]

Gombe was to be the next base of the Maitatsine attack, in April 1985. Here again, the group demonstrated an impressive level of sophistication in its military organization and in the mastery of weaponry; they are even believed to have benefited from the knowledge of an ex-Biafran soldier who served as a mercenary.[11] Here, over a hundred people were killed. By mid-1985, the Maitatsine uprising had been completely defeated, but its tactics would live on in the radical actions of others.

Overall, the Maitatsine uprising occupies an important position in the history of religious violence in Nigeria. Apart from producing a reference point by which future uprisings are measured, it also provides an intellectual basis for analyzing the motives of subsequent radical religious groups.

Post-Maitatsine Cases of Islamic Radicalization:
Dynamics, Causes, and Manifestations

Islamic radicalization after Maitatsine was more organized and based on clearer principles than the period before the unrest. Adherents of radical Islam during this phase did not immediately take to violence, instead spending time to strengthen the intellectual base of their arguments. Meanwhile, most governments during this time almost totally abandoned the socioeconomic infrastructure. The radicals were thus able to win more converts and to justify the need to fight successive governments, which they framed as being unresponsive to citizens.

Between the Maitatsine uprising and the development of Boko Haram, violence associated with Islamic radicalization in Nigeria claimed many lives. While most of the time these conflicts can easily be traced to radical religious views, sometimes global issues, ethnicity, and local politics conceal, even if superficially, the religious aspects of these conflicts. The formation of an Islamic government in Iran under the leadership of Ayatollah Khomeini in 1979 and the subsequent humiliation it meted out to the United States between November 1979 and January 1981 inspired Muslims the world over, convincing some youths that Islam was an alternative to the capitalism/communism binary. In the 1980s, young Muslims across the world, radicalized by the revolution, began formulating ideological variants of radical Islam: this was the beginning of what became known as the revival of Islam. The teachings of radical Islamic scholars now started arriving in Nigeria from other parts of West Africa, especially Senegal; it was not uncommon during this time to see audiocassettes containing these teachings in marketplaces and motor parks across northern Nigeria. This continued during the 1980s and 1990s. Then, shortly after the birth of democracy in 1999, one of the northern Nigerian states, Zamfara, adopted Sharia law; within a few months, other northern states did so also, and within two years, all the states in the northern part of the country had adopted Sharia to varying degrees.

Dynamics internal to Muslim groups shaped this second phase of radicalization. Muslim youths, assuming that Christians had enjoyed advantages under colonialism, spoke up forcefully for a new order that would restore balance. Although the largely Muslim north was very active in national politics during the first republic, Muslims found it difficult to advance any clear agenda because the administrative structures bequeathed by colonialism, including greater recognition for Western education, made this particularly difficult.[12] Recruitment into the membership of radical Islamic groups during this period took different forms, the most prominent being massive preaching, similar to Christian evangelism.

More of these new members were young people than in previous expansions, and more men seemed to gravitate toward radicalization than women. Muslim youths who pursued violence during this period fell into three categories. First were those who were genuinely committed to the religion and felt concerned about whatever they saw as a desecration of the religion. They may be described as genuine radicals. Second were those who may be described as ad-hoc radicals, who only became violent once there was an instruction to that effect from spiritual leaders and reverted to their ordinary ways of life afterward. The third were those who may be described as opportunistic radicals, who only seized the opportunity of the moment to loot and vandalize, after which they waited anxiously for another opportunity. However, in the process of militant activities, it is difficult to identify who belonged to which type among these individuals.

Some Muslim radicals during this period too sought to prevent a return to what they saw as the era of *jahiliyya*—the period of darkness or ignorance that preceded the coming of Islam and Christianity. Also, many protested what they saw as desecration, especially of the Holy Qur'an or the name of the Prophet Muhammad. In contrast to Christians, who can freely handle the Bible—for example, putting it under their pillows for protection and on their dining tables for use before meals—Muslims cannot touch the Qur'an without performing ablutions, nor can they leave copies in places where unwashed hands might touch them. Muslims understand this as a matter of respect, even reverence; when Christians do not treat the Qur'an in this way, problems have resulted. Cases in which this has resulted in violence are discussed later in this chapter. Similarly, radical Muslims are unequivocal in their demand for respect for the Prophet Muhammad, while Christians are less inclined to give the Prophet any special attention: though most respect the sensitivity of Muslims by not desecrating the name, they do not accord the name any special respect (for example, they will not say the usual "Peace be unto him" after the mention of his name). While many Muslims are willing to accept this, they take seriously any conscious attempt to desecrate the name. There are further nuances in interpreting whether a person intends the desecration, and we can discern four different layers of intention: deliberate desecration, where all sides seem to agree that the name of the Holy Prophet or the Qur'an has been deliberately desecrated; alleged desecration, where a third party alleges that someone has desecrated the name of the Qur'an or that of Prophet Muhammad; perceived desecration, where actions are seen, often wrongly, as desecrating the name of Prophet Muhammad or that of the Islamic holy book; and unintended desecration, where actions have unknowingly desecrated the religion or the name of the Prophet.[13] Again, this chapter discusses later how this has occasioned violence.

The focus group discussions undertaken for this book show a difference of opinion on how to understand the relation between desecration and violence. All those who took part in the discussions recognize that it is a major cause of violence. But some participants argue that it need not be a cause. That is, some of the Muslim participants claimed that they would be offended by any form of desecration of the Qur'an or the Holy Prophet, but they would not necessarily be violent over it.[14] Notably they were from the southwest; some of the participants from the north, however, said that there are legitimate grounds to be violent over any indication of desecration. To them violence in this case is meant to serve as a punishment for the desecration and as a deterrent to future similar action.

Along with seeking to return the country to an ideal past and protesting desecration, Muslim radicals committed violence in reaction to domestic issues. Of these, political differences, economic deprivation, and disputes over natural resources were the most important. Indeed, economic deprivation is at the center of many of these conflicts; many hold that politicians (and sometimes religious elites) have only exploited divisions to their own advantage. Finally, international events, especially as they relate to the Islamic world, shape radical Islamic violence, though far less than local political and economic issues. Radicals keep a close eye on the Middle East and express support for the Palestinians in their struggle against Israel; indeed, Israel's actions against Palestinians and other Arab countries have provoked riots in Nigeria. More recently, US activities in Iraq and Afghanistan stirred anti-Western feelings and further radicalized Muslims in Nigeria.[15] All these are discussed in chapter 8.

Ethnic and regional differences affect the behaviors of Muslims who take to violence. Muslim radicals in the north, especially in towns like Kano, Kaduna, Katsina, Sokoto, Maiduguri, and Jos, have been more likely to engage in religious violence. There are, however, some peculiarities. In Kano, although there is a large Muslim population, the centrality of trade has brought people of different ethnicities and other faiths into the city. For example, many Ibos from the eastern part of the country sell spare motor parts, just as Yorubas from the southwest are involved in the transportation business. This was to introduce ethnic coloration to the pattern of religious conflict in the town. In the case of Kaduna city, and indeed the entire Kaduna State, the perennial religious conflicts have strong historical and ethnic roots; although a largely Muslim area, some parts of the state, especially the areas known as southern Zaria, are predominantly Christian. Since the 1804 Sokoto jihad, people here have resisted what they saw as Hausa domination and have embraced Christianity in defiance of their northern neighbors. Jos, too, is mixed, with Christians and Muslims also following the lines of ethnicity. The intermix of religion and ethnicity has always manifested in the patterns of conflicts in these towns.

There were a number of riots believed to have been instigated by Muslims. One of the earliest religious conflicts after the Maitatsine riots were the Kafanchan riots in March 1987. Riots broke out when one Bello Abubakar, a recent convert from Islam to Christianity, allegedly extolled his new religion by denigrating Islam during an annual Christian week at the College of Education. Before the occasion, a bill advertising the celebration titled "Welcome to Jesus Campus" had infuriated the Muslims, and they had asked the Christians to withdraw it.[16] Perceived insensitivity created grievance. During the riots, twenty-five people were killed and sixty-one injured; forty churches and three mosques were destroyed; and the president had to send in troops from the first division of the army based in Kaduna under Brigadier Peter Adamokhai to quell a riot he described as the "civilian equivalence of a coup d'état."[17] What further complicated the problem is politics in Kafanchan that carried over from the days of Usman dan Fodio: the king of the town and his advisers are still Hausa/Fulani and Muslims, while the Kajes are the subjects and Christians. This again is discussed further in chapter 6.

In June 1992, the infamous Zangon-Kataf riots erupted from a monstrous gridlock of religion, history, ethnicity, and land ownership crises. In the previous month, it had become apparent that the face-off between the Kataf and the Hausa was assuming more religious dimensions. Citing different historical accounts, each side claimed the other was the stranger, but the impression of the Kataf people was that the Hausa were being shielded from the law and favored by the government. This story is also discussed in detail in chapter 6.

In December 1995, in the Gideon Akaluka incident, a group of Muslims actually beheaded a young Ibo trader and paraded his head around the city of Kano. One story said that a woman, supposedly Akaluka's wife, used pages of the Qur'an as toilet paper for her baby. Others said that she actually used the Arabic section of the manual for a transistor radio. In any case, the police arrested and imprisoned her husband, though he was not at home when the incident happened. Some Muslims broke into the jail and killed him.[18]

In September 2001 a major conflict emerged in Jos, Plateau State, when a woman attempted to pass through a barricade erected by Muslims during Friday prayers.[19] The Muslims prevented her from passing and allegedly attacked her, on the grounds that she was dressed in a manner that exposed parts of her body, which they found sacrilegious. In response, Christians fought back, and then the entire state went up in flames. The federal government sent in armed soldiers to quell the riots, and later declared a state of emergency. But the crisis in Jos can only be understood in light of wider national politics. Whatever the immediate cause, the trouble was larger: a political crisis within Plateau State and rising tensions between the major ethnic groups in the state. This was to be a recurring feature in the town (see chapter 6).[20]

Another political issue that created a religious conflict was the 2002 Miss World beauty pageant. Sometime in 2001, Nigeria was selected to host the Miss World Pageant.[21] Controversy began almost immediately after the announcement. Some people inside and outside the country objected—and some contestants withdrew from the competition—because, they charged, the country had a pattern of abusing women; they cited a Sharia court's condemnation to death by stoning of a Nigerian woman, Amina Lawal, for purportedly having a child outside wedlock, as a damning example. In contrast, some Nigerian Muslims criticized the competition as a debasement of women, promoting promiscuity and offending both female modesty and sexual morality. These objections remained contained until a columnist with a national newspaper, *This Day*, Isioma Daniel, criticized Muslims who opposed the competition and argued that Prophet Muhammad would probably have loved to marry one of the contestants. This was greeted with spontaneous riots across the country and a fatwa was pronounced on the writer, who was forced to flee the country.[22] Despite apologies by the newspaper, riots continued for many days, resulting in the death of more than one hundred people. Ultimately, the organizers of the competition moved it to London.

The fatwa pronounced on Isioma Daniel turned out to be very controversial, even among Muslim clerics and scholars, both within and outside Nigeria. Within the country, some argued that the fatwa declaration was inappropriate since Isioma is not a Muslim and as she and her newspaper had apologized.[23] Indeed, the Supreme Council for Islamic Affairs had accepted the apology and was not willing to enforce the fatwa. Some also argued that while Isioma not being a Muslim did not invalidate the fatwa, her apology did. Outside Nigeria, reactions seemed to follow the same line: an official of the Saudi Ministry of Islamic Affairs, Sheikh Saad al-Salah, said that it would be inappropriate to kill a person who is not a Muslim and who has apologized for her action. Finally the Nigerian government said that it would not allow the fatwa to be carried out. But meanwhile, the attendant Muslim killing of Ibos in northern Nigeria resulted in the reprisal killing of Muslim Hausas in Onitsha.[24]

A few violent conflicts have emerged as a result of the alleged desecration of the Holy Qur'an, two of which attained national prominence. In February 2006, an alleged desecration sparked riots when a schoolteacher seized a copy of the Qur'an in Bauchi from an inattentive student who was reading it during the lesson. This was considered a desecration, and in the ensuing riots, more than fifty Christians were killed.[25] Again, in March 2007, a Christian teacher, Ms. Oluwatoyin Olusesin, who was supervising an examination in Islamic religion in Gandu, Gombe State, caught a student allegedly cheating. After the end of the examinations, the student informed his colleagues that the teacher had desecrated the Qur'an, and she was killed.[26]

A few violent punishments have been carried out in compliance with Sharia law. In January 2000, the first amputation for stealing was carried out on Buba Jangebe for stealing a cow, and shortly afterward, one Lawali Isa lost his right hand for stealing three bicycles.[27] In both cases the victims claimed to be satisfied with the punishment and to be happy that they had become "better human beings."[28] In fact, in neither case was there any appeal of the initial sentence. What has again made Sharia the focus of controversy in Nigeria has been the alleged gender partiality of the punishments for sexual offenses. In 2001, in Zamfara State, a woman found guilty of fornication was given one hundred lashes, despite her protests that she had been raped.[29] Again in October 2001, in Sokoto, an Islamic court sentenced a thirty-year-old pregnant woman to death by stoning after she was found guilty of having premarital sex, while the man identified as her lover was released because of "insufficient evidence."[30] However, the sentence was never carried out. Again, in 2002, there was another punitive implementation of Sharia when a seventeen-year-old girl, Bariya Maguzu, was given 180 lashes of the whip for becoming pregnant out of wedlock.[31]

While it is impossible to identify all the radical groups that emerged in pre–Boko Haram Nigeria, some of their names and their origin can be identified here. One of the groups was the Al sunna Wal Jamma (Followers of the Prophet), formed around 2001. Its members were highly educated and experienced in the handling of weapons. It is believed that the group first set up a camp around Kanamma, a small town in Yobe, around late 2002 and early 2003. What first brought them to public attention, apart from their preaching and their calls for Islamic purity, was their total lack of respect for local traditions, especially property rights. They farmed and fished everywhere, especially on the bank of the Yobe River owned by families, claiming that "everything belonged to Allah."[32]

Another militant group, the Nigerian Taliban, believed by some to be the precursor of Boko Haram, emerged in 2002. They originally referred to them-

selves as Muhajirun (Migrants) and began attacking government establish-
ments, then launched a rebellion in Yobe State. Specifically, the group hoped
to create an Islamic state that would run in strict accordance with an extremist interpretation of the Muslim faith. After the army put down the uprising,
it alleged that the group had been funded by the Saudi al-Muntada al-Islami
"charity" whose other "good works" include educating aspiring African clerics
in Saudi institutions and setting them up in its own network of mosques and
schools back in their native lands upon graduation to members for extremist
groups.[33] In April 2007, there was a new wave of attacks in Kano, with radical
groups protesting that governments in northern Nigeria were not enforcing
Islamic laws strictly enough. They also attacked what they saw as an attempt
by Christians to Christianize Kano.

Yet another organization that later became prominent in the politics of radicalization is the Tebligh group. This group has a distinctive way of dressing:
their trousers are short, ending well above their sandals. They are like a Muslim version of the Franciscans; although they do not take an oath of poverty,
members nevertheless renounce all they acquired in life before joining.[34] Members of the group also undertake most of their journeys on foot, possibly to
conserve the little money they have. Like other Wahabi/Salafi-inspired groups,
they follow Ibn Taymiyyah's teachings for the most part. In the last decade, the
group has grown in membership and has also transformed into a larger movement called Ahlu Sunnah, meaning followers of Sunnah (ways of the Prophet
Muhammad and his immediate disciples). The Ahlu Sunnah derives its inspiration from the Wahabi strain of Islam, and it has benefited from the return
of clerics who studied in Saudi Arabia. In their preaching, the Ahlu Sunnah
defines its mission as to purify the practice of Islam with superior knowledge
and practice of authentic Sunnah of the Prophet. In this pursuit, the group has
not completely ruled out the possibility of violence. Sometime around 2001,
members of this group came into Ogbomosho, a town in Oyo State, and started
taking photographs of churches in the town. Residents were concerned and
alerted the *soun* (the paramount ruler), who ordered their expulsion from the
town with a stern warning that they should never come back.[35] Although the
activities of the Tebligh are discussed below, it should be noted that no actual
violence has been associated with them.

Another sect, the Kala Kato or Qur'aniyyun, emerged in August 2009 in
Zaria, Kaduna State, under the leadership of one Malam Isiyaka Salisu. Unlike
Muslims who believe in the Qur'an, Hadith, and the *ijma* (consensus of Islamic
scholars), this group only believes in the Qur'an: their conviction is that all
prophets of Allah were given only one revelation or book and that scripture is

the only thing that guides their worship and that of their followers.[36] Further, its members perform only two *raka'ats* of prayer (*salat*) in lieu of the compulsory five daily prayers stipulated for Muslims. The group also has dietary regulations. For example, its members do not eat fish unless it is slaughtered like a ram or cow, as their reading of the Qur'an says that all animals, including fish, must be slaughtered before they become pure for consumption.[37] Finally, the group's members do not observe funeral rites the way other Muslims do, as the Qur'an does not mention ritual baths, funeral prayer, or shrouding the dead.

Some have attributed the whole issue of Islamic radicalization to the broader ethnoreligious and socioeconomic differences that have historically permeated relationships among the Nigerian populace. For example, in the Sokoto focus group discussion, one of the participants pointed out:

> The blame trading is something that has not helped the discussion on the crucial issue of religious radicalization in Nigeria. There seems to be a "we" versus "them" culture between the Christians and the Muslims, which has again been crudely interpreted as being between North and South. If the Muslim population in the North was happy because of the attack on America, the Christians in the country have shown delight with the American attacks on Iraq. It is a case of "we" versus "them" that has been translated to even things that are of very remote relevance.

Others have different views. For example, a participant in the Makurdi focus group named another way through which militancy affects politics in Nigeria, pointing out that the root cause of militancy (in Nigeria) can be traced to the "numerous gaps" that exist in Nigerian society: "Gaps between ideals and reality; between needs and expectation; between what the government says and what it does; between what the preacher preaches and what he practices; and between what the masses want and what the elites are willing to concede. When the population reads about the disbursement of millions in the newspaper and yet nothing in their pot of soup, what do you expect?"

The extent to which the lack of formal education can be identified as an explanation for Islamic radicalization in Nigeria is controversial. A view often aired is that many of those taking part in militant radicalization are illiterates who have been manipulated by elites. While it is true that illiteracy could be a factor, we must be cautious of easy explanations. In the course of the Abuja focus group discussion, one participant pointed out that rates of violence and illiteracy do not rise and fall together: "I have witnessed a lot of religious riots. In some cases, I participated, and I want to debunk the idea that ignorance is the cause of the problem. For one, I am not ignorant. But apart from this, there was no major crisis over religion before independence. Does that mean that people were literate then or better informed? Of course, the answer is 'No.' So, we should probe deep and look for other answers." What all the discussions above show is that the dynamics of Islam's association with violence in Nigeria are complex, and the complexities have been further compounded when one sees the violence as a reaction to other religions.

Islamic Violence as a Reaction to the Perceived
Provocation of Other Religions

Some radical Muslims commit violence in reaction to what they interpret as the provocation of other religions. Muslims have often charged Christians with such provocation. Because the distinction between ethnicity and religion in the country is somewhat blurred, Muslims, especially those from the northern parts of the country, have claimed that southerners (who are often Christians) have made disparaging remarks about their ethnicity and their religion. This double insult of ethnicity and religion is something that Muslims in the north often point to as sources of great anger that provokes them to be violent. This, in a way, links to the north/south discussion earlier.

Sometimes Christians have heralded the invitation of foreign Christian visitors in ways Muslims thought implicitly reduced the importance of Islam. For example, in April 1982, Muslims violently protested when the visiting Archbishop of Canterbury, Robert Runcie, laid the foundation stone of an Anglican church in Kano. The protest was organized by the Muslim Students Union. Demonstrations later spread to Kaduna and resulted in the deaths of forty-four people. The worst of the violent protests in this category, however, was the riot in Kano in October 1991. The Kano branch of the Christian Association of Nigeria had invited Reinhard Bonnke, a German missionary, to Kano for a evangelical campaign. As part of the publicity for the event, announcements were made in the news media, for example, that "the anointed man of God is coming to deliver sinners and unbelievers to Jesus Christ." Many Muslims considered this to be insensitive at best. It was also rumored that Bonnke was planning not just a crusade but an invasion that would separate Kano from its Islamic roots.[38] Some youths claimed that Reinhard Bonnke was planning to blaspheme Islam, and this was the last straw. People rioted. In self-defense, the Christian community set up barricades and formed groups to protect nonnatives in the Sabon Gari area of the city.

Many Muslims worry about Christian radicalization: unless it is aggressively countered, they think Muslim youths will be converted to Christianity.

Speaking to a meeting of northern rulers at Arewa House, Kaduna State, Alhaji Abubakar Saad III—the sultan of Sokoto, the spiritual head of all the Muslims in Nigeria, and the president general of the Jama'atu Nasil Islam (JNI)—lamented the upsurge of Christian evangelization in Nigeria and vowed to counter it with the message of Islam:

> The rise of secularism and the increasing activities of western evangelical organizations have made it all the more urgent that the message of Islam shall be heard loud and clear and the JNI must play a leading role in this endeavor. The JNI, in the next few years, needs to establish a proactive and virile Da'wah (Preaching) agency to respond to these challenges. This agency must be able to deploy full-time Da'wah workers in its strategic areas of operation and make maximum use of emerging media technology. . . . We must first and foremost develop a five-year action plan to rehabilitate, reposition and expand the schools currently under the management of the JNI.[39]

While Muslim radicals are understandably opposed to the conversion of Muslims to Christianity, they are generally willing to ignore the new converts, provided they do not say or do anything that denigrates Islam in celebrating their newfound Christian faith. When Muslims who turned to Christianity have openly condemned Islam, there have been conflicts, with Islamic radicals often violently attacking those former Muslims. For example, in Iwo, Osun State, in October 2007, during a Christian crusade, a former Muslim who had become Christian told the audience, "if you want to know about God, go to the Qur'an, but if you want to know God, go to the Bible."[40] Local Muslims found this unacceptable, as they argued that the statement presupposes that the Qur'an only talks about God without really revealing God. They subsequently attacked the speaker. But while there were disagreements with other faiths, there have also been cases of violence among adherents of radical Islam.

Intra-Islamic Violence

As noted in chapter 1, the Qadriyya and Tijaniyya, the two major sects in Nigeria, have been at war with each other since the conquest of Sokoto caliphate by the British. The strained relations between the members of the Qādiriyyah and the Tijaniyyah Sufi brotherhoods in Nigeria improved due to the emergence of a group that was opposed to both of them, the Jamācat Izālatil Bidca wa Iqāmatus Sunnah (Movement against Negative Innovations and for Orthodoxy), widely known as the Izala, established in Jos in 1978 by the former grand kadi (*qādī*) of northern Nigeria, Shaykh Abubakar Gumi.[41] The group differed from the Muslim Brothers. The Izala movement did not, as a policy, challenge the state or political authority. Gumi was, in fact, an officially sanctioned scholar with unhindered access to the corridors of power in Nigeria. The Izala movement primarily attacked Muslim Sufi groups for innovation and apostasy, and it fought against such innovations as the Sufis' genuflection in greeting elders, the keeping of concubines by traditional rulers, celebration of the Prophet's birthday, Mawlid al-Nabī as Bidcah, as well as supplication to Allah through reading *Dalā'ilul-khayrāt* (a collection of prayers for the Prophet) and "al-Burdah," a poem on the Prophet chanted as a means of warding off evil and attracting prosperity, visiting graves and tombs of dead scholars, and denial of women's right to a proper education. In October 1987, there was a clash between the Izala and the Darikas.[42] Because of their perception that the Darikas are Kafirs, the Izala demanded a separate mosque in Zuru, but before this was done, they were to use the central mosque alternately. This, however, resulted in conflict. The Izala movement conflicted with civil, as opposed to political, social order, and Gumi was considered an enfant terrible by traditional rulers and traditional scholars. The organization has objectives that include "to promote the fundamental teachings of Islam as laid down in the Holy Qur'an and the Hadith of the Holy Prophet (SAW); - to revive in the minds of the followers of the Islamic religion the actual duties of true Muslims as are required of them by the Almighty God. - that we are determined to guard these principles at all cost without any options for compromise."[43] Prior to the formation of the Izala, Shaykh Gumi had written a book titled *al-cAqīdatul ṣahīhahin*, in which he condemned both the Qadriyya and the Tijaniyya for bringing unacceptable innovations into Islam. Gumi also wrote articles in *Gaskiya*, a Hausa newspaper, while he was also able to reach wide audiences on Radio Nigeria in Kaduna and Nigerian Television, also in Kaduna. Gumi's status as a former grand kadi must have contributed to his leadership position among the Western-educated civil servants and professionals in Kaduna who regarded him as the authority on Islam. The members later resorted to arming themselves with knives and inflicted injuries on members of the Tijaniyyah in particular while holding their ritual prayers and chased them out of mosques. The violent attacks, which led to serious public disorder in different towns and villages, cost some people their lives.

Islamic groups in Nigeria have clashed violently over doctrinal disagreements; many of these intra-Islamic conflicts have been between the Sunnis and the Shi'ites. There is the need to note the historical roots of this disagreement, because of its prominence in Nigeria's history: soon after the death of Prophet

Muhammad, there was a controversy over succession. One group believed that the leadership of Islam should pass to Ali, his son-in-law, but Abu Bakr was made the caliph instead, as he had stepped in to lead prayers when ill health prevented the Prophet from doing so. Those who supported Ali formed the Shi'ite group, elevating Ali to the status of a prophet. Some even went so far as to substitute his name for the Prophet's in their recitation of the *kalimat sha'hadt*. They formulated other doctrinal differences as well, one of which is that they observe the *ashra* (martyrdom) day of Imam Hussein, the grandson of the Prophet. They deepened their roots in Iran after the overthrow of the shah and the ascendancy of Ayatollah Khomeini. The Shi'ites are identified more strongly with fundamentalism, and their activism and martyrdom have proved attractive to many Nigerian Muslims, who see traditional Islamic religion in the country as being stagnant. While many other sects appear somewhat averse to challenging the Shi'as, the Sunnis have expressed their discomfort with Shi'a fervor, and conflicts have ensued.

Although there is more detailed discussion of the activities of the Shi'ites later in this chapter and in chapter 6, cases of violent interactions with the Sunnis can be identified here. In August 1996, Shi'ite groups in Katsina broadcast their interpretation of Islam in Sunni neighborhoods, organized citywide processions, distributed pamphlets on city streets, and engaged Sunnis in argument in mosques and religious centers. Verbal opposition turned into violence in Katsina as Shi'a groups clashed with other Muslims. A week later, in another clash between the two groups, people burned houses and wounded people. It was alleged even by moderate Muslims that some Shi'a activists' confrontational methods provoked violence. Certainly Shi'ites are zealous, and that religious passion is mirrored all over northern Nigeria. And as corruption and the northern economy worsen, Qur'an readings and Sufi brotherhoods attract more and more participants.

In the same month (August 1996), Shi'ite Muslims in Kano clashed with other Muslims.[44] Also, in 1996 and 1997, the Shi'ites engaged a breakaway group known as Yan Tauri in violent clashes.[45] The Shi'ites also incessantly clashed with Sunnis in Sokoto, which came into prominence in 2005, when Islamic Movement of Nigeria (IMN) imams sought leadership positions in Sokoto mosques, despite the town being predominantly composed of Sunni Muslims. Some IMN members that had become too radicalized for the group's philosophy had moved on to other more radical groups. The founder of Boko Haram, Mohammed Yusuf, for some time followed El-Zakzaky before Yusuf became Borno State amir of Jama'at al-Tajdid al-Islami (JTI, Movement for the Revival of Islam).[46]

The Shi'ites maintained limited contact with the Sunnis, who also tended to steer clear of them, especially in Zaria, where the Shi'ites constituted themselves as an autonomous group. A doctrinal issue that also served to win support for the group, especially among the youths, was its endorsement of temporary marriage, in which a young man could live with a woman before getting formally married, giving him time to gather money to pay the bride price. The Sunnis frowned on this and saw it as a way of letting young men have sex without responsibility.

The rhetoric of the Nigerian Muslim Brothers (before it evolved to become the IMN) had the kind of revolutionary idealism found in the works of Sayyid Qutb. His major work, *Al-Ma'alim fi'l-Tariq* (then widely circulated in English, with its translation known as *Milestones*) was compulsory reading for members. His thesis of an irreconcilable dichotomy between Islam and *jahiliyya*, or ignorance, played a critical role in shaping the mindset of this group, as it did in the case of many Islamist groups in the Middle East that went by the generic name of Al Takfir wa'l-Hijra. Although the Muslim Brothers in Nigeria started as a Sunni group, its close association with Iran (including scholarships for several of their members to study in the city of Qom) led to their switch to Shi'ite doctrine. El-Zakzaky was himself a Sunni before converting to Shi'ism. But this switch later led to rebellion and fragmentation in the movement. The splinter group that formed as a result was led by some of El-Zakzaky's most loyal members, including Abubakar Mujahid (Zaria), Aminu Gusau (Zamfara), and Ahmad Shuaibu (Kano). This group, however, maintained that its disagreement with El-Zakzaky was purely doctrinal in that they rejected Shi'ite theology but remained committed to the revolutionary process of Islamization.

The age-old enmity between Muslim scholars of the Ash-ari/Sufi tradition and the Wahabi/Salafi tendency also played itself out in the Nigerian scene. But the Muslim Brothers tended to stress the essential unity of the Muslim *ummah* and to see their principal conflict as being with political authority; its overthrow was their raison d'être. Where they had conflicts with leaders of civil society, it was whether they perceived them as in alliance with the forces of *jahiliyya* and against the revolution. By the late 1990s, El-Zakzaky was becoming more temperate in his radicalization, and some of his more radical followers had begun to look for another source of inspiration. This they found in Abubakar Mujahid, who broke away from El-Zakzaky to establish the Ja'amatu Tajidmul Islamia, the Movement of Islamic Revival.

In July 2007, soldiers and riot policemen were deployed to Sokoto following violent clashes between Shi'ites and Sunnis over the killing of Sheik Umaru Hamza Dan'Maishiyya at the Shehu Juma'at Mosque in Sokoto.[47] The Sunni cleric had been killed while preaching, allegedly by members of the Shi'ite sect. Immediately after, mobs torched houses, with hundreds of people storming through four neighborhoods of the city. The attempt by riot policemen to arrest the Sokoto governor-general of the Shi'ites, Mallam Kasimu Rimin Tawaye, culminated in the shooting of two policemen by members of the sect. As a result, soldiers were later brought in, and they eventually arrested the governor-general and about ninety of his followers at his residence in Kanwuri in Sokoto.[48] After intense police and military patrols intervened, calm eventually returned.

The Shi'ites have always argued that the Sokoto government has persistently shown hatred toward them—Shi'ite leader El-Zakzaky condemned successive Sokoto governments for what he considered to be their anti-Shi'ite stances—and that it fueled the Shi'ite-Sunni rivalry in the state.[49] But this last conflict between the Shi'ite and the Sunni had wider political ramifications. The Shi'ites argued that Dan'Maishiyya, who was killed while preaching, was not, as the state government put it, a major Islamic cleric, but a political thug who was so powerful that he determined who held key appointments in the state. Furthermore, the Shi'ites claimed that the state government killed him to create an opportunity to clamp down on Shi'ites in the state. Although the state denied these charges, this suggests that Shi'ites saw a major link between the state and Islamic radicalism.

The Shi'ites in Nigeria began seeing intra-Islamic conflicts as a mechanism by which the enemies of Islam in Nigeria divided the religion. El-Zakzaky argued that the killing of prominent Islamic scholars is just the government's attempt to reduce the number of radical Islamic scholars in Nigeria while at the same time giving the impression of intra-Islamic division. He said that the strategy used in the killing of Dan'Maishiyya in Sokoto was again attempted in Katsina, but that the plot was uncovered and the Islamic scholars whose killing by state security agents was to be blamed on Shi'ites were later taken to safety by that very Shi'ite group. El-Zakzaky also implicated the American government in the murder, as its attempt to foment Sunni-Shi'a discord in Nigeria.[50] In short, to El-Zakzaky, it is the state and the international community, and not the Islamic groups, doing the killings, with the sole intention of further dividing adherents of the religion.

Kano has also recorded several clashes among different Islamic sects, some of which brought members of some sects into conflict with the police. In a clash between Shi'ites and the JNI that took place largely in the Kofar Ran district of Bauchi city in Kano, a hard-line cleric, Saudi-educated Sheikh Jafar Adam, was shot while praying at the Dorayi Central Mosque. In April 2007, Muslim radicals sought to avenge the assassination. They burned down a police station in the Panshekara district, wounding two officers, and then ambushed and killed thirteen police officers who came to investigate. It was rumored that the attackers made it clear that they had nothing against civilians and that they were looking to kill police officers to avenge the death of Sheikh Jafar. It was not long before the riots were under control. Bauchi also saw clashes between different Islamic sects.

In another kind of intra-Islamic violence linked to the divergence in radical views, individual Muslims—not aligned to any specific organization—attacked other Muslims for allegedly doing things that bring Islam into disrepute, including allegedly desecrating the Qur'an. For example, in July 1997, six Muslims in Randalli village, Kebbi State, killed another Muslim, Abdullah Umaru, by slicing his throat for allegedly insulting Prophet Muhammad.[51] In their court defense, the six men pleaded not guilty even though they admitted to the killing, arguing that as Muslims, they had the duty to kill Umaru as written in the Holy Qur'an.[52] The court dismissed their claim of provocation and condemned them all to death.[53]

Another case of intra-Islamic violence over doctrinal disagreements was the fatwa pronounced by the JNI, the highest Muslim body in northern Nigeria, on Muhammadu Bello Masaba, of Bida (Niger State), for having married eighty wives, which the JNI said was contrary to Islam. It told Masaba to repent within four days and select only four wives from the horde, or the death sentence would stand, according to Sharia law. The Central Fatwa Committee of the JNI, in a statement signed by its chairman, Sheikh Abubakar Babatunde, and Secretary-General Abdulkarim Mu'azu, said that any Muslim who married more than the approved number of wives at a time, either by mistake or out of ignorance, is instructed to choose only four and ask for Allah's forgiveness. Masaba won support from civil society groups who considered the fatwa absurd. He refused to reduce the number of his wives, accused those who pronounced fatwa on him as being ignorant of the Qur'an—that it nowhere restricted the number of wives to four—and argued that there are emirs (rulers) who marry more than four wives, including uncountable concubines.[54] Nonetheless, the fatwa was never carried out, and Bello Masaba died in January 2017 at the age of ninety-three. This story shows that there are still major disagreements on fundamental Islamic principles even between radical groups.

Intra-Islamic controversies that have ultimately ended up underlining violence in recent times continue to have an ethno-geographical dimension, with Muslims from the south vigorously disagreeing with their northern colleagues over the timing of key Islamic events, like the Ramadan fast. Some Islamic celebrations depend on the sighting of the moon, which occurs at different times in different regions of the country. For years, people disagreed over who was doing the correct thing. Although all Nigerian Muslims are under the spiritual control of the sultan of Sokoto (in the north), southern Muslims sometimes resisted his instruction on when these festivities should begin as being from an earthly spiritual leader, and they insisted instead on getting heavenly guidance. Things came to a head in November 2008, when Muslims in the south argued that their spiritual leader in Sokoto was trying to make them disobey God by instructing them ahead of time when to celebrate Eid Al-Fitr.[55] The president of the Muslim Association of Nigeria, Alhaji Waheed Olajide (from the southwest), said in an interview, "The League of Iman and Alfas had fixed the date before the month came and in my point of view, it is not appropriate. What we are told in the Holy Qur'an is that if anybody sighted the moon, we should confirm if that person is a Muslim. The idea of determining what the day will be before the actual date, I found it difficult to believe."[56] In response, the sultan of Sokoto set up a twenty-nine-member committee in 2008 to address issues of moon sighting during fasting, education, commerce, and the declaration of public holidays. Despite these disagreements, Muslims also believe that there is a limit to how far divergence of views can go. In a veiled reference to Christians, the president of the Muslim Association of Nigeria, Alhaji Olajide, noted, "There is a limit to what you can disagree on [in Islamic religion]. You cannot disagree on the time of prayer (*salat*), you cannot disagree on where to face where you are praying, you cannot disagree on the month of Ramadan. . . . It cannot get to a stage when Yoruba service will be slated for 9 am, Igbo service for 10 am and English service for 7 am, as we have in other religions. So, Allah himself has put in place a kind of unity in Islam."[57]

Ethnonationalism has also started to cause intra-Islamic tensions. As far back as 1994, Yoruba Muslims from the southwest were resisting what they saw as Fulani domination. The allegation has always been that the sultanate only catered to northern Muslims. Ilorin, the capital of Kwara State, has always been at the forefront of this anti-Fulani sentiment. In September of that year, the chairman of the Afonja Descendant Union, Abdul-Kareem Kasumu, called for the reduction of the power of the sultan of Sokoto and for the creation of the Supreme Islamic Council of Southern States; he was arrested for alleged public incitement.[58] In October 1994, Sheikh Abdullahi Adam El-Ilori, deeply scholarly and highly respected across the southwest, was said to have embarrassed Dasuki, then a prince but later the sultan of Sokoto, for not being able to speak Arabic even though he was the spiritual head of all Muslims in Nigeria and from the family that claimed to be the custodian of the religion.[59]

Indeed, a new group traces the ascendancy of Islam in the southwest to periods long before the 1804 Fulani jihad. This group is now arguing that the control that the descendants of Uthman dan Fodio have over Islam is wrong, and that it is a kind of imperialism that should be resisted. Specifically, the group wants the Yoruba parts of the country (which the Fulani could not overrun during their jihad) to contest the supremacy of the sultan of Sokoto over all Nigerian Muslims. In Ilorin, Yoruba Muslims are now seeking greater collaboration with Yoruba from other southwestern states to fight what they see as the feudal tyranny of the Fulani-held caliphate system that is based in Sokoto. At a meeting of Yoruba Muslims, the head of the group in Ilorin openly criticized the sultanate and the emirate hierarchy that he claimed has misruled Islam, to the detriment of Yoruba culture. Specifically condemning the neglect of Yoruba names for the adoption of Arab names, Sheik Abdulraheem Aduranigba called on Yoruba in Ilorin to jettison Arab names and called for the total removal of the Fulani emir of Ilorin and the restoration of Yoruba rule. In conclusion, he called on pan-Yoruba militant groups like the Odua Peoples' Congress and the Yoruba antioppression group, the Agbekoya, to join hands with the Yoruba in Ilorin to remove the emir of Ilorin, forcefully if necessary.[60]

An issue that is now emerging—one that has started showing potential signs of intra-Islamic tension—is the extent to which indigenous culture should be acceptable in Islam. This issue is far more prominent in the southwest, where the dividing lines between religion and culture have been historically blurred. Broadly, the disagreement here pitched locally trained Islamic leaders against young Islamic leaders who had traveled outside Nigeria, mostly to Middle Eastern countries, to study. Locally educated Islamic leaders think that people should tolerate local traditions, especially other Muslims' use of local herbs and traditional medicines; as long as nobody chants incantations or invokes spirits, said the leaders, they do not affect Muslim practices. But the young Islamic religious leaders mandate that Islam be practiced in its pure and original form as it was done during the period of the Prophet Muhammad.

There are also rising tensions among Islamic groups in Yorubaland. Here again, the historical background is worth recording. Basically, there are three main Islamic movements in southwestern Nigeria: the Adabiyah, founded by the late Sheikh Kamaludeen Adabiyyah, with its headquarters in Ilorin, Kwara State; the Moricas, founded by the late Sheikh Adam Al-ilory, based in Agege, Lagos; and the Zummuratul, founded by the late Sheikh Yussuf Agbaji and Baba Lamunigun, which also has its headquarters in Ilorin. Over the years, adherents of these schools of thought have established branches all over southwestern Nigeria and in the diaspora, including the UK, the United States, and so on. Although there are internal differences among the groups, they also have a lot in common.

Allocation of offices and appointment into positions in mosques have also been known to cause violence. For example, in October 2021, four persons were injured when a clash erupted on who would become the chief imam of the Central Mosque in Inisa, Osun State. Riots allegedly broke out when one of the main contenders, Sheik Abdulakeem Muhammadu-Jamiu, gained entrance into the mosque to lead Friday Jumat prayers.[61] After a hot exchange between the pro- and anti–Muhammadu-Jimoh supporters, a free-for-all fight ensued, during which four members of the Muslim community opposed to his choice as chief imam sustained injuries. Muhammadu-Jamiu was also reportedly stoned by an antagonist, which led to the smashing of decorative glasses that adorned the imam's section of the mosque. In May 2021, the state government had ordered the closure of the mosque because of the possible breakdown of law and order in the town.

The Tebligh group is challenging the positions of the established order. Broadly, the group has four main theological differences with traditional Muslims. The first is their allegation that orthodox movements in Yorubaland do not practice pure Islam, and that certain elements of orthodox practice are fetish. Specifically, the group condemns the traditional Yoruba worship and alleges that spiritual rites have been mixed with Islam, including geomancy (*ite iyepe*, divination) and the offering of fruits and food (*sara*). Second, Ahlu Sunnah accuses the traditional Islamic movements of bringing innovation (*bid'iah*) into Islam. Among such innovations include burial prayers, *assalatu* gatherings, celebration of birthdays, traditional Yoruba greetings, the use of a rosary (*tesbih*), elaborate child-naming ceremonies, congregational night vigils (*tahajud*), drumming, and singing Islamic gospel music. Third is the group's rejection of *jalabi*, traditional clergy work in Yorubaland, wherein clergy pray for and on behalf of people, attending to people's spiritual needs and helping people resolve problems and challenges. To Ahlu Sunnah, the whole process of *jalabi* has given rise to the mixing of certain elements of traditional Yoruba spiritual practices with Islam. The group claims that rather than going to any *alfa* for prayers, it is the duty of Muslims to seek and find knowledge and do their own prayers and spiritual development individually. There are also disagreements over what should be the correct position toward the Hadith and the Sunnah. The Ahlu Sunnah adopt a more textual interpretation of the Qur'an and Hadith, while traditional scholars have tended to favor more contextual interpretation, and also reject certain Hadiths, especially those that appear to contradict the Qur'an. Their grounds for repudiating aspects of the Hadith are that it could have been corrupted over time, especially as the extant Hadith collections were made several decades after the death of Prophet Muhammad. Ahlu Sunnah resist selective acceptance or rejection of Hadiths by the traditional movements; rather, Ahlu Sunnah claim the need to accept all codified Hadiths.[62]

Since around 2019, tensions have been on the rise due to the activities of Ahlu Sunnah in Yorubaland. Although these are more visible via online platforms like Facebook and YouTube, they are also getting heated, with increasing exchanges of threats between members of Ahlu Sunnah and traditional movements. Some have also cursed and condemned each other to *jahanama* (hellfire). The disagreements include claims by scholars and adherents of the traditional movements that Ahlu Sunnah groups are being sponsored and financially aided by Saudi Arabia, in line with other groups like Boko Haram, al-Shabaab, and so on. They claim Ahlu Sunnah is part of the export of Wahabism to southwestern Nigeria. They also wonder why Ahlu Sunnah would solely focus on attacking and condemning fellow Muslims, when their job should be to propagate the religion to non-Muslims. In response to Ahlu Sunnah attacks, some adherents of the traditional movements have branded Ahlu Sunnah as Ahlu Fitnah (spreading *fitnah*, which means evil).[63] From the foregoing, it can be seen that intra-Islamic disagreements leading to violence are clearly occurring in Nigeria and have manifested in the country's numerous institutions of higher education.

Universities, Islamic Radicalization, and Violence

First, it needs to be noted that there is a subtle, nonviolent controversy between Christians and Muslims on the whole origin of tertiary or higher education. Muslim scholars often revisit the glorious past of Islam and celebrate its contribution to human civilization, asserting that, whatever Western or Christian civilization's claim to superiority might be, Islamic civilization also has achievements to celebrate, many of which far predate Western civilization. Muslim scholars argue that "Islamic civilization had started at the time when Western Europe was still grappling with the feudal system of the Middle-Ages," and that universities in Islamic societies predated Oxford, Cambridge, Harvard, and a host of others celebrated by the Western world.[64] Historical evidence agrees: the earliest universities included Al Quaraouiyine, founded in Morocco in 859, and the Al Azhar University in Cairo, established in 970; they grew out of Islamic madrassahs. It also shows, however, that the modern concept of universities as formal institutions of learning originated in medieval

Christian tradition. Indeed, modern university titles like chancellor, warden, registrar, dean, and so on, are Christian titles, and the practices and paraphernalia used in most universities today are adaptations from Christianity.[65]

In modern Nigeria, university campuses have been breeding grounds for all forms of religious radicalization. For example, El-Zakzaky, the noted Islamic radical, got his start at Ahmadu Bello University (ABU) in Zaria, and Ahmed Yerima, the governor who introduced Sharia in Zamfara State, was earlier a major actor in Islamic radicalism at Bayero University, Kano. Islamic radicals are often able to find intellectual backing for their arguments in universities. Particularly important in university Islamic radicalism has been the Muslim Student Society of Nigeria (MSSN). Possibly to counter the massive evangelization activities of Christians on university campuses, the MSSN too embarked on massive campaigns, inviting outsiders to come and share views with the students. Most of those invited hold radical views that are often compatible with the youthful disposition of MSSN members. The association almost always makes public their stands on key national and international issues.

In 1979, a radical wing of the MSSN attacked a gathering of the Palm-Wine Drinkers Club, popularly known as the Kegite Club, at the Samaru campus of ABU, inflicting injuries on many members. The attack, according to the report of an investigating committee set up by the university senate, was completely unprovoked. The committee recommended that disciplinary action should be taken against the erring MSSN officials. The offending students got wind of their impending punishment and mobilized their colleagues to attack the vice chancellor. After the Friday prayer at the university mosque on May 18, 1979, the MSSN militants attacked the vice chancellor's lodge with the intention of killing him, but the vice chancellor, who got wind of the impending attack, had escaped few minutes earlier. Some of the MSSN members who allegedly led the assault on the vice chancellor's lodge left the country and returned later to become key actors in the nation's religious radicalization politics.

In the mid-1980s, the University of Ibadan became the center of a major controversy that almost became violent. Some radical Muslim students, allegedly encouraged by Muslim politicians, argued that the Christian cross on campus violated the Islamic doctrine that forbids Muslims from seeing a cross, idols, or effigy during worship. The cross was erected in the 1950s to denote the Christian place of worship, which is in front of the Qiblah (the direction of the Ka'aba). In fact the church was built first, and the mosque came much later.[66] The Muslims insisted that the cross should be removed, while the Christians suggested Muslims move their mosque to another location if they found the cross objectionable. In the end, all agreed that the cross would remain in place, that a crescent (the symbol of Islam) would be installed beside it, and that a large structure would be erected to block the mosque's view of the cross. Although the matter was resolved, the fact that the controversy took place at a university in the south, often considered more tolerant in religious matters, was a wake-up call for Nigerians that university institutions can play a role in the formation of radical religious views.

Universities in the southwest were particular sites of violence, as Christian and Muslim populations were more evenly distributed. Muslim radicals were at the center of a series of disputes at Obafemi Awolowo University over several years. The university faced charges of unfairness on campus during the 1990s. Muslim radicals more broadly were alleging that higher education institutions in the southern parts of the country marginalized Muslims. The radicals argued that Friday evenings should be left free of events, lectures, and exams to enable Muslims to perform Friday prayers, just as Sundays were left free for Christian services. They noted that academic areas for prayers and religious activities also favored Christians.[67] Hence the Obafemi Awolowo University in Ile-Ife considered banning the use of lecture rooms and auditoriums for any religious practices.[68]

The Obafemi Awolowo University Muslims also played a prominent role in the politics of the Muslim Congress. The congress allegedly wanted to take control of the MSSN across the country; it had already taken subtle control of the MSSN at the universities of Lagos, Ibadan, and Ogun State. The MSSN at Ife thus saw itself as the body that had to stand up to the Muslim Congress. When the congress organized a holiday program for Muslim students at the Obafemi Awolowo University, Ile-Ife, in 1994, MSSN members invaded the venue, apprehended those who organized the program, and tied them up. It took the intervention of the university authorities to get the visitors released.[69]

Those who took over the affairs of the MSSN at the Obafemi Awolowo University around 1998–99 had become confrontational even in their attitude toward Muslim academics within the university. The students argued that the Muslim lecturers and other elders were not sufficiently pious. The lecturers and elders, for their part, started pointing out openly what they saw as the hypocrisy of the Muslim students, claiming that some of the students had done things that run contrary to Islamic doctrine, including getting married without the consent or even knowledge of their parents. Students also criticized the chief imam of the university. For example, the chief imam stipulated that there must be eight *rakah tara weeh* during prayer, whereas the students insisted that there must be ten. Students turned the annual Jihad Week, usually a social gathering, into a period of internal purification.

After the September 11, 2001, Al-Qaeda attack on the United States, Islamic radicalization in all Nigerian higher education institutions increased significantly. Many Muslim radicals found reasons for (if not justification of) the attack on the United States. They also foregrounded the plight of the Palestinians and the role of Israel in the Middle East. Many universities organized public lectures and symposia about these issues, where radical Muslim academics used the opportunity to express similar political sentiments.

Muslim radicals in universities have also tried to enforce what they consider to be minimum moral standards on campus, focusing largely on women's behavior and dress, and on sexuality in general. In 2008, radicals sparked a major riot at the Obafemi Awolowo University when they stormed a residence hall to stop other students from watching a pornographic movie on the grounds that it was immoral.[70] Other students challenged them and physically assaulted the massively outnumbered Muslim radicals. The university shut down.[71]

In 2006, a female Muslim student insisted on wearing a hijab to class and to write exams.[72] The university authority rejected this request. The student, allegedly with support from wealthy Muslims outside the university, took the university to court for violating her human rights.[73] Although the university won, tension remained between the university authorities and the Muslims on campus. Indeed, controversies over the wearing of hijabs by female students were part of this focus on morality, though they never degenerated into violence. The hijab controversy tends to be largely centered on students in public schools. The origin of the problem was the 1979 government takeover of all schools that had been established and managed by religious bodies. Parents of Muslim students at the Baptist High School Iwo insisted that female Muslim students should be allowed to wear the hijab to school. The school authority disagreed. Without official permission, female Muslim students started coming to school in hijabs. Then Christian students started wearing dresses that looked like Christian choir robes. To complete the web of mischief, some students began coming to school dressed like traditional herbalists. The government eventually had to intervene to restore order. Hijab controversies continued in subtle ways until another major crisis erupted in November 2018, when Muslim parents insisted that their daughters at the elite fifty-five-year-old International School at the University of Ibadan be allowed to wear hijabs to school (see chapter 6). Islamic professional associations were also a key voice in the larger debate on radicalization and violence on university campuses. Indeed, many were at the forefront of the expression of radical views, and they helped fund the MSSN and its propagation of radical Islam on many university campuses. The complications of Islam's connections with violence also intertwine with the media.

Role of the Media

The media has played a major role in the violent radicalization of religion in Nigeria.[74] Religion columns appear in virtually all national newspapers on Sundays and Fridays, for Christians and Muslims respectively. Although the content of many of these columns is temperate, sometimes it is less temperate and may even be competitive. Most parts of the country rely on print media for information about what is going on in other parts of the country and the world. But in the northern parts of the country, where conflicts over religion are most prevalent, there are more radios per person than in any other part of the country, and people have more access to foreign news than in any other part of Nigeria. Through the plethora of Hausa service programs available on global radio networks, the Hausa population in northern Nigeria learns more about events in other parts of the world than any other ethnic group in Nigeria. Thus people in the north are likely to react more quickly to global developments that they perceive as anti-Islam.

Films of the debates between a Muslim cleric, the late Ahmad Deedat, and a Christian writer, John Gilchrist from South Africa, circulated through Nigeria in the late 1980s and early 1990s. Deedat also debated some Christian leaders on video. The focus of one of the debates, with an individual known as Shorrosh, was "Which one is the word of God: Qur'an or Bible?" Deedat published and widely circulated books and video recordings that Christians alleged had been doctored. His videos were shown freely on television in northern Nigeria, but were not allowed to be shown in the southwest.

In more recent times, some Muslims have accused the media of further encouraging violence among Islamic groups, and particularly of exacerbating the long-running Shi'ite-Sunni conflict. Journalists allow their own beliefs and experiences to influence what they put out as news stories, the radicals say, and they twist the facts. For example, on March 8, 1987, after the Kafanchan riots, Radio Nigeria in Kaduna reported that Christians were killing Muslims in Kafanchan and that copies of the Qur'an and mosques were burned.[75] Controversies surrounding the Miss World competition underline this. In another example, the Islamic Council of Nigeria accused a national newspaper, the *Daily Trust*, of a "lack of all ethics and values of professionalism" for linking the IMN with the murder of Umaru Dan Mai Shiyya, whom they described as a "political thug," in Sokoto.[76] The council further expressed its disappointment with the newspaper for "preferring to be on the side of the irresponsible, morally degenerate Sokoto Governor, Aliyu Wammako . . . in his battle against the Islamic Movement."[77]

Moreover, most Nigerian newspapers are based in the south and are owned by southerners who are mostly Christians. Therefore, northern journalists say, most national newspapers are incapable of covering northern crises. They argue that northern journalists' coverage of the riots is more objective because they are usually geographically closer to those areas, and thus actually make the effort to be physically present to write their reports, and because they are familiar with the language and culture. But southern papers just send southerners who cannot penetrate the language or culture, and northern journalists accuse southern journalists of concocting reports. This has always been denied by southern journalists.

The media has also come under criticism for exaggerating the nature and extent of the problems of radicalization. During the November 2008 riots in Jos, both sides criticized the press for giving what they saw as wrong information on casualties in the conflicts.[78] The Christians criticized journalists for inflating the number of Muslim casualties while the Muslims did the same for Christians.[79] While, of course, accurate figures can never be obtained in situations like these, inevitably, the biases of media reports are also a factor to be considered.

The State and Islamic Movement of Nigeria (Shi'ites)

The activities of the Shi'ite sect in Nigeria have been personified by Ibraheem El-Zakzaky. Born in May 1953 in Zaria, he started his Qur'anic and Islamic education at a tender age. From 1971 to 1975, he attended the School of Arabic Studies in Kano, and he later attended ABU for a degree in economics.[80] While at ABU, he was an active member of the MSSN and championed the nationwide demonstration in support of the inclusion of Sharia in the constitution.[81] Because of their deep involvement in Muslim radicalization on the campus, nine students were expelled from the university; a Zaria-based charity then funded their continued studies in some Middle Eastern countries. El-Zakzaky went to Iran just when the revolution was brewing.[82] The Iranian experience fired him up, and he emerged as the leader of the group that described itself as "brothers" (Yan Brotha or Ikhwan).[83] Outsiders called this movement the Shi'ites, but it was later to become known as the IMN. El-Zakzaky has been jailed several times for sedition or inciting disaffection against the government.[84]

Fired up by the success of the Iranian people, many joined his group in his struggle to construct an Islamic state in Nigeria on the ashes of the existing state, which was built on ignorance (*jahiliyya*). The IMN soon established control over a ward in Gyellesu, in Zaria, where it allegedly lived outside the authority of the Nigerian state. It maintained its own security and ran extensive social welfare programs, feeding the poor, and providing ambulances and medical care—where the government was not providing these services. El-Zakzaky was accordingly able to recruit many followers.

The nature of the IMN's militancy needs to be properly defined. First, for most of the 1990s, their violent contacts were largely with members of the other sects of Islam, especially the Sunnis. Very rarely did the group engage in direct violence against the government during this period. Second, the group has strong views on contemporary international developments, and some of its pronouncements on these could have encouraged people to commit violence. The group's positions on the West and Israel are clear examples of views that have been linked to violent protests in Nigeria.

In terms of direct confrontations with the government, one early example was in April 1991, when there was a clash between Shi'ites in Katsina and security forces. Here, a Shi'ite leader, Yakubu Yahaya, a devout student of El-Zakzaky, and his followers confronted the military. The immediate cause of the violence was the December 1990 edition of *Fun Times*, a *Daily Times* of Nigeria publication, allegedly blaspheming both Muhammad and Jesus Christ. Once the crisis started, El-Zakzaky gathered more than a thousand supporters to come into Katsina to support Yahaya; they went around the town chanting war songs. The state military governor, John Madaki, read the riot act to them, declaring, "The leader of the Shi'ites should be aware that I am not afraid of him. . . . If he causes trouble again . . . we will go to his house, take him to the Polo ground and kill him publicly."[85] To this, Yahaya replied, "I am not afraid of a glorious death."[86] After this, Madaki was summoned to Lagos to meet with President Babangida. On his return, he reversed the death sentence and said that Yahaya was free to engage in peaceful demonstration and that, if there was a protest, he would take them through the due process of law. This did not satisfy the protesters, who insisted that the governor must come personally before their leader to revoke the death sentence and to apologize.[87] He ignored this demand.

El-Zakzaky and his fold have, however, come back to national attention in recent years. In July 2015, there was a clash between the army and the Shi'ites in Kaduna, during which four of El-Zakzaky's sons were killed, and another clash in December, during which the army killed 347 Shi'ite followers, including one of El-Zakzaky's wives, Zeenat, and his son Aliy.[88] The December clash between the army and the Shi'ites occurred in Zaria. The army chief of staff, Yusuf Buratai, was on his way from Dutse to pay homage to the emir of Zazzau before heading to the Nigerian army depot for a parade.[89] His convoy met a roadblock mounted by the IMN. Entreaties to remove the roadblock failed, and members of the Nigerian army opened fire on the IMN members, killing many of them; in return, members of the sect killed a soldier. Over the course of the following two days, soldiers attacked the residence of the IMN leader.

A judicial commission of inquiry, under Justice M. L. Garba, was set up by the Kaduna State government and concluded that the army used "disproportionate" force. The committee recommended the prosecution of IMN members involved in the killing of the only soldier who died but also indicted the general officer commanding the First Division of the Nigerian army in Kaduna, Major General Adeniyi Oyebade, as well as one Colonel A. K. Ibraheem, who led the operation. It also concluded in its report that "the high number of casualties cannot be justified."[90] Amnesty International also condemned the Nigerian security forces' excessive force and open deployment of lethal weapons against the Shi'ites. The Nigerian government subsequently detained El-Zakzaky and his wife. Several law courts ordered his release, but the government refused. The special adviser to the president on media affairs noted in an interview in July 2019 that El-Zakzaky's continued detention was because other cases against him were open, and all must be addressed before a release would be possible. Another round of protests came again in October 2018, when Shi'ites in Abuja organized a peaceful protest to seek his release. In July 2019, Abuja witnessed another round of Shi'ite protests, resulting in the deaths of a Youth Corp member and a deputy commissioner of police.

Meanwhile, the IMN had its own set of critics among top Muslim scholars, and despite the persecution of the group and its leadership that they alleged, it was not attracting sympathy. In August 2018, some Islamic scholars from northern Nigeria warned the government that Shi'ites were threats to Nigerian security and that the group's deliberate twisting of the Qur'an was un-Islamic.[91] The group also promised to "cut the sect down to size."[92] According to the JNI secretary-general, the only way to check the excesses of the Shi'ites was through the acquisition of superior knowledge to counter their position. But the Shi'ites have, ironically, shown friendship toward Christians and have even attended church celebrations to rejoice with Christians. For example, Shi'ites in Kaduna visited three churches during Christmas celebrations in 2017.[93]

On July 26, 2019, a high court in Abuja outlawed the IMN as a terrorist organization, sowing further division among Islamic groups in Nigeria. One prominent group, the Muslim Rights Concern (MURIC), immediately threw its weight on the side of the government, agreeing that the excesses of the IMN should be curtailed.[94] The Izala also issued a strong statement calling on the federal government not to handle the Shi'ites with kid gloves. And MURIC argued that "Boko Haram would not have festered so badly had former President Goodluck Jonathan taken action when he should." However, MURIC also used the opportunity to condemn Christians criticizing the government for the proscription, calling the action hypocritical and claiming their position was taken to further "decimate Islamdom, particularly in Nigeria." The group wondered why Christians should be defending "a Muslim group which even mainstream Muslims regard as dangerous," ending its press release by warning the Iranian government to desist from interfering in the internal affairs of Nigeria.[95] As of the end of 2021, the IMN remained banned.

Conclusion

Because of its deep linkages with politics and governance, Islam remains the religion most associated with global controversies. This, as noted in the introduction, is because Islam is more than a religion; it is a way of life. The fact that the religion has specific instructions on how governance should be undertaken has increased its propensity for controversies, especially in those communities where Islam has to contend national spaces with other religions, as is the case in Nigeria. I have tried in this chapter to discuss the issues that have brought Islam to the point of violence in postindependence Nigeria. While it is, of course, impossible to identify all the issues here, the key patterns of violence have been identified. Major issues like the zero-sum relationship with Christianity, doctrinal disagreements among various Islamic groups, and the breeding spaces provided by universities have all underlined the ways the religion has been linked to violence. This chapter has shown that the root causes of violence linked to Islamic religion in Nigeria are largely connected to internal issues, with occasional interjections of external factors that have been effectively internalized. Internal issues include ethnicity, past injustices (including colonialism), allocation of opportunities and privileges in national politics, natural resource management, and economic deprivation, all of which are complicated by global developments and exploited by the country's ruling elites.

Overall, before Boko Haram, the nature of Islamic radicalization in Nigeria was distinctly different from that of some other parts of the world in that there was not a single case of a suicide mission in Nigeria, despite the extent of religious instability in the country. Perhaps one reason was that the external dimension of ethno-patriotism in many other places was not present in Nigeria during this time. Consequently, the country's population had no reason to embark on extreme actions. But the key underlying issue that Islamic actors have always taken into consideration is the presumed zero-sum nature of the relationship with the other dominant religion in the country, Christianity, whose linkage with violence in Nigeria is the objective of chapter 3.

3. CHRISTIANITY AND VIOLENCE IN NIGERIA

Boko Haram is hereby warned that if it carries out any further attacks on Christians anywhere in the North, our Commandos will unleash deliberate attacks on selected targets in cities with majority Muslim populations in the North. Your people will see and experience what you have been doing to others firsthand. . . . Akhwat Akwop will match you blood for more blood, violence for more violence, and life for more lives. —Akhwat Akwop Manifesto, EMEKA MAMA, "Nigeria: Rival Group Drops Threat Leaflets in 10 Northern States"

You catch anyone that looks like them, kill him! There is no reporting to anybody. Kill him! Pull off his neck! And we spill his blood on the ground. What nonsense. Every agent of destruction in Government today, call fire down on their head. . . . Everyone sponsoring evil against the nation, let your fire fall on him! —DAVID OYEDEPO, pastor and founder of Faith Tabernacle Church

The idea of Christian radicalization or Christian religious violence in Nigeria is not as oxymoronic as most adherents of the religion within the country, and even sometimes outside, are often inclined to assume. Across the nation, Christians have engaged or threatened to engage in violence, with some even going as far as to form a radical group dedicated to armed militancy for the protection of Christian faith and values. Christian leaders have also been known to espouse radical views, sometimes strongly enough to threaten national unity. Consequently, therefore, any attempt to have a comprehensive discussion of religious violence in Nigeria must discuss the Christian angle, especially its causes, its patterns of expression, and the extent to which it is a reaction to the radicalization espoused by other religions, particularly Islam. It is also necessary to interrogate the issue of radicalization on the part of Christian leaders who espoused views that endorse violence.

Broadly, Christianity's association with violence in Nigeria has taken five somewhat interrelated forms. First, militant Christian youths informally took up arms to protect Christians against what they saw as Muslim attacks. Second, Christian leaders openly endorsed violence, either for spreading Christianity or in self-defense; some specifically instructed members of their congregations to carry out violent acts. Third, though many are not aware of it, a militant group announced its determination to defend Nigerian Christians by use of force. Fourth, Christians have turned to physical violence inside their churches to resolve interpersonal disputes, especially on money, leadership, and succession issues. Finally, Christian clergy instruct people to inflict violence on those, especially children, categorized as witches. In most of these five cases, the perpetrators of violence are often quick to add that they are acting in self-defense and that their actions are not a doctrinal violation of Christianity. In most cases, too, they are quick to point out that they have chosen violence because of the failure and/or inability of the government to protect them. The central argument advanced in this chapter is that Christianity, like Islam, has been associated with violence in postindependence Nigeria, even if aspects of the two religions' linkages with violence differ in some fundamental respects. The chapter also contends that violent Christian radicals may accuse the government of either not protecting them or even being in cahoots with those attacking them.

Activities of Militant Christian Youths

Between the end of 1999 and early 2000, militant Christian youths started demonstrating in opposition to states' imposition of Sharia law, objecting to the construction of mosques at places and in ways they considered insensitive to Christian concerns, and protesting what they saw as violent attacks from their Muslim neighbors. All of their actions involved violence.

Violent demonstrations against the imposition of Sharia started almost immediately after the law was imposed in some northern Nigerian states. Punishments stipulated by Sharia, including amputation and flogging, were viewed by Christians as a fundamental violation of human rights. Partly because they were not sure what the imposition meant, partly because they considered it illegal and as such to be resisted, and partly too because they were determined to fight for the freedom to practice their religion, Christian youths across northern Nigeria took to violence. They were particularly concerned about how much of the law would apply to them, as they had seen its extremity with the condemnation to death by stoning of Safiyatu Huseini, who was found guilty of adultery; the amputations of Buba Jangebe in 2000; and of Lawali Isa.[1]

One of the earliest acts of violence perpetrated by Christians against Muslims over Sharia came in February 2000, in Kaduna. Although the incident started peacefully, some Christian youths, allegedly in self-defense, employed violence.[2] Some of the protesting Christian youths smashed vehicle windshields and disrupted the flow of traffic in the Kaduna metropolis. A mosque was also burned down in the process.[3] Muslims also retaliated, and the Kaduna State governor, Ahmad Maikarfi, had to impose a dawn-to-dusk citywide curfew. Additionally, President Obasanjo and Muslim leaders from the north also met to discuss the problems associated with the implementation of strict Islamic law. By 2001, the number of violent Christian reactions to Sharia had increased. In June and July 2001, Christians protested in some parts of Bauchi State against the imposition. Also, in August 2001, Christians in the Tafawa Balewa local government council took to violence over alleged plans by the government to introduce strict Islamic law involving two communities: the mainly Christian Kutaru and the predominantly Muslim Zwall. This pattern of violent conflicts continued throughout the decade. Christian youths were taking the law into their own hands because they were convinced that even the federal government was unsure how to handle some states' decision to impose Sharia law. Christian youths felt that they had no choice but to fight to ensure their freedom and that of their religion.[4] For the most part, violent Christian reaction to the imposition of Sharia law during the first decade of its introduction was largely because of their uncertainty about what the future held and their lack of trust in federal and state governments' assurance that they would be safe.

Christian youths have also taken to violence in instances where they believe that Muslims had forced a conversion on a Christian. For example, in February 2017, in Kasuwan Magani, a town in Kurajuru close to the Kaduna metropolis, there was a major conflict between Christians and Muslims over a girl who allegedly agreed to convert to Islam after getting engaged to her Muslim fiancé; Christians in the predominantly Christian settlement said that the Muslim family had forced her to convert.[5] The Christians rioted and destroyed properties. This attracted the intervention of the commissioner of police in Kaduna

State and Major-General Mohammed Mohammed, general officer commanding I Division of the army, who intervened to stop the rioting.

Militant Christian youths were also demonstrating violently against the construction of new mosques in areas inhabited mainly by Christians. For example, in July 2010, Christian youths in the Wukari Local Government Area of Taraba State destroyed the walls and windows of a mosque that had just been built by a new police area commander, Mohammed Mustapher. Earlier, the youths had written a letter to the police area command office protesting the plans to build the mosque, which the area commander had ordered when he assumed office; the town's king, Shakarau Agyu Massaibi, had also warned the police commander against building the mosque, as it would affect intergroup relations in the community. The commander went ahead with the construction, and the Christian youths destroyed it. In retaliation, Muslim youths burned a Christian church. In the ensuing crisis, five people died.[6]

Militant Christian youths also took up arms to defend themselves against perceived attacks by their Muslim counterparts. By mid-2012, Christian youths had taken up arms to defend themselves, their families, and their belongings against what they saw as the onslaught of those they categorized as Islamic fundamentalists. Broadly, they took up armed resistance to local riots by Muslim youths, Boko Haram, and (starting in about 2014) groups they categorized as Fulani herdsmen who were allegedly attacking Christian churches. The dynamics of each fight differ, but what they all have in common is that Christian youths responded with violence to what they saw as threats. During communal conflicts in Kaduna, when youths from both sides carved the town into spheres of control, Christian youths were known to have attacked their Muslim counterparts who strayed onto their turf. The way they discerned the religious identity of any suspected intruder was to subject them to a quiz, asking them to complete the Christian phrase, "In the name of the Father, the Son, and . . ." They picked up this idea from their Muslim counterparts, who required their suspects to recite the Surah Al-Fatihah, the first chapter of the Qur'an. Those who failed the tests, whether Christian or Muslim, were attacked and sometimes killed.[7]

Some of these conflicts between youths started as socioeconomic clashes and then took on a religious coloration, especially in Jos and its immediate environs, and in Kaduna. The Christian militants involved are not necessarily particularly passionate about their faith. Personal issues also shape these conflicts: for example, in southern Kaduna, Christian youths attacked Muslim youths for snatching away their Christian girlfriends.[8] Indeed, interviews and focus group discussions carried out in 2018 pointed out that this was common around 2015 and 2016.

After Boko Haram insurgents began bombing churches, Christian youths responded almost immediately by forming armed groups specifically to protect churches. Some churches, especially those around Jos, encouraged their young members to do so. In some cases, these armed youths complemented the police. These people were not paid, and they claimed to be joining of their own volition and out of self-defense.[9] Although this is not officially confirmed, it is also likely that some of them took up arms more for necessity than conviction and that some Christian youths joined the Civilian Joint Task Force (see chapter 5) out of the necessity to bring an end to the Boko Haram insurgency.

Christian youths also responded to attacks on churches allegedly by those categorized as Fulani herdsmen (see chapter 6). The mere fact that churches were attacked gave many the impression that some of the perpetrators were either members of Boko Haram or sympathetic to its cause. While this may not necessarily be the case, some of the group's activities, including the arrest and killings of Christian leaders, were similar in pattern to those of the Boko Haram insurgents. When the Fulani herdsmen's attacks became common, Christian youths across different communities interpreted them as a direct assault, and in many cases, they planned ways of defending themselves, including organizing themselves into armed groups. They criticized the government for not doing anything to protect them from the attacks of herdsmen. Indeed, Christian youths claim self-defense against these attackers even more often than they do against other groups they attack. Fighting them is difficult, because the herdsmen come in groups and have superior firepower. Nonetheless, sometimes their self-defense looks like an attack. Five Christian youths in Adamawa State, sometime in January 2017, were charged with willfully and intentionally conspiring to attack three herdsmen tending cattle in Kadamun village in Demsa local government area and with killing a herder in the process. Alex Amos, Alheri Phanuel, Holy Boniface, Jerry Gideon, and Jari Sabagi were later convicted and sentenced to death, but this has not yet been carried out. Many Christians claim that it would be difficult to carry out the punishment when many Muslims who had been arrested and condemned for killing Christians have not been punished.[10]

In some instances, the youths clearly acted not in self-defense but in retaliation, with a time lapse between an earlier alleged Muslim attack against them and their own response. For example, in March 2012, in Jos, after a suicide bomber drove an explosives-packed car into the flagship church of one of Nigeria's largest denominations, blowing it up, angry Christian youths re-taliated by burning Muslim shops and killing nearby motorcycle riders.[11] Also, an August 2011 attack in Jos by Christians on Muslims during Ramadan was believed to be in retaliation for the Muslim attack on Christians in the area on the previous Christmas.[12] During the 2011 incident, Christians burned cars, and nine people were confirmed dead and 106 injured. The Christians used guns, machetes, and arrows to counter their opponents using similar weap-ons. Furthermore, in June 2012, after Boko Haram suicide bombers blew up churches in Kaduna, Christian youths, in retaliation, attacked Muslims and killed people.

An isolated incidence of spontaneous Christian violence took place in April 2019, when an officer of the Nigeria Security and Civil Defence Corps, ASC Adamu Abubakar, rammed his vehicle into a procession of a Christian youth group known as the Boys Brigade in Gombe, killing eight immediately and injuring thirty-five. The procession leader claimed that the driver was un-happy that the procession had blocked the road, and he drove into the children on purpose. The police, however, claimed that he lost control. The crowd then attacked Abubakar and beat him to death.[13] Three more boys later died. Chris-tians rioted for days over the killing.

There are similarities and differences between Christian youths who have taken to violence in the name of their religion and their Muslim counterparts discussed in chapter 2. The first similarity lies in the uniformity of their inten-tions, as both are ready to use force to propagate their faith. Another similar-ity is that most of those involved in violence in both cases are males, usually between the ages of eighteen and thirty years. The first major difference, how-ever, is that unlike the Muslim youths who occasionally claim that there are doctrinal justifications for their action, Christian radicals strongly base their grounds for violence on self-defense. Another major difference is that Chris-tian youths, more often than not, act of their own volition and not, unlike Muslim youths, under instruction of religious leaders.

The extent to which Christian youths who have taken to violence in de-fense of their religion could be described as genuine radicals is contestable. A critical look at most of the Christian youths involved in this category of violence shows that they see their Christian religion purely as an identity tag in the we-versus-them equation. While not standing on any Christian doc-trinal principle, they are of the opinion that Christian youths must stand up to match what they see as Muslim violence. But while the youths espoused radical reactions in defense of their religion, some Christian clergy were also advocating violence.

Beyond supporting the actions of militant Christian youths, there were Christian leaders who openly endorsed violence, either in the propagation of Christianity or in self-defense against perceived attacks by followers of other religions, especially Islam. Against the leaders' perceptions that militant Islam was growing because Christian doctrines focused on peace, some Pentecostal Christian leaders began preaching on the uselessness of pacifism and the need to meet militant Islam with violence. They urged Christians to adopt violence.

Among the earliest to call for violence in response to perceived attacks was David Oyedepo, the presiding bishop of Living Faith Ministry, widely known as Winners Chapel and generally recognized as one of Nigeria's largest Pentecostal churches. In a May 2014 sermon at his church headquarters in Otta, Ogun State, Oyedepo specifically instructed his members to kill "people who look like Boko Haram." He said, "If you catch anyone that looks like them [Boko Haram], kill him; no recourse to anybody." He said further,

> All the northern forces that are sponsoring this uprising and killings, I decree the curse of God upon them. Call down the Holy Ghost fire to descend on the camp of the enemy. Enough is Enough! What demonic devils. What Islamic demons. . . . I was even told from the report that they were targeting this church. . . . If you see anybody here kill him! Kill him and spill his blood on the ground. You catch anyone that looks like them, kill him. They said why should Christians say they could defend themselves, hold it! What stupid statement, why should Christians say they could defend themselves? So, they should watch for you to put a knife to their necks? You think we are dummies? What nonsense! Who born their mother, who born their father? They are too small. Come! Get excited and walk in confidence. Any devil that misbehaves around you will be slain by the fire.[14]

Like the militant Christian youths, Oyedepo argued that they have had to adopt this position because the government was not protecting them; they added that the government might even be complicit in the plans to attack them. In a somewhat veiled attack on the government's management of events, Oyedepo noted, "A Boko Haram agent was captured, and they said he had escaped. What demonic devils? What Islamic demons?"[15] Thereafter, he disclosed his newly given assignment: "God has anointed me to lead a revolution against Islamic Jihadists."

The clamor for militant self-defense became more pronounced around 2016 when Fulani herdsmen were allegedly attacking and killing Christians. Oyedepo

was more direct in his specific call to his congregants to fight the Buhari administration, which he accused of supporting the herdsmen, calling it an "Evil Government."[16] He asserted that Boko Haram members were masquerading as Fulani
herdsmen. He argued further that "this is an Islamic uprising, this is a strategic
jihad," but that "there is no day this country called Nigeria will become an Islamic
State." He concluded by noting that "we are not just believers; we are soldiers
of Christ. We are not dummies. We are spiritual soldiers."[17] Even before the
pronouncement, Oyedepo was known to tend to be expressive when angry.[18]

When in August 2019 people believed to be herdsmen killed one of his pastors, Jeremiah Omolewa, Oyedepo rained curses on the "killers and their backers." Citing several scriptural passages, he cursed the perpetrators and offered
his views about himself, Christianity, and intergroup relations in Nigeria when
he said, "This evil system will crash. And I am speaking as a Prophet. This evil
system that has no value for life, this wicked system—Fulani demons: In the
name of Jesus, their end has come. It's not by force that we live together. Nobody in this land has more stake than me in Nigeria. The church is not begging
to live. The church has the legal and divine right to live in this country."[19] It is
important to note that in all his spiritual condemnations of those he believed
to be acting against Christians, Oyedepo always focused emphasis on "the killers and *their backers*." Putting this in context with his other pronouncements,
there is no doubt that he had the Buhari administration in mind with this
innuendo. Because of the strength of his following, outsiders took his call for
violence very seriously, although there was no known case of anyone carrying
out his instructions.

Another Christian leader who advocated violence was Apostle Johnson
Suleman. Although the apostle had been in the ministry for a long time, he
made his debut in national politics shortly before the November 2015 Kogi
State governor's election with a prediction that any politician who attempted
human sacrifice in pursuit of political ambition would die.[20] He was particularly precise in his prediction: "Let me say this to Kogi State and all those politicians who are going out of the law. If you attempt [it,] you die." Shortly after
this, the leading candidate, Abubakar Audu, suddenly died, right before he was
declared the winner. (He was the former governor of the state.) Although there
was nothing to suggest that Audu's death was connected to Suleman's prediction, or that Audu was the person Suleman had in mind in his prediction, the
specificity of the prediction and the occurrence of the death of perhaps the
most important contestant in the election catapulted the apostle into the public eye and ensured his credibility. His subsequent predictions have, however,
failed woefully: for example, he predicted that the People's Democratic Party's

candidate (Kolapo Eleka) would win the 2018 Ekiti State governor's election, but it was eventually won by the All Progressive Congress candidate (Kayode Fayemi). He later claimed that a massive number of prayers counteracted his prediction. Nonetheless, he entered national politics with considerable decisiveness and focused his attention on Kaduna State, where he engaged in a running battle of words with the governor, Nasir El-Rufai. Some Christians in Kaduna State had charged that the governor supported the wave of anti-Christian sentiment in the state. Then the government decreed that Christian churches must secure permits for public preaching.[21] Vowing that he would never respect this law, Apostle Suleman released a bitter public outburst on the governor. After a public exchange that turned personal and insulting, the apostle again predicted in March 2016 that the governor would die. The governor sarcastically asked the apostle to be precise about the exact time of his death, saying that a general statement that someone will die does not say much since no one is immortal. As of the first quarter of 2021, the apostle had not gotten more specific and the governor was still alive.

Apostle Suleman again came to national attention in February 2017 when he, like Oyedepo, instructed members of his congregation to kill any Fulani person that they perceived as trying to attack his church. He noted, "Any Fulani herdsman that just entered by mistake, Kill Him. Cut his head. If they are busy killing Christians and nothing is happening, we will kill them and nothing will happen. Many people in Kaduna are now widows; many are fatherless; many are orphans because some people think that they hold power. Kill them. . . . We cannot be widows; we cannot be widowers because [of] some devilish people that say that they have a religion."[22] He made this statement against the background of so many unpunished Muslim/Fulani attacks on Christians. In response to this open incitement to violence, the federal government intervened: the Department of State Security attempted to arrest Suleman while he was in Ado Ekiti, the capital of Ekiti State, in January 2017, and take him to Abuja for questioning. He resisted arrest. The ultimate showdown was averted when the governor of Ekiti State, Ayodele Fayose, stepped in and used his immunity as a governor to prevent further attempts to arrest Suleman.[23] At the time, Governor Fayose was also engaged in an ongoing public disagreement with President Buhari, and he exploited the Suleman situation to criticize the federal government. After the arrest drama, Suleman crowed that members of his church lived across the world and that if he were to be arrested, his followers would attack the Nigerian embassies in all these countries.[24] Apart from his stance for self-defense by Christians, Suleman's disagreements with the government were also rooted in his belief that the government was behind allegations linking him to sex scandals.[25] Apostle Suleman has also called for minor violence to defend the Christian faith, including enjoining clergymen to slap any comedian who cracked jokes using the name of Jesus.[26]

Support for violence by Christians also came from another clergyman, Bishop Diamond Emuobor, chairman of the Christian Association of Nigeria. Justifying self-defense, the bishop turned to the scriptures, quoting the book of Luke (22:36) where Jesus Christ said those who have no sword should sell their coats and buy one for the defense of their lives.[27] Indeed, scriptural passage is popular among proponents of just war, especially Augustine, Aquinas, and Reinhold Niebuhr, who often cited it to refute the suggestion that Jesus was categorically opposed to the use of force.

Many other Christian leaders did not give such clear calls for violence as Oyedepo, Suleman, and to an extent Emuobor, but they signaled support for armed self-defense. For example, after the Christmas Day bombing of St. Theresa's Catholic Church in Madalla, near Abuja, by Boko Haram in 2011, which killed forty people, the national president of the Christian Association of Nigeria, Pastor Ayo Oritsejafor, declared that enough was enough, vowing that Christians would henceforth fight to defend themselves. He noted, "We have hitherto exercised restraint in our public statements on these matters. However, we cannot continue to do so indefinitely and are determined that in the year 2012, if these unprovoked attacks continue, and Christians remain unprotected by the security agencies, then we will have no choice but to defend our lives and property and take our steps to ensure our safety and security."[28] What made this declaration particularly important is that it was signed by an array of pastors, including those who had not themselves made any pronouncement on violence. Among those who signed the declaration were the general overseer of the Redeemed Christian Church of God, Enoch Adeboye; Mike Okonkwo of the Redeemed Evangelical Mission; David Oyedepo of Winners Chapel; Felix Omobude of the Gospel Light International Ministry; Uma Ukpai of the Uma Ukpai Evangelistic Association; Mercy Ezekiel of the Christian Pentecostal Mission International; and Paul Adefarasin of the Guiding Light Assembly. Leaders of the mainline churches—including the Roman Catholic, Anglican, Baptist, and Methodist denominations—were conspicuously absent here.

Another dimension of clergy radicalization comes from leaders who, though they do not call for outright violence, give subtle but enough encouragement to their audience to embark on violent reprisal campaigns. This encouragement increased during the run-up to the 2019 general election, largely in the form of Christian leaders preaching that Christians should obtain the Permanent

Voters Card to vote out the "anti-Christian" government of President Buhari. At the peak of the crisis over conflict with herdsmen-farmers (see chapter 6) some Christian leaders became convinced that the Buhari administration was against Christians, and with the election coming up, they encouraged their followers to vote them out.

It is also important to mention, even if briefly, that Christian radicals have also attacked traditional religion: for example, in January 2009 in Obosiland in Idemili North Local Government Area of Anambra State, a certain Pastor Ephraim, the founder of the Prophetic Healing and Deliverance Ministry, went about destroying ancient shrines.[29]

Establishment of a Christian Radical Group

Nigeria's radicalization picture changed, even if not drastically, sometime in 2011, when a Christian radical group in southern Kaduna announced its entrance into the political scene. Before this, many in the country indeed considered the idea of a Christian militia to be an oxymoron, as the general impression was that religious radicalization was the exclusive preserve of the Islamic religion; this impression was predicated on the preponderance of the radical activities of those who claim adherence to the religion, even if that affiliation was sometimes contested by fellow Muslims. The new Christian militant group, which called itself the Akhwat Akwop, stated clearly that its objective was to fight Boko Haram. Although its spread was never extensive, and its effects never widespread, its advertised intentions underline some of the wider underpinnings of religious radicalization's connection to political violence in Nigeria. Yet not many people know about the existence of Akhwat Akwop.

The camp of these Christian fanatics was at Dura Yadi village, Kwoi, in Jaba Local Government Area of Kaduna State. Right from the outset, the group made it clear that it was a response to the activities of Boko Haram and the spate of killings associated with Islamic radicalization. The first action of the Akhwat Akwop was in September 2011, when it issued an official statement making the following declarations:

1 Akhwat Akwop condemns in totality the recent charade in the name of Northern Traditional Rulers Council Meeting held recently in Kaduna.
2 Akhwat Akwop does not recognize the Sultan or any Islamic Traditional Ruler in any way or form.

3 It is resolved that for the desired peace and harmony to be achieved in the north, the Hausa Fulani must stop encroaching, stealing or laying claims to lands which by any stretch of the imagination do not belong to them.

4 Akhwat Akwop calls on all indigenous communities in northern Nigeria to as a matter of urgency call all Hausa Fulani on their lands to order. The Hausa Fulani must respect the norms, cultures, values, and traditions of their host communities.

5 Akhwat Akwop states unequivocally that the Hausa Fulani onslaught is aimed at:

   a Islamizing Christians in the north and Nigeria as a whole
   b Seizing, stealing and acquiring ancestral lands of indigenous communities in the north
   c Destabilizing the government of President Goodluck Ebele Jonathan
   d Seizing back political power by all means and at all costs.

6 Akhwat Akwop calls on all Christians and indigenous communities in the north and indeed in Nigeria as a whole to most vehemently resist these agents of evil and anarchy.

7 Akhwat Akwop calls on Nigerian Christians to wake up from their slumber. "Do not give what is Holy to the Dogs nor cast your pearls to swine lest they trample on them and tear you to pieces"—Matthew 7:9

8 Akhwat Akwop has identified the Islamic republics of Iran, Syria, Saudi Arabia, Mauritania, and Sudan as the sponsors of the Islamic onslaughts in northern Nigeria.

9 Akhwat Akwop states that nationals and diplomats of these countries are persona non grata in Nigeria and our commandos have instructions to hunt you down wherever and whenever they get you.

10 Akhwat Akwop is stating to members of Boko Haram and other Islamic fundamentalists/terrorists that you have tried us and not found us wanting. Akhwat Akwop will match your blood for more blood, violence for more violence, and life for more lives. It is better to jaw-jaw than to war-war. End the madness you have started, or we will be forced to permanently end it for you. A word is enough for the wise.

11 Akhwat Akwop states here that should President Goodluck Ebele Jonathan not want to continue as President in 2015, the presidency must and should remain in the Old Eastern Region of Nigeria.

12 Akhwat Akwop calls on all Christians to continue to pray for God's guidance and protection for Christians in the north, Nigeria and the world at large.[30]

The group dropped leaflets containing this statement in at least ten northern states: Benue, Taraba, Yobe, Borno, Bauchi, Adamawa, Plateau, Kogi, Nasarawa, and Kaduna. It also warned that it would liberate northern minorities from the stranglehold of the Hausa/Fulani who had been lording it over them, and causing havoc in the north and throughout Nigeria in the name of Islam. In one of its releases, the group addressed Boko Haram directly: "Boko Haram must not involve itself in the internal politics of Kaduna State and the Middle Belt, they are a no go area for Boko Haram. Our Commandos have advised you to stay in your Sharia-compliant areas. It is the Hausa Fulani Muslim men who wear jeans and T-shirts, sneak into our areas to drink alcohol."[31] The group further noted:

Akhwat Akwop says enough is enough. We also know that not all Hausa Fulanis are guilty. We shall try and avoid innocent casualties in our operations. We prefer peace but are ever ready for war. Akhwat Akwop is also aware that the ultimate aim of the Fulani terrorist is to create a situation of insecurity in southern Kaduna whereby our people will not be able to utilize this farming season thereby leading to hunger, deprivation, and famine in the land. Akhwat Akwop will declare "open season" on any Fulani found within their lands. Akhwat Akwop has watched with disgust the unrelenting murders and killing of our peaceful, innocent, and hardworking people by wandering bands of Fulani terrorist gunmen operating in southern Kaduna.[32]

The national executive committee of the group ended up making the following resolutions on June 3, 2012:

1   For so long we have restrained ourselves from reprisal attacks against these Fulani dogs from hell. We can and will no longer do so.
2   Today 3/6/12 Akhwat Akwop gives all Fulani within southern Kaduna 7 days to leave. After these 7 days of grace which expires on 10/6/12 Akhwat Akwop declares open season on any Fulani found within our lands.
3   Akhwat Akwop assures all our peace-loving and hardworking people of their safety in their homes, villages, highways and on their farms.
4   Akhwat Akwop reminds all that eternal vigilance in Christ Jesus is the price we pay for our freedom.[33]

Although it claimed to be a militant Christian group, Akhwat Akwop, right from the beginning, associated its struggle with that of other minority groups and with the situation in the Niger delta, where militant groups had been protesting against the government over environmental pollution and other perceived injustices. The group alleged that the violence being unleashed on the country by Boko Haram was intended to intimidate President Goodluck Jonathan and other Nigerians and thus to enable the Hausa/Fulani to seize power in the 2015 election. Consequently, Akhwat Akwop's objective was to checkmate the Boko Haram sect. Akhwat Akwop said that political power must return to the east after Jonathan in 2015. It further stated that it does not recognize any Muslim traditional ruler in any way or form in any part of the north, warning that for peace and harmony in the north and Nigeria in general to be maintained, the Hausa/Fulani who settled among the various minority ethnic groups in the north must stop oppressing their hosts in those areas.

The new group identified the target of its violence: women whose husbands were reportedly behind the violent activities of Boko Haram in the previous three months. Blaming the activities of Boko Haram on those not happy with the victory of President Goodluck Jonathan and Governor Patrick Ibrahim Yakowa of Kaduna State, both minority Christians, Akhwat Akwop posed seven rhetorical questions, including whether it was a crime for either Jonathan or Yakowa to become president and governor respectively, or if it was a crime for the Sawaya people of Tafawa Balewa in Bauchi State to be landlords in their ancestral land. The group also asked why the "innocent people of Plateau State have been made to pay so much in tears and blood" and "why the innocent farmers in Benue, Taraba, Kogi states have been continually attacked and killed by alleged terrorists as well as why Christians in Bauchi, Yobe, Borno states were being killed or whether or not it was a crime for northern minorities to say that enough was enough of Hausa/Fulani oppression." Putting these questions in context, they were all issues at the center of politics and intergroup relations in some parts of northern Nigeria.

The group said that they had already mobilized some unrepentant militants from the Niger delta as well as members of the Movement for the Sovereign State of Biafra. The unsigned twenty-page booklet that described its activities bore the inscription "Remain Blessed Akhwat Akwop" and stated at the end of each page: "Akhwat Akwop says enough is enough. We also know that not all Hausa Fulanis are guilty. We shall try and avoid innocent casualties in our operations. We prefer peace but are ever ready for war."[34]

By September 2011, the government had become aware of the group's activities. The Nigeria Security and Civil Defense Corps confirmed that even though the organization applied for registration as a private security company, it was yet to be registered because it had not met the required standards and, as such, was never registered. Following a tip-off, the Kaduna Police Command found the group's camp on the outskirts of Kaduna metropolis. A team of heavily armed antiriot policemen descended on the camp and arrested fifty-seven of its members. The tipster indicated that members, mostly youths ages twenty-three to thirty, might have been recruited from Kano, Kaduna, and Anambra states by the organization upon payment of unspecified amounts of money. The arrested head of the organization and coordinator of the training gave his name as Royal James. The state commissioner of police, Ballah M. Nasarawa, noted that the people arrested were being trained by a group known as the Advanced Homeland Security and Mountaineering Agency.[35]

The special adviser on Christian matters to Governor Patrick Ibrahim Yakowa, Rev. Joseph Hayab, lamented the intention of the group to wage a war against non-Christians in the southern part of the state, saying Christianity did not condone killings. Hayab said, "Within the week there was a statement going around within Kaduna State and the nation at large by a group 'Akhwat Akwop,' who in their statement gave [a] one-week ultimatum to Fulani herdsmen to leave the whole of Southern Kaduna or face spontaneous attacks by the militant sect of the said organization who were presented as Christian militias."[36]

Boko Haram responded to Akhwat Akwop on July 27, 2012, alleging in a terse statement titled "Past Time of Governors" that the governors of three northern states were actually the masterminds of the Christian radical group: Jonah Jang of Plateau State, Patrick Yakowa of Kaduna State, and Murtala Nyako of Adamawa State.[37] Beyond that sweeping allegation, Boko Haram did not offer any specific explanations of what any of the named governors had done in support of the group or to further its stated goals. Many of those interviewed during the research for this book, however, pointed out that while governors Jang and Yakowa are Christians, Nyako is a Muslim; they said it was therefore improbable that Nyako and the other two governors could ever have found a common political or religious interest.

Another reaction to the emergence of Akhwat Akwop came from the Islamic group Jama'atu Ansarul Muslimina fi Biladi Sudan. In an email sent by the group's spokesman, Abu Ja'afar, to the *Desert Herald*, a local newspaper, the group threatened to attack Akhwat Akwop over their warning to Fulani residents of the area:

We have received information from a group that is well known for its terrorist and atrocities on Muslims in Southern Kaduna known as Akhwat Akwop on the 5th June 2012 with the message that; a five-day notice is given to all the Fulani Muslim communities to vacate their motherland or face deadly attacks. This is not the first time, it can be recalled that the same group openly claimed the responsibility upon the brutality of the aftermath of the presidential election of 2011 in that region (on killing women and children including burning mosques and properties) which resulted to various refugee camps for many Muslims. We have also not forgotten the atrocities of Zamani Lekwot of the previous years.

Lastly, we are calling on all the Muslims to unite . . . against these terrorists. Any challenge to brothers and sisters in Islam of Southern Kaduna is also a challenge to the entire Muslim world because the prophet said; believers are like a single body if any part is troubled the whole body is troubled. Based on the Hadith it has become an obligation upon all of us to unite and face these infidels like the way they are united in fighting us. It can also recall that even of recent Thursday the 7th June 2012. Ali Kwara was able to uncover the smuggling of weapons by a Customs Officer, named Jack Bot to give them as his contribution to the fight against Islam and Muslims, and we are aware that so many of them exist. And at the end of the day Jack Bot will be free so why do the Muslims fear to render their assistance in fighting these infidels. Their biggest agenda is to illuminate [sic] Islam and Muslims wherever they are.[38]

The counterthreat promised by the Jama'atu Ansarul Muslimina fi Biladi Sudan was, however, not pursued.

In the history of religious radicalization in Nigeria, however, the Akhwat Akwop occupies a very unusual position, as more is unknown about it than is known. First, there is no known published material on the group's activities and neither have many of its members been interviewed. It also has no recognizable leaders, and little is known about its establishment. It is also worthy to note that despite all its threats, no specific violent activity has been attributed to the Akhwat Akwop Christian radical group. However, as noted earlier, its publicized intentions underline some of the wider underpinnings of religious radicalization's connection to political violence in Nigeria. Many Nigerian Christians see adherents of the Islamic religion as their main rival, and in the zero-sum nature of national politics, there was a need to create an armed group that would reflect Christian interests. Nowhere can this be better situated in northern Nigeria than in Kaduna State, where ethnicity and religion are inextricably intertwined.

Although the Akhwat Akwop were the Christian radicals most similar to Boko Haram (see chapter 5), they are not comparable, in either actions or commitment. Akhwat Akwop only threatened, but never used, violence. Indeed, compared with Boko Haram, the Akwhat Akwop had mere entertainment value. But while there are issues against Muslims and occasionally against the government, there are also cases of disagreement among Christians over the attitude toward violence.

Christianity's Internal Reactions to Calls for Violence

Some clergymen have spoken out against violence. For example, Femi Aribisala, of the Incisive Thoughts, Practical Faith Group, argues that Christians should follow the preaching of Christ and the teaching of pastors.[39] He notes that Boko Haram is not just the enemy of Christians; it is the enemy of every peace-loving Nigerian, and he cites instances in which Muslims have taken up arms to defend Christians. For example, he pointed out that in Minna, Niger State, Muslim youths formed groups to guard churches during Sunday services. He quoted their leader as saying, "We are protecting our fellow Christian brothers and sisters to show the world that our leaders cannot use religion to divide us."[40] Also, in Kano, Aribisala posits that Muslims under the leadership of Salihu Tanko formed a group called Concerned Citizens of Kano to reach out in support of aggrieved Christians, visiting churches to give speeches of friendship and solidarity.

The Centre for Social Justice, Equity, and Transparency also urged a range of church leaders—the spiritual director of Adoration Ministry in Enugu State, Rev. Father Ejike Mbaka; and the founder of the Synagogue Church of All Nations, Prophet T. B. Joshua—to admonish their followers against adhering to the hate message of Apostle Johnson Suleman. In an open letter to Father Mbaka and T. B. Joshua, titled "Hate Sermons: Urgent Need for Prayers and Understanding, in the Light of Prevailing Religious Tensions in Nigeria," the group alleged that Suleman was acting out a "script of external enemies by inciting Christians in Nigeria into a religious war." The group complained that:

> Apostle Suleman's inciting comments happen to be the trouble at the moment. Initially, he opposed the bill on prohibiting extreme religious views or preachments sponsored in Kaduna state and placed a curse of

death on Governor Nasir el-Rufai. But it never bothered anybody because it had a personal effect. But invoking the powers of God Almighty to herd Christians into killing and beheading all Fulani herdsmen on sight is not only ungodly but mocks the thinking of orthodox Christianity and reflects more the thoughts and actions of Nigeria's external enemies bent on destabilizing the country by causing crisis of genocidal proportion in Nigeria. . . . Calling for the mass killings of members of an ethnic group—the Fulani herdsmen, who pasture their cattle, because of the transgressions of a few criminals suspected to be their kinsmen, is tantamount to exterminating a whole race. This action would also be interpreted in Christian ethos as battling against flesh and blood, which true servants of God have repeatedly warned us that we cannot win any war against the spirit.[41]

The group went further to clamp down on other Christian leaders who, they believed, espoused views similar to Apostle Suleman's:

Similarly, we deem it extremely bad faith the tendency of some anointed and venerated clergy, who are advocating for the extrajudicial killing of Boko Haram terrorists in the presumption that they launched a war against Christianity. But the same Boko Haram insurgents also slaughtered fellow Muslims in their rage of raids. The bickering in the aftermath of the split in Boko Haram's leadership between Abubakar Shekau and Abu Musab Al Barnawi sufficiently placed this notion in the public domain. But in all, does it not betray the essence of being a good brother's keeper, love of neighbor and respect for the sanctity of human life as decreed by God Almighty for anointed men of God to mount the pulpit to preach internecine wars with the religious card?[42]

Another Christian who has challenged the violence call by Pentecostal pastors is Ifedayo Olarinde, popularly known as Daddy Freeze. After Oyedepo cursed those who killed his pastor Jeremiah Omolewa in August 2019, Olarinde attacked him for not showing a Christlike attitude in his actions. Like Oyedepo, he too quoted biblical scripture to condemn Oyedepo's stance on the matter.[43] Olarinde remains one of the strongest critics of Pentecostal pastors in Nigeria.[44] Although the extent of his criticism has caused some to doubt his Christian credentials, he maintains that he remains a Christian preacher who would not violate the Christian doctrines that he holds as important.[45]

Nigeria has recorded a number of disagreements within and between Christian churches. Indeed, virtually all mainstream churches have had reason to go to court to resolve differences, with some even reaching the Supreme Court, the nation's highest court. Occasionally, these disagreements have resulted in physical violence on church premises, resulting in the intervention of the police and the sealing off of the churches. Broadly, the issues that have resulted in violent conflicts within churches have centered on three things: church finances, doctrine and leadership styles, and succession after the death of a leader. Church members have disagreed about the alleged mismanagement of church funds, arbitrary increases in church worker salaries, and spending money without the permission of appropriate regulatory authorities. Disagreements over doctrine and leadership style have included congregants rebelling over doctrinal innovations of the pastors or protesting the high-handedness of methods of the officiating pastors, while succession disputes have often emerged when supporters of successor applicants alleged fraudulent hiring procedures.

A few examples are worth citing. In May 1985, physical violence broke out at the Methodist church in Ikoyi, Lagos, over who had the right to conduct service. The ecclesiastical feud had to be resolved with police using tear gas.[46] In December 2012, there was a physical fight at the Christ Apostolic Church (CAC), Palm Avenue Mushin, Lagos, over leadership, again resulting in police intervention. Also in July 2016, members of the CAC in Abule-Ijesha in Lagos threw out their pastor, Michael Oni, in a violent protest during a church service over disagreements on the disbursement of church funds and his monthly salary.[47] In another church in Yaba, disagreements over church funds resulted in a public fight in July 2018. In September 2014, two women got physical during the monthly evening program at the Cathedral Church of All Saints, Makurdi Benue State, after one accused the other of being a witch.[48] Violence broke out in the Glory House Parish of the Assemblies of God Church in Effurun, Delta State, in February 2016, when the church broke into factions and one of the factional leaders allegedly invaded the church with thugs, the military, and police.[49]

In Enugu in July 2015, two pastors, also of the Assemblies of God Church, and their loyalists engaged in a physical conflict that compelled police to lock the church premises: the crisis started when a pastor, Nathaniel Udeze, came with letters of posting as the new pastor to the Enugu parish to replace Reverend Amaechi Agbo, the serving pastor. Udeze and Agbo were members of different factions fighting over the national leadership of the church. Trouble started as early as 7 a.m., when supporters of both pastors arrived and started sharing different versions of the Sunday school manual in preparation for the main service. They engaged in fisticuffs. Divisional Police Officer Dennis Ayara, who later arrived on the scene, made frantic efforts to bring the situation under control through negotiation, but to no avail. The police, therefore, cordoned off the church and locked it, while the leaders of the two factions were asked to report to the station.[50] The latest case, in December 2019, was in Akure, Ondo State, when violence erupted after the disappearance of a one-year-old boy, Gold Kolawole, from the children's department of the Sotitobire Praising Chapel in the Oshinle quarter of the town. Angry members of the church and nonmembers alleged that the disappeared boy was a victim of ritual killing by the pastor of the church, Prophet Alfa Babatunde, and they burned the church down.[51] Also in August 2020, in Ibadan, Oyo State, church members beat up a pastor, Adebayo Bamidele, after his wife told them that he was using charms against them.[52] There was another case of a congregation rising against a pastor in Port Harcourt in October 2020. The pastor, David Alfred, the general overseer of Faithful People's Assembly Church, was accused of sending telephone texts and chats to men in the church to ask for sex. A number of men accosted the pastor over these allegations, and he was physically beaten.[53]

Not all cases of physical violence among Christians are, however, within the same church. There have also been physical fights between different churches located near each other. In February 2018, for example, police had to intervene when members of two churches, the Aladura Church and the Calvary Church, both in Idimu, Lagos, dropped their Bibles and publicly brawled over the ownership of plots of land in the area.

In most of the cases of violence within Nigerian churches, disagreements over money, position, and material things have been consistent factors. But there is another layer of Christian violence that is worth recording—that against vulnerable children.

Of Witches and Their Catchers

A type of Christian violence that is often not categorized as such is the attacks on young children called witches. First, it needs to be noted that belief in witches is part of the communal consciousness of many Nigerian communities, but it is more entrenched in some places than others. It is most prevalent among the Ibiobios in Akwa-Ibom and Cross River states, where up to fifteen thousand young children have been branded and subjected to severe beating, maiming, burning (by fire, boiling water, or acid), poisoning, attempts to bury them alive, abandonment, rape, and trafficking. They are further denied access to health care and vaccinations. And they are blamed when they become ill and their diseases spread to other members of the family and community. Victims have been as young as two years old. In some cases, disabled children have been called witches. Also, a child called a witch is believed to have the ability to transform into a cat, snake, viper, insect, or any other animal, and to be capable of wreaking havoc, like killing people (including their parents) or bringing disease or misfortune into the family.

According to an independent research group, the Conversation, "for some religious leaders there is the lure of economic gain attached to child witchcraft accusations. The purported capacity to deliver people from the power of witches can generate huge earnings for pastor-prophets who engage in deliverance sessions. . . . Religious leaders [thus] encourage congregants to repeatedly attend church programmes, pay tithes regularly and give offerings and vows, all with the aim of generating more and more income from their followers."[54]

A few Pentecostal churches have been at the forefront of labeling young children witches, and some have been complicit in the abuses inflicted on them. For example, Pastor Chidi Okonkwo, of Power Encounter Ministry, in September 2003 organized the Operation Kill Witches crusade. Some pastors teach their congregations that witches cause sickness and poverty. Religious leaders capitalize on the ignorance of some parents in the villages just to make some money off them, charging a fee for "deliverance"—anywhere from US$300 to US$2,000.

One of the most notable pastors in this witch-catching scandal is Helen Ukpabio of Liberty Gospel Church. Her 1999 film, the widely distributed *End of the Wicked*, depicts Satan possessing children; child rights groups have denounced the film. In her pamphlets, crusades, and preaching, Ukpabio has identified traits she says are symptoms of witchcraft in children: consistent sickness, deformity, bed-wetting, sleepwalking, often running off to play, talking in sleep, unusual intelligence, stubbornness, and so on. Chillingly, many of these are simply normal childhood behaviors. Yet as a result of her activities, many children have been denounced, abandoned, stigmatized, mobbed, rejected by family members, or even killed. Parents have also taken their children to her to be delivered from witchcraft and exorcised, for fees ranging from N200,000 to N400,000.[55] Most of these exorcisms are done under gruesome conditions, sometimes leading to severe injuries to the children. If parents can't pay the high fees, Ukpabio detaines the kids under horrendous conditions; many go without food for weeks. To make a fifteen-year-old girl confess that she was a witch, church members drove a three-inch nail into her skull; she suffered a brain injury before she died shortly afterward. A boy of nine was made to drink a concoction of cement; another was bathed in acid, all for the same reason. An NGO, the Eket-based Child Rights and Rehabilitation Network, has been formed by Sam Itauma to rescue and treat these children. The category of conflict here has also attracted the attention of Nigeria's media.

The Media and the Politics of Violence Perpetrated by Christians

A topic that has attracted considerable interest, especially during the period of incessant clashes between Christians and Muslims in Nigeria, has been the role played by the news media. There are allegations, mostly from Muslims, that the electronic and print media, largely dominated by Christians from the southern parts of the country, have inflamed violence because of their support for Christians. They charge that print media often ignore violence perpetrated by Christians (actual or alleged), while simultaneously oversensationalizing violence by Muslims (actual or alleged). Many Muslims perceive that print media misrepresent facts in their reportage on clashes between Muslims and Christians. They believe that the media constantly repeat some news items to entrench a particular narrative. This kind of bias, critics have said, created the image of Fulani herdsmen as violent toward Christians. There are many profound issues involved here. While the possibility of exaggeration may not be completely ruled out, it is also correct to say that the violence perpetrated against Christians is also real, and in some cases very gruesome. Media houses in Nigeria have also risen up to condemn all those who have been involved in accusing children as witches in the Niger delta.

Conclusion

The common nature of violence associated with Islam has given the impression in many circles that its counterpart religion, Christianity, is hardly linked to any form of violence. This assumption has again been further reinforced by the scale of violence associated with Islam and the extent of the publicity that has been given to it. Recent examples from across the world have, however, shown that Christianity has its own links to violence. I have tried in this chapter to identify and discuss the various ways that Christianity has been associated with violence in postindependence Nigeria. There are areas of convergence as well as significant differences in the causes and patterns of Christian and Islamic radicalization in Nigeria. In both cases, lives have been lost because of either strong determination to advance religion or to address the perceived unfair and unjust activities of the other. Also, as with the Islamic religion, there is no uniformity of positions among Christians on violence, either for propagation of Christianity or retaliation against Islamic practices. The differences come in terms of scale and targets. By comparison, incidents of Christian-induced violence are far less common than those rooted in Islamic radicalization.

But apart from reactions to Islam, other issues link Christians to violence, and these are equally damaging for the country, as it has been shown in the case of unfair attribution of witchcraft to children and the infliction of brutal reprisals on them. This is as condemnable as any other type of brutality, and there are clear signs that this is still going on in some parts of the country. The positions of some Christian clergy also underline the extent of doubts they have about the Buhari administration's sincerity in addressing the country's religious problem and its impartiality in the handling of Christian-Muslim disagreements. However, although Christians and Muslims are at the center of most of the controversies, also important in understanding all the ramifications of religious violence in Nigeria is the dimension of traditional religions, which is the subject of discussion in chapter 4.

4. TRADITIONAL RELIGIONS
AND VIOLENCE IN NIGERIA

When the Oro festival is on, no woman . . . should behold the Oro. No woman should behold Oro with her naked eyes. The penalty for such violation is death, no matter who the woman is. —FREDERICK FASEUN, OPC Leader, *Tempo* (Lagos), November 10, 1999

The *Egungun* festival [should] be used to showcase the rich cultural values of Egungun in the state and promote it beyond the shores of the country. . . . The ministry is set to project and package the entertainment value in a manner devoid of violence. —TOYE ARULOGUN, former Oyo State commissioner for information, culture, and tourism, "Oyo to Rid Egungun Festival of Violence, Hooliganism," *The News*, March 5, 2018

As with Christianity, not many people in Nigeria associate traditional religions with violence. They assume that religious conflicts are between Christians and Muslims, and that worshippers of traditional religions have been the magnanimous hosts of the two religions that were subsequently to drive them (traditional religions) into insignificance. The fact, too, that some traditional religions have long allowed polytheism was seen as a measure of tolerance and inclusiveness that precluded violence. But a close look at the politics of religious violence in Nigeria reveals a different picture. Indeed, like Christianity and Islam, traditional religions are linked to violence in postindependence Nigeria, in part by socioeconomic and ethnopolitical considerations. This chapter concludes the tripod of the key religions in Nigeria with a discussion of how and why Nigeria's traditional religions have been connected with violence, the patterns of that violence, and its relation to the politics of intergroup relations.[1]

A major point that should be noted from the outset is that traditional religions, unlike Christianity and Islam, often do not have dedicated buildings or structures as places of worship, which has made their associations with violence profoundly different from those of Christianity and Islam. This chapter advances four central arguments: first, the rituals of some of Nigeria's traditional religious practices do manifest in ways that could and do lend themselves to being perceived as violent; second, the reassertion of traditional values by some traditional religions have resulted in clashes with Christianity and Islam; third, like Christianity and Islam, the increasing ethnonationalism across the country has resulted in traditional religions underlining ethnopolitical conflicts across Nigeria; and fourth, criminal individuals have employed aspects of traditional religions in the perpetration of their crimes.

Traditional Religious Rituals That Involve Violence

In looking at the religious practices that have predisposed traditional religions to violence, two things have to be borne in mind. First, some practices in Nigeria's traditional religions are, by the standards of other places, considered violent, but are, in context, parts of the instrument of social and political order. As noted in chapter 1, what counts as traditional religion in Africa is essentially embedded in the way power and authority are constructed within the society. In essence, those practices seen as violent are not really about those traditional religions, but more about the systems and practices (rituals) of power and authority. Second, some traditional religions have practices that are restrictive and thus have the potential for evoking reactions that can result in conflict with those who don't belong to the fold.

In the category of practices that may be considered inherently violent, the Yoruba hold an annual religious festival across all Yoruba towns that honors departed ancestors, a masquerade known as the Egúngún festival. Supporters of different towns' masquerades use canes to beat each other, and they display other actions that appear violent. The festival is an occasion for the Egúngún to display charms and magical tricks in the form of a contest, with each Egúngún daring the other to cross his path or meet him during the procession.[2] The display of violence here is part of the festival and is purely theatrical. Consequently, it does not come squarely under the category of violence being discussed in this book.³ But recently rival supporters of different masquerades have gone much further, to display levels of violence that go beyond the limits of traditional practices, and several towns in the southwest have recorded cases of violence that resulted in injury and even deaths. Ibadan, the capital of Oyo State, seems to be the center of the most vicious incidents. Virtually every year in recent times, violence has followed every festival. Violence associated with the Egúngún festival reached an important peak in July 2012, when the police arrested perhaps the most important Egúngún in Ibadan, the Oloolu, after a street fight with Muslim youths and arraigned him in court on a three-count charge of arms possession, assault, and malicious damage. When the masquerade and his followers could not meet the bail conditions, they were held in custody at the town's notorious Agodi prison.

The circumstances that resulted in the violence are worth recording. During his annual outing, the Oloolu encountered Muslim clerics holding a memorial ceremony for a late chief imam.⁴ The clerics allegedly asked Oloolu not to pass or disrupt their ceremony. When he refused, he was attacked by Muslim youths, and in the process, he sustained injuries and had to be taken to the hospital by the police. The following day, supporters of the Oloolu group organized a reprisal attack and swooped down on the area. They unleashed mayhem, armed with charms, broken bottles, daggers, machetes, and guns. Some also used arrows, empty bottles, and stones. They attacked residents, smashed vehicle windshields, damaged property, and looted shops. When the Oloolu and his followers saw the police, they attempted to retreat, but not before some of the followers were arrested with dangerous weapons, including a locally made gun. At the conclusion of the case, the court warned them to be on their good behavior. Violence again emerged in July 2013, when supporters of Oloolu clashed with the loosely organized gangs of street children and teenagers known as Area Boys.⁵ Here again, supporters of the Oloolu wanted to forcefully exercise their right to freedom of movement that was challenged by the Area Boys.

In 2017, violence that trailed the Ege masquerade resulted in one death.⁶ Supporters, again brandishing machetes, guns, swords, cutlasses, broken bottles, stones, and charms, confronted the police team trying to stop them from further advancing toward a rival group. In the mayhem, pedestrians, motorists, commercial motorcyclists, and residents ran for cover and hurriedly shut the doors of houses and shops. The masquerade's supporters assaulted many people and destroyed properties.⁷ Again, in June 2019, five people were killed, with several others wounded, in Ibadan when supporters of the same Ege masquerade became violent in the city. Again brandishing dangerous weapons, these supporters went on a rampage attacking shops and commuters. Because of police intelligence that there would be riots during the masquerade's traditional visit to the *Olubadan* (the mayor of the town), the masqueraders were advised to shelve the idea of paying homage to the monarch. This development did not go down well with the masquerade team, but they took the advice in order to maintain law and order. The supporters, however, saw things differently, and they used the opportunity to attack other rival gangs. The policemen that intervened to bring order were also attacked. It was in the ensuing violence that the five people were killed. Thugs were also in the habit of taking advantage of the commotion usually created by the masquerade's presence to beat and rob unsuspecting persons.[8]

The constant violence that often trailed the festival later forced the government to work very closely with the various families involved in the festival and with the police. The state's former commissioner for information, culture, and tourism, Toye Arulogun, later declared that the "*Egungun* festival [should] be used to showcase the rich cultural values of Egungun in the state and promote it beyond the shores of the country."[9] Although the violence has reduced, it has not stopped altogether. In some other towns in the southwest, violence has been associated with the Egúngún festival, but they have been less serious than those in Ibadan. On the whole, the violence associated with the Egúngún is a case of an organized social order that was hijacked by worshippers who took traditional rites beyond legal limits. Ironically, the Egúngún festival among the Yoruba is also characterized by the renewal of relationship and family solidarity, and it has also helped to resolve agelong disputes and family and community problems. Also a bit of an irony is that, while masquerades have been associated with violence in the southwest, they have been instruments for conflict resolution among the Ibos in the southeast.[10]

In the second category—traditional religious practices whose restrictiveness has evoked reactions from others—the Oro festival, also celebrated in the southwest among the Yoruba, is at the forefront. Traditionally, the cult brings together prominent members of the community, notably kings, chiefs, and the rich.[11] It is a subcult within the Ogboni cult, so their memberships are often intertwined.[12] The festival differs from town to town, but everyone celebrates it annually for up to two weeks (it can also be called after the death of a reigning monarch or any prominent man). The usage of vulgar words is permitted during the festival. It is manifestly patriarchal, as it is celebrated only by male descendants of paternal natives in the location where the event is taking place. During the festival, women must stay indoors, lying down and covering their heads and those of their children; it is believed that women have died from beholding Oro. To ensure that women and nonnatives stay indoors during the period, notice is given throughout each town. Adherents observed these and other rituals freely in the precolonial era, but with the advent of colonialism devotees had to stay within the confines of government laws.[13] With independence, they reclaimed a measure of authority. As is shown in the next section, the Oro festival has become a serious issue of contention between Oro cult members and adherents of other religions (Christianity and Islam) in Yoruba society over the lack of consideration for other people's religious, civil, and commercial obligations.[14]

The Aluku festival is celebrated in some parts of Yorubaland, especially in Ifetedo, Osun State. This is very much like the Oro festival, except that it does not discriminate between male and female. During the festival period when adherents move around the town in the middle of the night, all the members of the population, regardless of gender, who are not initiated are forbidden from coming out to behold the worshippers, and those who do run the risk of being violently attacked.[15]

There are also traditional religious practices that involve cruelty toward animals. Two of these are particularly important. The first is the Ogun festival, celebrated among the Yoruba. The festival is often held around August or September, and it is more prominent in Ondo State and parts of Ekiti State. The festival involves the public beheading of a dog. Two people pull the dog in opposite directions, hence causing intense pain. The high priest kills the dog with a machete. The dog's blood is then mixed with salt, kola nuts, palm wine, and palm oil, and poured over the working tools of the worshipers, which are gathered in a bowl; this is believed to protect them from trouble and bring abundant profits. Ogun is the patron of those who make use of metals in their everyday work, such as blacksmiths, drivers, mechanics, and surgeons.

The second practice is Adiye Irana, the passage of the dead in Yoruba mythology. In the procession to bury a dead person who had lived a good life, local elders wearing white loincloths strapped around their waists grip a big and mature cock by its feet and pull off its feathers as they proceed to the graveyard, with the casket of the dead following them. The cock is believed to be the emissary that buys the right of way for the dead man as he embarks on his journey to the land of no return. It is only for a worthless dead man that the Adiye Irana ritual is not performed.[16] It goes without saying that this process is a painful way for an animal to die.

Also, certain acts may be considered abominations by worshippers in certain traditional religions, who may react violently to anyone who shows disrespect for their concerns. For example, drinking palm wine is an abomination for Obatala worshippers among the Yoruba. Consequently, the worshippers react violently to any attempt by nonworshippers to taunt them with palm wine. This caused minor violence in Ile-Ife in September 2007.[17]

The Reassertion of Traditional Values and the Resulting Clashes with Followers of Other Religions

As noted in chapter 1, Islam, Christianity, and traditional religion have historically coexisted in parts of Nigeria; in particular, traditional religions in southwest and southeast Nigeria were receptive to both Christianity and Islam. But traditional worshippers gradually began to resist the two religions, because of their demonization of traditional religion. Of the two religions, however, it was Islam that was more vocal in its denunciation of traditional religious practices. Indeed, a prominent scholar on traditional religions, Omosade Awolalu, reported that "traditional religious practices, including sacrifice—secret societies of all types—were condemned. . . . The Muslim leaders disregarded curfews imposed on women during Oro festival, and they also deprecated the Ogboni cult, disregarded the divinities and all their cults, and composed songs to ridicule the 'pagan' practices. All the people who practice these traditional rites were stigmatized as *Kafirs* (unbelievers) by the Muslims."[18]

The radical postures advanced by Muslims and Christians evoked objections from traditional religion worshippers, who came out forcefully and sometimes violently to prove to Christians and Muslims that religions were already present at the time of their arrivals. Indeed, around the 1970s, traditional religions experienced a bit of attraction among people who saw foreign religions as encroaching on traditional practices. In the bid to reassert themselves, adherents of traditional religions began adopting means that Christians and Muslims found inherently violent. As early as the late 1970s, traditional worshippers and Muslims were clashing, mostly during traditional festivals, especially masquerades.[19] While the activities of these people were largely spontaneous and often sporadic, they are worth mentioning in any study discussing violence. At the center of the clashes were Muslim radicals seeking to prevent the traditional worshippers from celebrating their festivals. In the southwestern town of Ibadan, a Muslim radical preacher, popularly known as Ajagbe-mokeferi (meaning the one who shouts or yells at the infidel) led Muslims in a revolt against one of the town's most sacred traditional religious activities, the Oloolu masquerade.[20] Under the tradition, women are forbidden from beholding the Oloolu and are required to remain indoors during his passage.[21]

Ajagbemokeferi, however, defiled this tradition by parading all the women in his household during the passage of the Oloolu. He also allegedly attempted to derobe the Oloolu. Violence ensued, and supporters of the Oloolu went on a rampage in the vicinity.[22] It took the intervention of the police to restore order. But from this moment, supporters of traditional religion began to seriously object to what they saw as the increasing effrontery of adherents of Islamic religion and, to some extent, Christianity.

The celebration of the Oro cult resulted in violence in Iseyin, in Oyo State, in September 2019. Worshippers announced a curfew in the town from 9 p.m. every day for seventeen days for the duration of the Oro festival. Almost immediately, the Iseyin chapter of the Nigerian Supreme Council for Islamic Affairs warned that it would not allow it.[23] The group argued that "the rights of freedom of Muslims and Christians to move about their daily activities cannot be sacrificed for a few, who are hell-bent on shutting down Iseyin for seventeen days."[24] This ultimately resulted in violence, with Oro worshippers attacking Muslims in their mosque.

There were also conflicts over restrictions imposed by the Oro worshippers on towns in Ogun State, until the Christian and Muslim communities in the state took the matter to court. The religious bodies officially complained that the festival's restrictions shut down social and commercial activities in the state. In February 2018, the Ogun State high court ruled in a case of the Christian Association of Nigeria and the Muslim Community in Ipokia local government versus the Oro cult, that the Oro cult should not celebrate their festival in the daytime; the court restricted the festival to the hours between 12 a.m. and 4 a.m.[25] In March 2020, in Ogun State, Oro worshippers again clashed with Christians and Muslims over another movement restriction, this time in the Yewa district of Idiroko, Oja-Odan, Ipokia, and other towns. In the conflict, Oro worshippers killed a Muslim and destroyed mosques, churches, and cars. The police stepped in and eventually brokered a peace.

In 2001, Muslim Hausa-Fulani residents attacked Oro cult worshippers in Sagamu, resulting in a temporary spread of social unrest, including ethnic dimensions, discussed later in this chapter. Followers of traditional religion also attacked Muslims in Offa, Kwara State, in February 2004. Muslims had insisted that the Shrine of Moremi, located at the palace of the king to commemorate the brave and altruistic Yoruba princess, must be removed because it was close to a mosque that was built more than a hundred years after the construction of the shrine.[26] In September 2005, the sleepy town of Iwo, Osun State, became a theater of violence when the community's masquerade cult took on a group of Muslims called Tahun in open combat.[27]

In looking at the cases of violence orchestrated by followers of traditional religion, a noticeable difference can be seen in comparison with Muslims and Christians. Adherents of traditional religions engaging in violence are mostly trying to reclaim the spaces believed to have been acquired by Christianity and Islam, and are not, unlike Muslims and Christians, trying to make any ideological claim of superiority. It is, however, not all the time that violence coming from the believers in traditional religion responds to Islam and Christianity. There are also cases when the violence is a by-product of political and socioeconomic concerns, as when the violence is geared to the politics of ethnicity in the country.

Ethnonationalism, Traditional Religion, and Violence

Again, as noted in the introduction, religion and national politics in Nigeria are intrinsically intertwined, and, just like Islam and Christianity, traditional religions in the country at some point became associated with the politics of ethnonationalism and conflicts. The resurgence of ethnoreligious nationalism in Nigeria began around 1993, after the military regime of Ibrahim Babangida annulled the presidential election that was won by the late M. K. O. Abiola, a Yoruba from the southwest. Although he was a Muslim, many Yoruba people looked beyond his religion and saw his electoral victory and subsequent annulment purely as an ethnic calculation of the Hausa-Fulani–Yoruba dichotomy, and they reacted as such. In the southern parts of the country, new groups began looking into their indigenous religions to find ethnic unity in what was seen as the zero-sum nature of national politics. In the southwest, for example, a pan-Yoruba ethnonationalist group known as the Odua People's Congress (OPC) was formed.[28] Although it was not a religious group, the OPC drew deeply on Yoruba religious philosophy and relied more on Yoruba traditional religion rather than Christianity and Islam, which the group saw as endorsing national institutions that were against their ethnic interests. Many members of this group used local charms and invoked traditional religion in their engagement of violence. Calls were also made to Yoruba people across the southwest to jettison foreign religions and support traditional religions in the fight for what was seen as an ethnic cause.

This soon became entangled with intergroup relations after the return of democracy in 1999, and increasingly, the Yoruba-Hausa political tension that existed in the run-up to the democratic transition developed religious connotations. The first major case of violence between the Hausa and the worshippers of Yoruba traditional religion during this period occurred in Shagamu, Ogun State, in July 1999, when some Yoruba youths celebrating the Oro festival killed a Hausa woman. Yoruba people said the woman had refused to obey the traditional rule requiring nonparticipants in the festival to stay off the streets.

After the death of the Hausa woman, Yoruba Oro worshippers rioted around the town, resulting in many deaths, mostly Hausa. The Hausa retaliated, attacking the Yoruba in Kano. It took the intervention of the federal government to restore some form of normalcy. Since the resurgence of ethnic tension that followed the activities of the Fulani herdsmen (see chapter 6), Yoruba people have further embraced traditional religions to seek unity in their perceived fight against those seen as Fulani invaders. It is not uncommon for OPC members to invoke the names of traditional gods.

However, of all the parts of the country where religion has been exploited to mobilize people for violent ethnonationalism, nowhere has it been as pronounced as in the oil-rich Niger delta region. Here, the Egbesu religious cult has been invoked to bring ethnic cohesion in the fight against perceived injustice. Among the Ijaws of the Niger delta, Egbesu is the deity of warfare and the spiritual foundation for combating evil. It can also be used in defense or in correcting injustice. In a way, the story of the Egbesu reflects some of the issues associating religion with ethnopolitical violence. The ancient Egbesu cult of the Ijaws declined after the British colonial conquest in the late nineteenth century, and for some time most Ijaws only knew of the cult through folklore. In recent times, however, members of the cult have been fighting against authorities in the Niger delta in response to environmental and other problems caused by oil exploitation and lack of investment of oil revenue in the local economy. Many young men have joined the cult, undergoing secret initiations by witch doctors who impart the supernatural powers of Egbesu. The initiation involves the subject being etched with scars on some hidden part of the body, and some members also wear amulets. The followers often believe the charms and cult initiations make them bulletproof. A scholar of the subject, Edlyne Anugwom, sums all this up effectively when he posits that "the asymmetric power between the federal government/trans national oil corporations (TNOCs) and the militias may have privileged the invocation of the supernatural as a critical agency of strength and courage by the youth militias."[29] He argues further that "the conflict in the region embodies a cultural revision which has been necessitated by both the uncertainty of the oil environment and the prevailing narratives of social injustice. Hence the Egbesu deity, seen historically as embodying justice, has been reinvented by the youth militias and imbued with the powers of invincibility and justice in the conflict with the government and oil companies."[30] In his study of the Egbesu, Anugwom identified some Ijaw traditional religious beliefs that may also have informed the popularity of the Egbesu among the youth fighters. One of the most important of these beliefs is the acquisition of membership in the group and all the rights and obligations therein through elaborate rituals. In this sense, one becomes Ijaw by performing such rituals of acculturation and then acquires the full rights and privileges of citizenship.[31]

Since the 1990s, Ijaw youths from the Niger delta region of Nigeria have been engaged in interethnic as well as oil-related conflict with the federal government.[32] In terms of their activities, a 2003 research report by the Centre for Development and Conflict Management Studies notes that "it is difficult to assign any specific actions or encounters to Egbesu Boys because their members in different militant organizations undertake most of the militant actions of the Ijaws towards the State, oil companies and other ethnic groups."[33] There have, however, been reports of Egbesu Boys being involved in the kidnapping of oil workers and the sabotage of oil installations, as well as attacks on Nigerian authorities.[34] The Egbesu Boys have also been involved in conflicts with the Itsekiri ethnic group in the Niger delta region.[35] There have also been reports of Egbesu Boys, among other militant groups, being used by politicians to "assassinate political enemies" and to "settle political scores."[36] The Egbesu Boys have been described as one of the "most daring" Ijaw youth groups and "more dangerous" than other armed groups in Nigeria, such as the Bakassi Boys.[37] It is believed that sources of funding to the Egbesu Boys include oil bunkering as well as "highly influential members of the community," which allows the group to buy its weapons.[38]

In concluding this section, it needs to be noted that in most cases of violence in this category, ethnic groups have dug into their culture to find aspects of indigenous religions that can assist in the zero-sum complexities of national politics. Indeed, it is also an implicit condemnation of Christianity and Islam for failing woefully to protect the people. Indeed, some of those taking part in this class of violence could also be either Christians or Muslims but, in the context of national political realities, find that indigenous religions provide answers to their problems and meet the conditions for endorsing what they see as necessary violence. In short, it is not that the religion itself is violent, but that it has been made to serve violent purposes. This in a way is very similar to how traditional religion has been made to serve functions in criminal activities, discussed in the next section.

Traditional Religion and Commercial and Criminal Activities

Traditional religions in Nigeria have had some association with illegal activities. There is, however, a need to put this in context to avoid misunderstanding. By their nature, traditional religions embed fears in (and some measure of power and authority over) citizens, often with the purpose of commanding obedience or hypnotizing victims. On the other hand, the mysticism constructed around traditional religions can be used in ways that make the impossible seem possible. It is in this context that some use traditional religious practices to ostensibly legitimize criminal enterprises. In addition, the fact that certain criminal agents use traditional religion parallels how other actors also use it in political contests. This shows that the instrumentalization of traditional religion, like other religions, is a consistent reality.

There are a number of criminal activities that, though not part of traditional religions, have used the religions in the pursuit of their actions. There have been cases of human sacrifice. In August 2004, at a shrine in Okija, Anambra State, police uncovered eighty-three corpses—including sixty-three that were headless—and twenty skulls; some were in coffins, others lying by the side of the path. They then arrested a number of people whom they suspected of being officials of the Okija shrine, most of whom appear to have been members of one extended family. Eventually, the police paraded thirty-one suspects before the press in the national capital, Abuja.[39] The extent to which the Okija incident can be associated with religion is tenuous, as there is no known case of any religion being propagated. But we can consider it as another case in which people have exploited traditional cults to perpetrate criminal activities.

But perhaps the most pronounced of the crimes that have used traditional religion is associated with money ritual. While again it is clear that no traditional religion in Nigeria endorses this criminal act, it is also something that has been done in its name. Cases of crime here are more frequent in the southern parts of the country. The practices vary, but essentially, they involve the removal of human body parts to be used for money ritual. For example, in December 2019, Segun Philip and Adeeko Owolabi were arrested by the Ogun State police command for killing a final-year sociology student at Lagos State University, Favour Daley-Oladele, for money ritual.[40]

Another crime that has employed traditional religion is human trafficking, especially for prostitution. Here traditional religion is exploited to extract an oath of silence from all those involved in the practice. This traditional control mechanism is designed to trap victims and put them in perpetual bondage. A scholar on the subject, Norah Hashim Msuya, notes, "Victims are subjected to the oath prior to their departure from Nigeria to ensure debt commitment and non-disclosure of the identity of the traffickers. However, in the event of non-compliance and violation of the oath by the victims and family members, illness and ultimate death may suddenly occur."[41] Victims of trafficking are subject to a popular traditional oath ceremony with a priest who is referred to as a "juju priest" before departure for their work abroad.

Also important in this category is oath taking. The resurgence of traditional religion among Nigerians has business and economic dimensions, as partners in business deals have gone to swear oaths before priests in local shrines. Indeed, the general assumption of many Nigerians is that traditional deities are swifter and more effective in dispensing justice than the Christian Bible and the Qur'an, and that those who swear by local gods are more likely to think twice before contemplating betrayal. A key ritual of traditional religions that potentially implies violence is a sworn oath of agreement, especially in southeastern Nigeria. Broadly, two people who want to seal an agreement with an oath go to a traditional priest and set out devastating consequences for betrayal by either side. Historically, such oaths concerned financial dealings, but, with the return of democracy, people started using them for elections and political office. When someone breaks a promise, as is often the case, either side in the agreement may employ the violence named in the oath.

Conclusion

There can be no doubt that traditional religions are the least politically active of the three religious divisions in Nigeria, and, as with the case of Christianity, have significantly reduced the extent to which people associate the religion with violence in the country. Indeed, like Islam and Christianity, traditional religions have been at the center of violence and controversies in Nigeria. However, much of this violence can be linked to the clash between tradition and modernity, as perceived by adherents of traditional religions and worshippers of the more modern religions of Christianity and Islam. In traditional religions, both Muslims and Christians, despite their profound antagonism, still found a common enemy. The violence associated with traditional religion also has similarities and differences with that perpetrated by Christians and Muslims. The first similarity is intention; in all cases, those involved believe in the superiority of their conviction, to the extent that they are willing to engage in violence to protect it. Another similarity is that violence associated with radical traditional religions, like Christianity and Islam, also affects intergroup relations and the governance of the country. On several occasions, central gov-is, in Christ God was reconciling the world to himself, not counting their trespasses against them, and entrusting to us the message of reconciliation." Also, Romans 5:10 reads, "For if while we were enemies we were reconciled to God by the death of his Son, much more, now that we are reconciled, shall we be saved by his life." Finally, Matthew 18:15 notes, "If your brother sins against you, go and tell him his fault, between you and him alone. If he listens to you, you have gained your brother." The Qur'an also underlines the importance of reconciliation. In Ash-Shura 42:40, it notes, "The Recompense for an evil is an evil like thereof; but whoever forgives and makes reconciliation, his reward is with Allah." Also, in Al-Hujuraat 49:9, it states, "And if two parties or groups among the believers fall to fighting, then make peace between them both. But if one of them outrages against the other, then fight you (all) against the one which outrages till it complies with the Command of Allah. Then if it complies, make reconciliation between them justly, and be equitable. Verily! Allah loves those who are equitable." Finally, Al-Hujuraat 49:10 declares, "The believers are nothing else than brothers [in Islamic religion]. So, make reconciliation between your brothers, and fear Allah, that you may receive mercy." Thus, both the Bible and the Qur'an teach reconciliation after a disagreement.

In the last decade, however, violence connected to religion has heightened, and this has been linked to radicalization, or the adoption of radical views by various religious groups across the world. Radicalization has become a trendy term and, like most words that have fallen into that category, it has become vulnerable to distortion. Its interchangeability, rightly or wrongly, with other terms like extremism, fundamentalism, and terrorism has added further layers of controversy and confusion to its conceptualization. Radicalization, in all its ramifications, has been studied rigorously by scholars, such that any detailed discussion in this chapter will not serve any additional purpose.[35]

In the context of this book, a radical group is one that professes a belief system that rejects the status quo and actively aspires to an idealized past or envisioned future, embedded in the paradox of past as future and change as a return to the past. Such a group calls for its adherents to use violent and unconventional means to realize that change. Its nostalgic view of aspects of the past and expectant view of the future signal a group's rejection of the present. Radicalization, then, is the process of transforming the mental and emotional motivations of a person or group to shift from peaceful to violent behavior.

Broken down further, six aspects of this definition are particularly important. First, radicalization is a process (with identifiable phases) and not an event, its dynamics formed by the complex interaction of multiple events, actors, relationships, beliefs, and institutions. Second, it emphasizes and aims a Jewess. He applied a Jewish law to the Jews (Leviticus 20:10 and Deuteronomy 22:22). He also applied the same law to two Muslims (Mā'iz ibn Mālik al-Aslamī and a Ghamidiyyah woman), apparently before the revelation of Qur'an 24:2–3, which appears to have been revealed to abrogate the punishment of adulterous Muslims by *Rajm*."[32]

Generally, the association between violence and religion has brought a number of political issues to the forefront. Issues like election and harmonious intergroup relations are factors in religion across the world. The practice of elections, central to political governance, appears in the central writings of Christianity and Islam. Christianity recognizes the practice; for example, in the book of Deuteronomy, 1:9–17, the people of Israel were instructed to choose among themselves those who would rule over them. Apart from this, the Bible also recorded several instances of the freedom of choice—the essence of an election—being given to the people of Israel. Election continues as a Christian practice today. Catholic bishops elect the pope, the head of the Catholic Church, and Anglican Church bishops also elect their head, the archbishop. In the Christian view, generally, taking part in a secular election is a civic duty, a demonstration of good citizenship, and emphasized by their religion. Similarly, while Islamic scholars posit that neither the Qur'an nor Hadith makes a categorical statement concerning elections (and neither uses the word), some argue that Islam has room for the related idea of representation. For example, H. A. AbdulSalam points out that the political system in Islam operates in three dimensions: *tawhid* (belief in God), *risalah* (messengership), and *khilafat* (vice regency).[33] According to him, *khilafat* also means representation, and anyone who occupies this position is expected to represent and lead according to the word of God.[34] The Qur'an also encourages mutual consultations in political matters and governance through *shura*, which means consultation, and the Hadith notes that leadership is to be chosen by consensus after due cognizance has been taken of the leadership and spiritual capabilities of all the people. The Hadith dictates that the best among the people in terms of knowledge and fear of God are selected as the leaders. The Prophet, however, further instructed that anyone who puts himself or herself forward for leadership should not be appointed. Further evidence that elections are not un-Islamic can be seen in the regular elections in predominantly Muslim states, including Egypt, Iran, and Pakistan.

Similarly, both the Bible and the Qur'an encourage the crucial practice of harmonious intergroup relations, focusing on reconciliation after a conflict. In the Bible's 2 Corinthians 5:18–19, it is written, "All this is from God, who through Christ reconciled us to himself and gave us the ministry of reconciliation; that ernments have had to intervene to ensure that social harmony is not affected and that peaceful coexistence between ethnic groups ensues.

But there are also remarkable differences. First, the extent to which radical traditional religions' adherents fall under the influence of spiritual leaders that can encourage violence is significantly reduced, compared to Islam and Christianity. Indeed, supporters of traditional religions who have taken to violence have done so without encouragement by spiritual leaders. This may have to do with the nature of the religious practices. With no stipulated times and days of regular worship (unlike Christianity and Islam), traditional religions are less vulnerable to the machinations that make the two foreign religions susceptible to violence. But while traditional religions have joined other religions in causing security problems for the Nigerian state, a greater security problem came from the activities of the group that went by the name Jamā 'at Ahl al-Sunna li-Da'wa wa-l-Jihād, more widely known as Boko Haram, the subject of chapter 5.

5. BOKO HARAM AND
THE NEW PHASE OF VIOLENCE

The enemies of Islam—the Jews, the Christians . . . as well as their hypocrite and the orientalist lackeys—have ignited the fire of a "world war" since their occupation of the lands of Islam. They have desecrated the sacred dwellings of Islam and changed the Sharia by enforcing the oppressive constitutions, the laws of the *jāhiliyya*, their tyrannous regimes, their devilish banners, their twisted secular studies, as well as their atheistic colleges and universities. Not only did they do all the above, but they also recruit people from us [Muslims] to carry on their goals: And they will continue to fight you until they turn you back from your religion if they are able. (Q2:217)
—MUHAMMAD YUSUF, founder of Boko Haram, "A Sermon on Colonialism," *Boko Haram Reader*

You are not a prophet. You have not yet proven your faith or moral character to your neighbors. If it took Prophet Muhammad twenty-three years preaching Islam, for how many years have you preached before you decided to judge Muslims as unbelievers because they have Western education? You did not have sufficient religious knowledge, or even enough general knowledge.
—SHEIKH JAFAR MAHMUD ADAM, erstwhile mentor of Mohammed Yusuf, "Me Ya Sa Suke Cewa Boko Haramun Ne?"

A new phase in religious violence in Nigeria came with the emergence of the Jamā'at Ahl al-Sunna li-Da'wa wa-l-Jihād, meaning People Committed to the Propagation of the Prophet's Teachings and Jihad but widely known as Boko Haram. In the last decade, the activities of this group have been the most profound security challenge the country has faced since the end of its civil war in

1970. At least three things make Boko Haram unique in the history of religious violence in Nigeria: its suicide operations; the sustained nature of its violence, such that the state is now looking for ways of addressing the issue apart from the use of force; and the extent to which the movement has keyed into global insurgencies. Writing about the Boko Haram insurgency in Nigeria at this time is, however, fraught with a major difficulty: the rebellion is still going on, thus making any conclusion about it tentative.

The central argument of this chapter is that the Boko Haram phenomenon is the inescapable consequence of the accumulated mismanagement of the political, economic, and intergroup relational aspects of the Nigerian state and that the problem has become intractable because the political, economic, and sociocultural frustration of a group of people found a pattern of expression in religion—undoubtedly the most emotional identity issue in the country. While the subject of Boko Haram has attracted a wide array of scholars, my objective is to situate the phenomenon within the broader picture of religion and violence in Nigeria, exploring its broad structural effects on the Nigerian state and its attempts to restructure the relationships between religion, violence, and intergroup dynamics.[1] Therefore this chapter addresses in turn the group's establishment, beliefs and doctrines, history of schisms, recruitment, funding, strategies and tactics, structures, activities, and targets. It also discusses the responses of the Nigerian state. But any discussion on Boko Haram should be prefaced with the assertion that several aspects of the group's activities are still shrouded in controversy, uncertainty, or both. Moreover, the problem is as yet unresolved, with scenarios previously considered unlikely. Consequently, conclusions can be at best tentative.

A note on terminology: The widely used name Boko Haram, translated as "Western education is forbidden," is, as explained by Andrea Brigaglia, only a nickname that "captures all the stereotypes that have daily currency in Islamphobic discourses: obscurantism, primitivism and the essentialist ferocity of Muslims. Indeed, the name is one that is strongly detested by the leadership of the group, which calls itself 'The People Committed to the Propagation of the Prophet's Teachings and Jihad,' *Jamā'at Ahl al-Sunna li-Da'wa wa-l-Jihād*."[2] This chapter uses the name, however, because of the wider global currency it has attained.

Birth of Boko Haram and the Shift to Radical Militancy

The Boko Haram group is such a complex organization that its birth can only be understood by discussing three overlapping accounts: the various versions of its creation; the biography of its founder, Mohammed Yusuf; and the phases of its evolution. Broadly, there are at least four versions of the birth of Boko Haram.[3] The first links it to the Maitatsine riots of the 1980s (see chapter 2), focusing on the aversion of both Maitatsine and Boko Haram to Western education. Scholars here include Pham, Onuoha, and Adesoji.[4] Indeed, both groups have engaged in revolutionary militancy in advancing their religious causes, and both have exploited disenchanted operational background, created by economic deprivation, to advance their causes.

The second version traces the formation to Muhammed Yusuf's link with the Shabab organization around 2001, which was purportedly associated with Sheikh Jafar Adam. Indeed, many see Jafar Adam as the spiritual mentor of Muhammed Yusuf.[5] Yusuf was the youth leader of Shabab but later fell out with Jafar Adam and established his own group to better advance Islam.

The third theory traces the birth of the group to the late 1990s, when it was formed as an unnamed study group in Maiduguri, led by one Mohammed Ali, a Nigerian allegedly radicalized in Sudan. It was he who purportedly converted Yusuf to a radical version of Islam. The group later established its base in Kannamma, in Yobe State, calling it Afghanistan because of their determination to replicate the country. According to Mohammed Kyari, it chose Kannamma strategically, for "its remoteness from the bases of power, far from the prying eyes of security and away from urban distraction. . . . [It] is also easily defensible as it was forested and located between two bodies of water."[6]

The fourth theory links Boko Haram's birth to local politics, and sees the group as an offshoot of "the ECOMOG boys," a group of political thugs formed by the former Borno State governor, Ali Modu-Sheriff.[7] The governor had used these thugs against his opponents in the 2007 election and promised to transform the state into a full Sharia state if he won the election. There was thus an agreement that the group would supply the name of one of its members to serve as the commissioner for religious affairs. A strong member of the group, Buji Foi, was thus nominated as a cabinet member. When the governor failed to keep this promise, the group called for the resignation of Buji Foi from the cabinet, and the road to the formation of Boko Haram began. Modu-Sheriff has persistently denied any connection with Boko Haram. All four of these theories may be relevant to the birth of Boko Haram. In any case, by 2003, the embryo of what would later become Boko Haram had been effectively formed and was about to take on the Nigerian state.

The central individual in the birth of Boko Haram was Muhammed Yusuf. There are disputes about his birthplace. While Walker puts it as Girgir in the Jakusko Local Government Area of Yobe State, Murtada cites Naiyyah in the Yunuari Local Government Area of the same state.[8] However, Yusuf grew up in Maiduguri, where he attended the Muhammadu Indimi Mosque and married Amma Fugu, whose father was his benefactor. Indeed, the parcel of land that Fugu gave him was where he built his headquarters. In the 1990s, Yusuf became a preacher at this mosque, where he also became the leader of the mosque's youths. He was recognized as a remarkable preacher.

In the early stages, Yusuf was a member of the Izala group, where he was tutored in the Saudi-oriented Salafi version of Sunni Islam. During this period, his mentor was Sheikh Jafar Mahmud Adam, who had attained wide popularity throughout northern Nigeria as an Islamic scholar. But soon his radical preaching brought him into conflict with Adam, the Izala, and mainstream Muslims. Yusuf founded the Ibn Taymiyyah Center in Maiduguri.[9] Nonetheless, he still had much in common with Izala, including the belief in the sinfulness of secularism and the condemnation of the heirs of Usman dan Fodio, the jihadist whose 1804 jihad changed the religious outlook of most of northern Nigeria, as unworthy representatives of their forefathers' legacy.

Around 2002, Yusuf started a group he called Ahl al-Sunna wa al-Jama'a (Companions of the Prophet), known locally as the Nigerian Taliban or Yusufiya (Followers of Yusuf), and became the Borno State representative on the Supreme Council for Shari'a in Nigeria. By 2002, the Nigerian Taliban had begun expressing antigovernment sentiments around Kannamma in the Yunusari Local Government Area of Yobe State. It also extended its activities to Damaturu, the Yobe State capital, and Damboa, Bama, and Gwoza in Borno State.

His group's first major confrontation with government forces was in December 2003, when it clashed with the police over fishing rights in a local pond. This was initially not a religious issue. The group overpowered the police and seized their weapons. For most of December 2003 and January 2004, the Nigerian Taliban attacked remote places like Geidam, Yunusari, Yusufari, and Damaturu in the forceful propagation of their version of Islam, and by mid-2004, they had spread to places like Gwoza and Kala-Balge on the Nigeria-Cameroon border and later to Bauchi. In response to all of these attacks, the Nigerian army led an attack on the group, killing up to seventy members. Mohammed Ali died of injuries sustained at Yajiwa around January or February 2004. Muhammed Yusuf took over the leadership of the group, whose members had scattered across towns in the region. Those who survived returned to Maiduguri, where they settled back into society under his leadership.

On the eve of the 2007 presidential election, Yusuf and his group killed the popular cleric and his former mentor Sheikh Jafar Mahmud Adam while he was praying at his mosque in Kano.[10] The killing of Adam was a turning point in Yusuf's story: it removed one of the few voices that could credibly challenge Muhammad Yusuf. In one of Boko Haram's numerous confrontations with the government, Muhammad Yusuf was arrested by members of the Nigerian army and handed over to the police, where he was extrajudicially murdered in July 2009. Attempting to cover up this killing made the police look ridiculous.

In July 2010, Abubakar Shekau became the new head of the group. One of the closest people to Yusuf, he was born in Yobe State and grew up in Shekau village.[11] He worked in Maiduguri's Monday Market, selling empty perfume and pomade bottles.[12] He probably attended the Borno State College of Legal and Islamic Studies. He subsequently fell under the influence of radical preachers and became militant. When he took over Boko Haram, another contender for the leadership position and a close follower of Yusuf, Abu Mohammed, left the group, taking his followers with him. Shekau was probably smarter than Yusuf, but he was not as gifted an orator and was far less emotionally stable.

There are broadly three phases in the evolution of the group. The first, the Kannamma phase, was between 2003 and 2005. During this time, the group fought against the Nigerian state, but the state almost effortlessly repelled it. The second phase began with the collapse of the Kannamma uprising and ended with the government's suppression of the group in July 2009. This period, the Dawah phase, was devoted to intensive proselytization, recruitment, indoctrination, and radicalization. It was also the period of its intense criticism of the governor of Borno State, Ali Modu-Sheriff, and it was during this phase that Mohammed Yusuf became prominent in the group. The third phase began with the government's 2009 suppression of the movement and the killing of Yusuf. During this time, Boko Haram went underground to reorganize, and it resurfaced with a vengeance in 2010.

Beliefs and Doctrines

Boko Haram is a grossly misunderstood movement, due in part to their own secrecy and in part to the media trivializing its messages. Broadly, Yusuf's teachings and the message of Boko Haram derived from and fed into the extant discourses of Islamism worldwide, denouncing secularism, democracy, Western education, and Westernization.[13] Yusuf promoted strict observance of *al amr bil ma'ruf wa-l-nahy 'an al-munkar* (enjoining the good and forbidding the evil) and avoidance of all forms of European enlightenment and Western civilization. To some extent these teachings had an ideological resemblance to other jihadi movements such as the Taliban in Afghanistan and Pakistan: seeing any form of Western influence as utterly un-Islamic and the root cause of the weakness of the religion. They were also specific to Nigeria: Yusuf said these Western views had permeated the conservative societies of northern Nigeria since the decimation of the Sokoto caliphate by the British colonialists.[14] In fact, Boko Haram was not the first Islamic group in northern Nigeria to promote contempt for Western education, norms, and values. Other Muslims advocated for "a complete rejection of Western education—especially after the British defeat of the Sokoto caliphate—based on the perception that Western schools are avenues for Christian missionary evangelism and thus a threat to Islam."[15] One notable example is a Hausa poet who satirized even Western-style stationery with letterheads and fountain pens:

> *Amshi takardunka da babu Basmala,*
> *Babu salati babu sunnan Allah,*
> *Alkalaminsu mai kamar masilla*

> Take your papers which bear no Basmala,
> No praise for the Prophet of Allah or his practices,
> their pen resembles a shaft[16]

After Western schools started including Islamic religious instruction and the Arabic language in the curriculum, Western education in northern Nigeria met with greater acceptance. But Boko Haram wanted to ensure complete cultural insularity, which meant rejecting the Western school system, or, as Abdulbassit phrases it, "the established secular systems often described as colonial constructs devoid of legitimacy and an obstacle preventing the restoration of the decimated Islamic caliphate in Northern Nigeria."[17] Also, in the attempt to acquire legitimacy, Boko Haram used the strategy of making reference to historical personages, especially Ibn Taymiyyah.[18]

Mohammed Kyari has identified four main concerns in the doctrine of Boko Haram: *taghut* (idolatry) of secularism, democracy, and partisan politics; Western education and Westernization; the charge of Kharijism (an Islamic sect known for extremism) leveled against the group by the local ulamas; and working for an un-Islamic government.[19] It is necessary to put each of these in context.

Taghut (Idolatry)

In his early preaching, Yusuf said, "We do not believe in democracy, which has appeared on the face of the earth at the hands of Allah's enemies—the Jews and the Christians. In the name of freedom and popular rule, they claim to be Allah, but we know absolutely that justice resides in that which Allah has revealed, not in that which human has made a system."[20] A statement issued by the group in Maiduguri in April 2011 restated its wish to abolish democracy and institute Sharia:

> We want to reiterate that we are warriors who are carrying out jihad in Nigeria and our struggle is based on the traditions of the holy prophet. We will never accept any system of government apart from the one stipulated by Islam because that is the only way that Muslims can be liberated. We do not believe in any system of government, be it traditional or orthodox except the Islamic system and that is why we will keep on fighting against democracy, capitalism, socialism and whatever. We will not allow the Nigerian Constitution to replace the laws that have been enshrined in the Holy Qur'an, we will not allow adulterated conventional education to replace Islamic teachings. We will not respect the Nigerian government because it is illegal. We will continue to fight its military and the police because they are not protecting Islam. We do not believe in the Nigerian judicial system and we will fight anyone who assists the government in perpetrating illegalities.[21]

In another statement, signed by one of the spokesmen, the group said it was content with preaching the Islamization of Nigeria until 2009, when it took up arms against the state. The statement accused some unnamed Muslim clerics and ward heads in the north of conspiring with the government and making it possible for the police to attack them in many states following the Maiduguri crisis in July 2009. The statement further noted, "For this reason, we would continue to fight until Islam is well established and Muslims regain their freedom all over Nigeria. We would never be ready to compromise, and we don't need amnesty. The only solution to what is happening is for the government to repent, jettison democracy, drop the constitution and adopt the laws in the Holy Qur'an."[22]

Western Education and Westernization

A close look shows that Boko Haram's objection to Western education has been blown out of proportion, to the group's annoyance.[23] Yusuf himself said in one of his public teachings: "Western education . . . includes Medicine, Technology, , Physics, and so on. . . . They can all be used if they do not clash with the teachings of the Prophet Mohammed and we can teach these subjects to our own children in our own schools, so long as they do not contradict Islamic teachings. If they do, then we should discard them."[24] The subjects that Yusuf found completely objectionable and thus forbidden included geography, geology, and sociology. He once stated, "These branches of knowledge are not knowledge but full of unbelief. Even those studying it are aware if they are fair to Allah, except if they haven't studied Islam. If you have read geography, you'll know that in geography there is danger. If you have studied Islam, you'll know, whoever you are, that in sociology there is danger."[25] Yusuf was specifically opposed to evolution on the grounds that it is not in line with the word of God about creation. Overall, he concludes, "We didn't say knowledge is bad but that the unbelief inside it is more than its usefulness. I have English books in my possession that I read regularly. I didn't say English amounts to unbelief, but the unbelief contained therein and the polytheism inside."[26] Again, such teaching may be permissible, provided it does not teach issues that contradict the Qur'an.

Although Yusuf had always been unequivocal about his stance on Western education, he struggled a bit when fellow Muslims challenged his position. In a debate in June 2006, he faltered several times against Isa Pantami, a Western-educated Muslim and fellow Salafi cleric.[27] The issue here, however, is that Yusuf was not known to have provided very clearly the criteria by which to determine the compatibility or otherwise of any branch or mode of Western knowledge with the Qur'an and Hadith. In several meetings in Saudi Arabia and Nigeria, many Salafis and scholars associated with the Izala movements tried to persuade him to change his ideological leanings.[28]

The Charge of Kharijism

Right from the beginning of his teachings, Yusuf had problems with other Muslims who did not share his doctrines. Specifically, he was opposed to local ulamas for their closeness with the government. In response, they charged that Yusuf and his group had the traits of the Kharijites, which were uncompromising views of Islam that put sinful Muslims in the same boat with unbelievers against whom a jihad was appropriate if they did not repent.

Working for an Un-Islamic Government

Yusuf also had problems with the ulamas and was violently opposed to the idea of any Muslim working for any government that was not based on Sharia; meanwhile, the local ulamas actually allied with the government to exterminate Yusuf and his group over their violent doctrine. Under Shekau's leadership, Boko Haram continued to oppose Muslims working for the government, and it did so with remarkable determination and violence. But during this time, Boko Haram was not only opposed to Muslims working for the government but indeed the whole northern political establishment and traditional elites such as emirs. It even attempted to assassinate the two main Muslim traditional rulers in Borno and Yobe—the *shehu* of Borno and the emir of Fika. In January 2013, its gunmen also attempted to assassinate the former emir of Kano, the late Alhaji Ado Bayero, but his bodyguards saved him; three of them died in the attack.[29]

Another concise expression of the position of the new Boko Haram can be seen in a letter it wrote to the former governor, Kashim Shetima of Borno, in response to his call for a ceasefire in 2011:

> We are calling on Muslims . . . to understand that we need fairness from everybody. . . . We do not believe in any system of government . . . except for the Islamic system and that is why we would keep on fighting against democracy, capitalism, socialism and whatever. We will not allow the Nigerian constitution to replace the laws that have been enshrined in the Holy Qur'an; we will not allow adulterated conventional education to replace Islamic teaching. We will not respect the Nigerian government because it is illegal. We would continue to fight its military and the police because they are not protecting Islam. We do not believe in the Nigerian judicial system and we will fight anybody who asserts the government in perpetrating illegalities. We want to reiterate that we will never kill pious Muslims and we will not take it lightly with any believer who attempts to kill any Muslim. The reason why we are at war is because our freedom has been curtailed.[30]

Again, the weakness of socioeconomic and political structures allowed such beliefs to thrive.

On the whole, there is no doubt that Boko Haram is determined to create its brand of the Islamic religion—supposedly purer because it is based on strict adherence to Sharia rules with no theoretical innovations—in northern Nigeria if not the whole country. In doing so, the group has benefited from local politics, even if one ignores the allegation that the group benefited from an alliance with the former governor, Ali Modu-Sheriff. It also benefited from economic hardship, as some became members of Boko Haram because of economic considerations. Boko Haram exploited global issues to their advantage as well. Finally, the group has thrived because of the weakness of the Nigerian state.

Disaffected youths, most of them unemployed, and students in traditional Islamic schools constitute the bulk of Boko Haram fighters. They joined for a variety of reasons. Some were genuinely inspired by the sermons they heard and by what they saw as the sincerity, righteousness, and piety of the original members of the group. Others were angry at what they saw as the indiscipline of successive governments in the country, and government counterinsurgency campaigns could also have pushed some youths into Boko Haram.

We know that ethnicity was a major factor in the early recruitment into Boko Haram, and that the Kanuri language was a unifying factor. This is the language spoken in Borno State and in some of the neighboring states around it. It is also spoken in some neighboring countries like Niger, Chad, and Cameroon. We can hypothesize about the possible models of recruitment employed by the terror group. Recruitment usually began with Yusuf propagating jihadi-Salafi ideology in a Nigerian community. Following the 2004 retreat of the Nigerian Taliban, Yusuf established the Ibn Taymiyyah Mosque in Maiduguri, whose members openly spread militant Salafism and anti-American and anti-Western propaganda, and incited each other to violence and confrontation with the Nigerian state. Muslims in Maiduguri already passively supported Islamist terrorist groups, and the proliferation of the ideology of militant Salafism amplified their imitative tendency. Yusuf and his students considered such groups to be the vanguard of the Muslim community.[31]

Boko Haram also forcibly conscripted people in some areas of Borno, and in other instances paid young men or boys to carry out attacks or burn schools. In a more complex scheme, they gave loans to young entrepreneurs in the northeast, targeting butchers, tailors, beauticians, and others in arrangements surreptitiously designed to fail; when the loans came due and the beneficiaries couldn't pay them off, the group gave them the choice of joining the group or being killed. Some people also felt obliged to join the movement after Boko Haram freed them from prison in jailbreaks. Indeed, Shekau's first military operation, in September 2010, released five hundred people from Bauchi prison in the process of freeing about fifty detained members of the group.[32] Like other militant groups, especially those in Asia, Boko Haram recruits members through social media platforms like Facebook, WhatsApp, SnapChat, Instagram, and YouTube. In August 2018, the Nigerian army announced that it had discovered the group's social media accounts.[33] The group has also recruited in Nigeria's neighboring countries, especially the Republic of Niger.

During the time Yusuf was the head of the group, the highest-ranking position in Boko Haram was the *amir ul-Aam,* or commander in chief, while the overall controlling body was the Shura, composed mainly of trusted individuals. In big towns like Kano, local emirs were responsible for the overall operation of the respective cells under their control. Next to the emir were local commanders. Depending on how influential they were within the group, some of the commanders were also members of the Shura. In turn, the commanders had deputies, the *nabin.* Despite their titles, the commanders and the *nabin* were foot soldiers, above only *mu'skars,* those who relay information.[34] Yusuf's main deputies were Abubakar Shekau, Mamman Nur, and Muhammed Lawan. Doctrinal differences sent Lawan (from Potiskim in Yobe State) to Izala in 2007. He later released an audio message attacking Yusuf, and Boko tried to kill him. Nur, probably of Chadian parentage, was born and raised in Nigeria; he met Yusuf when they were studying at the Borno State College of Legal and Islamic Studies.

After Yusuf's death, many thought that Nur would replace him, but Sanni Umaru assumed the interim leadership position of the group.[35] Then the Shura chose Yusuf's former second in command, Abubakar Shekau, as the leader. (Nur may have introduced Shekau to Yusuf.) Two possible factors could have tilted the balance in Shekau's favor: he was more radical than Nur and he was Kanuri, while Nur was of Shuwa Arab descent. Nonetheless, in 2009 when Shekau was shot by security forces and had to take time to recover, Nur stepped in as the commander in chief. In fact, Nigerian authorities believed that Shekau had been killed until he appeared in a video claiming leadership of the group in July 2010.

The Shura council continued to be the highest decision-making body of Boko Haram.[36] In a 2009 report prepared by the Da'wah Coordination Council of Nigeria, the organizational structure of Boko Haram was described as follows: at the top is the national emir, followed by state and local government emirs. Below the local government emirs are the remaining followers.[37] Some of the most important leaders and members of Boko Haram included Muhammad Yusuf, Abubakar Muhammad Shekau, Sanni Umaru, Mamman Nur, Suleiman Muhammad, Muhammad Zangina, Abu Qaqa, Abu Zaid, Abu Zinnira, Habib Bama, Kabiru Sokoto, Muhammad Abu Barra, Muhammad Manga, Abubakar Adam Kambar, and Khalid al-Barnawi.[38] While some of these people are now dead, others went on to play prominent roles in the organization's activities.

Aggressive military engagement and the incorporation of the Civilian Joint Task Force in 2012 (discussed below) resulted in the death of many older members of Boko Haram. According to Pérouse de Montclos, this generational loss robbed Boko Haram of a "uniting ideological axis."[39] The Shura was recomposed, with membership growing to thirty from the previous seventeen, and young and radical people who shared neither the temperament nor the ideology of the founders found their way into leadership positions.

Tactics and Targets

Over the years, Boko Haram has adopted a variety of violent tactics against a range of targets. Against the military, they have largely used an asymmetrical military strategy or guerrilla warfare against Nigerian and regional forces versed in conventional warfare. They have destroyed military barracks and killed soldiers, then carted away their arms and ammunitions. They have also killed individuals known to be associated with the government or the centers of power, even prominent Islamic clerics and informants of the government. Boko Haram has also sometimes practiced simultaneous attacks. For example, on the day they kidnapped the Chibok girls, in April 2014, they also attacked a bus stop in Abuja, killing nearly a hundred people.

One of the group's favorite strategies is suicide bombing, which has inflicted considerable damage on Nigerian society. This was the first time this occurred in the history of violence in Nigeria. While indoctrination into this strategy could have started much earlier, its first recorded case was in 2011. In the first quarter of 2015, Boko Haram carried out eighteen suicide bombings, resulting in the deaths of 211 people. This was to escalate significantly afterward, taking the figure of suicide bombing victims to five hundred or more by the end of 2015 in about seventy bombings in Nigeria, Chad, Cameroon, and Niger. Michael Nwankpa has given three possible reasons for this significant increase: more remote-controlled bombs, multiple simultaneous suicide attacks, and more attacks on soft targets like markets and mosques.[40]

Two aspects of Boko Haram's suicide missions are worth noting. The first is the gender dimension. In 2014, Boko Haram recorded its first case of a female suicide bomber, and the number of such bombings subsequently increased. The second, which is somewhat related, is the use of children, mostly girls, often as young as ten years old. Most of these children do not know what they are doing, and the bombs are detonated remotely. The extent to which these could be called suicide bombings is open to debate, as suicide is supposed to be undertaken after attaining a particular age, when it can be said the person undertaking it has sufficient conviction in the cause. The process for selecting who goes on Boko Haram suicide missions is still shrouded in controversy. Someone who claimed to be Abul Qaqa, the spokesman of the group but whose identity some members contested, asserted after his arrest, "It is a game of utmost loyalty by compulsion where a member handpicked by the group must comply because either way, being picked means being marked for death. You either accept the offer and end in death or refuse it to still end that way."[41] He also said that those who refuse to carry out such tasks are often killed in the presence of their family members.[42] The said Abul Qaqa also pointed out, "What is bad about those handpicked for the suicide mission was that all of them were non-Kanuris. They were always Chadians, Nigeriens, Cameroonians, Hausa, Fulani, and others. No Kanuri was ever selected."[43] What can be deduced from this statement is that even some members of the group may consider aspects of its policies unfair.

Another tactic is kidnapping. However, contrary to publicity generated by the 2014 kidnapping of the Chibok girls, kidnapping was not historically a Boko Haram practice: the group's supposed spokesman, Abul Qaqa, pointed out, "we have never been engaged in hostage-taking and it is not part of our style, and we never ask for ransom." Boko Haram's first kidnapping was in 2012, when it took two Europeans, Chris McManus and Franco Lamolinara, who were later to die in a botched rescue attempt. Since then kidnapping and ransom taking have become key strategies, whether as a result of desperation or the loss of initial focus as a result of the deaths of older members; in 2014 alone, Boko Haram kidnapped 1,298 people, as compared to 879 the previous year. Kidnapping is a source of revenue; Boko Haram has collected a huge amount of money for freeing kidnapped foreigners.[44] They also used victims for propaganda purposes, to show the effectiveness of the group and bargain with the government, as in the kidnapping of the Chibok girls. They have used the practice to build their own membership: some members of the group were originally kidnap victims. Scorched-earth tactics have also been used, especially in attacks against neighboring countries. Finally, they use victims as human shields against possible attacks by Nigerian or the multinational joint forces.

Boko Haram also uses a variety of weapons. They make their own improvised explosive devices (IEDs) in bomb factories across the northeast; perhaps as a way of attacking some alleged immoralities of Western culture, the group planted bombs in popular drinking places across the north and in Abuja. Firearms accounted for 30 percent of their attacks in 2013 and more than 50 percent in 2014; they could fire while riding a horse or motorcycle. Initially they used locally made pistols and targeted the chest or the forehead of their victims. A land mine–clearing agency, the Mines Advisory Group, pointed out that in the period between 2016 and 2018, mines laid by Boko Haram killed 162 people and wounded 277 more; land mine casualties in Nigeria "rose from twelve per month in 2016 to nineteen per month in 2017–18, making Nigeria's casualty rate from mines the eighth highest in the world."[45]

Boko Haram first targeted locals in Borno State politics, accusing Governor Ali Modu-Sheriff of being a "betrayer." Awana Ngala, whom they killed in October 2010, was the former national vice chairman of the All Nigeria's People Party, once a candidate for governor, an in-law of Sheriff Modu Gubio, and a cousin of Ali Modu-Sheriff. Abba Anas, whom they also killed, was the younger brother of the *shehu* of Borno. The reason for targeting local political figures was to hit at the heart of governance in the state, and their grudge for considering Modu-Sheriff a betrayer was his refusal to adhere to some of the promises he allegedly made to the group while trying to win their support during his electioneering campaign.

From the moment it took to using violence, Boko Haram has significantly altered its tactics and changed its targets. After the government suppressed the first round of protests in 2009, the group went underground and rebuilt its strategy. Since then, its tactics have included targeted assassinations, drive-by shootings, suicide bombings, deployment of IEDs and vehicle-borne IEDs, and lately kidnapping and hostage taking. From early 2012, Boko Haram started targeting telecommunication towers, especially around Mubi, Adamawa State, because it believes that the GSM Companies are aiding security agencies with relevant call information. Between July 2014 and March 2015, Boko Haram made considerable military gains, controlling considerable areas of Borno, Yobe, and Adamawa states. According to Nwankpa, during this time, the group also attained the unenviable reputation of being the world's most deadly terror organization, killing 6,644 people in 2014 alone compared to 6,073 killed by ISIS and 3,477 by the Taliban.[46] From this time, it attracted an extensive multinational force composed of people from Nigeria, Chad, Cameroon, Niger, and Benin.

Boko Haram has also planned its strategies taking into consideration the topography of targeted areas and the methods of Nigerian security. For example, once it realized that Borno and Yobe are big states that the Joint Task Force (JTF) could not patrol, the group entrenched itself in areas where there was a lighter military presence; in particular, it established camps in the savanna forest that extends across much of southern Borno and into parts of Yobe. Militants relocated from the forested bush, including the Sambisa Forest Reserve and surrounding areas, into villages in the Gwoza Hills—the northeastern extension of the Mandara Mountains that straddle northeastern Nigeria. Being a guerrilla force with cross-border mobility, Boko Haram has moved as far as northern Cameroon. They can melt into local population centers—towns and cities— even if there are signs that local populations are starting to challenge them.

Boko Haram does target Christians. One of the earliest cases of attacks on Christians was in Damaturu in Yobe State in November 2011 and the Christmas Day series of operations in 2011. This marked a departure from the group's strategy, as it had previously targeted Christians at random rather than making them a priority. An expert on the group's activities, David Cook, divided the new phase of attacking Christians into several target categories: "1) attacks against local Christians in Boko Haram's core operating area of Borno and Yobe states, and the adjacent state of Bauchi; 2) major suicide operations or bombing attacks of high-profile churches in Jos in Plateau State and the capital of Abuja; and 3) minor operations against church or parachurch personnel throughout the north and 'middle belt' regions of Nigeria. These operations represent a fairly major shift in the goals of Boko Haram, which are still squarely Nigeria-focused, and represent the opposition of certain elements of the Muslim north to the spread of Christianity in the region."[47]

But not all attacks on Christian churches are from Boko Haram. For example, in at least two cases, intrareligious disagreements among Christians were responsible for such attacks. In August 2011, one Lydia Joseph was apprehended while trying to burn down St John's Cathedral Church in Bauchi.[48] In January 2012, eight young Christian men were caught in an attempt to bomb the Church of Christ in Nigeria at Miya Barkate, Bauchi. As Kyari has noted, if these perpetrators had not been caught in the act, officials would have attributed the incidents to Boko Haram, and the group would have claimed them, because of its penchant for publicity.[49]

By around 2012, Boko Haram had evolved from an open-network model of insurgency to a closed, centralized system, shifting the center of its operations to Sambisa Forest. This literally changed the dynamics of the conflict, and in 2014 Nigeria was estimated to have had the highest number of terrorist killings in the world over the past years.

Along with physical violence, Boko Haram also mocks, taunts, and threatens the government. For example, Shekau, in one of his video releases, said:

You're funny! You call us Boko Haram and pretend you arrested some of our members during the Maiduguri attack. You take innocent people, townspeople, and you tie them up, you burn them alive saying that they are my men. You lie. Do you really think you're going to catch me and kill me? I swear, I'm the one who's going to kill you. In the name of the almighty Allah, killing is my mission now. Let's kill them, my brothers; let's kill them all. We'll depart this world if necessary, but let's kill them all. May Allah curse you. Almighty Allah guide us in our work. You see, your subjects are the ones helping Jonathan; Your subjects are the ones pretending to pray, but making fun of the Qur'an. Your subjects are the ones indulging in fornication. Your faithful subjects give us the strength and the courage to fight them, as You did when You guided us in the attack on the Giwa barracks. Allah, thanks to you, we killed, burned, and set free more than two thousands of our brothers. We destroyed, killed, and burned, and some of them were commandos![50]

Such statements seek both to dampen the spirit of the official fighting force and to discredit the government among the population.

They also direct such taunts at traditional rulers who support democratic institutions instead of Islam, combining them with physical attacks. This can be seen in the attempted attack on the emir of Kano and Shekau's pronouncement in December 2104: "Listen to me, Sultan of Kano. This is a warning to you because of your recent statements. . . . Sultan of Kano, Sultan of the banks, Sultan of money. Yes, you're Sanusi Lamido. Lamido is a Fula speaker, isn't he? You, Sultan of Kano, is this the way you practice religion? The religion of democracy, of the constitution, of Western education!" This was directed at Sanusi Lamido Sanusi as an individual and framed as a personal settlement of scores. But Sanusi was also more than an individual: he was Nigeria's Central Bank governor before he was elected emir of Kano in 2014. He was, however, deposed in March 2020, following a disagreement with the Kano State governor, Abdullahi Ganduje. Thus, he embodied both the Western liberal system and the federal government, two entities despised by Boko Haram. Furthermore, in a joint appeal with the sultan of Sokoto, the emir called upon the population of northern Nigeria to take up arms against the movement on December 15, 2014. So Shekau's pronouncement is also a contestation of the power of the aristocratic elite, a symbolic revenge. Shekau also issued a direct death threat to Sanusi, who had escaped a Boko Haram attack at the mosque two weeks earlier.

Funding

Where does Boko Haram get its funding? In a detailed study on the group's finances, Jason Rock pointed out that Boko Haram has sustained itself financially through a variety of sources, including "microfinancing, membership fees, external funding/sympathizers, extortion, bank robberies, kidnappings for ransom, and illicit trafficking."[51] The group set up a microfinancing system for members to open local businesses, especially in car and motorcycle taxis and subsistence agriculture. The income generated from these businesses was then directed back into operating Boko Haram as an organization. This strategy was adopted at the beginning and later reintroduced around 2016. The international organization Mercy Corps learned through field research that Boko Haram had been issuing microloans ranging from 10,000 naira (US$32) to 1 million naira (US$3,200).[52]

Boko Haram has also been the beneficiary of generous funding. While the significant external funding is discussed in chapter 8, local sources can be identified here. Local support has been known to come from businessmen and politicians. One of the identified early supporters was the late Alhaji Buji Foi, who was a powerful political figure in Borno State and, as mentioned earlier, was the commissioner for religious affairs in Borno.[53] Many northern Nigerian politicians have also been accused of giving Boko Haram financial support over the years. US government officials confirmed that a high-ranking Borno State politician supported Boko Haram financially until 2009.[54] Donations from members were quite crucial in the early years; committed members helped establish the group and its first evangelization, possibly by getting money from their immediate families. Closely related to this was money through membership fees and daily dues. On joining, members pay membership fees, followed up with the payment of dues of about one hundred naira. The payment of membership fees was believed to have stopped around 2012, when the group gained access to bigger sources of funding.

The group has also won financial sponsorship from local politicians and businessmen.[55] Some of these individuals were responsible for paying for training. For example, in 2006, a group of youths told officials that Boko Haram had sent them to an al-Qaeda training camp in Mauritania. State security services arrested a wealthy northern businessman, but he extricated himself by saying that he was innocently contributing *zakat*, charitable giving that is an obligation of wealthy Muslims.[56] A spokesman for Boko Haram said in 2012 that the Kano State governor Ibrahim Shekarau and the Bauchi State governor Isa Yuguda paid them monthly.[57]

Boko Haram also has gotten money by robbing local banks, particularly between 2010 and 2012. Indeed, in December 2011, a representative of the Central Bank attributed at least thirty bank attacks to Boko Haram that year alone. For example, in January 2010, four Boko Haram members tried to rob a bank in the Bakori Local Government Area of Katsina State.[58] In December 2011, Bauchi police commissioner Ikechukwu Aduba claimed that members of Boko Haram had robbed branches of Guaranty Trust Bank and Intercontinental Bank.[59] The group supposedly divided up this money between widows of members, *zakat*, less privileged members, the Shura, and members who stole or brought in the money. Boko Haram justifies robbing banks by saying the money it steals is "spoils of war."[60]

Boko Haram has also depended on extortion to procure funds, from business owners, politicians, and citizens. The group has persuaded business owners to donate financially to Boko Haram in return for protection. Politicians and citizens have been threatened with harm to themselves or their families if money was not paid. People have received text messages and phone calls demanding money with the threat of harm to the individual or their family if they refused. Wealthy individuals, especially politicians and business elites, pay the group protection fees in response to subtle threats. It is not uncommon for Boko Haram to send threats through text messages that being killed is a major certainty if the money is not paid. Thus to ensure permanent protection, prominent individuals have placed Boko Haram on security retainer.[61]

Another major source of funding for Boko Haram is illicit trafficking. Most recently, Boko Haram has engaged in selling stolen cattle as a source of income. Boko Haram has also engaged in weapons and arms trafficking, especially after the fall of the Gadaffi regime in Libya. In June 2014, a Chadian weapons trafficker who worked with a Boko Haram commander was arrested with US$15,000 on him from sales he made in Chad. Also in June 2014, Cameroonian authorities discovered travel documents in a Boko Haram camp that linked the group to Libya and Qatar. Two members of Boko Haram were arrested at the Burkina Faso–Niger border carrying weapons, ammunition, and 8 million CFA francs (US$13,500).[62] Upon interrogation, the members confessed that the weapons were acquired from an arms dealer in Burkina Faso. In June 2012, a courier for Boko Haram was arrested and during interrogation admitted that Boko Haram tends to use females to traffic weapons, ammunition, and cash.

As noted above, Boko Haram has made money through ransoms from kidnapping and bank robberies. For example, it is believed that the group received US$3.14 million from French and Cameroon negotiators for the release of a French family kidnapped in 2013. Kidnapping is now believed to be Boko Haram's main source of income, as they have earned millions of dollars conducting kidnappings over the years. Key among those who have been kidnapped include the French family just mentioned; the wife of Cameroon's deputy prime minister, along with the local leader of Kolofata and his family, bringing in US$600,000; and many local elders and Nigerian business owners. While these kidnappings do not earn millions of dollars per victim, numerous small payments add up because Boko Haram has kidnapped thousands of people over the past five years. Boko Haram's most notorious kidnapping made world news with the abduction of the Chibok schoolgirls.

In the beginning, Mohammed Yusuf was accused of receiving foreign assistance from Jewish people to infiltrate the Sunna and sow discord among Sunni Muslims because of the antipathy between Israel and the Sunnis. Yusuf considered this accusation so painful that he did a *mubahala*, saying in public in Bauchi, "If I, Muhammed Yusuf, sat together with the security forces either at home or abroad planning to destroy the Sunnis even on one occasion, may Allah do to me what He did to a zindiq [heretic]. On the other hand, if I did not plan with anybody, but someone said I did, may Allah forgive him."[63]

But by far the group's greatest source of funding has been from regional and global jihadist groups. The *Daily Beast*'s Eli Lake reports that the group received some early seed money from Osama bin Laden in 2002, through a disciple named Mohammed Ali, whom bin Laden sent to Africa with US$3 million for like-minded militant organizations. Support also came from the Al-Qa'ida in the Islamic Maghreb. And Boko Haram has gotten money from the Somali group al-Shabaab. It is also believed that the group is receiving assistance from other foreign financials (see chapter 8).

Activities

Accurate numbers of those who have died as a result of the activities of Boko Haram will never be known. The governor of Borno State asserted while delivering the annual Murtala Mohammed Lecture in 2017 that, based on estimates from community leaders, up to 100,000 people could have died as a result of Boko Haram's activities. This is the highest casualty figure ever provided by any government official.[64] According to a study by the National Consortium for the Study of Terrorism and Responses to Terrorism carried out in May 2014, Boko Haram most commonly targets private citizens and property (25 percent of attacks), police (22 percent), government agencies (11 percent), religious figures and institutions (10 percent), and the military (9 percent).[65]

As with most insurgent groups, the objective of most of the group's activities is to achieve maximum propaganda value for themselves plus maximum disaffection among the population with the government. Considerable success has attended the group's efforts, as the Nigerian population is increasingly concerned about the government's inability to protect them from Boko Haram.

After the death of its leader, Boko Haram vowed to continue with its war against the Nigerian state, threatening to carry out sustained attacks on the southern Nigerian cities of Lagos, Ibadan, Enugu, and Port Harcourt. It has also promised to make the country ungovernable by killing and eliminating supposedly irresponsible political leaders of all leanings. It promised to build "a corruption-free, Sodom free society where security will be guaranteed and there will be peace under Islam." In the aftermath of the 2009 conflict, the new leader of the group, Abubakar Shekau, declared in a message sent to the press, "In fact, we are spread across all the 36 states in Nigeria, and Boko Haram is just a version of the Al Qaeda, which we align with and respect. We support Osama bin Laden, we shall carry out his command in Nigeria until the country is Islamized, which is according to the wish of Allah."[66] The Nigerian security force dismissed this statement as mere entertainment. But they were wrong. In January 2012, northern Nigeria was again riven by terrorist attacks, with bomb blasts killing hundreds of people and putting further pressure on the government.

Between 2009 and January 2012, it has been estimated that the organization was responsible for the deaths of 935 people. In the early months of 2012, Boko Haram destroyed a dozen churches and schools and was suspected of a second suicide bombing, this time of a Catholic church in Kaduna, on Easter Sunday, killing forty. Just weeks later, on April 26, a bomber was captured after killing four at a newspaper building, again in Kaduna. At the same time, a third suicide bomber hit the offices of *This Day* newspaper (cited in this chapter) in Abuja, killing three more. In August 2011, the group also made another spectacular attack when it bombed the United Nations headquarters in Abuja, killing twenty-one people and injuring about a hundred.

The identity of arrested or captured members of Boko Haram turned out to be a major problem, which again affected the credibility of Nigerian security institutions. For example, the Nigerian security establishment on a few occasions claimed to have killed Boko Haram's leader, Shekau, only for Shekau to reappear again in another video release attacking the government. Similarly, at various times the Nigerian government has claimed to have captured or killed Abu Qaqa, reputed to be the official spokesperson for the group, but Boko Haram has denied this. The Nigerian government in late January or early February 2012 detained a man claiming to be Qaqa, but confirming his real identity proved to be a challenge since "Abu Qaqa" is an assumed name.

The bombing of the police headquarters in June 2011 introduced a new dimension, as it was the first suicide bombing in the country. In a position statement issued by Boko Haram after the attack, the spokesman noted, "Of recent he (Ringim the Inspector General) has been going to places and making unguarded utterances to the effect that he will crush us in some days. This is unfortunate. We attacked his base to show him that action speaks louder than words."[67] After the bombing of the police headquarters, the government again intensified its effort to address the menace of Boko Haram; in his meeting with his service chiefs in June 2011, President Jonathan even contemplated working with international security agencies, including the CIA, FBI, Metropolitan Police, Saudi Intelligence Agency, and the Israeli Institute for Intelligence and Special Operations (MOSSAD).[68]

Boko Haram's most spectacular operation happened in April 2014, when it kidnapped 276 girls from the Chibok Government Girls Secondary School. The kidnapping was shrouded in many controversies and was to become completely entangled in the intrigues of national politics, such that many people felt that it could have been a complex setup. The school authority released various versions of the story, saying the girls were kidnapped while they were writing their school certificate examination, and also while they were sleeping in their dormitory at night. School officials were rumored to be aware of the impending attack and had supposedly taken their children and wards from the school to safety; the school denied it, but the rumor persisted because their names were missing from the list of names of kidnapped girls. Amnesty International claimed that it gave the Nigerian armed forces at least four hours' notice of Boko Haram's impending attack on the school but that the government ignored the warning, a claim that the government denied.[69] The exact number of girls kidnapped was initially not known; sources cited figures ranging between 250 and 300. No explanation was given for the lack of clarity, except for the fluidity of the situation and the fact that some of the captives escaped. All these uncertainties gave many people, including, interestingly, the government, the impression that something bigger than Boko Haram was at work. Crucial questions remained: What did the government know about the impending attack and when did it know it? What determined the initial response from the government? How prepared was the security force to prevent a kidnapping of that magnitude?

From the account of the situation that can now be pieced together, the kidnapping appears more random than preplanned. From the diary kept by one of the released girls, we know that Boko Haram insurgents came into the school to steal one of the engine blocks being used for construction work in the school, possibly to use it to construct crude weapons. When this was not successful, the insurgents brought together all the girls around. After considering all their options for the girls they had assembled, including burning them alive or getting them back to their parents, the group decided that they should take the girls to Shekau, who would determine what to do with them.[70] Boko Haram members carted the girls away in seven trucks.

Neither the state nor the federal government seriously tried to rescue the captives immediately after their capture, thus losing valuable time. The Bring Back Our Girls campaign launched by civil society groups was to become one of the most successful campaigns in recent times, securing the support of many world leaders. They timed the campaign to coincide with Nigeria's hosting of the World Economic Summit, winning additional attention. Then the international public launched major media campaigns in global social networks to secure the release of the girls.

Still reeling from the attention it was receiving, Boko Haram's leader, Shekau, gave the Nigerian government a condition for the liberation of the abducted girls: the release of all jailed members of Boko Haram in government custody. Strategically, this condition was aimed at embarrassing the government. A monetary ransom would have been an easy way out for the government: it would have raised funds through a third party and probably secured the release of the girls while still maintaining its claim that it was not negotiating with terrorists. By giving a condition that would embarrass the government, Boko Haram was raising the stakes to the highest level. In the end, the Swiss government and the International Red Cross stepped in to mediate and won the release of some of the girls.

Boko Haram has abducted several other people since then. Some of those abducted secured their release, like the University of Maiduguri lecturers and policewomen abducted in 2017. In February 2018, Islamic State West Africa Province (ISWAP), a breakaway faction of Boko Haram (discussed later), struck with another major school kidnapping: they took 110 schoolgirls from the Government Girls Technical College in Dapchi in Yobe State.[71] This was a major embarrassment to the Buhari administration, for it had attributed the Chibok kidnapping to the weakness of Jonathan's government. Again, some alleged that it was preplanned, this time to demonstrate the government's decisiveness in recovering kidnapped girls, in contrast with the inability of the Jonathan administration to recover the Chibok girls.[72] But more seriously, an internal government memo said that the military had been informed of the plans by insurgents to attack and abduct in Yobe. The confidential memo, dated February 6, 2018, was titled "Plans by Boko Haram Terrorists to Carry Out Massive Attack on Maiduguri and Damaturu" and signed by Brigadier General E. A. Adeniyi.[73] It specified that defense headquarters was notified by the Defense Intelligence Agency. People wondered why the kidnapping was possible if there had been a warning. The Dapchi kidnapping also dented the government's claim that insurgents were "technically defeated." The Dapchi schoolgirls were later released, except for fifteen-year-old Leah Sharibu, whom ISWAP continues to hold for refusing to renounce her Christian faith.

Responses to Boko Haram

When Boko Haram began, the general impression was that the police would easily defeat it. The problem was too limited to warrant the involvement of the armed forces. But a problem that was to pervade the entire military response started very early, which was the credibility of the police. After the killing of the founder of Boko Haram, Mohammed Yusuf, the police first claimed that he was killed in a shoot-out while attempting to escape capture. But the army released a transcript of its interrogation of Yusuf that showed it handing him over to the police in handcuffs. Shortly afterward, a forty-second video clip surfaced that showed Foi, who was also killed, dressed in a long white gown with both hands and legs in chains, being taken out of the jail in a white Toyota Hilux pickup by an unidentified policeman. The policeman then left him to walk away from the truck alone. Seconds later, gunshots rent the air, with voices shouting, "Kill him" and "Ba an banda od aba?" In Hausa this means "Haven't orders been given [to kill him])?"[74]

The position of the governor of Borno State when Boko Haram began its activities was that the group's creation was an effort by the opposition to sabotage the government. This appeared initially to have some credibility when the leader of the All Nigeria's People Party, Modu Fannami Gubio, was killed. After Kashim Shettima won the election for governor in 2011, he confirmed that there were political tensions within the state but also that the Boko Haram insurgency was a real and separate movement. To dispel rumors of connivance in the extrajudicial killing of Boko Haram members in June 2011, the government prosecuted top police officers for it: David Abang and one Akira, both assistant commissioners of police, were made to face trial at a federal high court in Abuja.[75]

In September 2011, former President Obasanjo decided to intervene in the Boko Haram problem and sought permission from President Jonathan, who swiftly approved. The former president met with the brother-in-law of the slain Boko Haram leader, Babakura Fugu, and appealed to him to give peace a chance. He also sought the permission of Boko Haram to bring a form of settlement to its dispute with the government. The meeting was arranged by Shehu Sani, who was later to become a senator of the Federal Republic of Nigeria.

Fugu was said to have been pleased with the former president's visit, noting that Obasanjo was the first major person of note to reach out to them. Then forty-eight hours after the meeting, Fugu was killed by a group of people led by his brother. It also later came out that while Obasanjo was meeting with Fugu, other members of Boko Haram had debated arresting and killing him, but later decided against it because he was not known to be unjust to them. In a personal discussion with me, Obasanjo said it was only later that he realized how close he was to death.

The Jonathan administration faced the most profound of Boko Haram's challenges. On December 31, 2011, President Jonathan declared a state of emergency in fifteen local government areas in Borno, Plateau, and Yobe states. This was followed by a total declaration of a state of emergency on May 15, 2013, in Adamawa, Borno, and Yobe states. The army also created a Seventh Division in Maiduguri with the mandate to directly curb and rout insurgents. To give the requisite legal backing and effectively coordinate this counterinsurgency strategy, the Anti-terrorism Act of 2011 was amended to become the Anti-terrorism Act 2013 (as amended). The new act set the death penalty for terrorists and insurgents, and allowed the destruction of suspected terrorist enclaves. The Civilian Joint Task Force was created by the government to work with the military, but there was limited local support for it, which undoubtedly hindered effective counterintelligence-gathering activities. Within eight months of the establishment of the Seventh Division in Maiduguri, it had already gone through three general commanding officers and the redeployment of several field commanders.

President Jonathan also set up two further committees, including the Committee on Dialogue and Peaceful Resolution of Security Challenges in the North to constructively engage key members of the community in dialogue to end the problem and provide a long-term framework for resolution. Kabiru Tanimu Turaki, the minister of special duties, was the chairman of the committee alongside twenty-five other members. But the Jonathan administration also used excessive force against Boko Haram, especially in the near-terminal battle in Maiduguri in 2009; in the subsequent search for a survival strategy, the leaders of Boko Haram formed transnational connections with African al-Qaeda affiliates (see chapter 8). Several international nongovernmental organizations such as Amnesty International and Human Rights Watch have widely criticized the JTF deployed to northeastern Nigeria for their excessive use of force and human rights abuses, which contributed to local resentment and undermined the counterterrorism successes of the Nigerian government.[76] In

2013, the Nigerian military shut down mobile phone coverage in three northeastern states to disrupt Boko Haram's communication and its ability to detonate IEDs.

As noted earlier, the most profound challenge Jonathan faced was the issue of the kidnapping of the Chibok girls, and to some extent his loss in the 2015 election was due to how he handled the problem as much as to the mileage that was made of it by the opposition. Although discussed earlier, there is a need to put aspects of the kidnapping in context. Though the girls were kidnapped on April 14, 2014, it was not until May 4 that Jonathan spoke publicly about the kidnapping, and when he did, he said the government was doing everything to find them. He also blamed their parents for not supplying enough information to the police. From the outset, the insurgents seem to have hijacked the initiative from the administration, and all the government did was react to events. The parents' hopes were raised when the former chief of defense staff, the late Alex Badeh, in October 2014, said that a ceasefire deal had been reached with Boko Haram, which would result in the release of the girls. He also instructed all the service chiefs to comply with the ceasefire instructions immediately.[77] Afterward, then senior special adviser to the president on public affairs Doyin Okupe gave further details of the deal by revealing the role played by the prime minister of Chad, Idris Derby.[78] He confirmed that the negotiations had started months previously. Part of the deal was also to release the wife of the deputy prime minister of Cameroon, Chinese officials, and the traditional ruler of a border between Nigeria and Cameroon. But Boko Haram reneged, to the embarrassment of the Nigerian government that had heightened the expectations of the nation.

The Nigerian government has indicated its willingness to pursue negotiations with Boko Haram, but the well-intentioned agendas of the government are usually doomed from the start because of the failure to understand the grievances and ideology that drive Boko Haram insurgents. Every effort to bring the members of Boko Haram to a negotiating table has failed, partly because of the poor timing of engaging the group in such initiatives and because Boko Haram has remained firm and resolute in its terms of agreement, which can hardly be reconciled by dialogue or negotiation. Their spokesman reiterated their irreconcilable demands: "By the grace of God, we are responsible for all the attacks. There will never be peace until our demands are met. We want all our brothers who were incarcerated by the government to be released. We want full implementation of the Sharia system and we want democracy and the constitution to be suspended."[79]

Militarily, the situation at the end of the Jonathan era in 2015 was fluid. Although the military announced significant successes, not many Nigerians were impressed, as they believed that the insurgents were also making remarkable advances. Members of the armed forces were unhappy with the way the administration was treating them. Indeed, some members of the armed forces mutinied against their commander, who had sent them to confront Boko Haram with inadequate arms.[80] In September 2014, the government sentenced them to death; just a day later, the commander himself was retired from the army.

After the Nigerian military eventually recognized Boko Haram as a serious security threat, it started a concerted military operation. The affected areas were Adamawa, Borno, and Yobe states, which added up to about 152,000 square kilometers and about 16.34 percent of the country. Putting this in context, this is bigger than Portugal and Belgium put together and roughly about 62 percent of the size of the United Kingdom. The first military operation was code named Operation Restore Order and was launched on June 8, 2011, through a directive from the federal government to the defense headquarters to activate the JTF. The military activated Operation Restore Order III on September 13, 2012, to continue with the war. After a measure of success, the JTF was disbanded in August 2013, and the Nigerian army took over the operation and code named the initiative Operation Bayona in line with the state of emergency that was then declared in the three states. Operation Bayona later became Operation Zaman Lafiya (State of Peace), activated on August 22, 2013.[81] In November 2014, Boko Haram captured Mubi and renamed it Madinatul Islam (City of Islam).

By the time Buhari assumed office in May 2015, Boko Haram was the major security threat in the country. The first step the new administration took was the appointment, in July 2015, of Tukur Buratai as the army chief of staff. Fighting the Boko Haram insurgency was a factor in his choice, as Buratai was the force commander of the Multinational JTF under the auspices of the Lake Chad Basin Commission and the Benin Republic. Immediately, the military command and control center was relocated to Maiduguri. Buratai was also instructed by the president to defeat Boko Haram by December 2015. To secure international support for his determination to end the insurgency, Buhari also sought regional and global support and gave a sum of US$1 million to the Multinational JTF to assist in the war against Boko Haram.[82]

At the operational level, the Buhari administration tried to change the orientation and mindset of the troops from defensive to offensive. The name of the operation was also changed from Operation Zaman Lafiya to Operation Lafiya Dole, with the strategic objective of seizing the initiative and dictating the tempo of the exercise. Also, to facilitate this, new units were created, including the 157 Battalion, 158 Battalion, and 29 Brigade. The Third Division tactical headquarters and the 27 Brigade were moved to Damaturu and Buni Yadi, respectively. To address the specific problems emanating from the northern Borno axis, a new Eighth Division was created in Monguno. Against the realization that initial failures were due to an uncoordinated command chain and failure of junior leadership, efforts were made to conduct in-theater training, and the conduct of operations changed to asymmetrical tactics. Foot and mobile patrols were undertaken and ambushes laid; motorcycles were also introduced. In terms of manpower, from 2015 to the end of 2018, the number of military units increased from 58 to 112 and the number of troops committed increased by about 100 percent, from 18,350 to 36,500, during the same period.

In the military operation, the army collaborated more with other branches of the armed services. The air force provided close air support, aerial surveillance, casualty evacuation, and airlift logistics. Also, in September 2016, the air force conducted Operation Forest Storm, which attacked Boko Haram bases in the Sambisa Forest and assisted internally displaced people in the entire region. Meanwhile the navy, through its Special Boat Service, started operations from its base in Baga with the deployment of boats to conduct operations in Lake Chad waters. Moreover, the police, civil defense corps, immigration, customs, and other security agencies also joined the army in the war against Boko Haram.

To further enhance the capacity of the army, numerous field-training exercises were held. In April 2016 Exercise Shirin Harbi was held in Alkaleri Forest, and Exercise Harbin Kunama in Dansadau, Zamfara State, in July 2016. Battle exigencies and Boko Haram's constantly changing strategies have often required changes in the government's military responses. For example, a Theatre Command was created to improve coordination among formations. Also, new equipment—improvised explosive detectors, and Bozena-5 and Armtrac mine clearance vehicles—were introduced to improve mobility. A motorcycle battalion was also introduced as part of the effort to improve mobility.[83] In intelligence, the military has used human, technical, and signal intelligence sources. Drones, locals, and wire and communication intercepts have been used to obtain intelligence. Aerial surveillance using "Intelligence Surveillance and Reconnaissance platforms by the Air Force as well as support from the P-3 Partners (USA, Britain and France)" have been employed.[84]

Throughout, the army insists that it has done all it can to respect human rights, including expanding the Civil-Military Affairs Department and granting access to international NGOs to the war-affected zone. But some of these NGOs have come to indict the security forces for human rights violations, including the brutalization of civilians.

Buratai has identified some of the challenges facing the armed forces in the war against Boko Haram. First is the nature of the operational environment, which includes more than 6 percent of Nigeria's total area, so the troops can only be deployed selectively. The nature of the theater of operation, being sandy, mostly marshy, and vulnerable to flooding, also reduces troop mobility. The cross-border nature of the conflict has made it a beneficiary of conflicts in Chad and Libya. The border is porous, with footpaths leading to Cameroon and Chad that are in turn connected to Mali, Libya, and Sudan. Also noted by the army chief are insufficient international support, threats posed by mines and explosives, and a large number of internally displaced people.

The military has also made use of the media. As part of Operation Lafiya Dole, "regular media briefing, distribution of leaflets, enlightenment campaigns through Motorized Public Address vehicles and town hall meetings" were often undertaken.[85] Then Boko Haram was planting stories of military success in social media, such that the army director of public relations, Brigadier General Texas Chukwu, had to advise the population to be cautious of news about Boko Haram's successes.[86] The theater commander holds press conferences monthly and as needed, and regular updates are provided by the Army Public Relations Department. The Operation Lafiya Dole FM radio station releases information about its activities, messages to the local population on security consciousness, and tips on counter-IED measures.

Also important in the war against Boko Haram is the Civilian Joint Task Force, which was established in June 2013 to assist the military JTF in the war against Boko Haram. Its members included young and old civilian volunteers in Maiduguri and also volunteers from other parts of the northeast. Their weapons at the time of formation were basic and sometimes mundane, including bows and arrows, swords, clubs, and daggers. Sector commanders controlled their affairs. With their deep knowledge of the local environment and their enmeshment in the sociocultural life of the community, they proved very helpful.

The Buhari administration detained 2,321 suspected members of Boko Haram in October 2017. Of these, 1,670 were detained in Kainji while 651 were detained in Maiduguri. However, some people in Kainji were recommended for prosecution while some were suggested for deradicalization programs. The government was slow to prosecute them, it said, because some of the cases were poorly investigated "with confession being the only evidence."[87] To show the pains it had taken to ensure justice, the government categorized the suspects into four groups. The first group consisted of Boko Haram suspects investigated by the joint investigation team set up by the defense headquarters, whose case files were transmitted to the attorney general of the federation; after a careful review, it was discovered that they had no prima facie cases that would sustain a charge. Hence these suspects were recommended for release and rehabilitation and/or deradicalization. The second category included suspects that the attorney general found prima facie cases against; charges had already been filed in the federal court, Abuja Division. These suspects were mostly in detention facilities and would perhaps be willing to plead guilty to lesser offenses. The third category was suspects whose case files were either recommended for further investigation or had no investigations conducted on them at all, so the attorney general could not form an opinion on them. The fourth category was made up of suspects whose cases were reviewed and prima facie cases were found; these suspects might have been willing to opt for a full trial.[88]

The federal government also established what it called Operation Safe Corridor, aimed at rehabilitating Boko Haram terrorists who had been deradicalized through its policy. The Office of the National Security Adviser and the Nigeria Defense Headquarters through Operation Lafiya Dole oversaw this program. The government decided to recruit some of the deradicalized Boko Haram members into the police and the army. The Christian Association of Nigeria immediately criticized this action as a dangerous plan that could compromise the country's security system.[89]

Details of deals for the release of Boko Haram captives might never be known, including the possibility that the government paid ransom or swapped prisoners; some of these deals were made through intermediaries who have refused to divulge information. But the government has always been clear that the Boko Haram prisoners released were not the most violent ones. For example, after the liberation of the Dapchi girls, the former director of State Security Service, Lawal Daura, confirmed that the deal with ISWAP included freeing arrested members of the group who were not found culpable in any criminal activity. Between January and June 2018, the United Nations gave the number of those killed in conflicts connected to Boko Haram at 1,813—620 casualties in Boko Haram and 261 in the Nigerian security forces, across seventeen Nigerian states.[90] These numbers included 881 children, of whom 570 were killed and 311 were maimed. Operation Deep Punch, launched between

December 2017 and April 2018, finally dispossessed Boko Haram from Sambisa Forest; the Nigerian army recovered most of the weapons and equipment that had been seized by Boko Haram insurgents.

December 2019 recorded some major attacks by Boko Haram. On the second of the month, members killed four Chadian soldiers along the shores of Lake Chad; on the twelfth they executed four of the six aid workers they had held hostage since July; on the thirteenth, they killed nineteen Fulani cattle herders on the border with Cameroon; on the fourteenth, they killed fourteen people in the attack on Kaiga village in the Lake Chad basin; on the seventeenth, they killed six people and abducted five more; on December 22, they killed seven people in a raid near Chibok; on the twenty-fourth, they executed eleven Christians who were kidnapped from Maiduguri and Damaturu. The group said that this was in response to the killing of the Islamic State leader Abu Bakr al-Baghdadi. During the first week of January 2020, the theater commander of Operation Lafiya Dole, Major General Olusegun Adeniyi, came under Boko Haram attack while he was returning from the Jakana area of Maiduguri. The commandant later granted an interview, which went viral in social media, in which he subtly indicted the government: he said that the Boko Haram troops appeared better armed than his soldiers. He was removed from his position shortly afterward in what the army claimed was routine redeployment. Also in January 2020, insurgents abducted and killed the chairman of a local chapter of the Christian Association of Nigeria, Reverend Lawan Andimi.

By April 2020, the war against the insurgents had reached a decisive level. In the preceding month, Chadian forces had launched a major attack on the insurgents operating around Lake Chad, killing several. Now the Nigerian army, working on intelligence, launched an attack that killed 105 Boko Haram insurgents. Later that month, the army chief of staff, Tukur Buratai, moved to the northeastern region and promised not to come back until he had defeated Boko Haram. For most of 2021, Boko Haram continued launching attacks on the Nigerian state, with the Nigerian military also taking bold steps to counter the attacks. The persistent calls for the change of military service chiefs was eventually done at the end of January 2021, and Tukur Buratai was replaced by Major-General Ibrahim Attahiru as the Chief of Army Staff. Attahiru died in a plane crash in May 2021, and he was replaced by Major General Farouk Yahaya. During this time, too, significant developments were also going on within Boko Haram. Abubakar Shekau, the leader of Boko Haram, was killed during a clash with the Islamic State West Africa Province (ISWAP). During the attack, Shekau reportedly detonated his suicide vest, killing himself instantly. In a release by the group shortly afterward, one Bakura Modu, also known as Sahaba, was appointed as the new leader of the group to continue the war against the Nigerian state and other rival groups. This underlines the extent of schisms within the insurgent groups. ISWAP too continues its attack on the Nigerian military, and in November 2021, it laid an ambush that killed Dzarma Zirkusu, a brigadier-general and commander of the army's 28 task force brigade, and three other soldiers. As of November 2021, the senator representing Bornu South and the former senate majority leader, Senator Ali Ndume, noted that ISWAP was regrouping around the Lake Chad basin.[91] This is despite the fact that divisions still continue to exist among the insurgent groups. ISWAP again launched a series of attacks In December 2021. The first of these attacks, although foiled, resulted in the death of seven soldiers.[92] The same month, ISWAP again made a botched rocket attack on Maiduguri in the bid to overrun the Maiduguri International Airport and the nearby housing estate, but they were repelled by the military. The insurgents had earlier been dislodged from Gwoza, and they had reassembled in the village of Duwari before the attack on Maiduguri. In response to the renewed insurgence, the new chief of Army, Lt. Gen. Farouk Yahaya instructed the army to take the war to the insurgents.[93] He also warned them that 2022 would most likely be a more difficult year.[94]

Schisms

Boko Haram has experienced internal fighting. Early on, there were allegations of backstabbing and a divergence of views over tactics. Later, people disagreed over external interference in the affairs of the organization; some allegedly revealed the identities of other members to security forces, for which the organization sentenced them to death. Throughout, the greatest cause of infighting was disagreement over indiscriminate targeting of noncombatants. Some members felt that broad targeting of populations that included Muslims was unacceptable.

Two internal crises are particularly important, with one resulting in a breakaway faction and the other resulting in such internal destabilization that it affected the group's internal cohesion and external linkages. In 2012, the Jama'atul Ansaru Muslimina fi Biladis Sudan (Vanguard for the Protection of Muslims in Black Africa), more commonly known as Ansaru, broke away from Boko Haram under Khalid Barnawi and Abubakar Adam Kambar because of Boko Haram's brutality toward Muslims. Specifically, Ansaru was opposed to Boko Haram's killing of about 150 Muslims in Kano in January 2012. Ansaru's other close strategic objective, in contrast to Boko Haram, was to focus more on hard targets than on civilians. On a broader level, the objective of the new group was to "restore dignity and sanity to the lost dignity of Muslims in Black Africa and to bring back the dignity of Islam in Nigeria and the Sokoto Caliphate."[95] Personal issues also fueled the split. Some members believed that Boko Haram's leader, Shekau, favored Borno Kanuri members of the group over Hausa Fulani. Non-Nigerian elements of the group also protested, and were attracted to another foreign member of the group, Mammam Nur, who came from Cameroon.

Violent activities carried out by Ansaru, though significantly fewer than those of Boko Haram, were sometimes quite spectacular. In May 2012, the group killed a Lebanese and abducted another, and a German who was kidnapped also died in a botched rescue attempt.[96] In December 2012, a Frenchman, Francis Colump, was kidnapped but escaped, while a French Catholic priest, George Vandenbeush, who was abducted in November 2013, was released.[97] However, the most spectacular of the group's actions was the abduction and subsequent killing of seven foreigners (British, Greek, Italian, and four Lebanese) in March 2013.[98] Ansaru also committed violence domestically. For example, in November 2012, it attacked the Special Anti-robbery Squad (SARS) headquarters in Abuja.

Although Ansaru and Boko Haram disagreed on some fundamental principles, some scholars believe that they continued to collaborate with each other. For example, it was noted that during the attack on SARS headquarters in November 2012, Ansaru freed many members of Boko Haram, an action that was appreciated by Shekau.[99] Ansaru's attack also freed the wife of Kabiru Sokoto, the Boko Haram chieftain behind a Christmas Day bombing outside Abuja in 2011. By 2013, it appeared that Ansaru was on its way out as a coherent radical group in Nigeria. A major cause of contention was the nature of external linkage the group should have: some members saw an ally in the Islamic State of Iraq and Levant, but others preferred to be independent. The group eventually chose independence, and several members left the group and went back to Boko Haram. The group's leader was later arrested in April 2016.

Another schism in Boko Haram came into the open sometime in August 2016. Daesh's propaganda magazine, *Al-Naba*, named Abu Musab al-Barnawi, considered the late Mohammed Yusuf's son, as the new leader of ISWAP. Almost immediately, al-Barnawi openly condemned Shekau's leadership, especially for its attacks on Muslims, promising instead to focus attacks on Christians. He also accused Shekau of cowardice, being an infidel, and living a life of luxury while his followers wallowed in poverty. Shekau responded by claiming, in turn, that it was his critics that should bear the tag of being infidels. He said that he still maintained leadership of the group. Mamman Nur joined al-

Barnawi in the release of several audio criticisms of Shekau. In the exchange, both sides sought to attract the support of ISIS, the overall organization to which Boko Haram had only just declared alliance (see chapter 9).

In his detailed discussion of the subject, Freedom Onuoha notes that the breakup was rooted in something more fundamental than opposition to Shekau's approach to Islamic jihadism. According to Onuoha, Shekau's stand was predicated on the assumption that there can be no midway between being a Muslim and not being one. He notes, "I am against the principle where someone will dwell in the society with the infidels without making public his opposition or anger against the infidels publicly as it is stated in the Qur'an. Anyone doing that can't be a Muslim, thick and thin. This is what our ideology proved and that is where I stand."[100] Shekau's Boko Haram made no distinction between Christians or Muslims, and this is why his attacks focused on mosques, churches, markets, and other places that included people of all religions. But al-Barnawi's faction disagreed with this stance: "In the Qur'an, Allah forbids Muslims from killing one another . . . and He also taught against killing in secret. If it is a serious punishment, it must be public for people to know and witness it. But once you see killings in secret, there is something fishy, and this is what we noticed with Shekau."[101] They also accused him of autocratic tendencies, refusal to take advice, mismanagement of spoils, including money and captured women, and ordering the killing of senior militants who challenged his authority. Thus, according to Onuoha, "difference over 'whom' to kill and 'how' to kill, coupled with its impact on the sanctity of their jihadi insurgency underpinned the leadership feud within the Boko Haram."[102] The al-Barnawi faction made huge propaganda out of this as they persistently told villagers that the Shekau group had derailed because of its attacks on Muslims. The most immediate outcome of the infighting, however, was a lull in the activities of the group, as they expended more energies fighting each other than their previously common targets. Fighting broke out between the groups several times, including in September 2016 in the Monguno area of Borno State near Lake Chad. Some people believe that it was this lull in activity as a result of the internal schism that launched the government's feeling of euphoria that Boko Haram had been technically defeated.

The schism within Boko Haram was also related to ISWAP. In March 2015, Shekau, the head of Boko Haram, pledged his allegiance to the global ISIS leader, Abu Bakr al-Baghdadi, both in recognition of the expanding influence of ISIS and acknowledgment of the extent of the assistance of global ISIS to Boko Haram. Boko Haram now changed its official name to Islamic State West Africa Province (ISWAP). Soon after, two prominent members of the group,

Mamman Nur and Abu Musab al-Barnawi (the son of Mohammed Yusuf), led a group of senior members of the group to rebel against Shekau's leadership over his alleged un-Islamic methods. Their breakaway group retained the ISWAP logo, while Shekau retained the loyalty of the remaining group, now widely known as the Jama'tu Ahlis Sunna Lidda'awati wal-Jihad (JAS). Realizing the vital importance of external support from ISIS for their activities, both sides wanted ISIS recognition as the authentic side, and around June 2015, the nod was given to Nur and the al-Barnawi faction. Both sides made attempts at reconciliation, but these failed. Here ISIS seems to have been strategically cautious. While it favored al-Barnawi over Shekau, it also ensured that it kept Shekau within the fold, giving the latter the hope that he might one day find his way back into its favor. For ISIS, ISWAP provided a strategic outpost for publicity and activity in Africa, especially as ISWAP split from JAS at just about the time ISIS was losing its holdings in Iraq, Syria, and Libya. As of early 2019, ISWAP had between 3,500 and 5,000 fighters while JAS had between 1,500 and 2,000. The split between JAS and ISWAP was not just ideological but also involved violence.

Very early in its formation, ISWAP clearly defined its modus operandi: to avoid targeting civilians as well to aspire to win the hearts of those under its control. It established its base in Yobe State and on the banks and islands of Lake Chad in Borno State, where vegetation protects them from aerial bombardment from the Nigerian air force. ISWAP launched its inaugural attack on June 3, 2016, against Bosso town in the Republic of Niger, targeting military installations. The success of this operation was widely celebrated by global ISIS as a new dawn in ISIS activities in West Africa. But while the group basked in its success, they disagreed about how best to proceed. Some wanted to keep fighting while others believed that the group had gone as far as it could go militarily and that it was time to dialogue with the Nigerian authorities.

The relationship between JAS and ISWAP continued to be complex: they agreed on a ceasefire, and JAS released family members of ISWAP it had held captive since the ISWAP breakaway, but acrimony and tension continued. Their relationships with global ISIS remained a central tension. Shekau and JAS maintained their recognition of the late Abu Bakr al-Baghdadi as their head and kept sending messages that ISWAP was a fraud trying to trick ISIS. Shekau and JAS also publicly questioned the religious credentials of ISWAP and widely published its ISIS-style military strategies. Shekau's notoriety, especially after the kidnapping of the Chibok girls, made the military concentrate more attacks on JAS. ISWAP enjoyed this advantage and was able to develop with minimal government counterresponse. Its tactics of not attacking civilians also seem to have helped it avoid government reprisals.

After breaking from JAS, ISWAP increased its attacks on military targets to acquire the weapons it desperately needed. It is believed to have sophisticated intelligence. The group has continued to concentrate its attention on the banks and islands of Lake Chad. In September 2018, it overran the town of Gudumbali and seized a local government area; then in December it took over Baga and Doron Gowon. ISWAP has shown itself to be significantly different from other terrorist groups in its management of civilians under its control: the ISWAP emir ordered the execution of a fighter who killed a civilian, while ISWAP fighters who kidnapped for ransom were also expelled. There are significant concerns among the population that ISWAP is winning people over from the Nigerian military. Moreover, ISWAP provides social services in areas under its control: education (not Western) and basic medical care by militants or captured professionals; arrangements are made to transfer seriously ill patients to neighboring countries for treatment. Again, despite the controversies associated with polio vaccination in Nigeria, ISWAP allowed humanitarian workers to vaccinate people in its areas. ISWAP also ensures economic sustenance through its effective tax policies; detailed research carried out by the International Crisis Group reveals that most civilians under the jurisdiction of the group found the taxes being paid to be reasonable in terms of services provided. It encourages traders to bring in goods that people like. It pays fair prices for materials (and sometimes more than the asking price), which encourages the population to bring in goods and materials the group needs. Basic amenities like local toilets and microfinance opportunities are available, as are agricultural seeds and fertilizers. All this, however, should not be misinterpreted to mean that the group did not inflict harsh and violent treatment. Punishment for offenses that threaten its fiscal base (not paying requisite taxes or fishing without authorization) or its security (using a mobile phone, which is seen as spying) could go as far as execution.

In 2018, in a particularly deep moment of schism, ISWAP leadership detained and executed founder Mamman Nur. Nur was of the faction willing to negotiate with the Nigerian state, unlike the opposing side that was against any form of dialogue, and apparently some members of ISWAP did not approve of how he had handled the secret Swiss-mediated talks between the Nigerian government and ISWAP that resulted in the release of the Dapchi schoolgirls earlier that year; they took a more hard-line stance. After Nur's death, Abu-Musab al-Barnawi remained the head for the rest of 2018 even as two people known for their hard-line approaches, Abubakar Mainok and Mustapha Kirmima, fought to be the new leader. In March 2019, an audio recording by ISWAP said that ISIS had ordered that al-Barnawi be replaced by a similarly named but unrelated Abu Abdullah ibn Umar al-Barnawi. This seemed not to have worked and Abu-Musab al-Barnawi continued to be the head.

In November 2020, Boko Haram carried out one of its worst atrocities when it killed more than thirty people and wounded others when the insurgent group attacked farmers harvesting rice in the villages of Koshobe and Zabarmari near Maiduguri. Most of the victims were tied up and had their throats slit. The attack took place as voters went to the polls in long-delayed local elections in Borno State. The election itself had been repeatedly postponed because of an increase in attacks by Boko Haram and ISWAP. Most of the assailants came on motorcycles. The attack further reinforced the conviction of many Nigerians that the insurgent activity was far from over as the country moved into 2021. In October 2021, the Nigeria military announced the killing of the ISWAP leader, Abu Musab al-Barnawi. With the death of both Shekau and al-Barnawi, the insurgent groups in Nigeria now face a future that will have to come under new leadership.

Conclusion

Far more than ever before, the extent of violence associated with religion has captured global attention in the last decade and half. This is due largely to radicalization, a phrase which, though it may be blurry in meaning, is visible in consequences. The speed and extent with which groups in this fold connect and relate are quite phenomenal, and they have further made the extent of their impacts more devastating. Of all the radical groups in Africa, no doubt Boko Haram is one of the most prominent. Indeed, Boko Haram remains Nigeria's most profound security challenge, bringing out, in a complex way, issues enveloping Salafist indoctrination, ethnicity, socioeconomic conditions, corruption, state dysfunctionality, brutality, external interference, and a host of other factors in what is undoubtedly the most extreme case of religious violence in the country. I have tried in this chapter to discuss the ramifications of the group's activities in Nigeria, tracing its history, its transmutation to revolutionary militancy, the sources of its funding, its activities, its internal schisms, and the way the group has been engaged by the Nigerian state. In all, I have contended that many of the issues surrounding the emergence and activities of Boko Haram have existed since the country's independence, and were only brought into the open by contemporary local, national, and global developments. Since the Maitatsine riots discussed in chapter 2, widespread disenchantment had pervaded the country, waiting for an opportunity to find practical expression. This, to a large extent, was what Boko Haram offered. Many Nigerians are now beginning to lose hope that there can ever be a victory over the group, and they are thus calling on the government to concede to the inevitability of having some form of dialogue with the group. The challenges faced in addressing it also reflect the contradictions that have underlined the politics of governance and intergroup relations in Nigeria, which is the subject of chapter 6.

6. NATIONAL POLITICS, INTERGROUP RELATIONS, AND RELIGIOUS VIOLENCE IN NIGERIA

It is wrong to think that the rivalry between Christians and Muslims is an inseparable part of the game. The country belongs to all of us. . . . The hypothesis of separation between north and south is totally unfeasible. The reality is that there are Christians who not only live in the north, alongside the Muslim Hausa-Fulani, but also originate in the north, while almost fifty percent of my Yoruba ethnic group . . . is composed of Muslims. So, where do we draw the line on which to build our trenches if someone leads us to fighting. . . . The religious conflict hides another truth. The struggles have tribal, political and economic origins—also linked to the unequal redistribution of oil wealth . . . and are tied up with the semi-failure of the central government. —Bishop JOHN ONAIYEKAN, former Catholic archbishop of Abuja, "After the Christmas Massacre, Terrorism Comes from Afar"

I have said it so many times, those people picking up arms killing people are criminals and whoever you are, whether you are Igbo, Hausa or Yoruba or Fulani, you have no right to take up arms and kill anybody. If you see such thing happening, then there must be a failure of government. But if government wakes up to their responsibility, some of these things will not happen. We keep on calling on everyone to please maintain peace and allow the constituted authority to take up these issues. —SA'AD ABUBAKAR, Sultan of Sokoto

The objective of this chapter is to situate religious violence and controversies in Nigeria within national politics and the complexities of intergroup relations. The chapter specifically details how successive administrations have responded to religious issues, controversies, and violence, and the extent to which they have considered prevailing political contexts of the nation and the predilections of incumbent leaders in dealing with the issues. Violence over religion in Nigeria has, to a large extent, been rooted in and shaped by national politics and the intrigues of intergroup relations in the country. In responding to the violence associated with religion, successive leaders have tried to delicately balance their religious convictions, national security, national intergroup relations, and the sociocultural configuration of the country. The extent to which success has attended their efforts in this direction has, however, varied.

Religion and Conflict in Politics and Intergroup Relations during the First Republic

From the moment self-rule began, preceding independence, religion entered Nigerian politics, but conflict did not. As Muhib Opeloye has noted, the National Youth League was the first Muslim political party, formed in 1955, growing out of the Muslim Congress of Nigeria that had been formed in 1950. The congress was formed to protect the interest of Muslims in the western region, and it saw the Action Group party that governed the western region as a Christian party.[1] Specifically, the National Youth League challenged "the alleged neglect of Muslim schools, non-inclusion of Arabic and Islamic studies in the school curriculums, conversion of Muslim children to Christianity and most importantly, inadequate representation of Muslims in the Executive Council in the region."[2] For example, the party pointed out that of the twelve regional ministers between 1951 and 1957, only one was a Muslim. As soon as it started making its policies and stances clear, Chief Obafemi Awolowo, the region's premier, realized that the league was targeting the Action Group. Consequently, he did all he could to frustrate the party.[3] In the north, connections between religion and intergroup relations shaped politics. During the time when Ahmadu Bello was the Sardauna of Sokoto, subtle efforts were made to convert people in the Middle Belt to Islam. One of the strategies used was to tie promotions in the civil services and even of traditional rulers to membership in Islam. The father of the former minister of foreign affairs, Joseph Garba, was converted to Islam but came back to his Christian faith after Sardauna's death.[4]

During Nigeria's first republic, religion played a minimal role in the politics of intergroup conflicts. Even where extreme violence characterized intergroup relations, as in the May 1966 killings of Ibos in the north, people blamed it on ethnicity and commercial rivalries, rather than religious differences. The few religious differences that occasioned violence were largely internal (within the same religion). There were, indeed, no major security issues, nationwide, connected to religion exclusively. By the time the country moved into the first era of military rule in May 1966, subtle issues about religion and security began creeping into politics, and leaders had to begin crafting responses to the link between religion and ethnopolitical issues.

Politics and Intergroup Relations

The January 1966 entrance of the military into politics, though violent, did not bring religion into the equation. Although the military coup that ended the First Republic was carried out by army officers that were almost all Christian, the fact that their victims cut across religious divides signaled that considerations other than religion were the motivating factors. Even the countercoup of July 1966 was motivated more by ethnicity than religion. The officers behind the coup, though mostly from the north, were both Christians and Muslims. Some scholars have described some of its consequences in terms of religion, but again these were not violent.[5]

Although the cause of the January 1966 coup cannot be linked to religion in any significant way, some scholars have attributed some of its consequences to religion. Iheanyi Enwerem has identified two of those in this category. First, some claimed that members of the Kano People's Party and the local Tijani-yya Mallams celebrated Sardauna's death, in an extension of the Tijaniyya-Qadriyya rivalry; and Christians in the Middle Belt, many of whom had considered the late Ahmadu Bello as religiously oppressing them and forcefully converting people to Islam, were not sorry that he had died. Second, some Christians from the south welcomed his death, or at least hoped for a reversal of whatever political gains the Islamic north had made on the Christian south. Feature stories by southern-based publications told this story. For instance, the *Daily Times*—then the country's national newspaper—in its subsidiary publication, *Drum Magazine*, showed a picture of Ahmadu Bello floating in limbo and confessing his sins of "mixing politics with religion and playing the role of Prophet-cum-Caesar."[6]

The first national security issue that brought religion into the picture, albeit indirectly, was the Nigerian civil war.[7] At the beginning of the war, ethnicity was the proclaimed issue, but then Biafra, as part of its propaganda, framed the war as an attempt by Hausa Muslims to exterminate Christian Ibos. In fact, religion played a minimal role in the outbreak of the conflict. At the same time, as Samuel Daly has rightly argued, it "shaped how people believed and worshipped" in the face of the war: "Biafrans turned to new devotional practices to grapple with the circumstances in which they found themselves. In the context of hunger, violence, and constant, ambient fear of annihilation, many people found consolation in charismatic Christian churches. Others turned to faith-healers and ritualists, who offered more potent forms of protection than the scapulars and St. Christopher medals of the Catholic tradition."[8]

A major political issue that was to become more prominent in later years began during this period: Nigeria joined the Organisation of Islamic Cooperation (OIC). In 1969, Nigeria was invited to the inaugural meeting, which took place in Rabat, Morocco. But the Nigerian leader, Yakubu Gowon, considered it unwise for Nigeria to send an official delegation as Islam was not the country's official religion. Although a delegation from Nigeria, led by Abubakar Gumi, attended the meeting, Gowon wrote a personal letter to King Hassan of Morocco, making it clear that the delegation was not official; the Murtala/Obasanjo administration could not go for full registration of the OIC. The delegation was granted observer status.[9] Although members of the Supreme Military Council, like Murtala Mohammed, Sheu Yar'Adua, Ibrahim Babangida, and Muhammadu Buhari, were believed to be in support of full membership, other equally prominent members of the council, like Theophilus Danjuma, Isa Doko, and Michael Adelanwa, the heads of the army, air force, and navy, respectively, were against the idea.[10]

The coup that killed Murtala Mohammed in 1976 created a subtle religious tension. Those who organized the coup were mainly Christians, while Murtala Mohammed and Ibrahim Taiwo, the two most senior victims, were Muslims. Olusegun Obasanjo, who succeeded Mohammed, noted that apart from ethnicity, one of the balancing acts that brought Shehu Yar'Adua in as the chief of staff supreme headquarters (vice president), was religion, as Yar'Adua was a Muslim.[11] After Obasanjo succeeded Murtala Mohammed, he maintained Nigeria's observer status at OIC.

The politics of Sharia law and its application brought Islamic religion to the fore of violence and controversies in Nigeria. The roots of the controversy can be traced to 1979 when a new constitution came into force, as part of the transition to civilian rule that the Obasanjo administration shepherded. During the proceedings of the administration's Constitution Drafting Committee, many committee members from the north ensured that the new constitution included Sharia laws. Indeed, only one member of the committee, Paul Nnongo, was against including them. Once he failed, he sought and won election to the Constituent Assembly that was to ratify the constitution. Here, he joined other members from the Middle Belt and from the southern minorities of then

Bendel, Rivers, and Cross River states to challenge the Sharia parts of the constitution. A member from the east, Mudiaga Odje, moved for the removal of Sharia from the constitution. The debates had their own intrigues that are now coming to light. A member of the Supreme Military Council, the army chief of staff Yakubu Danjuma, held meetings with Christian members of the assembly, encouraging them to fight for the cause and promising to protect them as necessary from hawks in the Supreme Military Council, especially the chief of staff supreme headquarters, the late Shehu Yar'Adua.[12] This encouragement was all the more necessary when some Ibo members of the Constituent Assembly were showing indications of wanting to give up.[13] Finally it was resolved that Sharia would not be included in the constitution. Nonetheless, when the report was submitted to the Supreme Military Council, the council included Sharia laws.

During the Second Republic, Sharia became a topic of national debate, but overall, violence over religion was not a common phenomenon.[14] The Shagari administration did not push for a full-scale Islamization of the country between 1979 and 1983. The major religious occurrence during the Second Republic was the Maitatsine riots (chapter 2); they did not make any major impact on national politics. Most people in the south saw the incidents as a national tragedy (even though the riots barely affected their region), but they did not attribute the riots to politics or ethnic differences. As Akin Alao has noted, it is plausible that the nature, character, and profligacy of the political class that wielded authority during this period did not provoke any antagonistic religious claims.[15] It, however, provoked military intervention.

Politics and Intergroup Relations during the Second Military
Interregnum, 1984–1999

The Buhari administration that overthrew the Shagari government was so preoccupied with fighting "indiscipline" in the country that religion was not a major concern.[16] The fact too that the regime was determined to end all forms of indiscipline meant that it was not inclined to exploit religion for selfish motives. This was something of an irony because the new head of state had been a hard-core advocate of the Islamization of Nigeria during the Murtala/ Obasanjo era. Moreover, both Buhari and his deputy, Babatunde Idiagbon, were Muslims, and people expected them to care more about religion than they did. But then Babangida overthrew Buhari in turn, while his deputy and the strongman of the administration (Idiagbon) was performing holy pilgrimage, a matter some radical Muslims later identified as a source of some of the problems that affected the succeeding Babangida administration, especially some of the economic problems that came with the imposition of the Economic Structural Adjustment Program.[17]

During Babangida's administration, the first major issue about religion was again Nigeria's membership in the OIC, although it did not come to violence. In January 1986, an invitation to the OIC meeting in Morocco came to the government. The permanent secretary of the Federal Ministry of Foreign Affairs, against protocol, took it to President Babangida, who, instead of passing it through the minister of foreign affairs, Bolaji Akinyemi, accepted it. In fact he authorized the attendance of a Nigerian delegation at the conference, again without informing the minister of foreign affairs.[18] The standard practice at the time was for the Nigerian ambassador in Morocco to attend with observer status. The new delegation—Rilwan Lukman, the minister for mines and power; Alhaji Alhaji, then a permanent secretary; Abdul Kadir Ahmed, then governor of the country's Central Bank; and Ibrahim Dasuki, later the sultan of Sokoto—later applied to the OIC for full membership for Nigeria. The OIC should have taken a year to process the application, but approved it immediately. Meanwhile, because it was never discussed at the Armed Forces Ruling Council, the supreme authority in the country, many in government did not know about it until it was announced by the French News Agency. This created immediate confusion in the country. Ebitu Ukiwe, then a navy commodore and second in command to President Ibrahim Babangida, declared publicly that the decision to join OIC was not discussed at any level of government; in retaliation, he was forced out of government.[19] To diffuse national tension, Babangida set up a committee headed by the late John Shagaya, a loyal officer, but the report was never made public. Since then successive administrations have maintained Nigeria's membership in the OIC.[20]

Few religious riots took place during this period. One was the Kafanchan uprising in 1987, mentioned in Chapter 2.[21] A more profound ethnoreligious conflict, however, was the Zangon Kataf conflict, which began in February 1992. The conflict was caused by the relocation of the Zangon Kataf town market by the local government chairman. The market, which was originally located in the largely Muslim Hausa section, was relocated to a neutral place by a new Christian chairman. The relocation was resisted by the Hausas, who accused the chairman of ethnic and religious partisanship. This degenerated into bloody communal violence, with an official death toll of three hundred and unofficial estimates of a few thousand. The Zangon Kataf conflict recurred in May 1992 over allegations that some Hausa people had trespassed on a farm belonging to Kataf and uprooted yam seedlings. The Kataf people retaliated by destroying Hausa farms. The tit-for-tat developed into another ethnoreligious conflagration, and for three days, war raged in Zangon Kataf town.[22] This round of conflict resulted in the deaths of more than four hundred people and the destruction of the town.

The initial official response to the second Zangon Kataf conflict of 1992 was to ban all ethnic-based groups and to set up a judicial commission of inquiry to investigate the conflict, the Civil Disturbances Special Tribunal, before whom six prominent Katafs, including Major-General Zamani Lekwot, a former military governor and ambassador, were charged with complicity in the sectarian disturbances.[23] In September 1992, a total of fourteen people were sentenced to death by two different tribunals, including Major-General Lekwot. The federal government, however, commuted their death sentences to five years of imprisonment each.

Indeed, Zangon Kataf occupies a very important place in the politics of ethnoreligious conflict in Nigeria, and a brief discussion of the roots of the various conflicts in the place is worth noting, especially because of the perennial nature of conflict in the region. The roots of the crisis can be traced to the British indirect rule policy, through which British colonial territories were ruled by local rulers with the British masters providing overall supervision. After imposing colonial rule on northern Nigeria, the British imposed district heads from the minority Hausa ethnic group on the predominant ethnic groups of the area, the Katafs and the Atyaps.[24] The Katafs and Atyaps have always objected to traditional Hausa leaders, who are appointed by, and under the patronage of, the emir of Zaria. The atmosphere in Zangon Kataf was charged, with the Hausas accused of marginalizing the Katafs and other indigenous groups by taking over their lands and dominating the political and economic opportunities of the area under the protection of the emir of Zaria.[25]

There was a general sense that there might have been more to the handling of the 1992 Zangon Kataf riots than ordinarily suspected, and there were connections between the riots and the larger politics of the Babangida administration's transition to democracy. The ethnic politics and alliances of that transition program were believed to have figured in the outbreak of the violence; thus, the riots might not be unconnected to Babangida's reluctance to hand over power. With riots of this nature, the Babangida administration felt that there may be grounds to subvert the ongoing transition program.

The annulment of the June 12, 1993, election by Babangida brought ethnicity and religion to the fore of national politics, as it divided Muslims across the nation. In Yorubaland, where Moshood Abiola, the multimillionaire who was believed to have won the election, came from, opinions on the annulment were divided. People known to have benefited from the military, like Arisekola Alao, supported the military against Abiola, while many others were against Sani Abacha's assumption of power after the removal of the interim administration that came after the annulment.[26] The sultan of Sokoto, Dasuki, first issued a press statement urging Babangida to hand over power to Abiola, but he changed his position later to say that the annulment was an "Act of God."[27] Many Yoruba Muslims found it a completely unacceptable way to treat a fellow Muslim.

After Babangida himself was eventually forced to relinquish power, an interim government headed by Shonekan sat uncomfortably in power for less than thirty days before it was overthrown by another military regime under Sani Abacha. Although widely believed by many to be Nigeria's most brutal dictator, largely because of his imprisonment of Moshood Abiola, the winner of the election that Babangida annulled, and the killing of Ken Saro Wiwa and other Ogoni activists, he was not known to have used religion to his advantage in any significant way. Relying solely on threats and brute force, he was able to intimidate and silence the population until his mysterious death in June 1998. He was succeeded by Major General Abdulsalami Abubakar and it was he who handed power to the Fourth Republic.

Religion and Conflict in Politics and Intergroup Relations during the Fourth Republic

By the time of Nigeria's Fourth Republic, the links between religion, violence, and intergroup relations in Nigeria had become more complex, and all the administrations during the period faced profound challenges.

The Obasanjo Phase

With the coming of the new democratic dawn in 1999, the link between religion and national politics assumed another dimension. The political struggles that had followed the 1993 presidential election in the country had meant that a Yoruba from the southwest would be president of Nigeria after the end of the military dictatorship, as for the first time in the history of the country, the two main presidential candidates were Yoruba. Almost implicitly, the power shift would come with a religious shift, as both candidates were also Christians.

The most significant link between religion and politics during the Obasanjo civilian administration came with its adoption of Sharia. Sharia policy is inextricably linked with politics, as it connects elected governors in many of the affected states to the deeply religious Muslim masses. Indeed, some argue that the governor who first introduced the Sharia penal code, Ahmed Sani of Zamfara State, did so to avert impeachment; his party's representatives in the state House of Assembly were in the minority. By introducing Sharia, he took refuge in Islam and became seen as a defender of the faith.

Muslims in general are divided between those who genuinely support Sharia and those who are merely political in their support. Overall, many northern politicians have supported Sharia from personal conviction, political realism, political opportunism, or a sense that they should represent the wishes of those who elected them. Which of these takes precedence in any given situation is a matter of opinion, but the general belief in many of the places where the policy has been adopted is that it is more rooted in hidden expectations of political advantage than in the desire for pious living.[28] There is a wide gap between what government officials say in public about radicalization and what they do in private. Indeed, some believe that even the leaders of the Jama'atul Nasril Islam (JNI) are not totally committed in their support for Sharia law, while the emirs and other key officeholders in northern Nigeria are accused of being insincere in their support. Abdulkadir Balarabe Musa, a radical politician, said in his foreword to a book written by Mallam Lawan Dambazau that "traditional rulers in Muslim Communities in this country are opposed to the Sharia because the Sharia does not allow political oppression, economic exploitation or hereditary succession to public office. And since the basis of their position is hereditary succession, they do not actually like Sharia."[29] Participants in focus groups told me that they believe that top politicians and even senior military officers have sought and received support from radical Islamic scholars, sometimes imported from Senegal to come and pray for government officials.[30]

In focus group discussions and interviews conducted in the southwest, many people argued and even claimed to find evidence that there were diabolical motives behind the Sharia introduction and that those who introduced it had no pious intent. One said that it was an attempt by the Hausa Fulani north to frustrate a Yoruba presidency (under Obasanjo), thus making it easy for northerners to interpret such a failure as an ethnic failure. Others said that virtually all the governors who claimed to be pious in introducing Sharia law were later indicted for massive corruption by the Economic and Financial Crime Commission and, thus, they could not have been morally upright. Many southerners argued that Sharia controversies and agitations ended the moment Obasanjo left office and a northerner, Umaru Yar'Adua, was elected president. This, to them, was a confirmation that the Sharia façade had completed its destabilizing assignment and could, therefore, be put to rest.

A few violent religious conflicts did occur during the Obasanjo phase. The first of these was the 2001 Jos riots, which left several people dead. Although religion was a crucial dynamic, the crisis emerged from a long struggle for control of political and economic power between those categorized as indigenous and nonindigenous residents of the area. Tensions had been brewing since around 1994 over how political offices were shared among the various identity groups. More immediately, the appointment of Mukhtar Muhammad, a Hausa Muslim, as the poverty eradication coordinator in Jos North was the spark. He had been forced to step down from a previous appointment on allegations of credential falsification, and the non-Hausa/Fulani Christians considered his appointment an affront. Conflict soon broke out. Both sides had appealed to religious sentiments to manipulate popular emotions. Eventually such appeals inflamed the situation to a level where it could no longer be controlled. All groups were both perpetrators and victims of violence.[31]

Not long after the Jos crisis, another ethnoreligious conflict occurred in Yelwa, located in the south of Plateau State under the administrative control of the Shendam Local Government Area with headquarters in Shendam. At the ruling People's Democratic Party (PDP) ward congress in Yelwa, in April 2002, violence broke out as voters supported candidates along religious lines. Yelwa is predominantly a Muslim community, while Shendam, almost the same size, is largely Christian, including most local government officials and traditional leaders. Here again, the dispute involved many ethnic groups, but the main ones were the Gamai, the majority ethnic group in Shendam Local Government Area, and the Jarawa. The Gamai, who include both Christians and Muslims, consider themselves to be indigenous and regard the Jarawa as settlers, while the predominantly Muslim Jarawa claim to be the founders of Yelwa. Like most ethnoreligious conflicts, the crisis here is deeply rooted in history, dating back to the nineteenth century and the early twentieth century, over competing claims to the status of indigenous. But this issue has also been a hot one fairly recently: until 1990, the Jarawa, and other predominantly Muslim groups such as the Borghom and the Pyem, were granted indigenous certificates, but they claim that from then on, the traditional leader of Shendam, known as the Long Gamai, began denying them indigenous rights. Important historical disputes were over the process of selection of traditional chiefs and, more recently, political rivalry in local elections, particularly elections for the chairmanship of the PDP.

An issue that was to became a major problem in later years also occurred during the Obasanjo administration—the activities of Fulani herdsmen in the southwestern parts of the country. The largely Muslim Fulani herdsmen have had persistent disagreements with farmers in the Oke-Ogun part of Oyo State, with the local farmers accusing the herdsmen of destroying their farms. In the ensuing controversies, violence often broke out. After one of those conflicts, Muhammadu Buhari, then a retired general in the army, led a group of eminent Fulani elders (including the former Lagos State governor, Mohammad Buba Marwa) to the office of the governor of Oyo State, the late Lam Adesina, to protest the killing of Fulani herdsmen in the Oke-Ogun area of the state: allegedly, the bodies of sixty-eight Fulani cattlemen had been recovered that May and buried under the supervision of mobile police from the Oyo State command. General Buhari also gave a subtle indictment of the state government, claiming that those arrested for the killing were released without trial. Understandably angry, General Buhari and his team strongly expressed their displeasure with the way the matter was handled by the Oyo State government. In response, the governor invited the police commissioner to report on the matter to General Buhari and his team. The police commissioner debunked everything that General Buhari said and gave a version of the story that, indeed, indicted the Fulani herdsmen. The director of the State Security Service was also invited to give his report and again contradicted what General Buhari said: while confirming that some people were killed, the director said that five people were sadly killed in the dispute, not sixty-eight. The governor then called his deputy, Iyiola Oladokun, and the secretary to the state government, Michael Koleoso, both of whom came from the area, and their reports were along the same lines as those of the security chiefs. After all the exchanges, the governor delivered a parting shot to the visitors, which, according to an eyewitness, went something like this:

> Before I thank you for this visit . . . I also want to appeal: General Buhari has been a former Head of State, Brigadier Marwa has governed Lagos State . . . so you are the national leader of this country. Even though by accident of birth, you are from the North. . . . My appeal will be that efforts must be made to unite this country and that will be in the best interest of all Nigerians. I am appealing to the Arewa Consultative Forum, under which auspices you are here; in recent times, they have been sending wrong signals to a number of us who believe in the unity and peace of Nigeria. . . . I am saying this because Nigeria at this point, cannot afford to break and the words you northern leaders utter are very weighty. . . . I want to say also that we have to appeal to our people, the itinerant Fulani people that they should be less aggressive. It is not good, it is not right just coming from somewhere then you just pass through farmlands cultivated

maybe with the person's life savings and then overnight everything is gone. That is not right, even Allah does not approve of that. We even wonder when they talk about these people carrying dangerous weapons, I say do they believe in Allah? When you just take life like that and go away! Are we not forbidden not to take a human life? So, I think General Buhari, General Marwa, you have to be educating them.[32]

As is shown later in this chapter, many in later years claimed that Buhari's visit to Lam Adesina showed that he was a regional rather than a national leader.

In February 2004, another round of violence occurred in Yelwa. The immediate cause was a clash between some Fulani, who were angry at the alleged theft by Christians of their cattle, and Christians from Langtang South who chased the Fulani into Yamini. Both sides lost people in the clashes that ensued.[33] Violence occurred again between the two groups in May of the same year. It lasted two days but was on a larger scale than any of the previous attacks in the area. Reports of the clashes submitted by the international organization Human Rights Watch claimed that the majority of victims in the February 24, 2004, attack were Christians, while the majority of victims in the May 2004 attack were Muslims.[34] Such events continued until Umaru Yar'Adua became president.

The Yar'Adua Phase

In May 2007, Umaru Yar'Adua assumed office in an election that even he admitted was flawed.[35] In November 2008, violence broke out in Jos and up to eight hundred people died.[36] Here, the immediate cause was the result of a local government election. Even before the official report of the winner, rumors went around that a member of the ruling PDP, Timothy Buba, had won against a Muslim from the All Nigeria Peoples Party. The Muslim Hausa community rioted because they allegedly could not fathom a Christian victory. The conflict brought out key issues in the pattern of religious radicalization (both Christian and Muslim) and political violence. Jos occupies a very important place in the politics of ethnoreligious affairs in Nigeria. The population is highly mixed, as it is situated between the largely Muslim north and the essentially non-Muslim south. Combined with its temperate weather and wildlife, Jos is one of Nigeria's most metropolitan cities, with inhabitants from all over the world. However, the moment there are ethnoreligious riots, people from neighboring regions come to the town to assist their compatriots. Moreover, while most of the indigenous population in Jos is Christian, Hausa Fulani have settled in the town for more than a century. Their strong determination not only to hold on to their ethnicity and religion but also, if possible, to convert the indigenous population strengthens the overall political power of the Hausa Fulani in the wider national politics but has also created tension and rivalry with Christians.

The November 2008 riots started when a local government election was allegedly rigged. The most affected areas were densely populated places—Ali Kazaure, Angwar Rogo, Gangare, Nasarawa, Katako, and Dogon Dutse—where Christians and Muslims live together. The pattern of the conflict was that in the places where Muslims were in the majority, they attacked Christians, while the latter did the same in places where they had the numerical advantage. Reactions to the November 2008 Jos crisis incorporated the usual controversies that often underline the politics of religious violence in Nigeria. President Musa Yar'Adua and his wife, Turai, sent two separate emissaries to Jos to sympathize with those affected by the crisis, but neither visited the state governor. This gave many people the impression that the president and his family were supporting their fellow Muslims/Hausa Fulanis and were opposed to the governor who, along with being a Christian, was from the indigenous group.[37]

But just as the country was recovering from the Jos crisis, another religious problem emerged in Bauchi, in February 2009. Although Bauchi was not a stranger to religious riots, the riots caught the nation by surprise.[38] The trouble started in the railway area with a complaint by the Church of Christ in Nigeria that the prayer gatherings at Fantami Mosque across the street often blocked their entrance. Two factions of the Izala Islamic sect agreed to hold their Jumat prayer at different times: one between noon and 1 p.m. and the other between 1 and 2 p.m. But one Friday, one of the groups held its prayers from noon to 2 p.m., thereby depriving the other of the chance to observe prayers. The deprived group protested, and clashes ensued. An objection by the church members that evening led to violence, with people using guns and machetes, but state security men apparently got the situation under control. That night unidentified persons set the Fantami Mosque ablaze. Muslims claimed that it was done by Christians, and soon churches, mosques, and other properties went up in flames too.

The January–March 2010 riots in Jos also mixed religion with ethnicity and economic realities. Again, as in most conflicts in Nigeria, casualty figures ranged between three hundred and a thousand. Houses, churches, and mosques were destroyed. Some cited the immediate catalyst as the attack by a set of Muslim youths on a Christian church; others blamed disagreements over the building of a Muslim home in a Christian area. The Plateau State Christian Elders Consultative Forum considered it another stage in an organized jihad.

Indeed, the Anglican archbishop of Jos, Benjamin A. Kwashi, noted, "What seems to be a recurring decimal is that over time, those who have in the past used violence to settle political issues, economic issues, social matters, inter-tribal disagreements, or any issue for that matter, now continue to use that same path of violence and cover it up with religion."[39] The rivalry between the Hausa and the Berom people was dynamic. Religious leaders saw the hidden hand of nonreligious considerations in the crisis. For example, the Catholic archbishop in Abuja described the crisis as a classic conflict between pastoralists and farmers, except that the Fulani pastoralists are Muslims and the Berom farmers are Christian. Where this assertion, however, runs into some difficulties is that most ethnic groups in Plateau State are predominantly Christian, share the same sentiments on land and property rights with the Berom, and collectively see an Islamic threat to their lands. The Berom have often been accused of not being accommodating and of often being unhappy at the economic progress being made by settlers in their midst. Meanwhile, most natives of the state see themselves as victims of neglect by successive federal administrations.

An issue that later caused minor ripples but not violence in some parts of the country, especially the southwest, during this period was the decision by some governments to hand over schools to the missionaries. During the colonial era, many Christian missions established primary and secondary schools, which they managed without government interference. Muslims too established their own schools. Then, in October 1979, when civilian rule was reintroduced in the country and the Unity Party of Nigeria took over the administration of the states in the southwest, the government took over all the schools under its Free Education Scheme. The decision now to revert to the old order and hand schools back to their original owners was seen by Muslims as a way of bringing back a structure skewed in favor of Christians. All over the southwest where this policy was being considered, radical Muslims have been coming out to speak forcefully against it.[40]

But undoubtedly the greatest issue during Yar'Adua's tenure was the emergence of Boko Haram. When Boko Haram first struck, President Yar'Adua was on his way to a twice-postponed official visit to Brazil, and all he could do was to instruct his security forces to manage the situation in his absence. When eventually Mohammed Yusuf was extrajudicially killed, pressure mounted on the president to resolve the crisis. The president's initial reaction was to direct the national security adviser to study the killing and to ask the nation to avoid hasty judgment. This, however, was a strategic deception: as the press secretary to the late president, Olusegun Adeniyi, was to confess later, there was, indeed, no investigation into how Yusuf was killed.[41] By the time Umar Farouk Abdulmutallab attempted to bomb an American Airlines flight in December 2009, President Yar'Adua was already seriously ill in Saudi Arabia, and his speech was so badly impaired that he could not conduct telephone discussions with US President Obama.[42] The mantle of responsibility fell on Vice President Goodluck Jonathan, and he had to assume full responsibility when he became president.

Goodluck Jonathan Administration

The Jonathan administration faced the most profound of Boko Haram's challenges. As noted in chapter 5, for a long time, the administration interpreted the activities of Boko Haram as part of the grand strategy of failed politicians to undermine the government. This gained some credibility when the All Nigeria Peoples Party governor candidate Modu Fannami Gubio was killed.

Of all Boko Haram's insurgent activities, the greatest challenge to the Jonathan administration was the kidnapping of the Chibok girls. Jonathan's position was not made easy by comments from the international community about his administration's management of the tragedy. The former British high commissioner, Sir Andrew Pocock, said a couple of months after the kidnapping that American drone technology witnessed the seizure of up to eighty of the girls: the girls, a camp, and evidence of ground transport vehicles were spotted next to a local landmark called the Tree of Life in the Sambisa Forest—but that the Nigerian government had failed to act on this information.[43] The *New York Times* also reported that when the Pentagon came up with actionable intelligence from drone flights that might indicate the location of some of the girls and turned it over to Nigerian military commanders to follow up, they did nothing with the information.[44] The *Times* cited African High Command officials in Stuttgart, Germany, as its source; it reported that shortly after the United States offered to help rescue the girls, it flew several hundred surveillance drone flights over the vast, densely forested regions in the Sambisa Forest. Jonathan also made some gaffes that played into the hands of his opponents, especially when he said he believed the girls were still alive because Boko Haram would have displayed their bodies if they had been killed. The opposition All Progressives Congress (APC) immediately described this as "callous, morbid and insensitive."[45]

An amorphous group that went by the name Bring Back Our Girls, led by prominent citizens including Oby Ezekwesili, a former minister in the Obasanjo administration, made the strongest criticism of the Johnathan administration, organizing several protests. Police opposed them, with a commissioner of police, Joseph Mbu, trying to disrupt their nonviolent protests, but the inspector general of police distanced himself from efforts to arrest members of the group. At one stage, the Bring Back Our Girls campaign also fell into the murky waters of national politics when key members of the Jonathan administration started alleging ulterior motives for Ezekwesili's actions; the special assistant of the president on public affairs, Doyin Okupe, claimed that Oby's gripe was her inability to accept Ngozi Okonjo-Iweala's (another female member of the cabinet from the same region as Oby) supremacy in national politics.[46]

It would, however, not be correct to see the whole situation only through the prism of difficulties. Individual initiatives indicate possible harmony between different religious groups. Pastor James Wuye and Imam Mohammed Ashafa, leaders of the youth wings of, respectively, the Christian Association of Nigeria (CAN) and the Islamic Society of Nigeria, came together with trepidation to form the Pastor and the Imam Project, which tries to heal the divide between Nigeria's Christians and Muslims across the country. Both men have been violent radicals who forcefully propagated their faith. Both had personal tragedies in the roles they played: both lost members of their families in riots, and Wuye lost one of his arms. The project has won several national and global awards. Pastor Wuye said in a February 2001 interview, "We are now like husbands and wife that must not divorce: if we divorce, our children will suffer—and our children in this context are the Nigerian youths whom we must not allow to suffer. So we have vowed to stay together."[47] Their work was a glimmer of good hope as the Buhari administration assumed power.

The Buhari Phase

The Buhari administration rose to power by promising security, economic improvement, and a war against corruption. But it also still faced troubles at the intersection of religion, violence, and intergroup relations from Boko Haram, the herdsmen and farmers, and Shi'ite groups. Of all these, the one for which the government was prepared effectively was the Boko Haram crisis. During the campaign that preceded the 2015 elections, security and Boko Haram were at the top of the national agenda. The opposition APC campaigned on the idea that President Jonathan had been weak in facing Boko Haram. Indeed, Buhari made an emphatic promise about the Chibok girls, saying, "I want to assure all of them and particularly the parents, that when my new administration takes office at the end of May, we will do everything we can to defeat Boko Haram.

We will act differently from the government we replaced."[48] In another campaign speech for the 2015 election, Buhari reiterated his commitment to rescue the girls:

I have had the opportunity to serve my country in the military up to the highest level as a major general and the commander-in-chief of the armed forces. In the course of my services, I defended the territorial integrity of Nigeria and if called upon to do so again, I shall rise to the occasion. As a father, I feel the pain of the victims of insurgency, kidnapping, and violence. Under my watch, no force, external or internal will occupy even an inch of Nigerian soil. I will give it all it takes to ensure that our girls kidnapped from Chibok are rescued and reintegrated with their families.[49]

However, perhaps Buhari's strongest commitment to rescuing the girls was in his presidential inaugural speech: "we cannot claim to have defeated Boko Haram without rescuing the Chibok girls and all other innocent persons held hostage by insurgents."[50]

Indeed, the government changed tactics by modifying its military strategy after the Buhari administration assumed office. But as if to show Nigerians that nothing had changed with the new president's assumption of office, the next few months after his inaugural speech witnessed increased Boko Haram activities. Shortly after the inauguration in May 2015, Boko Haram insurgents killed 97 persons, and in June, July, August, September, and October 2015, the sect killed 368, 635, 431, 267, and 279 people respectively.[51]

On the matter of the Chibok girls, the government and International Red Cross negotiated with Boko Haram and secured the release of about one hundred of the captured girls in May 2017. The terms of the negotiations were not released to the public, nor were the criteria for the selection of girls. Some senators hinted that the release involved the payment of a ransom to Boko Haram, but the government denied it.[52] The International Red Cross later confirmed that its role was only to implement the deal between the government and Boko Haram, not to give input into the actual deal.[53]

After the release of the girls, the president said that the government would intensify efforts to secure the release of the other girls. However, starting from November 2015, the number of persons that Boko Haram killed dipped, with November recording 81 and December 136. In December 2015, Buhari said he was willing to negotiate with Boko Haram for the release of the girls without preconditions. He confirmed on national television that he had no information on the whereabouts of the girls. The number of Boko Haram killings in

January 2016 was 104. But former President Obasanjo said in February 2016 that it was unlikely the girls would return alive:

> Nobody can bring back the girls for they are nowhere to be found. So, if any leader is promising to bring [back] Chibok girls, he is lying. The majority of these girls would have died, while those alive would have been married off and others will be victims of sexual violence and human trafficking. Nigerian leaders should stop deceiving the populace as Chibok girls cannot return. The disappearance . . . is a result of the nonchalant attitude of the previous leaders, who did not swing into action immediately which constituted an impediment to their return. Seventy-two hours after the Chibok girls were abducted was too late for their rescue, talk less of two years.[54]

Boko Haram killings kept declining, for the most part: in February of 2016 they were 90, in March 20, in April 43, and in May 12.[55] But in September 2017, the United Nations Office for the Coordination of Humanitarian Affairs said that at least three local government areas in Nigeria were still cut off due to the presence of Boko Haram insurgents—contradicting the government's long-standing claim that no part of the northeast was under the control of Boko Haram.[56]

When in December 2017 the federal government announced that it was taking one billion dollars from the Excess Crude Account to prosecute the war against Boko Haram, there was concern and criticism, especially from the opposition PDP. Most members of the opposition believed that the government would use this money to fight the 2019 election, and that Boko Haram had become a cash cow for military and political leaders in general. The critics of government found greater strength for their argument because the government had previously claimed that Boko Haram had been technically defeated. Among those who were critically vocal of the expenses was the former Ekiti State governor, Ayodele Fayose.[57] The pan-Yoruba group Afenifere, described the approval of money from the Excess Crude Account as the "foisting of the greatest heist in the country."[58]

Buhari and the Shi'ites

Since its inception, the Buhari administration has been contending with what is often widely described as the Shi'ites issue. As discussed in chapter 2, the Shi'ite group under the leadership of El-Zakzaky had constituted itself as a force in the country and had violent disagreements with military and civilian authorities. At the center of most disagreement is the assumption by the civilian and military authorities that the Shi'ites are refusing to subject themselves to the laws of the land, and the contrary conviction of the Shi'ites that the government and the majority Sunni Muslims are doing all they can to oppress them because of their minority status. The initial position of President Buhari on the Shi'ites was tactical indifference, though, like many in previous and present governments, he believed that the group had to be curtailed because of what he saw as their excesses. When the insurgents attacked the convoy of the army chief of staff and suffered injuries themselves, the president said that the group must have been aware of the dangers and consequences of their actions, but otherwise he did nothing. In an endorsed (if not authorized) biography of the president, John Paden enumerated the questions raised by the Shi'ite crisis, any one of which could have been on the president's mind: "Could the Nigerian military avoid such a crisis in the future? Was the military equipped to handle a domestic crisis of this sort? Should new localized police initiatives be developed to preempt such situations? Were state-level authorities able to deal with such crisis or should the Federal be involved? . . . Were religious enclaves such as the one in Zaria a prelude to demands for autonomy from the Nigerian state? Could clashes with a Federal force (or with the military) produce new forms of insurgency?"[59]

The December 2015 military clampdown on the Shi'ites forced the government to be somewhat more cautious, without changing its definition of what it considers fundamental to national security. The president initially did not make any pronouncement until after the Commission of Inquiry (set up by the Kaduna State government) submitted the report of its findings. Partly in response to the criticisms that attended the clampdown on the Shi'ites, the Nigerian army announced the creation of the Human Rights Desk within the Ministry of Defense to address all forms of individual complaints against military operations.

The continued detention of the leader of the Shi'ite group, Sheikh El-Zakzaky, raised considerable legal and human rights concerns. A court judgment had stipulated that the government had to construct him a new house in the location where his previous home was destroyed, and then release him to it. But the government claimed that his erstwhile neighbors no longer wanted him in their vicinity, so that it was difficult to get a place for him. Thus, the government claimed, it had a reason to keep him in protective custody. The government also cited security reasons for holding him. The government did grant El-Zakzaky and his wife permission to travel to India for medical treatment, but he ended up returning to Nigeria without undergoing the treatment.

On September 1, 2019, the inspector-general of police, Mohammed Adamu, ordered the arrest of all identified Shi'ite leaders across the country, blaming them for the killing of the deputy commissioner of police in charge of the operations of the Federal Capital Territory Police Command, Umar Usman, and a National Youth Service Corps member, Precious Owolabi.

In July 2021, the court acquitted El-Zakzaky of all eight criminal charges against him, including culpable homicide and unlawful assembly, as none of the fifteen prosecution witnesses proved he committed the offences. Following the ruling, the couple's lawyer, Femi Falana, wrote separate letters to the Nigeria Intelligence Agency (NIA), the State Security Service (SSS), and the attorney general of the federation to demand the release of their passports, allegedly seized after the Indian trip. El-Zakzaky also used the opportunity to say that the India medical trip was supervised and controlled by the NIA and the SSS. El-Zakzaky and his wife later filed a N4 billion suit against the government.

The Herdsmen Controversy

But while the Shi'ite problem continued, another national security problem that had been latent came to have a strong bearing on the politics of religious and ethnopolitical violence: the activity of those widely described as Fulani herdsmen. By 2015, the herdsmen issue had become connected with religious radicalization, and by around 2017, it had created casualties almost to the proportions of Boko Haram.

Ethnicity, religion, and vocation all rolled into one in the herdsmen controversy. Most of the conflicts involve Fulanis, who are herdsmen and mostly Muslims, against indigenous communities, who are largely Christians and commonly farmers. The controversies here began before the Buhari era and are largely rooted in clashes over land: Because of climate change, grazing lands available to herdsmen have shrunk, and looking for land for their stock inevitably put them in a clash with farmers. The problem has been more profound in the Benue River confluence, where Benue State historically has been the nation's breadbasket. Pastoral-related conflicts are some of the most controversial natural resource conflicts in Africa, especially because belligerents often do not recognize boundaries.[60]

The Fulanis have one of their original homes in the Futa Jallon area in present-day Guinea, and probably migrated from North Africa and the Middle East. Another initial home was in the Futa Toro area, along the banks of the Senegal River in present-day Senegal. Although they have had contact with people in northern Nigeria, the Fulanis' relationship with Nigeria increased significantly as a result of the jihad of Uthman dan Fodio (a Fulani) in the early nineteenth century. After conquering most of northern Nigeria, the Tivs fiercely resisted dan Fodio's attempt to spread his jihad to the present-day Nigerian Middle Belt. He sustained an injury in April 1817 in this war, from which he later died, and Fulani expansion toward the southeast ended. The remaining Fulanis reached a truce with the Tivs, which led to a relationship known as *abokanin wasa*, meaning "playmates." Middle Belt areas such as Jema, Lafia, Keffi, Jere, Wase, and others remained largely Fulani and non-Muslim. While most of the Fulani population in present-day Nigeria live in cities, a sizeable percentage remain nomadic, herding their cattle. Presently, most of the Fulanis in Nigeria operate under an umbrella organization known as the Miyetti Allah Kautal Hore under the honorary chairmanship of the incumbent sultan of Sokoto, Sa'ad Abubakar.

For most of the postindependence period, the Fulanis have played a significant role in the political leadership of the country: of Nigeria's previous and present rulers, four have been Fulani: Shehu Shagari, Murtala Mohammed (through his mother), Umaru Yar'Adua, and the incumbent Muhammadu Buhari. While they have lost out and have, indeed, been victimized in other parts of West Africa, they have been associated with power and influence in Nigeria. This has shaped how people have interpreted Fulani activities and the government's treatment of them.

The Fulanis are mostly nomads. Although nomadism was historically known across Nigeria, with the occasional but manageable crisis with farmers and other local inhabitants, climate change, modern land-use policies, and urbanization in the last few decades sent the practice into decline. Then local (and sometimes national) politics, historical considerations, intergroup relations, and elite greed brought herdsmen issues into the politics of religious and ethnopolitical violence in Nigeria. Before 2015, when the Buhari administration came to power, the herdsmen wreaked havoc in certain communities in the Middle Belt region of Nigeria, but later, the rate at which they committed these crimes increased exponentially. Although alleged violent activities of herdsmen were prevalent across many states, they were more serious in the states of the Middle Belt region, especially Benue, Nasarawa, and Plateau. Benue State in the central part of Nigeria occupies a very important position in the politics of herdsmen and religious conflicts. As one of Nigeria's most fertile areas, it is attractive to farmers and herders alike. With the increasing desertification of the Lake Chad region, the state has further attracted greater importance in the politics of agriculturalist/pastoralist relations.

The ethnoreligious composition of the state is quite significant in the Christian/Muslim divide. Although it has a sizeable Muslim population, the state includes more Christians. There has, however, been violence in their relationship. Indeed, according to statistics provided by the Institute for Economics and Peace, 1,229 people were killed in 2014, up from 63 in 2013, and Benue State seems to be the hardest hit in recent times.[61] Barely five days before the end of Governor Gabriel Suswam's administration in May 2015, over one hundred farmers and their family members were reportedly killed in villages and refugee camps located in the Ukura, Per, Gafa, and Tse-Gusa local government areas of the state. In July 2015, suspected herdsmen attacked Adeke, a community on the outskirts of the state capital, Makurdi. In December 2017, six people were killed in Idele village in the Oju Local Government Area.[62] A reprisal attack by youths in the community saw three Fulani herdsmen killed. The problem later spread even to the southern parts of the country. Indeed, the former secretary to the federal government, Olu Falae, was kidnapped in September 2015.[63] From 2016 to 2018, more violent incidents with Fulani herdsmen were recorded. In February 2017, as a result of a clash between herdsmen and farmers in Benue State, 40 more people were killed, about 2,000 displaced, and no less than 100 seriously injured.[64] In short, by 2014, the activities of herdsmen had begun causing serious security concerns across the country.

Local populations in some parts of the Middle Belt also believe that they are victims of the security forces as much as they are of the herdsmen. There have been instances of alleged brutality by security forces. For example, soldiers sacked Agasha community in Plateau State in April 2018 after the people killed a soldier they mistook for one of the herdsmen terrorizing them. The governor of Taraba State, Dairus Ishaku, accused the soldiers of taking over police duties and of flagrantly abusing youths, including indiscriminately arresting them.[65] The governor was specific that the armed forces were arresting the population instead of protecting them from killer herdsmen. In April 2018, women protested against the soldiers' abuse of power.

The killings came to the center of national attention when someone killed Catholic priests inside their church in April 2018. The CAN asked the president to suspend his campaign for a second term and concentrate on bringing peace to the country.[66] Expressing the same sentiment and protesting the killings, Catholics marched in seven states: Edo, Oyo, Benue, Lagos, Kaduna, Adamawa, and Kwara. Critics have compared the government's response to the herdsmen's activities to the way the government handled the protests for the sovereign state of Biafra, which they alleged was firm, brutal, and decisive. The governor of Benue, Samuel Ortom, also wondered why the priests would be the target of the herdsmen.[67]

Reactions to the killings fell into predictable patterns. The reluctance of the government to condemn the herdsmen was interpreted as an implicit endorsement of the killings. Many of the victims said that the federal government appeared nonchalant about the killings because the president was a Fulani man and would never openly condemn his kith and kin. The federal government emphatically denied this and publicized statistics to prove that the violence had started during the Jonathan era. For example, in 2013, there were nine cases of herdsmen violence in Benue State and more than 190 were killed. In 2014, there were sixteen such violent contacts, resulting in the death of 231 people, and between January and May 2015, when the government changed, there were six attacks that left about 335 people dead.[68]

The government of Benue countered that the federal government was still showing more sympathy for the herdsmen than for the suffering people of Benue, and that between January and May 2018, about 492 people had been killed and over 180,000 internally displaced.[69] Ironically, the Fulani herdsmen also believed that the president was not protecting them. A representative of the group said, "Instead of backing us, we the Fulani are now accusing Buhari of allowing other ethnic groups to continue to rustle our cattle and killing our people. . . . He does not care about us and if things don't change, we will fight him back."[70] Fulani herdsmen also argue that they were carrying arms because the government was not doing enough to protect them.

In response, the federal government established ranches for the Fulani and their cattle in ninety-four locations across ten states of the federation: Adamawa, Benue, Ebonyi, Edo, Kaduna, Nasarawa, Oyo, Plateau, Taraba, and Zamfara. The initial cost of this was put at N70 billion, with a sum of N170 billion to be spent over the next three years. The minister for agriculture used the word *colony*. To many, this was a sad reminder of British colonial rule and an evocation of the expansive 1804 Fulani jihad that took their independence from them.

The federal government also promulgated an open grazing law, under which land was to be designated for grazing. Some states, especially those in the southwest, resisted the law; in fact, Benue State instantly passed an antigrazing law. In Ekiti State, Governor Ayodele Fayose (known to be opposed to the president) unequivocally condemned the open grazing law. Governments in the Middle Belt also disagreed with it. There are, however, those who supported it. For example, the governor of Plateau State, Simon Lalong, gave his endorsement and saw the violence that engulfed his neighboring Benue State as a vindication of his position. He even said that he warned his Benue counterpart of the dangers and consequences of challenging the federal government.[71] But the state whose opposition to the law met with the reality of Fulani herdsmen activities was Benue. After the state passed its antigrazing law, the leader of the pan-Fulani group Miyetti Allah Kautal Hore, Alhaji Bodejo, openly announced that Benue's law put the Fulani under siege and that Fulani across West Africa would occupy Benue. This threat was carried out on January 1, 2018, leading to the deaths of ninety-seven people. The group went to court to challenge the antigrazing law but lost.

The federal government's handling of the whole matter evoked many negative reactions. For example, the Tiv Youth Organization called for the federal government to increase its efforts to address the herdsmen's activities and to arrest and prosecute the leaders of the Miyeti Allah.[72] The group described as preposterous the claim by Fulanis that they were the original owners of the Benue valley and vowed to resist, at all costs, the government's confiscation of their land and its transmutation into grazing land for Fulani herdsmen.[73] Even those initially reluctant to criticize Buhari found it difficult to remain silent about the activities of the herdsmen. Indeed, Nobel laureate Wole Soyinka told the president to wield a big stick against the herdsmen.[74]

The politics of the competing narratives have been complicated and have shaped how incidents were reported. Sometimes the activities of the Fulani herdsmen have been reported as indicating support of the presidency and the endorsement of Islam, such as that the herdsmen, after successful attacks, were shouting "Allahu akbar"—Arabic meaning "God is great," often used in a revolutionary or violent context—and also sometimes thanking the president for his support.[75]

The military soon started what it called Operation Whirl Stroke to address the herdsmen's activities in Benue State and appointed Adeyemi Yekini, a major general, as its commander. In August 2018, the military deployed an Mi-35 helicopter against the Fulani, resulting in the deaths of twenty-one militant herdsmen and one soldier. A wanted militia leader, Terwase Akwaza, popularly known as Gana, was suspected to have been killed during the attack.[76]

The governor at the center of the problem was Governor Ortom of Benue State. He made several efforts to enlist the sympathy of the federal government, writing letters to the acting president on June 7, 2017, to the president on

October 27, 2017, to the inspector general three times (June 7 and October 17, 2017, and January 2, 2018), to the director-general of the Department of State Services on June 7, 2017, to the National Security Adviser on three occasions (June 7, October 17 and 27), and to the National Assembly on June 7, 2017.[77] This is important because it shows the lengths to which the governor claimed he went to ensure peace.

Realizing that the security forces could not protect them, farmers, hunters, and youths started amassing arms to protect themselves from the Fulani herdsmen. When a newspaper reporter asked where the vigilante groups got their weapons, one of their members responded, "First ask the Fulani herdsmen to tell you where they got their weapons from before you ask me to tell you the sources of our weapons."[78] In Ekiti, the National Youth Council of Nigeria formed to meet the herdsmen's threat with force. In the southeast, there was rising local resentment. In Enugu State, for example, farmers promised to meet the herdsmen with force. The same sentiment was expressed in Owerri, Imo State, while in Ogun, the Council of Obas met to address the situation.

The Fulanis have an answer to the allegations leveled against them. According to Mohammed Nuru Abdullahi, the chairman of the Miyetti Allah in Plateau State, "Fulanis do not have any security back up because they are in the rural areas where the security operatives may not go. . . . Therefore, Fulani herdsmen will do everything possible to protect their lives and property themselves since the government has failed to do so."[79]

Ethnic Dimensions of the Herdsmen Issue

By December 2019, the Nigerian population seemed to have divided between pro-herdsmen and antiherdsmen. The pro included those in the core northern parts of the country—Fulanis, Hausas, and Muslims—except for the minorities. The anti were largely southerners, plus non-Muslims in the north, especially in the Middle Belt. In short, the conflict had assumed an ethnoreligious coloration. Those accusing Buhari of complicity in the killing by Fulani herdsmen were quick to point out his October 2000 visit to the late governor of Oyo State, Lam Adesina, mentioned earlier.

Many of President Buhari's critics believe that he has not freed himself from the ethnic prejudice that drove him to visit the Oyo State governor in October 2000 and that it was this, added to his religious belief, that underlines what they see as his nonchalant attitude toward the activities of the herdsmen and his partisan position on this issue as a military leader.

Religious Dimensions of the Herdsmen Issue

Indeed, the activities of herdsmen fall into the category of religious violence. For one thing, Boko Haram members have been mistaken for Fulani herdsmen, or, put inversely, it has been said that Boko Haram members might be operating as herdsmen, and they have reacted against the herdsmen accordingly. Indeed, the identity of the Fulani herdsmen can be blurry, as it also involves people from other West African countries. But it is very difficult to correlate the activities of Boko Haram terrorists with those of the Fulani herdsmen. Boko Haram has utilized explosives carried by suicide bombers or hidden in a target, but the Fulani herdsmen are mainly concerned with gaining greater access to grazing lands for livestock; moreover, after the February 2017 attacks in Benue, the leadership of the Fulani group openly admitted that its members carried out the attacks. The herdsmen-farmer crisis also counts as religious violence because Christian churches, especially those with Pentecostal leanings, say that Fulani herdsmen who kill Christians should be met with violence. Indeed, as noted in chapter 3, a few prominent Pentecostal pastors (including Apostle Suleiman of Omega Ministries in Kaduna and David Oyedepo of Winners Chapel in Ota) openly told members of their congregation to kill any Fulani herdsman that they saw around the church. And some Christians viewed the sudden increase in violent activities of Fulani herdsmen as being similar to Boko Haram's strategy of Islamizing Nigeria. A vocal former Anglican primate, Peter Akinola, drew this parallel between the Fulani herdsmen and Boko Haram:

> They both [Boko Haram and Fulani herdsmen] want a society where Islam and its dictates govern the society. Banking, education, health, military, governance, everything . . . should be governed by Sharia. . . . It is their faith that is fueling their activities. So as Boko Haram continues to fight, we claim that we have technical victory . . . then the Fulani herdsmen started their own. . . . They go to the southern parts of Borno, which is dominated by Christians, to Chibok, and to Adamawa. Those places are largely Christian areas. They come to the southern parts of Kaduna. . . . So why are they carrying out their killings in those areas? What has the killing of innocent people got to do with feeding cattle if they have no hidden agenda?[80]

Oyedepo was more emphatic in his February 4, 2020, pronouncement in his church, when he described the Buhari administration as the "most murderous system" in the history of the country. He opined that "it is impossible for the killers to be on the loose without some authority backing them up." He concluded by prophesying that "the days of . . . irresponsible system are numbered."[81] While many Christian leaders may not share the venom of his attack on the Buhari administration, they share his views that the administration was not doing enough to protect Christians. They equated the activities of herdsmen to the Islamic religion, seeing the whole development as part of the grander design to Islamize Nigeria.

Religious considerations soon affected ethnic responses to the activities of Fulani herdsmen and the alleged complicity of the Buhari administration. A group that identified itself as the Muslim Community of Oyo State (under its chairman, Alhaji Ishaq Kunle Sanni) held a major press conference on July 5, 2018, in Ibadan. The group specifically accused the Yoruba Council of Elders (YCE, also known as the Afenifere) of fraud in its claim to be representing the Yoruba in the fight against herdsmen and the Buhari administration. It further alleged that the YCE was an "amalgam of Christian predators" with the agenda of the "furtherance of Christian political domination in the southwest."[82] The press release also complained that all those in the YCE leadership were Christians and wondered why the group failed to include Muslim Yoruba people in its leadership. After listing the names of key Yoruba Muslims that qualified for inclusion, the group concluded that what disqualified these Muslim leaders was "the agenda of the group for Christian proselytization hiding under the canopy of Yoruba irredentism."[83]

Some Christians in the Middle Belt, especially Benue, interpreted all the killing as a continuation of a jihad that radical Muslims have vowed to undertake. For example, the director of communication in Catholic dioceses in Makurdi, Rev. Father Moses Iorapuu, argued that grass for grazing had nothing to do with the killing.[84] Some also see the herdsmen's actions against the background of religious history: that it has been the jihadists' goal since the 1804 jihad of Uthman dan Fodio to conquer Benue and the Tiv people, who resisted their advances into the Middle East and the eastern part of Nigeria.[85] Thus they pointed to motives of religious cleansing and ethnic or expansionist tendencies.

Senior Christian military officers from the Middle Belt have played a role in the politics of religion and intergroup relations in the Middle Belt. Many of the Christian generals from the region, including Yakubu Danjuma (former army chief of staff) and Lawrence Onoja, have been united in their position that the Buhari administration was partial in its management of herdsman activities— in fact that the government was against Christians. Danjuma even went so far as to allege that the armed forces were deliberately killing Christians. The government and the army emphatically denied this charge.[86] Danjuma's opposition to the Buhari administration put him in the company of other generals who had other reasons to be opposed to the president, including the former president Obasanjo.

In June 2019, General Danjuma took his protest against General Buhari to the British Parliament. In a paper presented in the name of a group that called itself the Northern Christian Elders Forum, Danjuma, along with retired general Zamani Lekwot and a senior advocate of Nigeria, Solomon Asemota, accused President Muhammadu Buhari of pursuing a jihad or Islamization agenda and of not being serious about tackling insecurity arising from the Boko Haram insurgency and the herdsmen-farmer crises in the country. The paper, titled "Competing Ideologies of Democracy and Sharia in Nigeria; The Nuance Understating of the Drivers of the Conflict in Nigeria by Farmers and Herders," was presented to the All Party Parliamentary Group for International Freedom of Religion or Belief, UK Parliament, in June 2019.

In understanding the complaints of Christians in the northern parts of Nigeria about the incessant insecurity in the region, this paper is particularly important and worth discussing. In the paper, the group noted that President Buhari had, in pre-2015 comments, given reasons "why he could die for the course of Islam, why they could not be blackmailed into killing the sharia idea, why sharia must be spread all over Nigeria, why Boko Haram members should be given VIP treatment and not killed, and why Muslims should only vote for those who will promote Islam." The paper then gave a long history of instances when northern Muslims had tried variants of jihad against the Nigerian state, including the coups of January and July 1966, the Civil War of 1967–70, and the Maitatsine riots, which they said provided an excuse to attack and kill Ndigbo, especially shop owners, and loot their shops, along with the overthrow of Christian general Yakubu Gowon and a moderate Muslim president, Shehu Shagari.

It would appear that the government took the submission to the British All Party Parliamentary Group very seriously, as the Nigerian high commissioner in London, Justice George Oguntade, wrote two letters, one to Reverend Philip Mounstephen, a former secretary of the Church Missionary Society and head of the Independent Review of Foreign and Commonwealth Office Support for Persecuted Christians, and one to Baroness Berridge, the chair of the All Party Parliamentary Group for International Freedom of Religion or Belief. In the letter, Oguntade argued that allusions to the effect that Boko Haram terrorism served a government agenda against Christians were ridiculous and laughable.[87]

An individual whose position has been somewhat precarious is the vice president, Yemi Osinbajo, a Pentecostal Christian. Many Christians expected that he would be able to curtail excesses that have threatened the religion. Without mentioning any names, the head of Winners Chapel, David Oyedepo, described as a "fool" anyone occupying an office without making any impact.[88] Some expected him, as a legal practitioner of the highest level in the country, to address the problem in the courts. The fact that he is a pastor and the vice president has also been used by supporters of the government as an indication that the Buhari administration takes the concerns of Christians seriously. Indeed, the Nigerian high commissioner, Justice Oguntade, mentioned this in the letter above to the All Party Parliamentary Group. Some, however, believe that Osinbajo has not been able to strike a balance between his faith and his position in government, and that all he has been able to do is attend funerals, pay condolence visits, and promise that the government will "find the killers and punish them." In short, they think that he is helpless. In May 2018, the bishop of Gboko Catholic diocese, William Avenya, openly confronted him and bluntly accused him of subtle complicity in the attempt to Islamize Nigeria: he said, "a day is going to come when you as vice-president, the injustices in our land . . . when the issues and the records are raised, you too will bear the brunt of the problem. So, as a Christian, exonerate yourself from this situation."[89] Osinbajo took this opportunity to address the whole question of those who see his apparent silence as a subtle endorsement of Buhari's perceived ethnic agenda: he openly declared that he would rather resign from the office of vice president than compromise his faith or endorse injustice in any form.[90]

Many Christians have accused Buhari of openly skewing his appointments of heads of security and law enforcement agencies in the country in favor of Muslim Hausa/Fulanis, with the government sometimes showing blatant favoritism. For example, they claim that when two people, Babachir Lawal and Ayo Oke, were removed from their positions as secretary to the federal government and director of the National Intelligence Agency respectively, Babachir was replaced by his townsman, Boss Mustapha, while Ayo Oke, a Yoruba, was replaced by someone from the president's home state of Katsina.[91]

Some criticize the media for oversimplifying the herdsmen issue. For example, the federal minister for information sees the media's blaming of the Fulani as mischievous stereotyping that trivializes a problem with wider ramifications—that the "insurgency, terrorism and criminality is an overflow of regional and socio-political and economic crisis and conflicts raging in the region."[92] He thinks that the Fulani grazing crisis alone does not explain the violence: the huge amount of armaments, explosives, and devices that they are surreptitiously importing or smuggling into the country; the cattle rustling, kidnappings, and huge ransom payments; or various other criminal undertakings. A death sentence was passed on some Christians—Alex Amos, Alheri Phanuel, Holy Boniface, Jerry Gideon, and Jari Sabagi—for attacking three herdsmen and killing one of them, Adamu Buba, in June 2017.[93] The CAN immediately warned the Adamawa State government not to carry out this sentence, arguing that Fulani herdsmen had killed several hundred Christians without anybody being arrested for it.[94] Bishop Kukah seems to have addressed the issue of Islamization:

> We are not talking about Islamization here in terms of direct conversion or that we are dealing with people who genuinely are concerned about religion as such. We are dealing with people who are concerned about holding on to power by appealing to those base sentiment[s]. However, if you make an appointment on these lines, you leave people with no choice but to become conscious of certain identities. There is no doubt of the fact that today, Muslims need to save their religion from the clutches of politicians whose manipulation has neither improved the life of Muslims nor has it given Islam a good face as we all know.

He notes further:

> If those who want to Islamize Nigeria are serious, should we not see a sign from the states that are predominantly Muslim, where an attempt has been made to create an Islamic State? Zamfara was supposed to be the poster child of an Islamic state, but today it is the theatre of the worst violence in Nigeria and the worst social development indices, with the highest national poverty levels leveling at over 90 percent. The Emir of Kano spoke to these issues most eloquently. If this is what their Islamic state will look like, then I do not believe the Muslims themselves will want it.[95]

Views from Christian Ibos have been largely similar to those of southwestern Christians. A prominent Ibo clergyman, Archbishop Emmanuel Chukwuma, specifically noted that the Fulani herdsmen issue was a "time-bomb" whose explosion was imminent because of the kid gloves with which the Buhari government was handling it.[96] The archbishop put aside religion and drew parallels with the activities of the Indigenous People of Biafra when he noted:

> The members of the Indigenous People of Biafra (IPOB) were agitating for their rights but were declared terrorists. It is unfair. This is what I meant

by selective negligence. These herdsmen are killing people and you are talking about giving them colonies; they don't deserve it. If any governor tries it in the South East, we will be out for him. This is a Christian zone, and nobody can use colonies or ranches to Islamize us. Our IPOB is keeping quiet but if we are pushed to the wall, they will defend us. If [herdsmen] come to this area with their nonsense, we shall bring out IPOB to face them.[97]

His interpretation of the reason for setting up cattle colonies was poignant: "By setting up these colonies, they will gradually and indirectly influence the areas with Islamic populace. . . . Some of them are Fulani herdsmen who have come for real jihad and what we are seeing today is Jihad in disguise. . . . The truth is that we can never be Islamized in this country. If they want to Islamize Nigeria, we will also Christianize the country. . . . The government should be careful. They seem to be taking sides with the Fulanis."[98]

In a counterreaction, the JNI advised CAN that it should register as a political party if it wanted to test its popularity. The secretary of the group, Khalid Aliyu, accused the Christian body of "unnecessarily overheating the polity": "Why is the whole herdsmen issue heightened now (i.e. 2018)? Simply CAN is unnecessarily overheating the polity because 2019 is around the corner."[99] Aliyu said the "herdsmen debacle" is a product CAN uses as a franchise to perpetrate evil, as witnessed in the Boko Haram tale. He noted, "The herdsmen debacle—it must be understood that this is a coinage mischievously invented by CAN over time and its biased errand boys among media practitioners to stereotype an ethnic group and achieve a preplanned agenda."[100] He added that CAN is a problem to the country rather than a solution. He alleged that CAN had devised a new approach of destabilizing Nigeria to achieve its agenda: "selective amnesia," or only reporting issues that involve Christians, due to its "height of enmity against the Muslims and Islam."[101] Another Muslim group agreed that CAN tried to use the herdsmen's situation as a means to perpetrate evil:

Is CAN not supposedly representing all Christians? If not so, why forget to mention the gruesome attack in Rivers? Is it because no Muslim is involved, and therefore it's not a crime? Talking about the killings in Benue state, why did Asake remain mute on the arming of thousands of ethnic militia by the Benue state government (as reported by some sections of the media), an act which is seen as a prelude to the most unfortunate spate of horrendous experiences in the state. To put the record straight, JNI condemns the killings of innocent souls wherever they happen and whoever is involved. JNI also condemns the generalization of criminals as representatives of the whole, thus leading to unjust stereotyping and name-calling. CAN and other Christian leaders such as Bishop Mathew Hassan Kukah, Pastors Oyedepo, Suleiman and recently El Buba should not take the Nigerian Muslims' patience for foolishness, as their hate speeches are becoming provocative and outlandish. Hypothetically, as a religious body, they are expected to be part of the solution rather than the problem they have now become. The Muslims know that "Nigeria is secular" sloganeering is mere mendacity seeing that the government and its policies are more tilted towards Christianity and Christian signs and practices. So, CAN should free us from the hypocritical secularity claim.[102]

The Miyetti Allah Cattle Breeders Association of Nigeria did not necessarily support the establishment of cattle colonies. The chairman of the group in Anambra, Alhaji Sadiq Gidado, said that such a thing was unnecessary in his state because of the harmonious relationship between its herdsmen and farmers. He also condemned the practice: "In the South East, the proposed cattle colonies can't work; you cannot just take somebody's land and give to another person to conduct his own business; it is not right."[103]

Fulanization, Islamization, Professionalization, and Violence

By the end of the first quarter of 2019, the link between religion, ethnicity, and professionalization or land use had become profoundly serious, with both Nigerians and even external commentators giving apocalyptic warnings about the future of the country.[104] Although the roots of the issues here are much longer, they became more distinct shortly after President Buhari won a second term in office and the administration came up with the policy of Ruga settlement, which it thought would resolve the issue of herdsmen-farmer clashes across the country. Under this scheme, the federal government would acquire lands from states that would be used for the settlement of herders.

Some Nigerians supported the initiative, seeing it as a way of addressing the problem significantly, if not permanently. They argued that it could even bring greater intergroup harmony. Perhaps unsurprisingly, those with this opinion were largely herders, most operating under the group Miyetti Allah. The group pointed to the fundamental human right of Nigerians to move and settle freely across the country and practice their vocations. To drive home the point, the group drew a parallel with people of other ethnic groups living and practicing their vocation in the northern parts of the country.

Others were opposed to the entire idea, seeing it as an attempt by the Buhari administration to Islamize and Fulanize Nigeria. Former President Obasanjo delivered a public lecture at the Cathedral Church of St Paul's Anglican Church, Oleh, in Delta State, in which he accused the Buhari government of trying to Fulanize Nigeria.[105] Pan-Yoruba and pan-Ibo groups also opposed the idea, with the former head of the pan-Yoruba organization the Odua People's Congress, Gani Adams, seeking an audience with the US embassy to discuss the fear of war in Nigeria, while more acerbic criticism, colored by politics, came from the former minister for aviation, Femi Fani-Kayode, representing the opposition party in the southwest.[106]

Then there were those, including the national president of the All Farmers Association of Nigeria, Kabir Ibrahim, who thought that Ruga was a good idea wrongly presented. They roundly criticized the decision of the federal government to undertake the step without due consultation with the state governments and other stakeholders, especially as the federal government has no control over what has been constitutionally placed under the state governors. A subsection of this group also argued that the entire idea was not new and that it had been practiced during the First Republic by notable politicians like Obafemi Awolowo. A representative of this group is the national president of the All Farmers Association of Nigeria, Kabir Ibrahim.

At the center of the greatest controversy about Ruga was the president, especially after he won a second term in office. Many people focused on what he stood for, whether he had a hidden or blatant agenda, and what it meant for the nation. Some thought that the president, being of Fulani ancestry, was determined to advance a Fulani agenda, as evidenced by appointing Fulani people as strategic staff members and using kid gloves when fighting criminal Fulani herdsmen. The government has persistently denied this. Also at the center of this controversy are the multiple layers of identity and the zero-sum nature of the relationships between them. At any point in time, any actor in the controversy has three identities that can be flagged—ethnicity, religion, and profession—each of which offers justification for violent extremism.

Another major ethnoreligious issue that has emerged is the alleged presence of ISIS in some parts of the southwest, particularly in the Oke-Ogun area of Oyo State. Although there had been rumors of the presence of "foreign-looking" people attacking farmland and killing innocent farmers in the area, the first formal allegation of ISIS presence in the region was made by Gani Adams, the *are ona kakanfo* of Yorubaland, in August 2020.[107] The Yoruba generalissimo categorically stated that the "terrorists are already in the Lusada thick forest with over 500 sophisticated bikes loaded with current fighting equipment that could destroy a nation." He also raised the issue of the allegations against the head of the Muslim Rights Concern (MURIC), Professor Isiaq Akintola, by the person monitoring terrorists in Mali that ISIS gave MURIC money to recruit for them in the southwest. Adams further called on the governors in the southwest to come together as a matter of urgency to find a way to avoid this calamity. He also warned residents living in Ibarapa, Oke-Ogun, Saki, and Igbo Ora to be extra cautious and for people to come and apply for gun licenses. He was emphatic that al-Qaeda and ISIS were already camping in southwestern Nigeria with plans to carry out deadly massacres on Yoruba citizens.

The coordinator of defence media operations, John Enenche, had once said in a press conference,

> Our attention was being drawn to the fact that terrorists from other zones are coming here. There is no doubt that we already have that challenge as far back as when the war in Libya was declared, and even in Iraq. Have we not captured foreigners among the people that have been terrorizing us in this country? Recently, we captured some in Niger state from our neighboring country. Where are they coming from? Why do we have ISWAP here now? Was ISWAP indigenous to Nigeria? No! It's just like a wakeup call, which is readily welcome. All the security agencies have that at the back of their plan and they factor it in implementation. The general public should not be afraid of that at all. It's not a new thing. it's already in our schedule of activity.[108]

A number of issues make this development important for religious violence in Nigeria. First, it is coming with the backdrop of the warning by the commander of the US Special Operations Command, Africa, Dagvin Anderson, that al-Qaeda and the Islamic State are silently taking over northwestern Nigeria and also expanding to other parts of southestern Nigeria. The warning and the alleged sighting of foreign individuals in a part of the southwest that has a long history of tension between Fulani herders and the indigenous population can only imply something sinister for harmony in the region. Second, the allegation that MURIC, an organization headed by a Yoruba Muslim, is involved in any arrangement with foreign bodies against the people has serious implications for intergroup relations. Third, the ease with which it was dismissed by the security forces gave many the impression that the allegation was not properly investigated before it was dismissed. In a climate where there are already mutual suspicions, this does not solidify confidence. While at the time of writing the validity of the presence of al-Qaeda and ISIS in southwestern

Nigeria is not confirmed, the implications of such confirmation will be serious indeed for national security.

Conclusion

The vicissitudes of colonial division, which made most African countries multiethnic, introduced major complexities for postindependence intergroup relations, and religion inevitably became entangled in the complex web of identity crises that bedeviled many of the countries. To be added to the catalog of "us" versus "them" that this evokes are the complex issues of the personal religious convictions of the leadership, the politics of natural resource governance, the intrigues of party politics, and other socioeconomic issues. Because of the extent of its diversity, this has become particularly difficult for Nigeria. The country's distinction of having one of the largest populations of Christians and Muslims coexisting has underlined many challenges. In this chapter, I have argued that the primary factors in most religious violence in Nigeria have been domestic socioeconomic and political issues. Successive governments have had to contend with different issues and have addressed them with different approaches. The zero-sum relationship between Christians and Muslims has also meant that each has interpreted the actions of successive governments in power in the way that best suits them. Under the present arrangement, most Christians and their organization (CAN) are of the strong opinion that the Buhari administration favors Muslims and that some of the activities undertaken by herdsmen across the country and the unfolding developments in some parts of Kaduna State could only be taken with the tacit endorsement of the government in power. This, as would be expected, has been denied by the Muslims. But religion, in its links to violence, has also brought some other special considerations, especially the issue of ethnicity and land. Here, mobile populations want lands allocated to them in a country where people have a fixed concept of the resource. This and many other issues make the economic dimensions of religious violence the focus of discussion, which is the subject of chapter 7.

7. THE ECONOMICS OF RELIGIOUS
VIOLENCE IN NIGERIA

We have seen . . . in recent years, how corruption directly fueled the terrorist insurgency in the North-East. And how in turn that has led to one of gravest humanitarian disasters in the world. —Vice President YEMI OSINBAJO, "Corruption Responsible for Insurgency in North East"

The whole thing is economy manifesting in religion; those people protesting are doing so because of economic reasons and the elites in government responding are also doing it for economic reasons. For example, the government can eradicate Boko Haram if they want to; but because of the money they make from it, they don't want to. —Participant in focus group discussion in Abuja

A comprehensive look at economics is crucial to understanding the politics of religious violence in Nigeria. One school of thought, with a significant following, sees many of the uprisings—especially key ones like the Maitatsine riots and the Boko Haram insurgency—as manifestations of the economic deprivation of marginalized sections of the community. Moreover, exploring the cost of violence to the country and its immediate neighbors helps us appreciate the ramifications of the problem, even if sometimes some of these are not easily quantifiable. And waging war against insurgent movements and the bringing of riots and protests under control has economic consequences; indeed, allegations have been made that fiscal mismanagement and graft in weapons purchases are a major cause of the prolongation of the Boko Haram insurgency.

Most violence over religion in Nigeria is rooted in disagreements over faith, with leaders of movements and some followers exploiting economic considerations as opportunities to spread violence. Religious violence in the country has negatively affected the local and national economies, further affecting the abilities of locals to contribute to those economies. Also, excuses to fight violence have created their own economy, which has created servicing structures that run contrary to the national interest.

The Economy and the Causes of Religious Violence

Academic writings abound on the link between the economy and religious radicalization, with most focusing on how economic deprivation has been a factor in the outbreak of religious violence.[1] In a study on the subject, for example, Thomas Straubhaar noted that "religiousness and religious violence are the consequence of specific economic, political, or social conditions but are more importantly the result of strategic goals of religious clubs and their efficiency in organizing and mobilizing their members."[2] The standard Marxist explanation sees religion as functioning primarily to fill the void created by economic deprivation. But this is a grossly inadequate account of the relationship between religion and economics (or other spheres of life for that matter), for it ignores the phenomenological integrity of religion as a meaning-framing/giving reality, a system of meaning that provides what Peter Berger calls "a plausibility structure" for its adherents.[3] Rather than understanding religion as a reactionary phenomenon, this Weberian approach interprets religion as serving as the basis or foundation upon which people build their normative expectations of life and society.[4] People draw upon their religious ideas and beliefs to understand how politics, economics, and the government should work or function; when these vectors of society fail to function as expected, people are bound to react angrily and even violently. In this case, religiously grounded responses cannot be interpreted as reactionary but as punitively expressive.

In Nigeria, we can gauge the economic motivation of radical groups by comparing cases where the violence was spontaneous and where it was carried out by formal radical groups. In spontaneous religious riots, economic motivation was a major factor for many participants, who saw them as opportunities to loot shops, with shops of Ibo motor spare parts traders in some key northern Nigerian towns the most vulnerable targets. Chapter 2 categorizes them as "opportunistic radicals."

At a broad level, it can be said that violence over religion became a more common feature in the 1980s when the country's economic situation began its first plunge downward. The 1970s had witnessed the positive effects of the oil boom, but toward the end of the decade the military administration of General Olusegun Obasanjo embarked on economic measures to tighten loopholes and avoid wastage. The economic situation had declined further by the time the Shagari administration assumed office, not further helped by the corruption and profligacy of the administration. From this time onward, economic deprivation became a feature of Nigeria's life, one that was waiting to be exploited by any coherent rebellion.

Also important in the link between economic considerations and the emergence of religious violence, especially the Boko Haram insurgency, is the patrimonialism that has pervaded Nigeria's prebendal politics.[5] According to Mohammed Usman:

> Politics and undue emphasis on the acquisition of power primarily for access to resources and wealth play a role [in violence]. . . . The unabashed contest for political patronage by various social groups gives the impetus to engage in acts that are inimical to the interests of other contestants and groups. Politicians aggrandize wealth in the office with the aim, amongst other things, of "settling" members of their "constituency." Therefore, funds designated for various public works are embezzled, leaving infrastructure to decay to the stage they become un-repairable and contracts have to be awarded at highly inflated prices to enable contractors to pay kickbacks. Schools, hospitals, roads are in such a state of disrepair that everyday life has become hectic for the common citizen. The hope of redemption by religious men becomes an attractive alternative and any call to change the course of decay and reformation is keenly heeded to, as many believe the "prophets" who shall raise the nation to greater heights have come at last.[6]

Finally, religious violence arguably came because of the climate change that has resulted in the shrinking of the Lake Chad basin and simultaneously reduced economic opportunities coming from it. Indeed, the Lake Chad dimension in the cause of the Boko Haram insurgency has attracted its own array of scholars.[7] A crucial factor in the insurrection has been the desertification of the Lake Chad basin. Through climate change, overuse, and conflict, the basin has shrunk about 90 percent since the 1960s. The attendant displacement of up to 5 million people from the countries in the basin has been identified as a major cause of the war.

There are also scholars who have identified oil as a major factor in Boko Haram. For example, Tochukwu Omenm argues that "the attack on the Nigerian oil exploration team in the Lake Chad basin, and the continuous exploitation of oil and gas by Chad, Niger, and Cameroon" are the main motivations for the Boko Haram insurgency.[8] Although the article's argument that the economic motivation played a more important role than religious factors is less convincing, it succeeds in offering strong economic motivations for the insurgency.

Having noted all these general links between economic deprivation and religious conflicts in Nigeria, we need to be cautious in pointing to deep economic considerations as the actual causes of some of the early uprisings. Indeed, going specifically into the causes of religious violence, it will be difficult to draw any direct economic connections to the two major insurrections that occurred: the Maitatsine riots and Boko Haram. The leaders of both rebellions cited government corruption and the attendant economic hardship as among the reasons people should repudiate the government in power, but otherwise nothing economic was in the listed causes of the protests. As noted in chapters 2 and 5, the leaders of both revolts identified poverty in the land as one of the reasons why the population should revolt against the government, and apart from this peripheral linkage, economic issues were not among the links between religion and violence. The main causes of the two insurrections were religious. Indeed, both Mohammed Marwa and Mohammed Yusuf, but more especially Yusuf, assured their followers that they should be ready for more privations, and neither promised an economic boom here on earth. The leaders in both cases had strong convictions in the religious justifications of their respective causes and were determined to fight them through. Undeniably, there were economic dynamics. Both leaders in the uprisings had access to wealth and influence through contacts with those in the corridors of power. Their determination not to stay under a government where corruption had created economic problems was a causal factor for the uprising and insurgency in both cases. Boko Haram has taken money for ransom and has been involved in other lucrative illegal activities. But again, these only became factors after the rebellion had taken off and the group needed resources to expand it. Thus, in looking at economic consideration as a cause of both the Maitatsine and Boko Haram conflicts, scholars seem to have been looking in the wrong direction. The error here could have been influenced by the role economic considerations played in the groups' initial recruitment of followers.

But a link between economics and ethnoreligious issues is clear in the conflicts in the Middle Belt between the largely Muslim Fulani herdsmen and the mainly Christian farmers. It would be inaccurate to tag these as mainly religious conflicts; in this case, economic considerations were the main cause of conflicts that later attained religious dimensions. In particular, as shown in chapter 6, the economic importance of land was the main cause, and religion and ethnicity were just attendant issues. But if there are doubts about the role economic considerations played in the initial causes of some of the religious violence in Nigeria, the same cannot be said about the role economics played in the motivations of people to join various uprisings once they had begun.

Economic Considerations and the Prolongation of Religious Violence

Generally, however, the economy became an issue after the conceptualization of the initial idea. In assessing this dynamic, however, broad generalizations may not be particularly helpful, as there are issues that create distinctions in different cases. In the two most important cases of violent extremism in Nigeria, the Maitatsine riots and Boko Haram, looking at the economic situation prevailing during those periods offers some explanation of the motivations for joining. In 1980, when the Maitatsine riots took place, Nigeria's economy had started to show signs of strain due to dependence on oil and the effects of the profligacy of the ruling National Party of Nigeria. However, in most of the areas affected by the insurrection, the extent of poverty was already quite remarkable, with lots of people homeless and many young children and youths both out of school and jobless. Those who took part in the Maitatsine riots were mostly young and poor men, artisans and low-paid workers displaced by the oil boom; many had migrated to Kano in search of Islamic education. Their social and economic marginalization made them vulnerable to Marwa's revolutionary message and exclusivist religious outlook. The report of the investigative panel set up after the riots by the federal government alluded to the role played by economic factors in the spread of the insurgency. The spontaneous nature of the insurrection and the short duration, compared to that of Boko Haram, also support the thinking that random economic consideration was an important factor in the spread of the insurrection.

The role of economic considerations in the recruitment of people for the Boko Haram insurgency also appears very significant. While, no doubt, some of those who joined did so because they were sufficiently indoctrinated or found themselves located in the region at the time the rebellion started, many also joined because they had become disenchanted with the government due to economic deprivation. Also, as noted in chapter 5, Boko Haram lulled many vulnerable people into the fold through loans whose terms turned out to be impossible to meet. Having fallen into the trap, many of them found it difficult to leave the group. In the ethnoreligious crisis in the Middle Belt, the economic situation of those who joined each side is somewhat complex. While many joined to protect their group's economic interest, whether herdsmen or farmers, each group's identity was already interwoven with issues of religion (see chapter 6).

Wars generate their own economies, and the war against the Boko Haram/ ISWAP insurgents created its own complex economic web, from which insurgents and members of the Nigerian security forces alike have made considerable financial gains. It turns out that Boko Haram has sustained its activities in part through international trade in smoked fish and red pepper since around 2015, and that Nigerian security forces are also involved.[9] Before the emergence of Boko Haram, the World Food Programme estimated that the combined fish and red pepper trades contributed 28 billion CFA francs (US$48 million) to the economy of Niger, with most of this coming from exports to Nigeria. The red pepper (or red gold) farming and trade was estimated to employ over 300,000 people.[10] The insurgents took strategic steps to control and reorder trade in both products. Because the structures of both the production and trade had collapsed, the ISWAP leadership reorganized the structures and invited back those who had been moved to internally displaced person (IDP) camps to come back and recommence their work under their watch. The Nigerian military have been allegedly involved in this through the collection of money from seizing of items.[11]

Nigerians reacted to the downward plunge in their economic well-being in ways linked to religious violence. Many people, unaware of any other ways of meeting the pressure created by the change in the economic tide, turned to religion. But the economic deprivation that is most relevant to the politics of radicalized violence is the vulnerability and exclusion it has created for youths in the country. Many youths, unable to make a living, became tools in the hands of those with hidden agendas. Homeless youths in northern Nigeria, popularly known as *almajiris*, are key participants in most of the cases of religious violence across the whole country.[12]

Economic Consequences of Religious Violence

Once they start, conflicts involving religion have been known to leave strings of economic consequences in their wake. Nigeria's religious conflicts have left a series of economic consequences, many of which have become more impactful because of their association with preexisting socioeconomic challenges in the country. In their manifestations, however, consequences have varied in their patterns and effects. Because the Maitatsine riots were somewhat spontaneous and took part in several locations over a specific period of time, the economic implications of the group's actions were comparatively limited. Indeed, they were limited largely to the group's physical destruction of property; places that were destroyed during military actions; the shutdown of businesses and the inability of people to work during periods of unrest; and the shops and properties looted (whether by members of the group or opportunists).

The economic impacts of the persistent clashes between the military and the Shi'ites is somewhat difficult to quantify. The relationship between the Shi'ites and some of their neighbors, especially around Kaduna, has not been particularly friendly, and a few of the neighbors complained that their economic activities had been affected by what they said was the domineering behavior of the Shi'ites, including putting in place other laws apart from those established by the government.[13] But the physical destruction of properties in the various riots in Abuja, Kaduna, and other places was far more serious; also important are the legal costs of the various litigations between the government and the Shi'ites and the cost to the government of holding El-Zakzaky and his wife in custody.

Unsurprisingly, the religious violence of the Boko Haram insurgents has been the most costly. Focusing on Pakistan, Arshad Ali pointed out results of the insurgent activities of Boko Haram when he notes that "the burden on a state managing a terrorism problem may be enormous, serious and unmanageable and has severe consequences on its economic outlook":

- Increased costs of maintaining law and order, including military, paramilitary, police, and associated judicial costs.
- Costs for Humanitarian aid to conflict-affected people, including IDPs and refugees.
- Fiscal costs, including lost revenue and funding programs for growth and to rebuild society.
- Economic costs, including reduced investment, a flight of capital, and lower growth rate.
- Social costs, such as reduced living standards, including health care and education, and higher vulnerability. Conflict often harms the poor the most.
- Cultural costs, including severe and long-lasting damage to social conventions and structures.[14]

Ali also notes that economic costs also include issues like

a fall in production and a related drop in exports; lower domestic sales; and disruptions of international markets. Shift from tradable to non-tradable sectors, due to, e.g., the undermining of banks and failure of transport system, increased foreign borrowing and aid. Sharp fall in government capital formation and private investment, due to budgetary restrictions and increased uncertainty. Budget deficit due to increased spending, the increased share allocated to the military, making it difficult to sustain social and economic expenditure. Heavy human costs: increased infant mortality rates, deteriorating nutrition, health, and educational standards, as a result of falling entitlements and war-induced famines. Heavy development costs due to the destruction of capital and reduced investment.[15]

The Nigerian government has statistics specific to the country. The former army chief, Tukur Buratai, estimated the economic impact of Boko Haram activities on the northeast at US$9 billion (N274.5b).[16] General Buratai said that the greatest impact was on Borno State, estimated at US$5.9 billion (N180b), and that Boko Haram damaged 95 percent of the 400,000 houses there; and the loss of agricultural production in the northeast caused by Boko Haram activities amounted to US$3.5 billion (N107b).[17] In Yobe State, the militants destroyed almost 1 million properties, including more than 986,000 homes, 5,335 classrooms, and over 200 health facilities and hospitals, according to Yerima Saleh, the permanent secretary of the Yobe State Ministry of Reconstruction, Rehabilitation, and Resettlement.[18] More than 1,600 water facilities, 726 power stations and transformers, and 800 public services structures, including police stations and prisons, have also been destroyed.[19] "The quantum of destruction caused by insurgents is monumental, resulting in a serious humanitarian crisis. . . . The destruction has rendered 22 out of the 27 local government council areas uninhabitable."[20] Schools were primary targets, where an estimated 600 teachers were killed. In the health and nutrition sector, of the 788 reportedly damaged facilities, 45 percent, including twenty-one hospitals, were destroyed.[21] For a region with an already weak medical infrastructure, this was a major cause of concern. In the housing sector, it was estimated that 431,842 housing units (68 percent) were destroyed, most of them in Borno. The estimated cost of damage to the housing sector stands at US$12 billion.[22]

The most important impact of Boko Haram, of course, is the loss of life. Estimates put the deaths at 20,000, at least. Although the figure of 100,000 deaths given by the governor of Borno State, Kashim Shetima, is no doubt an exaggeration, figures toward 30,000 may not be completely misplaced, and the Global Terrorism Index put the number of deaths in 2014 alone at 6,644.[23] The conflict has also displaced 2.3 million people and has affected 14.8 million. Boko Haram's scorched-earth policy has also further affected the economy of the concerned areas.

As agriculture is the economic mainstay of these areas, the prolonged conflict has prevented farmers from cultivating their land for several years. Vast amounts of arable land are lying fallow. Access to fertilizer is limited because it is also used by Boko Haram to manufacture IEDs. The planting of some agricultural products like sorghum and maize was discouraged in the theaters of conflict because they can hide insurgents, even though these are staple crops. Along the course of the Yobe River and the shores of Lake Chad, Boko Haram has banned the tomato and pepper trade as well as fishing and the fish trade since early 2015. The Nigerian government estimated the loss to the agricultural sector at US$3.7 billion.

In the three most affected states (Adamawa, Borno, and Yobe), the conflict impacted the economic livelihoods of the population. Before the conflict, women were able to manage and run businesses and get to the market to sell farm products, but they can no longer do so for safety reasons. Men were involved in trading, unskilled labor, masonry, artisanry, electrical work, and farming, but they stopped for fear of their safety. They effectively lost their livelihoods. Of all of these, farming is the endeavor most affected by the activities of the insurgent Boko Haram and the government's responses to it.[24]

In terms of livelihood and employment, labor force participation was concentrated in agricultural activities (43 percent) and the largely informal, non-agricultural sector (39 percent). With the onset of the conflict, the proportion of labor participation in agriculture declined to 27 percent in 2012–13, as the continuing conflict limited people's access to land for crops and livestock, and curtailed agricultural activities significantly.[25]

The conflict severely affected food production and agricultural productivity, particularly in the three most affected states. The hostilities and conflict resulted in numerous casualties and continued population displacements, preventing households from pursuing their typical livelihoods and interrupting trade and market functioning. In February 2016, markets were closed in Borno and Yobe states by the authorities, including the cattle market in Maiduguri (one of the biggest in West Africa), to curb transactions with Boko Haram, which resulted in food price increases. Restrictions on food availability and access to farms and markets in Borno, Yobe, and Adamawa generated localized crises of acute food insecurity during the lean period.[26]

The timing of most Boko Haram attacks had further impacts on agricultural production. For example, in Gombe, the 2013 attacks came just before harvest; and people returned to their farms to find their crops further destroyed by animals. In 2014 and 2015, farming was completely insecure. The insecurity of farmland due to fear of attacks or IEDs and unexploded ordinance also meant another reason for low harvests. So 2016 was the first harvest in four years, but with seeds and farm equipment lost or destroyed plus an overall lack of capital, it was a small one. Many women took in those displaced from places that were even more insecure, adding to their households. The deaths of many victims further meant that many women, in addition to caring for their own children, took in unaccompanied and separated children whose parents had been lost or killed, and they were struggling to cater to them all. Some women were looking after grandchildren in addition to children, elderly or sick parents, and/or other relatives alone. The cost of renting land has also increased, as people did not have money and wanted to get as much as possible for their land: what used to be N5,000 increased to N15,000.[27] Some roads in the three states were also blocked either by the insurgents or by the military, further resulting in the reduction or complete loss of livelihoods.

In some communities, such as Simari in Jere Local Government Area, a significant number of the men were economic migrants who sent money back from other parts of the country to support their families, leaving women responsible for managing their family, household, and finances. Husbands who hadn't left were not always able to fulfill their previous breadwinning roles, as their businesses had also been affected. Places most touched were Kaga, Dikwa, and other towns in the Jere Local Government Area of Adamawa State.[28]

Also, since the commencement of the operation, foreign direct investment (FDI) in Nigeria has reduced quite significantly. Indeed, according to the World Investment Report for 2013, FDI flows into Nigeria dropped by 21.3 percent in just one year—from US$8.9 billion in 2011 to US$7 billion in 2012. The economic challenges have been increased by the lack of insurance coverage for victims of terrorist attacks.[29]

Banking activities have also been significantly affected. The decision by many to leave the region affected the profitability of businesses in the region. The attendant reduction of economic activities eventually resulted in banks closing branches, while those who retained their jobs were seeking to be transferred to safer areas. Once the "banks and other businesses decide to pack up and move elsewhere, it leaves the region in a state of economic depletion, and one that won't easily be regained."[30]

As is discussed later in this chapter, some in the military have benefited economically from the Boko Haram conflict. As a September 2017 study carried out for Feed the Future, a US government global hunger and food security initiative, has noted, "not only has the conflict given the military a position of significance and power . . . but levels of funding are seen as not matching the quality of guns and other equipment used by soldiers and there are stories of the military using tractors to relocate tanks. Money is seen as going to the top brass rather than being seen on the field."[31]

The insurgent activities of Boko Haram have negatively affected the productive capacity, employment, and livelihoods of over 6 million people in the northeast. Studies by the federal government and the international community have shown that the six states have been unevenly and differently affected: "Adamawa, Borno, and Yobe have experienced significant physical destruction and massive movements of displaced persons, which undermined their local economies and livelihoods."[32]

In terms of macroeconomic and fiscal effects, it is noted that before 2010, the performance of the northeastern economy continuously lagged behind the national average and deteriorated further between 2011 and 2015, as measured by GDP, inflation, and food prices. It is estimated that the region suffered an accumulated output loss of N1.66 trillion (US$8.3 billion).[33] Borno suffered from the largest loss, as output fell by US$3.54 billion. At the regional level, prices for all items rose by 5.4 percent annually from 2011 to 2015, while prices for food items rose by 7.5 percent annually. Prices for food and all items rose in four states, except in Bauchi and Taraba.[34]

Looking at the effects on the private, trade, and financial sectors, first, physical destruction affected the private sector by undermining the operation of small and medium-sized enterprises and open-air (street) markets. Markets were also regularly attacked, and the army also closed some markets for security reasons (to avoid attacks or to disrupt supplies to Boko Haram). As of December 2015, most markets in Borno had minimal or no activity or were significantly disrupted, with limited activities. In Yobe, around half of the markets had minimal or no activity and the other half have reduced activity. The situation markedly improved in Adamawa between October and December 2015, with most markets having normal activities, except in northeastern Adamawa, where markets faced significant disruption because of insurgent activities. The economy was also significantly affected by reduced connectivity as people fled their villages, and others were isolated. Trade has been disrupted as mobility of humans, goods, and services is curtailed by damaged infrastructure, continued insecurity, and closed borders. Trade had long been strong in the northeastern region, and its contribution to the national economy was especially pronounced in Borno, Yobe, and Adamawa. The volume of trade severely diminished as all the major trade routes became inaccessible. Traders from all over the country have taken alternative (longer) trade routes to reach Maiduguri, negatively affecting the roads and bridges in the states of the alternative routes.

Most households depending on the income from other occupations (traders, shop owners, artisans, etc.) lacked access to infrastructure, tools, and most importantly customers with sufficient purchasing power.

The economic situation of IDPs is dire as they lack regular income. Specifically, IDP households used to earn their income from farming, but lost access to their land or any land when they were displaced. The only IDPs still able to earn a living appeared to be local government employees. Large-scale displacement also caused significant stress for the host communities and family members supporting IDPs, as more than 90 percent of IDPs lived in host communities with relatives or friends or in accommodations they rented or could use free of charge. Competition for jobs also put a strain on the host communities. Jobs were scarce in the region, and IDPs often ended up competing with locals also desperately looking for work or income-generation opportunities.

The Boko Haram insurgency hurt economic activities in the Lake Chad basin. Even before the Boko Haram crisis, "the Lake Chad region was one of the poorest in the world, with high demographic growth and vulnerability to extreme weather and climate change."[35] This "fragility was heightened by its position as a climatic, cultural, and geopolitical intersection between West Africa and Central Africa, dry Africa and wet Africa."[36] Climate change has shrunk the lake by up to 90 percent since the 1960s. The fishing industry in Lake Chad, where the borders of Nigeria, Niger, Chad, and Cameroon meet, had especially suffered, with the fish shortage being felt for hundreds of miles within each country. Nonetheless, the region was becoming a beneficiary of gradual urbanization, where "the two N'djaména and Maiduguri metropolises, other cities such as Maroua, Garoua, Yola, and Gombe, and a growing number of towns and market towns—powered a buoyant system of generally informal, regional, and even cross-border trade."[37]

The economic impacts on the neighboring countries have also been pronounced, with Cameroon bearing the brunt of the damage. The far northern region had contributed 20 percent to Cameroon's national GDP, but it has been the most affected and now contributes a very negligible percentage, according to the minister of economy, planning, and regional development, Emmanuel Nganou Djoumessi. Tourism has also been affected: "Waza National Park, once

TABLE 7.1 Overall Recovery and Peace Building Needs by Component (US$ Million)

	Adamawa	Borno	Yobe	Gombe	Taraba	Bauchi	Federal/ Regional	Total
Peace building/ social cohesion	27.5	37.8	22.5	13.6	19.4	23.9	5.7	150.5
Infrastructure and social services	594.9	3,933.3	668.3	129.1	144.9	202.9	94.7	6,040.1
Economic recovery	37.6	68.8	30.7	22.3	27.7	41.4	245	473.5
Total	660	4,040	721.5	164.9	192	268.2	345.4	6,664.1

Source: World Bank Group. 2015. North-East Nigeria Recovery and Peace Building Assessment: Synthesis Report. World Bank, Abuja, Nigeria. © World Bank. https://openknowledge.worldbank.org /handle/10986/25791 License: CC BY 3.0 IGO.

TABLE 7.2 Overall Recovery and Peace Building Needs by Component (US$ Million)

	Adamawa	Borno	Yobe	Gombe	Taraba	Bauchi	Federal/ Regional	Total
Safe and voluntary return of IDPs	9	11.3	7.5	5.2	7.1	8.6	0	48.7
Reconciliation, peace building, and community cohesion	3.7	4.7	3	1.9	2.8	3.5	0	19.5
Local governance and citizen engagement	9.3	11.9	7.5	4.9	7.1	8.8	0.2	49.7
Community security, justice, human rights, mine action, and small arms control	5.6	9.8	4.6	1.7	2.5	3.5	.6	32.6
Total	27.5	37.8	22.5	13.6	19.4	23.9	5.7	150

Source: North-East Nigeria: Recovery and Peace Building Assessment, Federal Republic of Nigeria.

TABLE 7.3 Overall Recovery and Peace Building Needs by Component (US$ Million)

	Adamawa	Borno	Yobe	Gombe	Taraba	Bauchi	Federal/Regional	Total
Energy	31.9	15.9	3.3	N/A	3.4	N/A	92.5	147
Environment	10.6	235.9	15.9	15.6	34.4	2.7	N/A	315.1
Information and communications technology	N/A	N/A	N/A	N/A	N/A	N/A	N/A	272.1
Public buildings	40.3	295.9	22.7	2.7	5.8	6.7	N/A	374.1
Transport	74.5	337.5	126.7	37	N/A	N/A	N/A	575.8
Water and sanitation	25.9	115.3	17.2	3	4.7	5.8	N/A	171.9
Education	83	513.6	77.1	6.8	17.4	23.5	N/A	721.4
Health and nutrition	50.6	481.7	86.2	4	12.7	29.3	2.2	666.7
Private housing	15.7	1,097.4	46.6	1.8	2.2	0.7	N/A	1,164.4
Social protection	93.8	180.3	69.6	34.3	30.6	91.1	N/A	499.5
Agriculture	141.1	485.4	170	18.5	29.7	36.6	N/A	881.4
Community infrastructure	27.4	174.4	33	5.4	4.1	6.5	N/A	250.8
Total	594.9	3,933.3	668.3	129.1	144.9	202.9	94.7	6,040.1

Source: North-East Nigeria: Recovery and Peace Building Assessment, Federal Republic of Nigeria.

a major tourist attraction, has lost its former glory, as safari tourists now face a 50 percent chance of being kidnapped," according to Nouma Joseph, the commander of a specialized military unit tasked with fighting Boko Haram.[38] Indeed, the 2013 kidnapping of a French priest visiting the park took an almost immediate toll on tourism, in which French visitors figure prominently; the French ambassador to Cameroon cautioned French citizens to leave the far northern region. (Cameroon later negotiated the release of the hostages.)

The customs department in the region used to collect about $8.64 million per year, said the Cameroonian minister of territorial administration. That figure dropped by almost 30 percent, to $6.2 million. For example, the customs department was expected to contribute $1.3 billion—about 24 percent—to the national budget in 2015 but was not able to come even close to this figure.[39] The decline in customs was also seen on the ground level. Low-quality fuel from Nigeria was in short supply, and Nigeria had supplied 80 percent of foodstuffs and necessities to northern Cameroon since the two countries gained independence. The shortage, coupled with the abandonment of farms by residents fleeing the area, has caused a food crisis in northern Cameroon.

The Economic Costs of Responding to Insurgency

The military response to the religious violence has also been costly: conservative figures put it at millions of dollars, especially as they used heavy artillery and aerial bombardment. All the military expenses in suppressing various riots and insurgencies are, however, quite insignificant when one considers the expenses Nigeria has incurred fighting Boko Haram. Nigeria's security bill rose to 20 percent of spending in the 2012 budget, from 16 percent in 2010, leaving less money for much-needed infrastructure projects, especially reforms to power and other social and industrial sectors. (The 2011 budget did not break down security costs.) Similarly, Cameroon, which deployed seven thousand soldiers to fight Boko Haram at the time, was spending close to US$800,000 per month in the antiterror campaign.

The aspect of the economic cost of fighting Boko Haram that seems to have attracted most attention from the nation is corruption in arms procurement. The money that was supposed to be used for arms was diverted, thus exposing those at the forefront of the war to greater danger. Most of the news about this came out when Muhammadu Buhari was elected president.

This corruption has included bribery, kickbacks, inflation of contracts, awarding of contracts to spurious companies, and fake contracts for equipment that was never delivered. The scheme unfolded between 2007 and 2015 and became known in the country as Armsgate. All this has been made possible because of weak or nonexistent oversight of the security sector. The deals allegedly benefited some senior military officers, politicians, government officials, businessmen, and their families to the tune of least US$2.1 billion, and possibly as much as US$15 billion of extrabudgetary funds.[40]

At the center of the corruption allegations was Col. (Rtd.) Sambo Dasuki, President Jonathan's national security advisor. The Buhari government first made public the interim report of the investigative panel it set up in November 2015. The report stated that between 2007 and 2015, there had been "extrabudgetary interventions'" for arms procurement totaling NGN (Nigerian naira) 643.8 billion and that the "foreign currency component" was US$2.2 billion.[41] At the time, the Nigerian naira was exchanging for less than 200 US dollars. This would thus put the entire "extra-budgetary interventions" at between US$4.5 billion and US$7.2 billion, depending on the timing of the naira transactions and the exchange rate at the time. Specifically, the report noted that "of 513 contracts awarded at US$8,356,525,184.32; 2,189,265,724,404.55 Naira and EUR 54,000.00; Fifty-Three (53) were failed contracts amounting to US$2,378,939,066.27 and 13,729,342,329.87 naira respectively."[42]

This thus added up to around US$2.5 billion worth of "failed contracts"—that is, contracts for which no goods or services were delivered—between 2007 and 2015. On top of this, the report counted "fictitious and phantom contracts worth US$1.7 billion for the procurement of four Alpha jets and twelve helicopters, as well as bombs and ammunition, which were never delivered."[43] Most of these contracts were allegedly awarded to two companies that have a history of nonperformance. These numbers might well be low. For example, in May 2016, Nigeria's chief anticorruption body, the Economic and Financial Crimes Commission (EFCC), reported that a previously quoted figure of US$2.1 billion related to just one transaction, and in total US$15 billion went missing.[44] Even given an allowance for exaggeration, this was an excessive amount of money to be missing from Nigeria's national treasury.

Another high-profile person that was charged with corruption in the fight against Boko Haram was the former chief of defense staff, the late Air Chief Marshall (Rtd.) Alex Badeh, who was investigated for the award of contracts worth US$930.5 million. This was in addition to other charges relating to "nonspecification of procurement costs, absence of contract agreements, the award of contracts beyond authorized thresholds, transfer of public funds for unidentified purposes and general non-adherence to provisions of the Public Procurement Act." Badeh included the withdrawal of N1.1 billion from air force accounts to buy a mansion, N650 million for another property, and N878 million for the construction of a shopping mall, all totaling N3.97 billion (US$19.8 million). Investigations were still going on when Badeh was murdered in December 2018 by unknown gunmen.

Many people used the fight against Boko Haram as an opportunity for personal gain. A few senior military officers and some civilians with connections to the former ruling party, the People's Democratic Party, were also arrested and charged with involvement in arms deals connected to the fight against Boko Haram.

Another major controversy came when, in September 2014, the South African government impounded a private jet belonging to a Nigerian pastor, Ayo Oritsejafor, allegedly carrying US$9.3 million.[45] The Nigerian government was to admit later that the money was meant for the procurement of black-market arms.[46] That the government would involve itself in getting arms on the black market surprised many Nigerians. There were allegations in some quarters that the private jet was a gift to the pastor from President Jonathan. Oritsejafor, however, clarified that the plane was a gift from members of his congregation to mark the fortieth year of his being called into the ministry.

Camps hosting Boko Haram refugees have also been plagued with financial impropriety. Indeed, at one stage, the person who is technically the number five citizen in the country, the secretary to the government of the federation, Babachir Lawal, was alleged to have been involved in an N270 million fraud. The money was supposed to pay for cutting grass in the IDP camps in the northeastern part of the country but did not.[47] After considerable national outcry, the federal government set up an investigative panel; it ultimately recommended his removal from office. Some aid workers also stole funds that were set up to support victims of insurgency.

A 2017 report by the United Nations Development Program and the National Human Rights Commission showed that officials of the Presidential Initiative on the North East stole IDP money at an alarming rate between 2015 and 2017.[48] The report also alleges that the bulk of the resources were found to have immensely benefited some public officials. The 103-page report reveals that out of the N8.352 billion released by the initiative in 2016, only N6.326 billion was actually spent as allocated, leaving N2.026 billion unaccounted for. All this triggered violence by IDPs in Borno camps in August 2017, with the displaced people protesting against government's handling of their welfare.

The EFCC later seized a hotel worth between N650 million and 1 billion from one Ima Niboro, a spokesman for former President Jonathan, said to have been connected to the US$5.9 million released by the Office of the National Security Adviser (ONSA) for international image laundering for the Jonathan administration on its handling of the Chibok issue.[49] It also seized an N500 million property in Maitama belonging to Alhaji Ibrahim Maahe, an associate of Dasuki.[50]

Conclusion

In concluding this chapter, we may ask what we can understand of the big picture now that we have worked our way through all these details. There is no doubt that economic considerations have been factors in the cause and prolongation of religious violence. Although most of the attention in the case of Nigeria has been paid to the activities of Boko Haram, largely because of their long duration and extent, other cases of religious violence have also had economic implications, even at the local level. Although the nature of the problem and the pattern of manifestation make the availability of statistical data difficult in some cases, most of the time, the effects are real and visible, and they have further assisted in understanding the various ramifications of the problem and the ways through which enduring solutions to it can be sought. Even though the extent to which economic considerations featured in the commencement of violent uprisings like the Maitatsine riots and the Boko Haram insurgency is contestable, the same cannot be said about the way religious violence has been linked to economic devastation. Also undeniable are the economic implications of having to respond to the insurgency wars caused by the activities of Boko Haram, especially the opportunities it has given for civilian and military elites to illegally deplete the national economy. But just as the economy assists in understanding the complexities of religious violence in Nigeria, so too do the global ramifications, and these are the subject of discussion in chapter 8.

8. NIGERIA'S RELIGIOUS VIOLENCE IN THE CONTEXT OF GLOBAL POLITICS

The problem is even older than us; it has always been there, but now [is] made worse by the influx of armed gunmen from the Sahel region into different parts of the West African sub-region. These gunmen were trained and armed by Muammar Gaddafi.... When he was killed, the gunmen escaped with their arms. We encountered some of them fighting with Boko Haram. —President MUHAMMADU BUHARI

Al-Qaida are our elder brothers. During the lesser Hajj, our leader travelled to Saudi Arabia and met al-Qaida there. We enjoy financial and technical support from them. Anything we want from them we ask them. —ABU QAQA, Boko Haram spokesman, in Zimet, "Boko Haram's Evolving Relationship with Al Qaeda"

Religious controversies in Nigeria, right from their earliest occurrences, have always had a wider external connection, either as a cause, a pattern of manifestation, a reason for prolongation, or even as a consideration for resolution. While the earliest controversies did not lead to actual violence, they planted the seeds for major violence in later decades. The external dimension has also shaped how successive governments have patterned their responses to the phenomenon, and external assistance, especially in recent times, has taken into consideration the wider global implications of religious violence and radicalization. Religious violence in the country has both benefited from global religious violence and contributed to it; and over the decades, the global rivalry between Christianity and Islam has influenced politics and violence in Nigeria. But even though global events affected religious violence in Nigeria, that violence has almost always erupted locally.

This chapter first provides the historical background of external influences on religious politics in Nigeria, before discussing the key global issues that have underlined the politics of religious violence in the country. There is also a discussion of the global intervention in the fight against the activities of the Boko Haram insurgents.

Early Global Involvement in Nigeria's Religious Politics

Right from independence, politicians have also tried to bring other countries into the controversies of religion in Nigeria, particularly the we-versus-them dynamic. The first country it enlisted was the state of Israel. The relationship with that country started off as a secular one. However, shortly before independence in 1960, the western and eastern parts of Nigeria established a close relationship with Israel, obtaining its financial assistance, especially with agriculture.[1] The north, however, maintained its distance. Consequently, the line was informally drawn between the north and the south over the relationship with Israel. This continued into the time of independence. The Balewa government that took over at independence sought and obtained a loan from Israel, but the premier of the northern region, Ahmadu Bello, rejected his region's share of the loan.[2] This created some controversy, such that the prime minister warned against the introduction of religion into the country, predicting, quite correctly as it turned out, that such an introduction would mean "the end of happiness in Nigeria."[3] The northern premier, however, remained adamant and even went further to say, "to my mind, it [Israel] does not exist."[4] As if to respond to Ahmadu Bello, two high-ranking officials of both the east and the west, Chief Michael Okpara and Chief S. L. Akintola, respectively, gave positive assessments of Israel. During a state visit to Israel, Chief Okpara noted, "I am almost an Israelite. I love and admire Israel for my part. I shall always visit Israel."[5] Chief Akintola went along the same line: "You can be assured of our friendship and support at any place and we promise never to withdraw this."[6]

When it appeared that the Islamic world did not appreciate his rebuff of Israel, Ahmadu Bello, in a speech delivered at the 1964 World Islamic League, pointed out his disappointment to his audience that international solidarity and mutual assistance, which he called the backbone of Christian success around the world, was lacking among Muslims, and said that this was having an impact on Muslims in Nigeria. He then cited the example that "two years after his government had turned down a sizeable Israeli loan to Nigeria, even though all the governments of the Federation had accepted the loan, he was yet to get any assistance from any of our sister Muslim countries."[7] He noted, "I have only given these examples to show how genuinely we in Northern Nigeria have been at times suffering and how single-handed we have been working for the cause of Islam, and which we shall continue so long as our lives last. I have earlier spoken of conversions of non-Muslims to Islam. I would like to say that this is only the beginning as there are other areas we have not yet tapped. I hope when we clean Nigeria we will go further afield in Africa."[8] To many Christians, this remained the guiding position of the northern Nigerian oligarchy. This strategy to win the sympathy of the Muslim world seemed to have worked, as some countries immediately responded to Ahmadu Bello's clarion call, with Saudi Arabia alone donating 100,000 pounds to northern Nigeria in 1964 and other countries like Kuwait adding significantly more.

While Obafemi Awolowo, Ahmadu Bello's counterpart in the southwest, was not as blatant, he had his disdain for the Arab world and favored Israel. He did not consider Egypt part of Africa and particularly detested the Egyptian leader Gamal Abdel Nasser, whom he accused of "undisguised totalitarianism at home and territorial ambitions in Africa and the Muslim world."[9] As Ibrahim Gambari has noted, Awolowo's party spokesman on foreign affairs, Anthony Enahoro, wanted Arab North Africa excluded from any discussion on pan-Africanism.[10] In April 2018, the Israeli government, as part of its seventieth anniversary, conferred a posthumous award on Obafemi Awolowo for promoting economic ties with Israel.[11]

For average Nigerians, the first external dimension to religious radicalization in Nigeria was largely the messages of foreign preachers coming into the country. The messages of radical Islamic preachers, mostly from Senegal, freely circulated across northern Nigeria on audiocassettes. Christian tracts, mostly from evangelizing missions in the United States, similarly circulated to Nigerian Christians. Most of these messages were not preaching violence.

Mohammed Marwa, who led the Maitatsine riots, as noted earlier, came from Cameroon and brought religious radicalization to Nigeria. When the riots initially occurred, they were widely suspected to have external influences, but because Nigeria's foreign policy was conservative, accusing fingers quickly pointed toward Gadaffi's Libya, then brandishing a brand of radicalism. The fact too that Libyan troops were then fighting in neighboring Chad further facilitated these rumors.[12] Quite surprisingly, there were also allegations of Israeli support for the Maitatsine group. The Aniagolu Commission of Inquiry set up by the Nigerian government to investigate the riots, however, dismissed all these forms of external involvement as unsubstantiated. But apart from foreign sponsorship, the physical involvement of non-Nigerians in the riots was not in doubt: of the 449 people imprisoned in Kano Central Prison after the riots, 135 came from the Republic of Niger, and between 1983 and 1985, many illegal immigrants from West African countries were expelled from Nigeria for breaches of national security.

Before the Boko Haram insurgency, some global developments heightened the propensity for religious radicalization and political violence in Nigeria. As noted earlier, one of the earliest of these developments was the successful revolution of the Iranian people against their shah; the Arab-Israeli conflict and the Arab Spring also affected Nigeria. The Islamist revival began in the 1980s, as young Muslims everywhere, radicalized by these revolutions, began introducing variants of Islam that were more radical in their own countries. The effects of this were most prominent in Nigeria, where the Muslim Brotherhood started clamoring for a repudiation of the old order for the establishment of an Islamic state.

The Arab-Israeli Conflicts

As noted earlier, the Middle East had been connected to the politics of religion and ethnicity in Nigeria since independence. The system of government during the First Republic allowed for regional autonomy in international affairs, and it seemed to have laid the foundation of some of the ethnoreligious conflicts that subsequently emerged in the country. Also, as noted earlier, during the First Republic, there was a close relationship between the largely Muslim north and Saudi Arabia; the premier of northern Nigeria, Ahmadu Bello, had a particularly close relationship with the king of Saudi Arabia. But while the north had an anti-Israeli position, the east went all-out in friendship with that country. Some very enthusiastic Ibos even believed they had ancestral roots in Israel, though that has never been scientifically established.

There were rumors of Israeli support for Biafran secession. Although this was emphatically denied by Emeka Ojukwu, the Biafran leader did confirm in an interview with Maren Milligan that "a small number of Israeli individuals with business interest in Eastern region acted as intermediaries for arms acquisition and humanitarian aids."[13] During the war, the Biafran secessionists used religion selectively and cynically, drawing parallels between their war and the genocide against the Jews. According to Maren Milligan, the "propaganda war echoed those deployed by Israel's international campaign during the 1967 war, including the David and Goliath metaphor coupled with heavy use of references to jihad."[14] Ojukwu was to confess in a later interview his deliberate and repeated use of the term "pogrom" in Biafran propaganda, stating "one thing that will wake up Europeans is to see the type of massacre that happened to the Jews."[15]

A major turning point in the politics of external involvement in Nigeria's religion crisis occurred in 1973, when Nigeria, in response to a call from the Organization of African Unity (OAU), cut off diplomatic relations with Israel during the oil crisis of 1973 and the Yom Kippur War.[16] The OAU bowed to the heavy pressure applied by the Arab League and passed a resolution recommending that member states sever relations with Israel. The rationale presented by the Arabs was that Israel, by crossing the Suez Canal, had occupied African land. The cutting off of diplomatic relations was widely supported by the largely Muslim northerners. The Nigerian leader at the time was a Christian, Yakubu Gowon, which made it somewhat difficult for Christians to read religious meanings into it. Nonetheless, Christians (especially those in the south and their press) urged the government to reconsider what they saw as a wrongly advised move.[17] General Obasanjo, also a Christian, who came in after the brief administration of General Murtala Mohammed, made it emphatically clear that he was pursuing the path of not establishing diplomatic relations with Israel.[18] The Shehu Shagari and the Buhari administrations followed the same position, saying that Israel had to establish cordial relations with its Arab neighbors before looking for any change in its relationship with Nigeria. Reactions in Nigeria fell largely along religious lines, with the Christian Association of Nigeria and one of its key members, Cardinal (later Archbishop) Olubunmi Okogie, calling for restoration and key Muslim leaders from the north arguing against it. However, some did not see things through this religious prism. Bolaji Akinyemi, former director of the Nigerian Institute of International Affairs, himself the son of an Anglican clergyman, said that Nigeria should not establish a relationship with Israel as it would be a betrayal of the Palestinians, who had always supported the African cause.[19] (Ironically, it was to be the same Bolaji Akinyemi who was to start the process of formal normalization with Israel when he became Babangida's minister of foreign affairs.) Another turning point in the external dimension of Nigeria's religious controversies came when Nigeria joined the Organization of Islamic Cooperation in 1985 (see chapter 6). To douse the controversies that ensued, the Babangida administration reestablished relations with Israel in 1992.

The impact of the Middle East crisis on the ethnoreligious conflict in northern Nigeria can be seen in the unilateral renaming of districts and localities in key cities, especially Kaduna. The Hausa-Fulani majority renamed the section of the town that they occupied Mecca, while the minority Christian population residing in the south renamed their district Jerusalem.[20] Although these names were never officially recognized, they showed the extent to which key actors in the politics of religious radicalism in Nigeria have also used the developments in the Middle East as a rallying point for bringing attention to what they perceived as global injustice.

The situation in the Middle East has been a subject that unites all Nigerian Muslims, Sunni or Shi'ite, and all the known Islamic radical groups in Nigeria agree that Israel's treatment of Palestinians is unjust. Sheik El-Zakzaky, in May 2008, claimed that the state of Israel was created "on the basis of terrorism, and what is not yours, is not yours, no matter years of oppression and hostage it would slip someday along with those supporting them. Israel will fall with her allies certainly."[21] He was even more forceful in attacking the notion that the success of the Jews in the Middle East was due to their "smartness" and "intelligence," saying, "They are not smart, intelligent and strategic, they are just human beings, their aims are just unjustifiable and inhuman, do you call people that perpetrated all these inhuman acts smart, they have no human standard and there is no point of praising them, it is just like saying armed robbers are smart and intelligent."[22] When Israeli Foreign Affairs Minister Avigdor Lieberman visited Abuja in 2009, El-Zakzaky said that Nigerian security forces targeted the Islamic Movement of Nigeria (IMN) for Israel because "Iran is waxing stronger in Nigeria through me, and this is why they want to attack us, to finally slay the growing Iranian influence and our movement."[23] All this shows that the international politics of the Arab-Israeli conflict was a major factor in explaining actions and reactions in Nigeria's religious controversies. As mentioned in chapter 2, the access of the population of northern Nigeria to an array of Hausa services on global media outlets like the BBC and the VOA has exposed them to news about the developments in these parts of the world.

The Iranian Revolution

The Iranian revolution of 1978–79 is also deeply connected with the politics of religious radicalization and violence in Nigeria. Apart from encouraging general revolutionary fervor among Muslims, the most important aspect for Nigeria was the ascendancy of Shi'ite doctrine, largely through the activities of Sheik El-Zakzaky. As Jacob Zenn has noted, "while the group was virtually non-existent 30 years ago, they now comprise about five percent of Nigeria's

80 million Muslims [in 2013]."[24] Indeed, Nigeria now has the largest population of Shi'ites in Africa.

The extent to which Iran was involved in exposing El-Zakzaky and his group to violence is still controversial. Iran has persistently denied this and so has the IMN. But a former Iranian career diplomat, Adel Assadinia, who was also Iran's consul-general in Dubai and an adviser to the Iranian foreign ministry before he defected, claimed that Iran trained the IMN "in guerrilla warfare, bomb-making, use of arms such as handguns, rifles, and RPGs, and the manufacturing of bombs and hand grenades."[25] The sole objective of all this, he said, was to model the IMN on Hezbollah—the Shia Islamist militant group and political party based in Lebanon.[26]

When the military clamped down on El-Zakzaky and his group in Nigeria in December 2015, after the group's clash with the army chief of staff, Tukur Buratai, Iran became particularly concerned, describing it as unacceptable and summoning the Nigerian chargé d'affaires in Tehran to the Foreign Office in protest.[27] The Iranian president, Hassan Rouhani, also called the Nigerian president, Muhammadu Buhari, demanding that Nigeria compensate the families of those killed and injured.[28] In the end, the Iranian Foreign Ministry came up with a mildly veiled criticism of Nigeria's handling of the problem: "Nigeria is now dealing with problems arising from extremism and *takfiri* terrorism and we hope that in these conditions preservation of calm and national unity in battling terrorism is prioritized while rash and unconstructive measures are avoided."[29] None of this affected Iran's interest in deeper collaboration with Nigeria. In February 2018, as part of the thirty-ninth anniversary of the revolution, the Iranian government announced its intention to build a university in Nigeria.[30]

Nigeria's banning of the IMN in July 2019, however, brought concerns to many in Nigeria about the possibility of Iranian intervention in Nigeria's religious affairs. The Islamic organization the Muslim Rights Concern, known for its opposition to the Shi'ites, warned Iran not to interfere in the affairs of Nigeria. It noted, "Iran is known to have executed Sunni Muslim leaders in its domain even without the latter engaging in any criminal activity. Therefore, Iran has no moral right to dictate to the Nigerian government how to handle Shiite excesses. This is a sovereign nation and any attempt to export the Ayatollah-style bloody revolution to Nigeria will be stiffly resisted by mainstream Muslims in the country."[31] A Christian and a known critic of the government, Femi Fani-Kayode, warned the Nigerian government about the possible reaction from Iran:

The Shia Muslims have strong, battle-hardened, war-tested, well-armed, well-motivated, well-funded, highly professional, functional, active, experienced standing armies and militias in Lebanon, Iraq, Yemen and Syria and a strong military presence all over the Middle East. They are supported, backed and funded by Iran and they have warm relations with Qatar. By murdering, maiming, detaining, persecuting, torment-ing, clamping down on and banning the 26 million strong Shia Muslims of Nigeria Buhari is dragging us into a Muslim sectarian conflict and an Arab versus Persian proxy war which may never end. This is what happens when an unrepentant Salafist and hard-line Islamist Wahhabi jihadist that is in the pocket and under the control of Saudi Arabia sits on the throne.[32]

None of these fears had, however, manifested as of the end of 2021, although the general assumption that Iran is deeply interested in the affairs of Nigeria remains.

The Effects of the Arab Spring

The Arab Spring was one of the most important factors in Islamic radical-ization in Africa. It further revealed the weakness of state structures on the continent, especially those not based on credible and sustainable democracy. Within a few months, dictatorships that had existed on the continent for de-cades collapsed. When Libya collapsed, thousands of Tuaregs that had fought in Gadaffi's army migrated into northern Mali, where they reinforced an in-surgency that was to engulf the whole of the Sahel region. The loss of the rule of law created a power vacuum that allowed militant groups—particularly the Islamic State of Iraq and the Levant group (ISIL) and al-Qaeda—to thrive in Syria, Iraq, and Afghanistan.

The Arab Spring, and more precisely the collapse of Gadaffi's regime in Libya, had an indirect effect on Nigeria. Nigerians suspected that the Arab Spring would have local connotations in their country. Chukwuma Osakwe, a Nigerian academic, wrote at the time:

[A] religious threat to national security is a ripple out of the Arab Spring. In the countries of the Arab Spring, the major plays are between the Sunni and Shia religious sects. The intra-religious conflict between these sects is predominantly mid-wifed by two godfathers, Saudi Arabia to the Sunnis and Iran for the Shia sect. [A] religious threat to national secu-rity in Nigeria is plausible. In fact, [scholars] using Sokoto and Zamfara

TABLE 8.1

Rank	Terrorist/Rebel Group	Killed	Injured
1	Boko Haram	2,924	268
2	Islamic State (IS)	1,459	517
3	al-Shabaab	1,136	671
4	al-Huthi rebels	584	163
5	al-Qaeda Arabian Peninsula (AQAP)	509	184
6	Taliban	384	278
7	Jabhat al-Nusrah	298	252
8	Donetsk People's Republic (DPR)	295	0
9	Islamic Front	247	68
10	Seleke	229	107

Source: Ioannis Mantzikos, "Boko Haram Attacks in Nigeria and Neighbouring Countries: A Chronology of Attacks," 63.

States, contend that ethnoreligious conflicts essentially derive from intra-religious conflicts as opposed to inter-religious conflicts. Although it is still of importance to Nigerian national security, it would be of a sectional, albeit of a regional dimension. It will not play out in Nigeria as a Sunni or Shia conflict but will be rooted in the cultural practice of religion.[33]

This was how it manifested before Boko Haram came into the picture.

The Boko Haram Dimension

As discussed in chapter 5, even by global standards, Boko Haram was an organization of enormous concern. In a report released in July 2014, Boko Haram was at the top of the list of the world's ten most deadly groups, according to Intel-Centre, a US-based center looking at counterterrorism and intelligence (table 8.1). These ratings are based on incidents between January and July 2014.

There is now established information that there are links between Boko Haram and global insurgency groups. Broadly, apart from the relationship with the Islamic State in Iraq and Syria (ISIS) discussed in chapter 5, Boko Haram has had links with several external organizations. The three that are particularly important are al-Qaeda, the Movement for Oneness and Jihad in West Africa (MUJAO), and Al-Qa'ida in the Islamic Maghreb (AQIM). All are linked to the larger global jihadi network.

The link between Boko Haram and al-Qaeda became more pronounced after Abubakar Shekau took over and effectively transformed the group into a total jihadi group. His first video in 2010 called on the leaders of al-Qaeda for support, and it worked. The support from al-Qaeda was not only in terms of ideology but over time included financial, technical, and training assistance. The International Crisis Group said that in 2000 Osama bin Laden gave up to US$3 million to militant Islamic organizations in Nigeria; Yusuf got a significant percentage of this to fund Boko Haram.[34] Yusuf had always admired al-Qaeda, and had identified Osama bin Laden as one of the "four pure Salafists" that Muslims should follow.[35] As early as the first decade of the 2000s, Yusuf sent some of his followers to Algeria and Mauritania to train with AQIM for them to "gain the strength to succeed" in jihad.[36] The link between Boko Haram and al-Qaeda was later confirmed by the spokesperson of Boko Haram.[37]

Al-Qaeda in the Islamic Maghreb (AQIM)

At its establishment, AQIM's primary objective was to overthrow the Algerian government. It originated as the Salafist Group for Preaching and Combat, but changed its name to AQIM in 2007. Although initially suspected, links with al-Qaeda were confirmed in 2006 by al-Qaeda's second in command, Ayman al-Zawahiri. Its members came from all the states in the Sahel region, although the main base was in northern Mali. Its known sources of funding included ransom money, and drug and cigarette smuggling. It was believed to have spread to all the countries in the Maghreb, and its membership was thought to be between six hundred and one thousand. It was suspected to have links with Nigeria's Boko Haram. Among the violent activities associated with it was the December 2007 bombing of the UN offices in Algiers.[38]

Abdelmalek Droukdel, the leader of AQIM, confirmed that the organization was working closely with Boko Haram. Their relationship became strained around 2012, and increasingly AQIM started distancing itself from Boko Haram. The group also no longer saw Boko Haram as a credible representative of al-Qaeda. What seems to be at the center of this was Boko Haram's indiscriminate attacks on Muslims. Indeed, in 2013, a leader of AQIM, Abu Mundhir, issued a fatwa condemning Boko Haram's killing of students: "Targeting schools to kill young students is impermissible since they have not yet joined the ranks of the apostate military.... This will allow the enemies of the religion and Western media to exploit these scenes to prove to Muslims that the mujahedeen are far from Islam."[39] The relationship between the two was believed to have later been reestablished. Documentary evidence to show this link between Boko

Haram and AQIM has now come into the public domain. Letters between Ab-delhamid Abou Zeid, a former commander of AQIM, killed in Mali in 2013, and the leader of al-Qaeda's North African branch, Abdelmalek Droukdel, written in August 2009, detailed how Shekau deployed some of his members to estab-lish ties with al-Qaeda. Boko Haram's emissaries included Abu Muhammad Amir al-Masir, Khalid al-Barnawi, and Abu Rayhanah, who were all allegedly selected because Abou Zeid knew them from their time in the ranks of the AQIM-affiliated Tariq Ibn Ziyad Battalion. In March 2016, another undated let-ter uncovered from the bin Laden cache showed Shekau requesting to speak with bin Laden and requesting greater collaboration with al-Qaeda.[40]

Movement for Oneness and Jihad (MUJAO)

The Movement for Oneness and Jihad in West Africa was a splinter group from AQIM, allegedly because it wanted to create a voice for Black African members of AQIM. It was established around mid-2011, and it looks to Black figures like Usman dan Fodio as sources of inspiration and wants to ensure the spread of radical Islam across West Africa. Its members are youths from across Mali and other Sahelian states. Funding for its activities comes from taking hostages for ransom (for example, it exchanged two Spanish and one Italian hostage for US$18 million in 2012) and smuggling. It has spread across West Africa but aspires to greater associations with groups in Algeria and Mali. Associated vio-lent activities include the suicide bombing of the Algerian National Gendar-merie regional command center in downtown Ouargla in June 2012 and the Tamanrasset suicide attack in March 2012.[41]

Boko Haram first linked with MUJAO when both raided the Algerian con-sulate in Mali's Gao region in September 2012. Here Boko Haram was said to have contributed about one hundred members.[42] Also, in November 2012, Boko Haram joined MUJAO and AQIM in the capture of Menaka in the same region. Again, in January 2013, Boko Haram joined MUJAO, AQIM, and Ansar Eddine in the attack on Kona, central Mopti region. Several independent sources have also confirmed the link between Boko Haram and MUJAO, including displaced persons from Gao, former military officials from Niger, US Africa Command General Carter Ham, the US ambassador to Nigeria, the Nigerian minister of foreign affairs, the Malian foreign minister, and the Algerian minister for Maghreb and African affairs.

The AQIM and MUJAO links reinforce the importance of Mali. Indeed, Jacob Zenn has given evidence of Boko Haram's deep involvement in Mali, including: (1) news reports from Mali of Boko Haram militants involved in the raid on the Algerian consulate in Gao and kidnapping the vice consul; (2) confirmation by displaced persons from Gao, including a former parliamentarian, who said that Boko Haram was training at MUJAO-run camps; (3) statements by military officials from Niger that Boko Haram militants were transiting Niger en route to Mali on a daily basis; (4) a MUJAO commander confirmation in an interview with a Beninese journalist for Radio France Internationale that Boko Haram members were arriving in Gao en masse; and (5) General Carter Ham's confirmation that Boko Haram militants train in camps in northern Mali and most likely receive financing and explosives from AQIM. All these links within the region assisted Boko Haram's activities within Nigeria and into neighboring states.

ISIS

In March 2015, Shekau swore allegiance to the leader of the Islamic State in Iraq and Syria (ISIS) or Daesh, Abu Bakr al-Baghdadi. The Daesh leader endorsed the alliance and described Boko Haram as "jihadi brothers." Before this formal announcement, Shekau had given indications of wanting some form of friendship with the group. Apart from following some of the templates of ISIS, including the declaration of his caliphate, Shekau had sent open greetings and praise for al-Baghdadi. The alliance request was accepted, and Boko Haram was renamed the Wilayat al-Islamiyya Gharb Afriqiyah or the Islamic State West Africa Province (ISWAP).

There are grounds for interpreting the alliance as a sign of Boko Haram's desperation. Boko Haram had just suffered a series of military setbacks. The group had lost territory in the effective military response by the Nigerian military to the group's action in Baga in January 2015. A nascent multinational force of troops from Nigeria, Niger, Chad, Cameroon, and Benin joined in the pressure on Boko Haram. Indeed, just a few days before the announcement, Niger and Chad had launched a ground and air offensive into Boko Haram–held territory, and the African Union had approved a regional force of ten thousand troops with headquarters in the Chadian capital, N'Djamena, with the objective of "eradicating the presence" of Boko Haram.

Wider global connectivity in training and support of logistics can also be seen in the case of Ansaru, the group that broke away from Boko Haram in 2012. That group's leader, al-Barnawi, was a close associate of AQIM's leader, Moktar Belmokhta. Ansaru seemed to be more concerned with external issues than with internal contradictions in the Nigerian states. Apart from its focus on the kidnapping of foreigners discussed in chapter 5, some of the things the group reacted to were somewhat more international. For example, in January 2013, the group killed two Nigerian soldiers who were on their way to Mali for deployment. Also, the demand that was made for the kidnapped German (who later died during the botched rescue attempt in 2012) was that Germany release a Turkish-born female jihadist whose German husband had been arrested for attempting to bomb a German military base. But apart from all the extensive links Nigeria's radical groups have with global insurgents, another set of external links comes in the responses to insurgent activities.

Global Connectivity in Training and Logistical Support

In the beginning, the international community thought Boko Haram could never be a global threat. Indeed, WikiLeaks documents noted as early as 2004 that the group did not present an international threat and likely had no links to international jihadist organizations. Once it established itself as a strong insurgent movement, however, several African countries pursued individual strategies in dealing with Boko Haram, with no success; then international collaboration against Boko Haram started. The main joint military action against the Boko Haram insurgents was undertaken by the countries in the Lake Chad basin: Cameroon, Chad, Niger, and Nigeria, with the involvement of the Republic of Benin. In 2014, countries in the Lake Chad basin decided to establish a Multinational Joint Task Force (MNJTF) to address Boko Haram's insurgent activity under the leadership of Nigeria's General Tukur Buratai. Cameroon initially refused to join, intending to pursue its own strategy: sending the Boko Haram fighters back to Nigeria. Boko Haram exploited this disunity, going through the long and porous border between Cameroon and Nigeria to wreak havoc on both countries.

It was at this stage that the French president, François Hollande, organized a security summit in Paris in May 2014 to get all the countries in the Lake Chad basin together. The meeting was also attended by representatives of the United Kingdom, the United States, and the European Union. It had four main objectives: (1) dismantle all Boko Haram bases in Cameroon, Chad, and Niger; (2) block arms supply to the insurgents; (3) allow allied forces access to the airspace of Cameroon, Chad, and Niger to monitor the insurgents; and (4) the possibility of rescuing the Chibok girls.[43] The Paris meeting was followed by another meeting in Niamey, Niger, in October 2014, where attendees decided to deploy seven hundred troops from each state immediately, that is, by November 1, 2014. The overall mandate of the MNJTF was to "create a safe and secure environment in the areas affected by the activities of the Boko Haram

TABLE 8.2 Proposed Number of Staff to Be Deployed

Staff (Military, Police, and Civilian)	Proposed
7,500	Recommendation by the AU PSC in January 2015
8,700	Recommendation by meeting of experts in February 2015
10,000	Recommendation by the AU PSC in March 2015
11,150	Announced by LCBC states and Benin in August 2015
8,500	Announced by Nigerian President Buhari in May 2016

Source: Assanvo, Abatan, and Sawadogo, "Assessing the Multinational Joint Task Force against Boko Haram."

TABLE 8.3 Evolution of the Total Recommended Number of Staff for the MNJTF

Countries	Announced/Recommended	Deployed/Committed
Nigeria	3,750	
Chad	3,000	
Cameroon	2,250–2,550	
Niger	1,000	
Benin	750–800	150

Source: Assanvo, Abatan, and Sawadogo, "Assessing the Multinational Joint Task Force against Boko Haram."

and other terrorists [insurgents] . . . facilitate the implementation of overall stabilization programs by the LCBC Member States and Benin in the affected areas, including the full restoration of state authority and the return of IDPs [internally displaced persons] and refugees; and facilitate, within its limit of capabilities, humanitarian operations and the delivery of assistance to the affected populations."[44]

After this, contributing members disagreed on issues like the location of the MNJTF headquarters and the control of the command structure. To solve such problems, they mandated the African Union as a regional body to put together and fund a Strategic Concept of Operations for troop deployment. Foreign ministers and defense chiefs of these countries met to finalize all the details of the collaboration. The details of the deployment are listed in tables 8.2 and 8.3.

By the time the heads of government of the states met again, in June 2015, Buhari had become the new Nigerian leader. At the meeting, his request that command of the force should no longer rotate between countries (as previously agreed) was accepted and Nigeria, being the country with the largest number of troops, became the permanent head. The position of deputy commander was given to Cameroon, while Chad provided the chief of staff. With all logistical issues sorted out, the force became fully operational in August 2015, after ceremonies for the transfer of authority were done, from national forces to the MNJTF.

Although the MNJTF is a joint mission of countries in the Lake Chad basin (Nigeria, Niger, Chad, Cameroon) and Benin, and its mandate is theoretically to tackle Boko Haram, in reality, it is designed only to prevent the insurgents from invading all the member states. The operation is broken down into three main sectors and a subsector: sector 1 stationed in Mora in Cameroon; sector 2 at Baga-Sola in Chad; sector 3 in Baga in Nigeria; and subsector 3 in Diffa in Niger, while Benin, whose troops are stationed at the headquarters in N'Djamena, Chad, provides a quick response force. This arrangement implied that the MNJTF was not designed to operate as an integrated regional force with joint patrols and operations but focuses on coordinating national contingents that operate on their terms and report back to their capitals.[45] Indeed, individual initiatives to address Boko Haram were still in the hands of national forces, as with the case, for example, of Operation Lafiya Dole in Nigeria. The idea was that these individual initiatives would drive the insurgents to border regions where the MNJTF would bring them down.

This arrangement has recorded appreciable gains in countering Boko Haram, liberating territories that were previously under Boko Haram's control, rescuing women and children held captive, and seizing and destroying caches of weapons. Many of the identified Boko Haram camps, hideouts, and bomb-making factories were destroyed by the MNJTF, thereby exerting more pressure on the insurgents. Many Boko Haram insurgents could not withstand the offensive operation and began to flee toward the borders with neighboring states, where the MNJTF arrested them, as envisioned.

The MNJTF has recorded some achievements. The force was able to recover some of the territory taken by Boko Haram. In the process, too, many hostages were freed. Operation Gama Aiki, which involved aerial bombardment and ground troops, was launched from all four sectors, resulting in significant degrading of Boko Haram troops and the fall of the Sambisa Forest. Major villages, including Diran-Nairi, Faide-Imba, Yebi-Tasagia, Yemi-emi, Alli-Kanori, Yebi-Tumanbi, and Aligarno, were also recaptured from the insurgents. The attack also resulted in weapons seizures. It was on the strength of the successes that attended this initiative, especially the fall of Sambisa Forest, that Nigerian President Buhari announced that Boko Haram had been "technically defeated." The UN under-secretary-general for political affairs, Jeffrey Feltman, shared this excitement: "We commend the Lake Chad Basin Countries' efforts to combat Boko Haram. The regional offensive involving Nigerian, Chadian, Cameroonian, and Nigerian troops operating under the Multinational Joint Task Force (MNJTF) has captured 80 percent of the areas once under Boko Haram control, freed thousands of captives and prevented territorial attacks."[46] A major phase in the combined effort came in April 2020. Toward the last week of March 2020, Boko Haram launched an ambush on Chadian soldiers at Bohoma and killed more than ninety soldiers. In retaliation, Chad launched Operation Bohoma Anger, during which it claimed it killed up to a thousand Boko Haram members and destroyed fifty motorized canoes.

There have, however, also been some operational challenges: the absence of a well-defined command and control structure; a lack of sufficient funds; a lack of trust between the contributing states; inadequate logistics, equipment, and manpower; the proliferation of small arms and light weapons; and local support for Boko Haram.

The regional responses to counterinsurgency measures have also received forms of assistance from countries outside of Africa. For example, Britain has sent some military assistance.[47] A British military training team was sent to Nigeria to provide the country's armed forces with the necessary skills to tackle and defeat Boko Haram. Britain deployed successive short-term training teams to aid the Nigerian armed forces to improve their readiness and forestall possible attacks from Boko Haram. For example, over six weeks, more than sixty personnel of the 5 Force Protection Wing from RAF Lossiemouth trained the Nigerian air force in warding off threats from terrorist groups, handling improvised explosive devices (IEDs), tracking insurgents, identifying weapons caches, navigation, and improving ground-to-air coordination. The British Army Corps of Royal Engineers and troops also went to Nigeria in 2016 to train the Nigerian army and navy during a four-month deployment at the Nigerian School of Infantry. Similarly, engineers from the 101st Engineer Regiment shared their expertise from Iraq and Afghanistan, focusing on how to disable IEDs. In total, between 2015 and 2017, more than 350 British troops trained the Nigerian armed forces, benefiting around six thousand troops. The program also offered medical training, infantry skills, media operations, command and leadership, and support to Nigerian military training schools. In December 2016, the British government officially announced the creation of a regional British Defense Staff for West Africa to support the Nigerian government in fighting terrorism. This defense staff is based in Abuja, Nigeria's capital, and represents a permanent British commitment to the country. Through the permanent British Military Advisory and Training Team and the successive Short-Term Training Teams, Britain has helped scale down the threats of terrorist organizations. This cooperation with Nigeria is also an opportunity to exchange skills between the British and Nigerian armed forces.

The Boko Haram insurgency also brought into existence the first-ever UK-Nigeria Security and Defense Partnership. Between 2015 and August 2018, the UK had only trained Nigerian soldiers individually—not full fighting teams—helping to improve the skills of some thirty thousand troops. In August 2018, after the partnership was announced, the British government declared that it would train Nigerian army counterterror squads to fight Boko Haram. The British government agreed to work with Nigeria to implement a new Nigerian crisis response mechanism, similar to the UK's COBRA system, to help the government respond to terror attacks and cut the number of recruits joining Boko Haram by tackling the lies and false information spread by the group to attract new members—including working with communities to push out counternarratives and drawing on the UK's experience of countering terrorist propaganda at home and as part of the global campaign against Daesh. General Sir Mike Jackson, the UK chief of general staff from 2003 to 2006, however, notes that despite the British army's valuable expertise and ability to successfully deliver such operations, UK support for West African states was dwarfed by that of both France and the United States.

During 2018, the United States doubled its assistance to the anti-insurgent operation in Africa's Sahel region to US$111 million, as the fight against the far-from-defeated Islamic State shifted further afield. The United States also formed the US/Nigeria Bi-national Commission in October 2010. Its Anti-Terrorism Assistance Program provided training and equipment. And it created a Counter-Terrorist Finance Intelligence Unit, working with Nigeria to address Boko Haram's revenue streams, with a special focus on kidnappings and bulk cash smuggling. But the United States' efforts to cooperate with Nigeria in freeing the Chibok girls faltered, largely due to mutual distrust and the alleged infiltration of the Nigerian military by Boko Haram. It was said that once the United States suspected that Boko Haram had infiltrated, it became wary of sharing raw intelligence data with the Nigerian military and vice versa, which affected the use of US drone flights in locating the kidnapped Chibok girls.

Conclusion

The nature of global politics is such that rivalries over religion would permeate any society where internal divisions exist that would allow opportunities for interference. How deep external intervention can go would depend on issues like the extent of internal divisions, the activities of political and religious elites, the prevailing complexities of global politics, and the ways all these are administered by the government in power. Why all this has become more profound in the case of Nigeria is that the country has almost equal populations of Christians and Muslims, and both have external resources they believe they could call upon to intervene on their behalf in the country's zero-sum politics. What I have tried to argue in this chapter is that at every stage since its independence, Nigeria's religious politics has always attracted external interests, largely because of the ethnoreligious setup of the country and the zero-sum nature of the relationship between the two major religions, Islam and Christianity. Local politicians have also exploited this, both for personal gain and also to advance the interests of their religions. I have also argued that religious violence in Nigeria has exploited global political developments and has equally contributed to them. Although the recent connection of Boko Haram with global Islamic radicalization is the most pronounced example of this dynamic, the roots are far deeper, and the ramifications more extensive. Since just before independence, external dynamics influenced the politics of religion in Nigeria, and this continued into the immediate postindependence period. Other global events have been external factors in Nigeria's religious radicalization, including the Middle East crisis and developments in Iran. With this discussion on the external dimension of religious violence in Nigeria, this book now seems to have come to the end of the key issues surrounding the nature and politics of religious violence in Nigeria.

Conclusion. THE IMPOSSIBILITY OF THE BEST AND THE UNLIKELIHOOD OF THE WORST

Everything Religion should be against is what it stands for in Nigeria; we Nigerians are deeply religious but totally godless. —YUSUF OLAOLU ALI (SAN)

All religions accept that there is something called criminality. And criminality cannot be excused by religious fervor. . . . [Trying to] create a religious Maginot Line through which nothing should penetrate [is] not religion; that's lunacy. . . . This is not taking arms against the state, this is taking up arms against humanity. —WOLE SOYINKA, "The Igbos Were a Victim of Genocide"

In a way, it is impossible to conclude a book of this nature; one can only pause, as developments continue to unfold in ways that make the issue of finality somewhat difficult, if not impossible. By the end of 2021, the various controversies associated with religion had raised Nigeria's security challenges to the highest level since its civil war, and concerns continued to dominate the minds of the population about whether the government had solutions to mammoth security problems that were linkable, directly or indirectly, to religion. Indeed, there were already calls from important interest groups that the government should consider hiring mercenaries, since the security forces were "tired."[1] This concluding chapter attempts four main things: to identify and discuss issues that have caused religious violence in postindependence Nigeria; to provide a critique of how the problem has been addressed; to discuss the current situations and their various ramifications; and to revalidate the central arguments laid out in the introductory chapter.

Broadly, one can distill the root causes of religious violence in Nigeria into about six factors. The first has to do with the composition of the country: it is clear, as noted in the introduction, that the vicissitudes of colonial division created long-lasting implications for ethnoreligious violence in the country. Also linked to this are the effects of the political situation, which have been as profound. The period between 1980 and 2007 was one of significant political developments in Nigeria, and their lasting legacies and consequences can be seen in the country's massive move toward religious violence. During the period, the country experienced issues like economic depression, acrimony in intergroup relations, brutal dictatorship, the end of military rule, and many other developments that affected how the country had been shaped since its independence.

A second cause is the intense rivalry within and between the two major religions in the country: Christianity and Islam. All the multiple reasons for this rivalry can be narrowed down simply to disagreement over the approach to worshipping God. The utter divergence of perception over how to worship and the concept of salvation are rooted in the doctrines of the two religions. Christians and Muslims rarely doubt that their religion is the authentic one that leads to salvation. While many may not say it openly, most believe that those of the opposing religion are not on the right path. Neither Christianity nor Islam has middle ground on the definition of salvation, and both believe that their holy books endorse their positions. Christians cite standard scriptural verses like John 3:10, John 3:16, John 3:36, John 10:9, John 14:6, Acts 4:12, or 1 Timothy 2:5, among others, to validate the sole way to eternity and the total exclusion of other faiths. In the same way, Muslims see the validity of the exclusiveness of their path in the relevant Qur'anic verses, like Surah 3:19, Surah 3:85, and Surah 48:28, all of which endorse the Islamic religion to the total nonrecognition of others for the qualification of eternal blessing. Undeniably, the zero-sum perception of each other in terms of qualification for eternal bliss at the end of our sojourn on earth is a key issue in the perception of Christians and Muslims in Nigeria. Even a Christian in name alone is in no doubt about this position, as are Muslims. Indeed, of all religions in Nigeria, only the traditional religions recognize a multiplicity of channels to salvation and eternal life. It is the monolithic perception of salvation that is at the root of militant preaching and the breeding of intolerance. Why this is a greater problem in Nigeria than in other places is because of its combination with other existing contradictions in the country, especially ethnicity.

The third cause of religious violence is radicalization, the process whereby individuals become sufficiently convinced and/or indoctrinated to carry out violence in the name of religion. While this has existed for centuries, it became a factor in postindependence Nigeria in the 1980s with the Maitatsine uprising and, after a brief lull, resurfaced with vengeance in the late 1990s with Boko Haram. The resurfacing is largely because of the ethnopolitical and socioeconomic challenges that have confronted the country. These challenges rapidly increased the number of people and groups willing to take up violence for their religion. Indeed, what is perhaps the greatest security problem that is facing the country recently, the Boko Haram insurgency, is mainly an issue of radicalization.

Political and religious elites have exploited religion to advance their political causes, especially during elections, constituting a fourth factor in the cause of religious violence in Nigeria. They have also exploited the interlinkage between religion and ethnicity, especially in places like the Middle Belt region. Violence over religion has given them opportunities for graft, as demonstrated in chapter 6, further encouraging religious violence. Many Christian and Muslim religious elites have manipulated their followers for selfish motives, and the fanatical obsession of many followers with their religious leaders means that they are gullible consumers of leaders' language of hate. While the excesses of many Christian leaders, especially those of the Pentecostal flavor, for material acquisitions have been subjects of concern, derision, and criticism, critics are starting to see that their Muslim counterparts could be similarly encouraging their followers into a culture of hate.

Events on the global scene provide the fifth cause. As shown in the preceding chapters, but especially in chapter 8, some religious violence is connected with wider global religious politics and radicalization. While, of course, the occurrence of religious violence in Nigeria has local content, the connection with wider global radicalization cannot be denied, as clearly manifested in the metamorphosis of Boko Haram into Islamic State West Africa Province (ISWAP). The extent to which Boko Haram has also connected with other African insurgent groups also underlines the role of external factors in the pattern of expression of religious violence in Nigeria. Also, Iran has been deeply involved in issues connected to the affairs of the Shi'ites. Closely linked to this also is the impact of globalization. The compression of time and space that globalization entails has brought about increasing interconnectedness among the world's regions, nations, governments, institutions, communities, and individuals, which has benefited the politics of religious violence in Nigeria. Indeed, globalization features like the synthesis of culture, the deterritorialization of borders, the revolution in the flow of information, and changes in the means of transportation have all assisted in solidifying the impact of external development.

Socioeconomic considerations are the last major factor in the occurrence of religious violence in Nigeria. In the parts of the country most affected by religious violence, the statistics on economic deprivation are profound. While, as argued in chapter 7, economic considerations might not be a strong factor in what motivated the leaders of the two major violent acts of radicalization in Nigeria, the Maitatsine riots and Boko Haram, it fueled their followers' violence and brought more disenchanted individuals into their fold. Apart from the violence that manifested in the Maitatsine and Boko Haram situations, the incessant clashes between Christians and Muslims also bear clear indications of economic deprivation. Closely linked to this is the issue of youth vulnerability and exclusion, which has made a stream of unemployed youths vulnerable to religious manipulation. The millions of jobless youths across the country represent a source of vulnerable people for religious violence. Finally, also coming under economic considerations are issues relating to climate change and the complexities of economic relations among communities in the Middle Belt and also in the Lake Chad basin.

While successive governments have tried to address the religious violence that has confronted them, the degrees of success that have attended these efforts have varied because of the extent of the challenges they faced, the level of sincerity of intervention, the nature and extent of external involvement, and changing ethnopolitical and socioeconomic conditions. At least on the surface, successive governments have tried to address the issues, but interventions have been largely haphazard, often uncoordinated, usually weak, and most of the time insufficient. In several instances, the government completely misread the situation and applied the wrong responses. Also, governments have struggled to balance the competing and connected forces of ethnicity, religion, and politics.

Following up on the above, also important in explaining the weakness of successive governments is the inability to address the interwoven nature of identity that often exists within the country. Three layers of identity—ethnicity, religion, and vocation—often come into consideration. It is thus sometimes difficult to discern whether to interpret violent actions as a clash between different ethnic groups, religions (Christians and Muslims), or vocations (herdsmen and farmers). What has made the problem particularly difficult for the government is that perpetrators of such violence also often do not distinguish between these layers of identity and do not interpret their actions at any particular time as falling into any of these three layers. People of a particular ethnic group would belong to a particular religion and engage in a particular type of vocation, while those they are opposing will belong to different sectors of these identities.

Also important in addressing the challenges is the crucial role of perception of the population. Over all the postindependence years of Nigeria, this has underlined the politics of how governments address religious issues. People often have the impression that actions and inactions are rooted in the personal attachments of successive leaders, who act because they are either Christians or Muslims. Even previous actions and utterances by individuals before they attain positions of political leadership are often brought up to explain their actions in office. This can be true for groups as well: both the Christian Association of Nigeria and Jama'atu Nasril Islam have had reason to interpret the government's actions in particular ways largely based on their perceptions of key officeholders.

The nature and extent of external interventions are often beyond the control of governments. While the activities of global insurgent groups like al-Qaeda and ISIS, and even African ones like MUJAO, AQIM, and so on, are completely beyond the reach of the Nigerian government, their effects on Nigeria's religious violence are real and devastating. Although the government continues to work closely with other global governments and institutions to manage the problem, its failure to influence how this affects Nigeria's internal religious violence remains one of its most painful difficulties.

The government has also caused problems itself, and has yet to end its own corruption, as in the war against Boko Haram and the indictment of top military leaders and other government functionaries, and its own abuses of civilians, including those in the IDP camps.

Religious violence continues to confront Nigeria: in the Boko Haram/ISWAP insurgency; the Shi'ites, the herdsman issue, which in a way has been widened under the broader theme of attempts to Fulanize or Islamize Nigeria; and the violence in Kaduna State. Taking them in order: the Boko Haram/ISWAP situation is one of the most critical hydra-headed problems facing the stability of the Nigerian state. Although the heads of both organizations have been killed, their activities are far from over. Analytically, one can conclude that the failure to completely bring an end to the Boko Haram/ISWAP insurgency stems from the little effort devoted to the proper understanding of the group and the firm conviction that military force alone will end the insurgency. This "enemy-centric" approach is not known to have worked, and it is increasingly certain that not much success will ever attend the strategy. The government has also not been able to cut the sources of Boko Haram funding. In its 2021 Mutual Evaluation Report, the Inter-Governmental Action Group against Money Laundering in West Africa, established by the Economic Community of West African States, says ISWAP moved about N18 billion (US$36 million) generated from trading and taxing communities in the Lake Chad region through the Nigerian financial system annually.[2] The report also notes that Nigeria "lacked an explicit policy to confiscate proceeds of crime or property of equivalent value, including terrorism financing."[3] Also noted in the report is that the Nigerian government failed to confiscate the assets of terrorists as stipulated in the global anti-money laundering and counterterrorist financing standards. The Financial Action Task Force assessment gave a subtle indictment of the government when it noted that Nigerian authorities did not prioritize terrorism financing investigations, as there were only a few terrorist financing prosecutions and convictions, which do not reflect the country's risk profile in terrorist financing. Specifically, the Task Force noted that "no individual, body or corporation has been convicted in Nigeria for funding terrorism since the insurgency started in 2009." Finally the Task Force noted that

> "Nigeria has a significant but incomplete understanding of its TF (terrorist financing) threats and risks. It lacks adequate insight into Boko/ISWAP's international linkages and abuse of the formal financial and commercial sector. The authorities do not prioritise TF investigations, as there are only a few TF prosecutions and convictions which do not reflect Nigeria's TF risk profile. The Department of State Services, Nigeria's lead counter-terrorism agency, has significant ability to identify and investigate TF activity. It conducts parallel financial investigations in conjunction with terrorism investigations. However, there is little evidence of the effectiveness of such efforts."[4]

Although some security responses to Boko Haram have had some isolated success, overall, the war against the insurgents has been mired with setbacks and errors that undoubtedly contributed to the escalation of the insurgency.

Meanwhile, the Shi'ite issue is yet to be completely resolved. Although their leader El-Zakzaky has been released, many fundamental issues are still yet to be resolved, including the banning of the Islamic Movement of Nigeria. Indeed, further Shi'ite violence could bring further acrimony to intergroup relations and intra-Islamic harmony. The Movement now sees itself fighting on three fronts: against the Nigerian government, against global forces led by Saudi Arabia, and against Sunni Moslems back at home in Nigeria. In fact, more sympathy seems to come from Nigerian Christians than from fellow Moslems.

The links between religion, ethnicity, and violence are now blurring in a way that portends the greatest threats to Nigerian's existence, through the entrance into national dialogue of the double terms and dynamics of Fulanization and Islamization. As noted in chapter 6, identity lines, especially when it comes to illegal acts, have become unclear—actors in violent acts and those interpreting those acts alike have multiple identities that can be deployed at any time. People have interpreted the government's plan to establish settlements for Fulani herdsmen in both religious and ethnic terms, and getting into it or out of it remains the unwinnable option that the Buhari administration must contend with for the remaining part of its term.

The crisis in southern Kaduna continues to attract attention, with its religious dimensions becoming apparent amid its ethnic connotations. The incendiary language of political elites has also not helped matters, and they oscillate between outright insensitivity and lack of appreciation of the complexities. People are being killed in southern Kaduna, and the federal and state governments should put rhetoric aside and address the situation. Publicity about the brutal killings on social media further inflames anger. The government's identification of the problem as rooted in "an evil combination of politically-motivated banditry, revenge killings and mutual violence by criminal gangs acting on ethnic and religious grounds" is not enough; sincere efforts should be made to put an end to it.[5]

Having provided a panoramic survey of the causes of religious violence in Nigeria and the situation report, this conclusion now revalidates the central arguments posited by this book. The first is that violence associated with religion in Nigeria is rooted in the numerous contradictions that have underlined the establishment of the Nigerian state. The vicissitudes of colonial division that brought disparate communities together without cognizance of their history stand accused here. The frequency with which this factor has been cited in Africa's postindependence challenges does not reduce the strength of its validity. Also indicted are the injustices—real and imagined—of colonialism, especially in the advantages that Muslims believe it gave Christians, and, by inference, southerners. Violence associated with religion in Nigeria is also rooted in the numerous contradictions that have underlined the establishment of the Nigerian state. Politics and intergroup relations have intermixed with religion since independence. This left issues that explain some aspects of religious violence in postindependence Nigeria.

A second thesis that this book has tried to establish is that incidents of religious violence in Nigeria are, contrary to widely held assumptions, not a monopoly of the Islamic religion, even if the occurrences of violence that have made the country the focus of global attention have been. Taking a broader definition of violence, we can see that the Christian and even traditional religions in Nigeria have also been associated with violence in a variety of ways. For Christianity, these include public calls by prominent clergymen to respond violently to perceived attacks; responses to real and perceived attacks from Muslims; the formation of a Christian militant group—even if it's not operational; acts of physical violence in churches over disagreements about money, leadership, and succession; and infliction of violence on young children alleged to be witches, while for traditional religions, acts of violence include cases of physical violence involved in some religious practices and attempts to regain ground lost to Christianity and Islam, among others. All these too are acts of violence associated with religion, and the fact that they did not result in massive causalities or gain wide publicity does not diminish this fact. Consequently, this book argues that in looking at the link between religion and violence in Nigeria mainly through the prism of the Islamic religion, scholars and observers seem to have been looking in the wrong direction.

The role of the elites, especially the political and religious elites, is also an identifiable feature in the politics of religious violence in Nigeria. Undeniably, various acts of religious violence in Nigeria have been associated with elite manipulation. Indeed, the situation in the Middle Belt, especially in Plateau State, has shown how quickly political elites can use religion in political calculations. Even major uprisings like the Maitatsine riots and Boko Haram have also been linked—even if allegedly—to political machinations of the elites. While it may not necessarily be a major cause, the role of political elites in the pattern of manifestation and the reasons for prolongation is plausible. Even religious elites have been involved in the politics of religious violence in Nigeria, by exploiting the ignorance of their followers. Across the nation, religious leaders have deliberately or unwittingly encouraged their followers to violence and have also subjected their followers to manipulation.

The fourth argument posited by this book is that issues surrounding religious violence are largely internal, either in terms of cause or in the pattern of manifestation. Even when external considerations, like the situation in the Middle East or developments in Iran, have been factors, local idiosyncrasies have always affected the ways they are expressed. The rapid increase in global incidents of religious violence introduced by groups like al-Qaeda and ISIS significantly impacts Nigeria, including the ways it brought radical groups on the continent together. Despite this, however, violence in Nigeria remains local. External considerations often revive dormant local issues to be fully expressed in conflict. Even external sponsors have always identified the importance of local issues, and this explains their deep interest in local peculiarities.

The final argument is that recent cases of religious violence in Nigeria have benefited from some of the consequences of globalization. This can be seen in the ways insurgent groups and perpetrators of religious violence have exploited the information revolution to propagate and advance their activities.

In October 2020, while Nigeria was still handling the minimal challenges posed by the COVID-19 pandemic, a nationwide protest of unprecedented proportions, tagged #EndSARS, occurred across most of the states in the country and the federal capital territory, Abuja. The original objective of the #EndSARS movement was to protest against the activities of the Special Anti-robbery Squad (SARS), the special section of the police that was ostensibly formed to fight crime but had become a source of intimidation, corruption, and oppression to the majority of the population, particularly youths.[6] Exploiting their knowledge of social media, youths across Nigeria and even abroad were able to organize a sophisticated and nonviolent campaign that won national and global admiration. The #EndSARS goals were later widened to include other issues and encompass various indices of bad governance in the country. Nonviolent and organized marches were made across the country. At some stage, however, the group was infiltrated by those with other objectives, and the protests became violent, resulting in the looting of shops, arson, and destruction of property across Lagos and many other state capitals. Prisons were invaded and inmates released. In response, the security forces attacked protesters, and some people were killed, especially in Lagos.

Although largely political and socioeconomic in origin, the #EndSARS protests, quite ironically, had links with the politics of religious violence in Nigeria. Coming when many Nigerian clergy were critical of the government, with the introduction of the Companies and Allied Matter Act that regulates the activities of religious organizations, many religious institutions were poised to respond to government policies that they found unacceptable. Broadly, the interconnections between the #EndSARS movement, religion, and violence came in two different phases: before the protests became violent and afterward. During the first phase, most religious leaders gave tacit support to youth protests against brutality, and the leaders were impressed at the maturity and orderliness exhibited by the protesters. Some Christian clergy and a few Muslim clerics encouraged their members to participate. Among others, Christian clergies like Paul Adefarasin, Ituah Ighodalo, Tosyn Buknor, and a few others saw justification in the complaints of the protesters and openly aligned with their causes. Even Pastor Adeboye of the Redeemed Christian Church, known for his caution on political issues, endorsed the orderly protests, having a few weeks earlier called for the restructuring of Nigeria, a position widely seen by many as calling for a reduction of perceived northern Muslim control of political events in the country.[7] These Christian leaders also justified the peaceful protests and saw them as a way to bring the Buhari administration to the path of what they saw as fairness in balancing the country's ethnic and religious affairs. While few Islamic clerics also saw justification for the peaceful protests, those in the category were fewer, and the intensity of their endorsement for the peaceful protests was less vociferous. The endorsement all these religious leaders gave could also have been because many of their members had been victims of police brutality. In all their endorsements, however, they insisted that the protesters should remain peaceful. Many other pastors and a few Muslim clerics in their various sermons were critical of the extent of social injustices in Nigerian society, and they used the opportunity to justify, even if they did not say that they endorsed, the protests.

During the second phase, religious leaders condemned the way the peaceful protests were hijacked by those with far less honorable intentions. When the violence was forcefully repressed by the government, another set of reactions emerged from religious leaders. Most of the religious leaders that commented during this period expressed shock and dismay. Again, two sets of reactions could be noticed at this stage: first were those of Christian clergy who took the "I warned you in advance" position. Those in this category claim to have warned the nation in advance of the dangers and consequences of electing Buhari president, either before he assumed office or early in his administration. Consequently, those included here had critically expressed unfriendly views about the president before the protests. Two of the clergymen that are prominent here, again, were David Oyedepo of Faith Tabernacle and Johnson Suleman of the Omega Fire Ministry International. Shortly before the forceful repression, Oyedepo had said,

> I kept quiet for a while because in 2015 I warned this nation, vehemently, consistently . . . because I saw the dangers ahead and you can tell. The most gruesome season in the life of this nation is in the last five years, where lives have no value, wanton killings here and there. Now, they have faced the youths; and because they don't know who is next, they have a right to say enough is enough. Any system that has no value for human lives is irrelevant. If they were killed when they were youths, will they be here today? Now, it will be a sacrilege to shoot the protesters who are not looting, who are not ravaging.[8]

On his part, Johnson Suleman said that he saw the protests as a spiritual move to teach Nigerian leaders a lesson that youths cannot be taken for granted.[9]

But apart from these two clergymen, many others also condemned the brutal repression but did not set it against any "I warned you in advance" precedence. Tunde Bakare, known for his radical stance on national issues and who had earlier called the Special Anti-robbery Squad the "State-Aided Robbery Squad," pointed out, "This is not the nation we hope to bequeath to our children. We will build this nation, not upon the altar of the blood of our young people, but on their visions and aspirations."[10] The general overseer of the Redeemed Christian Church of God, Pastor Adeboye, also condemned the attack on #EndSARS protesters, expressing dismay that "prior to the [attack on protesters] the Nigerian Police failed to arrest the weapon-bearing hoodlums who were attacking the well-organized and non-violent #EndSARS protesters."[11]

After the forceful suppression of the violence, religious leaders who were critical of the handling of the #EndSARS protesters were also disturbed at the refusal of the president, despite repeated calls by the Senate, the House of Representatives, and key individuals, to address the nation. For example, Pastor Olumide Emmanuel of Calvary Bible Church called out the president and accused him of insensitivity and arrogance. When eventually the president addressed the nation, the criticism increased because of what some clergymen saw as the insensitivity and lack of empathy in the broadcast.

A young Nigerian pastor, however, faulted the views in certain quarters of the country that the president ought to have addressed the youths in his capacity as the father of the nation. In a discussion with me, Pastor Tunde Adeyemi pointed out the fallacy in this assumption, which he said underlines the faulty paternalism that has bedeviled Nigeria. According to him, President Buhari should not be seen as the father of the youths, but as their employee. He noted, "He applied to us for [a] job by contesting; we reviewed his application by studying his manifesto, and we appointed him for the job by voting for him. So he is our employee and not our father. We pay his salary." He wondered why Boris Johnson was not seen as the father of British youths. Consequently, he saw the government's handling of the #EndSARS protests as falling significantly short.

The discovery of warehouses where food items that ought to have been distributed to the population several months previously for COVID-19 relief also brought violent anger from some religious leaders. Here Muslim clerics were unequivocal in their condemnation of various state governments. For example, in Ilorin, Kwara State, a Muslim musician with a considerable following among youths, known as Labaeka, went on social media to heap curses on the political elites for starving the population. Quoting verses from the Qur'an, he vented anger on the elites and warned them of serious spiritual repercussions if they did not ask for forgiveness. Although there was no known official endorsement by any religious leader of the looting of the COVID-19 supplies, there was also, quite significantly, no serious rebuttal, possibly indicating that some saw justification in their actions.

The involvement of religious leaders in the #EndSARS protests was not lost on the government, and the special adviser to the president on media and publicity, Femi Adesina, openly blamed churches and mosques "for promoting messages of hate." Adesina said many churches and mosques used the campaign to spread messages of hate and division: "When things boil over in graphic demonstration of hatred, it is a culmination of negative sentiments and tendencies. They come in persistent negative postings on social media, which generate and stimulate hate." He was more specific when he said that hate came "from hateful messages from the pulpit, as if that was the message of love, Jesus Christ handed over to his followers [and] from unduly critical messages during *Jumat* services."[12]

But beyond all the interpretations of the actions and inactions during the #EndSARS protests, there also emerged more fundamental issues in the protests that linked religion to violence in Nigeria. Three of these are particularly important. First, they united Nigeria across ethnic and religious lines. Never in the history of the country had Christians, Muslims, and traditional worshippers come together to fight for a cause. The holding of Jumat prayers on the streets on Friday and the conduct of Sunday Christian services at the same venue showed the level of harmony that can exist between Christians and Muslims if they are not divided by the selfish political motives of the elite class. Indeed, more than ever before in the country, the youths realized the importance of a unity devoid of elite interference.

Second, the handling of the protests also raised questions about the attitude of Nigerian security forces in addressing insurrections. There are indeed clergymen who argued that the same brutal force that the security forces had used to address the Boko Haram insurgents, which had proved ineffective, was also used against the protesters. There are those who believe that the Nigerian military should have realized the uselessness of this method of response. That the military adopted this approach in attempting to end internal protests showed some that they are yet to learn anything from what they saw as their failure in the handling of the Boko Haram conflict.

However, what seems to be the most important connection between the #EndSARS protest and the whole issue of religion and violence in Nigeria is the potential of the protests for redrawing the Nigerian state. Indeed, the conclusion from all over the country was that never before in the history of Nigeria had the elite class been so threatened to the point of recognizing the need to take seriously the call by many to address what they saw as the unworkability of the structure called Nigeria. The nature and extent of the protests showed the Nigerian political class that the days of continuing with the old order are numbered, and that the number is small indeed. Under the envisaged new Nigeria, issues underlining religious violence will, hopefully, be addressed.

A subject of controversy is the extent to which religion endorsed the violence associated with the #EndSARS protests. Here again, there are two mutually reinforcing types of violence: physical attacks on police officers and violent attacks on warehouses where food that should have been distributed to the population as COVID-19 relief was kept. While all religions oppose violence against police, they all seem to feel that looting the food is understandable, if not, in fact, legitimate.

In conclusion, perhaps a thought can be shared on the management of what is perhaps the most profound of the religious challenges facing Nigeria—Boko Haram. After more than a decade of living with the problem, the time seems to have come to take stock, especially in two directions: in the practical dimension, what operations work and what do not; and the extent to which scholarship has assisted in bringing us nearer to the resolution of the conflict. It can be concluded that some of the strategies adopted so far have secured very minimal success, and it is time to go back to the drawing board to develop new strategies. The excuse that the largely conventional tactics of the Nigerian defense forces cannot match the guerrilla method of the Boko Haram insurgents is no longer tenable after more than a decade of military engagement. The factionalized insurgent groups have also accrued more resources for themselves. More people, especially those outside the conflict zones, are gradually developing a sense of detachment from the Nigerian government. Rather than seeing the conflict as the tragedy that it is, the conflict is now wired into a war economy where both local and foreign agencies wrestle for seemingly limitless opportunities for self-enrichment.

Scholarship, too, has failed dismally to address Boko Haram effectively. Several hundred reports, articles, books, and conference papers, in addition to expert workshops, symposiums, and intervention/deradicalization programs, have been written and organized around the subject of Boko Haram, with little or no success in ending the conflict. Indeed, all that Boko Haram seems to have done is to provide scholars, Nigerian and non-Nigerian alike, with opportunities to publish books and journal articles for career progression. In a way, studying

Boko Haram has become a form of conflict profiteering, just as the Liberian and Sierra Leone civil wars were in the 1990s. The Boko Haram–affected regions have become reservoirs of research data where foreign researchers pay token fees to residents and local researchers in exchange for massive amounts of data that they then publish and disseminate through media unavailable to residents and local researchers. Yet they do not, in any way, assist in addressing the problem. Understandably, residents and local researchers are becoming increasingly wary of the avalanche of researchers who see them solely as sources of data collection in what has now become a form of humanitarian pornography.

INTRODUCTION

1. "Nigeria Leads in Religious Belief," BBC News, February 26, 2004, http://news.bbc
   .co.uk/1/hi/programmes/wtwtgod/3490490.stm.
2. Global Terrorism Index, Institute for Economics and Peace, National Consortium
   for the Study of Terrorism and Responses to Terrorism, University of Maryland,
   2018, 8.
3. Batson, Schoenrade, and Ventis, *Religion and the Individual*.
4. McGuire, *Religion*; Seul, "'Ours Is the Way of God.'"
5. Yinger, *The Scientific Study of Religion*, 33.
6. Huntington, *The Clash of Civilization and the Remaking of World Order*, 27.
7. Pargament, *Psychology of Religion and Coping*, 2.
8. Eitzen and Zinn, "Religion."
9. Recent books on violence include Alvares and Bachman, *Violence*; Larkin, *When
   Violence Is the Answer*.
10. David Rapoport has done a study interrogating how three main religions have been
    associated with violence; see Rapoport, "Fear and Trembling."
11. Abd Aziz, "Terror in the Name of God," 61.
12. Horsley, "The Sicarii."
13. For more on the Assassins, see Hodgson, *The Secret Order of Assassins*.
14. Abd Aziz, "Terror in the Name of God."
15. Mayall, "Jihad and the Clash within Civilization," 27–40.
16. This jihad occurred in most parts of present-day northern Nigeria, discussed exten-
    sively in chapter 1.
17. For more on revivalist Islam in North Africa, see El-Khawas, "Revolutionary Islam
    in North Africa."
18. Adam, "Islam and Politics in Somalia."
19. See Hallaq, *The Impossible State*; Sabet, *Islam and the Political*.
20. Davidson, *Islamic Fundamentalism*, 39.
21. Salvatore, *The Sociology of Islam*.

22. A'la Maududi, *Jihad in Islam*.
23. I owe this point to Abdulbassit Kassim, who is quoted here. Personal communication, June 15, 2019.
24. Juergensmeyer, *Terror in the Mind of God*, 11.
25. I thank Professor Simeon Ilesanmi for drawing my attention to this.
26. Esposito, *Unholy War*.
27. Ayoob, *The Many Faces of Political Islam*, 143.
28. This can be seen, for example, in the celebration of Husain, the third Shi'ite imam, who died while rebelling against Yazid, who practiced an adulterated version of Islam. See Olomojobi, *Frontiers of Jihad*, 94.
29. Olomojobi, *Frontiers of Jihad*, 95.
30. Interview with Alhaji Sule Baba Ali, November 2007.
31. Quadri, "All in the Name of God."
32. Quadri, "All in the Name of God."
33. AbdulSalam, "Islam and Public Life," 261.
34. AbdulSalam, "Islam and Public Life."
35. See, for example, Ranstorp, *Understanding Violent Radicalisation*; Peter Neumann, "Introduction," in Neumann, *Perspectives on Radicalization and Political Violence*.
36. Bourne, *Nigeria*, ix.
37. Adisa Adeleye, "Amalgamation of 1914: Was It a Mistake?" *Vanguard*, May 18, 2012.
38. Most of the officers who staged the coup were Christian Ibos, and those assassinated were Hausa and Yoruba, including two of the highest-ranking Hausa army officers, Prime Minister Tafawa Balewa, Northern Region Premier Ahmadu Bello, and the Western Premier Ladoke Akintola.
39. For more on the civil war, see Stremlau, *The International Politics of the Nigerian Civil War*. Nigerians who participated in the war have now contributed to the literature, including Obasanjo, *My Command*; Alabi-Isama, *The Tragedy of Victory*.
40. This is the process whereby offices were allocated to ensure some form of ethnic and religious balance.
41. See Ali, *Anatomy of Corruption in Nigeria*.
42. See Owele, "Class of 1999 Governors," 33.

CHAPTER ONE: RELIGION AND NIGERIAN SOCIETY

1. See Idowu, *African Traditional Religion*; Awolalu, *West African Traditional Religion*; Olupona, *African Spirituality*; among others.
2. For example, human sacrifice was known to be practiced among the Gauls in Europe.
3. Mbiti, *African Religions, and Philosophy*.
4. Olupona, "15 Facts of African Religions."
5. Olupona, *African Religions*.
6. Olupona, *African Religions*.
7. Olupona, *African Religions*.
8. Olupona, *African Religions*.
9. Olupona, *African Religions*.

10. See Bala, "Da'wah towards Alleviating Spirit Worship and Devil Possession."

11. For more on Igbo traditional religion, see Arinze, *Sacrifice in Igbo Religion*.

12. For more on Olódùmarè, see Bolaji Idowu's seminal study, *Olodumare*. A study that discusses the role of sacrifice among the Yoruba is Awolalu, *Yoruba Beliefs and Sacrificial Rites*.

13. For more on Ile-Ife, see Olupona, *City of 201 Gods*.

14. See Abimbola, "The Place of African Traditional Religion in Contemporary Africa."

15. Balogun, "History of Islam up to 1800," 211.

16. Balogun, "History of Islam up to 1800," 24–25.

17. For more on this, see Morgan, *Islam, the Straight Path*, 247.

18. See Falola, *Violence in Nigeria*, 24

19. The Wangarawas were mainly people of Malian origins who operated long-distance commerce across West Africa. See Akinwumi and Raji, "The Wangarawa Factor in the History of Nigerian Islam."

20. Hunwick, "Songhay, Borno and Hausa States," 338.

21. Kenny, "The Spread of Islam in Nigeria."

22. Balogun, "History of Islam up to 1800," 213.

23. Adeleye, "Hausaland and Borno," 618.

24. Adeleye, "Hausaland and Borno," 619.

25. For example, Sarkin Kano, Kumbari dan Sharefa (c. 731–43), was said to have imposed illegal taxes on the Kurumi market, while another king, Baba Zaki (1706–76), was noted for oppressing his subjects. See Adeleye, "Hausaland and Borno," 621.

26. See Crowder, *The Story of Nigeria*.

27. Malumfashi, The Spread and Development of Islamic Civilization."

28. Malumfashi, "The Spread and Development of Islamic Civilization."

29. Akintoye, *A History of the Yoruba People*, 333.

30. Akinjogbin, "The Expansion of Oyo and the Rise of Dahomey."

31. Gbadamosi, *The Growth of Islam among the Yoruba*; Makinde, "The Institution of Shari'ah in Oyo and Osun States."

32. Gbadamosi, *The Growth of Islam among the Yoruba*.

33. Akintoye, *A History of the Yoruba People*, 334.

34. Gbadamosi and Ajayi, "Islam and Christianity in Nigeria," 347.

35. Gbadamosi and Ajayi, "Islam and Christianity in Nigeria," 348.

36. See Islam in Yorubaland, https://dawahnigeria.com/articles/knowledge/islaam -yorubaland.

37. Opeloye, "The Yoruba Muslims' Cultural Identity."

38. Rufai, "A Foreign Faith in a Christian Domain," 137.

39. See Nwaka, "The Early Missionary Groups and the Contest for Igboland."

40. Kukah, *Religion, Politics, and Power in Northern Nigeria*.

41. This was the view of Alhaji Fuad, a Muslim scholar who runs an Islamic school in Abuja.

42. See Falola, *Violence in Nigeria*, 27.

43. Interview with Alhaji Suleiman Baba Ali, former Kogi state commissioner for health, September 2009.

44. Interviews conducted in Kano, Kaduna, and Sokoto, June 2008.

45. See Bello, "Jos Crisis and Ethnic Animosity in Nigeria."

46. Bello, "Jos Crisis and Ethnic Animosity in Nigeria."

47. Umar, *Islam and Colonialism*.

48. Umar, *Islam and Colonialism*, 33.

49. Umar, *Islam and Colonialism*, 35–38.

50. Peter Clarke and Ian Linden pointed out that many Muslims believed that this would be in 1949 (1400 AH). They further noted that the siege of the Grand Mosque in Mecca coincided with this date and that the first Maitatsine riots in Kano occurred one year after. See Clarke and Linden, *Islam in Modern Nigeria*, 43.

51. For a discussion on the relationship between the Qadriyya and the Tijaniyya, see Loimeier, "Nigeria."

52. Kenny, "The Spread of Islam in Nigeria," 9. There have been attempts, historically and recently, to force a change in this dominant attitude toward religion and religious politics by some leaders in the Yoruba Islamic community. However, these efforts have largely failed, despite the ascendancy and dominance of Yoruba Muslims (organized around Governor Bola Tinubu) in Yoruba-Nigerian politics for the first time since the 1950s. For more on this, see Adebanwi, *Yorùbá Elites and Ethnic Politics in Nigeria*, especially chapter 7.

53. This is discussed at some length in Uzoma, "Religious Pluralism, Cultural Differences and Social Stability in Nigeria," 651–64.

54. Dike, "Origins of the Niger Mission."

55. Dike, "Origins of the Niger Mission."

56. Dike, "Origins of the Niger Mission."

57. See Ajayi, *Christian Missions in Nigeria*; Ayandele, *The Missionary Impact on Modern Nigeria*.

58. Akintoye, *A History of the Yoruba People*, 352.

59. Ayandele, "The Missionary Factor in Northern Nigeria," 503.

60. Ayandele, "The Missionary Factor in Northern Nigeria."

61. Ayandele, "The Missionary Factor in Northern Nigeria," 351.

62. Ayandele, "The Missionary Factor in Northern Nigeria."

63. Ayandele, "The Missionary Factor in Northern Nigeria."

64. Gbadamosi and Ajayi, "Islam and Christianity in Nigeria," 352.

65. Omotoye, "A Critical Examination of the Activities of Pentecostal Churches."

66. Omotoye, "A Critical Examination of the Activities of Pentecostal Churches."

67. For more on John Elton, see Abodunde, *Messenger*.

68. Abodunde, *Messenger*.

69. Ojo, "The Contextual Significance of the Charismatic Movement."

70. Ojo, "The Contextual Significance of the Charismatic Movement"; and Ojo, *The End-Time Army*, 24–25.

71. A survey carried out at the Obafemi Awolowo University, Ile-Ife, in the country's southwestern region reveals that no faculty in the university does not have a staff member also serving as a pastor or assistant pastor of a Pentecostal church.

72. Gbadamosi and Ajayi, "Islam and Christianity in Nigeria," 353.

73. Gbadamosi and Ajayi, "Islam and Christianity in Nigeria."

74. Jimoh, "The Growth and Development of Islam in Epe," 6.
75. Interview with Professor Simeon Ilesanmi, March 15, 2019.
76. Interview with Ilesanmi.
77. Interview with Ilesanmi.
78. Yesufu, "The Impact of Religion on a Secular State."
79. These include Bienen, "Religion, Legitimacy, and Conflict in Nigeria"; Clarke, "Islamic Reform in Contemporary Nigeria"; Adebanwi, "The Clergy, Culture and Political Conflicts in Nigeria"; Kukah, "Christians and Nigeria's Aborted Transition"; Kukah and Falola, *Religious Militancy and Self-Assertion*; Olupona and Falola, *Religion and Society in Nigeria*; Obadare, "Pentecostal Presidency?"; Agbaje, "Travails of the Secular State"; among others.
80. Kukah, *Religion, Power and Politics in Northern Nigeria*, 115.
81. Ilesanmi, *Religious Pluralism and the Nigerian State*, 158–70.
82. Ilesanmi, *Religious Pluralism and the Nigerian State*.
83. Ilesanmi, *Religious Pluralism and the Nigerian State*, 170–72.
84. Falola, *Violence in Nigeria*, 37.
85. Vaughan, *Religion and the Making of Nigeria*.

CHAPTER TWO: ISLAM AND VIOLENCE IN NIGERIA
1. Falola, *Violence in Nigeria*, 5.
2. These are some of the views expressed during focus group discussions held across the country, especially in some parts of northern Nigeria.
3. The name Maitatsine was given to Marwa because he often ended his public preaching with the Hausa saying, "Wanda bata yarda ba Allah tatsine" (May God curse whosoever does not agree with me). Consequently, *Maitatsine* in Hausa means "the one who causes." On the riots, see, among others, Adesoji, "Between Maitatsine and Boko Haram"; Lubeck, "Islamic Protest under Semi-industrial Capitalism."
4. Isichei, "The Maitatsine Risings in Nigeria."
5. Isichei, "The Maitatsine Risings in Nigeria."
6. Quoted from Omolesky, "Dwelling in the Fire."
7. Comment from a noncommissioned officer who fought against the group during the riots in Kano.
8. O'Leary and McGhee, *War in Heaven/Heaven on Earth*, 147.
9. Isichei, "The Maitatsine Risings in Nigeria."
10. Isichei, "The Maitatsine Risings in Nigeria."
11. Isichei, "The Maitatsine Risings in Nigeria."
12. One issue was not to go to work on Friday—in line with the Christians, who have their holy day, Sunday, as a work-free day.
13. Focus group discussion at Kano.
14. Focus group discussion at Ile-Ife.
15. This came out of some of the focus group discussions that took place in the north. It is important to note that very few mentioned it in the south.
16. Dare Baabarinsa and Yakubu Mohammed, "Fire of Religion," *Newswatch*, March 30, 1987, 8–14.

17. *Newswatch*, March 30, 20; *Tell*, October 28, 1991.
18. Karl Maier, "Beheading Stirs Nigerian Tension," *Independent* (London), August 16, 1995.
19. Obed Minchakpu, "Religious Riots in Nigeria Leave Hundreds Dead," *Christianity Today*, October 1, 2001.
20. In November 2008, allegations of corruption in a local government election later assumed religious connotations when some alleged that positions on the matter were taken on the basis of religious sentiments. This resulted in a riot that killed many people. See Madueke, and Vermeulen, "Frontiers of Ethnic Brutality in an African City."
21. Among the reasons why Nigeria was selected to host the competition was that the previous year a Nigerian, Miss Agbani Darego, had won the competition.
22. Weimann, *Islamic Criminal Law in Northern Nigeria*, 152.
23. Discussion with Alhaji Abdul Razak, Abuja, March 2009. See also "Nigerian Muslim Body Overrules Miss World Fatwa," *Irish Times*, November 28, 2002.
24. Christian Allen Purefoy, "Five Days of Violence by Nigerian Christians and Muslims Kill 150," *Independent*, February 24, 2006, https://www.independent.co.uk/news /world/africa/five-days-of-violence-by-nigerian-christians-and-muslims-kill-150 -6108388.html.
25. Obed Minchakpu, "Muslim Youths Destroy 10 Nigerian Churches," *Compass Direct News*, March 26, 2006.
26. Ben Adaji, "Killing in Allah's Name," *The News*, April 9 2007.
27. Sam Olukoya, "Eyewitness: Nigeria's Sharia Amputees," BBC News, December 19, 2002, http://news.bbc.co.uk/2/hi/africa/2587039.stm.
28. Olukoya, "Eyewitness."
29. Ivan Watson, "Nigerian Girl Flogged for Premarital Sex," *San Francisco Chronicle*, January 23, 2001.
30. Human Rights Watch, "Nigeria: Women Sentenced to Death under Sharia," October 2001, https://www.hrw.org/news/2001/10/23/nigeria-woman-sentenced -death-under-sharia#.
31. "Nigeria: Teenage Mother Whipped," Human Rights Watch, January 2001, https:// www.hrw.org/news/2001/01/23/nigeria-teenage-mother-whipped.
32. I thank Abdulbassit Kassim for drawing my attention to this.
33. The activities of Muntada al-Islami Trust continue to be very controversial. In 2012, the *Nigerian Tribune* alleged that the Trust was sponsoring Boko Haram. This was repeated two years later in a letter signed by fourteen members of the US Congress to President Obama. The Trust, however, continues to deny this. See Alexander Thurston, "How Far Does Saudi Arabia's Influence Go? Look at Nigeria," *Washington Post*, October 31, 2016.
34. Berkley Center for Religion, Peace, and World Affairs, Georgetown University, "The Religious Landscape of Bangladesh: A Primer," policy brief no. 12, November 2014, https://s3.amazonaws.com/berkley-center/141101WFDDPolicyBriefReligiousLandsc apeBangladeshPrimer.pdf.
35. I am grateful to Dr. Makinde for drawing my attention to this.

36. Mustapha and Bunza, "Contemporary Islamic Sect and Groups in Northern Nigeria."

37. Bala and Sa'id, "Qur'anists' Deviant Da'wah as Reflected in Their Trends of Tafsir."

38. Dare Babarinsa, "Allahu Akbar! Allahu Ak-War!," *Tell*, October 28, 1991.

39. John Shiklam, "Nigeria: Sultan—We Must Counter Christians," *Daily Champion*, July 3, 2007.

40. Interviews in Iwo, Osun State.

41. In terms of its origin, the group is believed to be an offshoot of the combined reign of Abdulaziz and Sheikh Mohammed Abdelwahab in Arabia in the eighteenth century, both of whom were determined to get Arabian society back on the path of Islam after slipping away from the dictates set by the Holy Prophet.

42. "Many Voices of Islam," *Newswatch*, October 10, 1988, 20.

43. Gumi, *Where I Stand*.

44. Ade Olorunfewa, "Jitters Over Kano Riots," *Tell*, August 26, 1996, 10.

45. Adesoji, "The Boko Haram Uprising," 99.

46. JTI was a Kano-based IMN breakaway group founded in 1994 that continued El-Zakzaky's confrontational stance toward the government but through Salafist doctrine and whose members reportedly carried out the beheading of a Christian trader in Kano. Adesoji, "The Boko Haram Uprising."

47. Abdallah El Kurebe, "Islamic Preacher Shot Dead in Sokoto," *Vanguard*, July 20, 2007.

48. Sheriff Bello, "Riots in Sokoto," *Nigerian Tribune*, June 20, 2007.

49. Interviews in Sokoto, December 2007.

50. This is contained in WikiLeaks: "Nigeria: Shi'a Leader Implicates U.S. in Sunni Imam's Killing," Cable 08ABUJA321, February 21, 2008, https://wikileaks.org/plusd/cables/08ABUJA321_a.html.

51. Abubakar, "Nigeria's Blasphemy Laws and the Competing Rights."

52. Abubakar, "Nigeria's Blasphemy Laws and the Competing Rights."

53. Samuel Nkanu Onnoghen and Ibrahim Tanko Muhammad, "Supreme Court Upholds Two Death Sentences for Murder," *Vanguard*, October 8, 2007.

54. Hannah Punitha, "Finally, the Nigerian Man with 86 Wives Slapped with 'Fatwa,'" https://www.medindia.net/news/finally-the-nigerian-man-with-86-wives-slapped-with-fatwa-43361-1.htm.

55. I was in Nigeria during the time, and there were several phone-in programs on radio stations in the southwest, with some callers calling on Yoruba Muslims to no longer recognize the sultan of Sokoto as their spiritual leader.

56. See interview granted by Alhaji Waheed Olajide, *Nigeria Tribune*, January 23, 2009, 47.

57. Olajide, interview, *Nigeria Tribune*.

58. Olajide, interview, *Nigeria Tribune*.

59. "Dasuki's Albatross, June 12 Divides Muslims," *Tell*, October 10, 1994, 10.

60. The video clip of this went viral on social media.

61. Francis Ezediuno, "Four Injured as Opposing Groups Clash over Inisa Chief Imam," *Daily Post*, October 17, 2021.

62. I thank Dr. Olawale Ismail for drawing my attention to this point.
63. I thank Dr. Olawale Ismail for drawing my attention to this point.
64. See Adeniyi, "Evolution of Islamic Education in Nigeria."
65. Asaju, "Restoring the Religious Factor in Education," 95.
66. For details, see Falola, *Violence in Nigeria*, 175–77.
67. Discussion at Obafemi Awolowo Unversity, June 2008.
68. Discussions at Ile-Ife.
69. I thank Dr. Olawale Ismail for drawing my attention to this.
70. Alao, "Islamic Radicalisation and Political Violence in Nigeria."
71. Zakariyya Adaramola, "Africa: OAU Clash: MSS Denies Launching Attack," *Daily Trust*, March 15, 2006.
72. Focus group discussion at the Obafemi Awolowo University, June 2008.
73. Interviews at the Obafemi Awolowo University, June 2008.
74. Indeed, an international conference to appreciate the key importance of the media in understanding religious violence in Nigeria was scheduled to take place in the capital, Abuja, in July 2008.
75. Dare Babarinsa and Yakubu Mohammed, "Violence in Kaduna: Religious Fanatics on the Rampage," *Newswatch*, March 30, 1987, 10.
76. Alao, "Islamic Radicalisation and Political Violence in Nigeria."
77. Alao, "Islamic Radicalisation and Political Violence in Nigeria."
78. Interviews in Jos, December 2008.
79. Interviews in Jos, December 2008.
80. Davis and Manya, *An Account of Ibrahim Zakzaky*
81. Davis and Manya, *An Account of Ibrahim Zakzaky*.
82. See Paden, *Muhammadu Buhari*, 170.
83. Paden, *Muhammadu Buhari*, 171.
84. See the official website of the Islamic Movement of Nigeria, http://www.islamicmovement.org.
85. Yakubu Mohammed, "Now, the 'War': Shi'ite Muslim Leader Defies Orders and Riots Engulf Katsina," *Newswatch*, April 29, 1991, 18.
86. Yakubu Mohammed, "Now, the 'War': Shi'ite Muslim Leader Defies Orders and Riots Engulf Katsina," *Newswatch*, April 29, 1991.
87. Yakubu Mohammed, "Now, the 'War': Shi'ite Muslim Leader Defies Orders and Riots Engulf Katsina," *Newswatch*, April 29, 1991.
88. "The Continued Detention of El-Zakzaky," *This Day* (Lagos), May 15, 2018.
89. This was the parade for the 73 Regular Recruit intake. Henry Umoru, Luka Binniyat, Joseph Erunke, Mayen Etim, "Army/Shiite Clash: I Escaped by the Will of God," *Vanguard*, December 15, 2015.
90. Henry Umoru, Luka Binniyat, Joseph Erunke, Mayen Etim, "Army/Shiite Clash: I Escaped by the Will of God," *Vanguard*, December 15, 2015.
91. This was at the launching of a book titled *Fallacies of Shi'ite Beliefs*, written by Umar Labdo of the Maitama Sule University, held under the auspices of the Mahdi Foundation and the International Institute for Islamic Research and Development. See Godwin Isenyo, "Shi'ite, Threat to Nigeria Says Islamic Scholars," *Punch*, August 13, 2018.

92. Isenyo, "Shi'ite, Threat to Nigeria."

93. Caroline Mortimer, "Shi'a Muslims Visit Nigerian Churches to Celebrate Christmas with Christians," *Independent* (London), December 28, 2017.

94. Fikayo Olowolagba, "El-Zakzaky: MURIC States Position on the Proscription of IMN," *Daily Post*, July 29, 2019.

95. Olowolagba, "El-Zakzaky."

CHAPTER THREE: CHRISTIANITY AND VIOLENCE IN NIGERIA

1. The condemnation to death by stoning of Safiyatu raised considerable controversy with the former minister of justice, the late Bola Ige, who described it as "harsh and crude." There was also international condemnation, and the sentence was not carried out. Jangebe, who was from Jangebe village in the Talata Mafara Local Government Area of Zamfara State, was the first victim of Sharia amputation. Isa was the second and last person to suffer amputation in Zamfara State under Sharia law. He said he received calls from those who wanted him to sue the government, but he refused. Karen Macgregor, "Spread of Sharia Law Does Not Threaten Nigeria, Says President," *Independent*, May 21, 2002, https://www.independent.co.uk/news /world/africa/spread-of-sharia-law-does-not-threaten-nigeria-says-president -189216.html.

2. Interviews carried out in Kaduna in October 2005 confirmed that Christian youths, envisaging a counterresponse from their Muslim counterparts, prepared for violent confrontation.

3. Gilbert Da Costa, "Twenty Killed In Nigerian Sectarian Riot," *Washington Post*, February 22, 2000.

4. Discussions during the field trip.

5. See "Bloody Clashes in Kaduna as Christian Youths Resist Dating and Conversion of Christian Girls Share," *World Watch Monitor*, March 8, 2018.

6. Ben Adaji, "Five Killed, Houses Razed as Christians, Muslims Clash in Taraba," *P.M. News*, July 13, 2010.

7. A popular Nigerian newspaper columnist, Olusegun Adeniyi, noted that this identity verification by examination was confirmed to him by the former governor of the state, Ahmed Markarfi. Adeniyi mentioned the case of a hapless Muslim youth who was subjected to the Trinity question. Ignorant of the answer to complete the statement "in the name of the Father, the Son and . . . ," the hapless Muslim youth said, "and the Mother." See Olusegun Adeniyi, "Mass Murder on a Market Day," *This Day*, October 25, 2010.

8. Interviews in Kaduna, February 2009.

9. Interviews in Jos, April 2009.

10. Discussions in Kaduna, March 2018.

11. Discussions in Jos, April 2009.

12. Interviews and discussion in Jos, April 2009.

13. Chima Azubuikwe, "Gombe Easter Killing: Youth Boys Brigade Clash," *Punch*, April 28, 2019.

14. 'Dotun Akintomide, "'If You See Any Boko Haram Member, Kill Him, Spill His Blood,' Oyedepo Tells Members," *New Diplomat*, accessed January 7, 2022, https:// newdiplomatng.com/if-you-see-any-boko-haram-member-kill-them-spill-their -blood-oyedepo-tells-members/.

15. The Boko Haram fighter that was caught but who the government claimed alleg- edly escaped was Kabiru Sokoto. He escaped from prison in January 2012.

16. John Owen Nwachukwu, "Your Government Is a Failure, God Is Angry with You— Bishop Oyedepo Blasts Buhari," *Daily Post*, April 22, 2018.

17. "Mass Shooting in Church: Bishop David Oyedepo Says This Is an Evil Govern- ment," Starconnect Media, April 29, 2018, https://starconnectmedia.com/mass -shooting-in-church-bishop-david-oyedepo-says-this-is-an-evil-government/.

18. On one occasion, Oyedepo physically assaulted a young lady who called herself a "witch for Christ" during a deliverance service that took place at his church. The video of this incident went viral.

19. Kazeem Ugbodaga, "Daddy Freeze Attacks Oyedepo for Cursing Fulani Herds- men," PM News, August 11, 2019, https://www.pmnewsnigeria.com/2019/08/11/daddy -freeze-attacks-oyedepo-for-cursing-fulani-herdsmen/.

20. Allegations of human sacrifice have always been made against politicians pursuing their political ambitions.

21. The Kaduna State government came up with the law requiring public preach- ers to obtain a permit in March 2016. Those who violated the law would be fined N200,000. This was challenged in court, and the government lost.

22. Eromosele Ebhomele, "Kill Any Fulani Herdsman Trying to Attack My Church— Pastor Suleman Tells Members," Legit, January 21, 2017, https://www.naija.ng /1083888-kill-fulani-herdsman-attack-church-pastor-suleman-tells-members .html#1083888.

23. Kamarudeen Ogundele, "Drama as Fayose Foils DSS Plan to Arrest Apostle Sule- man," *Punch*, January 25, 2017. Immunity is the constitutional provision that pre- vents a governor from being arrested or prosecuted. This has often been assumed to extend to anyone in their company.

24. BVI Channel 1, "Apostle Suleman at War with Buhari, DSS & Fulani Herdsmen," YouTube, January 25, 2017, https://www.youtube.com/watch?v=a0WgJRoMfsE.

25. Josiah Oluwole, "Sex Scandal: Fayose Defends Apostle Suleman," *Premium Times*, March 15, 2017, https://www.premiumtimesng.com/news/more-news/226219-sex -scandal-fayose-defends-apostle-suleman.html.

26. Fikayo Olowolagba, "Slap Any Comedian That Cracks Jokes against Jesus— Suleman Tells Pastors," *Daily Post*, August 29, 2018.

27. "Buy Swords to Defend Yourselves—CAN Tells Southern Kaduna Christians," *Metro: Nigerian Bulletin*, January 26, 2017.

28. "Boko Haram Attacks: Adeboye, Oritsejafor, Oyedepo SpitFire," *Vanguard* (Lagos), December 28, 2011.

29. Abdulrazaq O. Hamzat, "Why Islam in Northern Nigeria Is Different From the South" (Part 2), *Modern Ghana*, August 15, 2014, https://www.modernghana.com /news/563804/why-islam-in-northern-nigeria-is-different-from.html.

30. "Akhwat Akwop Militia Surfaces in Northern Nigeria . . . Vow to Stop Boko Harram," *Nigerian Voice*, September 28, 2011, https://www.thenigerianvoice.com /news/70913/akhwat-akwop-militia-surfaces-in-northern-nigeria-vow-to-st.html.

31. Emeka Mama, "Boko Haram: Rival Group Drops Threat Leaflets in 10 Northern States," *Vanguard* (Lagos), July 24, 2011.

32. Sammy Zacks, "A New Deadly Sect 'Akhwat Akwop' to Challenge Boko Haram," Nairaland Forum, July 20, 2011, https://www.nairaland.com/717004/new-deadly -sect-akhwat-akwop.

33. "Christian Militants in Southern Kaduna Threaten Fulani Herdsmen, Give Seven Days Evacuation Notice," Sahara Reporters, June 4, 2012, http://saharareporters .com/2012/06/04/christian-militants-southern-kaduna-threaten-fulani-herdsmen -give-seven-days-evacuation.

34. Samuel Aruwan, "Nigeria: Security Agencies Trail Boko Haram's Rival Group," AllAfrica, July 25, 2011, https://allafrica.com/stories/201107261685.html.

35. "Flashback (Nigeria): New Christian Terrorist Group Uncovered," *Beegeagle's Blog*, October 8, 2011, https://beegeagle.wordpress.com/2011/10/08/flashback-nigeria-new -christian-terrorist-group-uncovered/.

36. "Ultimatum Issued by Christian Militia Group, Akhwat Akwop; Kaduna State Government React," *Beegeagle's Blog*, June 7, 2012, https://beegeagle.wordpress.com/2012 /06/07/ultimatum-issued-by-christian-militia-group-akhwat-akwop-kaduna-state -government-react/.

37. See "Boko Haram Alleges 3 Governors Are Sponsoring Rival Group, Akhwat Akwop," Safer Nigeria Resources, July 29, 2011, https://saferafricagroup.wordpress .com/2011/07/29/boko-haram-alleges-3-governors-are-sponsoring-rival-group -akhwat-akwop/.

38. "Jama'atu Ansarul Muslimina fi Biladi Sudan Threatens Southern Kaduna Militant Group, Akhwat Akwop," *Desert Herald*, June 11, 2012.

39. Aribisala made this known in many of his online writings.

40. Aliyu Hamagam, "Muslim Youths Guard Churches in Minna," *Daily Trust* (Abuja), January 9, 2012.

41. Seun Opejobi, "Advise Your Members against Teachings of Apostle Johnson Suleiman—Group Begs Mbaka, TB Joshua," *Daily Post*, January 31, 2017.

42. Opejobi, "Advise Your Members."

43. See Ugbodaga, "Daddy Freeze Attacks Oyedepo."

44. Olarinde has focused his attention on what he considers the excesses of the pastors, especially in how he thinks they are manipulating and misleading their followers to get money from them.

45. "I Remain a Christian Preacher Teacher Says Daddy Freeze," *Vanguard*, June 6, 2020.

46. Dele Olojede, "Sermon of Crisis," *Newswatch*, July 14, 1986, 12.

47. See "CAC Congregants Fight, Throw Out Pastor over Disbursement of Church Fund," *Vanguard* (Lagos), July 25, 2016.

48. Deolu, "Witchcraft: Two Women Fight Inside Church," Information Nigeria, September 25, 2014, https://www.informationng.com/2014/09/witchcraft-two-women -fight-inside-church.html.

49. John Owen Nwachukwu, "Factions of Assemblies of God Church Use Soldiers to Fight Each Other in Delta," *Daily Post*, February 15, 2016.
50. "Police Shut Enugu Church, as Pastors, Members Fight Dirty over Church Leadership," *News Chronicles*, July 20, 2015.
51. "Missing Child: Three Killed, Ondo Church Set Ablaze," *Punch*, December 19, 2019.
52. Wale Odunsi, "My Wife Ruining My Calling: Pastor Tells Court," *Daily Post*, August 25, 2020.
53. "Pastor David Beaten to Coma for Allegedly Sending Nude Pictures to Fellow Men," *Idoma Voice Newspaper*, October 27, 2020.
54. "What's Behind Children Being Cast as Witches in Nigeria," *Conversation*, April 15, 2016.
55. See "Children Are Targets of Nigerian Witch Hunt," *Observer* (London), December 9, 2007.

CHAPTER FOUR: TRADITIONAL RELIGIONS AND VIOLENCE IN NIGERIA

1. Osaghae and Suberu, *A History of Identities, Violence, and Stability in Nigeria.*
2. Makinde, "Potentialities of the Egúngún Festival."
3. For a detailed study of all the ramifications of violence associated with the Egúngún festival, see Campbell, "*Eegun Ogun* War Masquerades in Ibadan."
4. John Thomas Didymus, "Nigeria: Police Arrest Oloolu Masquerade, Spirit of the Ancestors," *Nigerian Tribune*, July 10, 2012.
5. The term Area Boys is the nomenclature for loosely organized gangs of street children and teenagers, mostly males, who roam the streets of major cities in Nigeria. They extort money from passersby, public transporters, and traders; sell illegal drugs; act as informal security guards; and perform other odd jobs in return for compensation.
6. "Egungun Festival Turns Bloody as One Confirmed Dead, Others Injured in Ibadan," *Vanguard*, July 17, 2017, https://www.vanguardngr.com/2017/07/egungun-festival-turns-bloody-one-confirmed-dead-others-injured-ibadan.
7. "One Dead, Others Injured in Egungun Festival Violence," *Guardian*, July 18, 2017.
8. "Day I Was 'Sentenced to Death' for Taking Photograph of Oloolu Masquerade," *The Sun*, August 24, 2016.
9. "Oyo to Rid Egungun Festival of Violence, Hooliganism," *The News*, March 5, 2018.
10. Amaechi, "The Use of Masquerade Cult and Umu-Ada Fraternity."
11. Daramola and Jeje, *Awọn Àṣà ati Òrìṣà ilẹ Yorùbá.*
12. For a more detailed discussion on the Ogboni fraternity, see Idowu, "Law, Morality and the African Cultural Heritage."
13. For a study of how the Ogboni fraternity was viewed during the colonial era, see Dennett, "The Ogboni and Other Secret Societies in Nigeria."
14. Akanji and Dada, "Oro Cult."
15. I thank Mallam Yusuf Ali (SAN) for drawing my attention to this information.
16. Olomola, "Contradictions in Yoruba Folk Beliefs Concerning Post-life Existence."
17. Interviews at Ile-Ife, August 2018.
18. Awolalu, *Yoruba Beliefs and Sacrificial Rites*, 190–91.

19. I was in Ibadan during this time and witnessed some of the violence associated with this clash between Muslims and supporters of the Oloolu.

20. For more on Ajagbemokeferi, see Azeez and Sarumi, *Ajabemokeferi the Missionary*.

21. Adelowo, "Mission Education and Yoruba Missions of Nigeria."

22. Toki, Gambari, and Hadi, "Peace Building and Interreligious Dialogue in Nigeria."

23. Ademola Babalola, "We Won't Allow 17 Day Oro Restriction in Iseyin," *Punch*, September 16, 2019.

24. Babalola, "We Won't Allow 17 Day Oro Restriction."

25. Daud Olatunji, "You Can't Impose Daytime Curfew: Court Tells Oro Festival in Ogun," *Vanguard*, February 22, 2018.

26. Tunde Sanni, "Nigeria: Moremi Shrine: Offa Muslims Reject Peace Committee," *This Day*, February 27, 2004.

27. Interviews and discussions in Iwo.

28. Guichaoua, "The Making of an Ethnic Militia."

29. Anugwom, "Something Mightier," 3.

30. Anugwom, "Something Mightier."

31. Anugwom, "Something Mightier."

32. Courson and Odijie, "Egbesu."

33. Quoted in "Responses to Information Requests (RIRs)," Immigration and Refugee Board of Canada, February 16, 2006, https://www.justice.gov/eoir/page/file/940936/download.

34. Mohammed Ibrahim, "An Empirical Survey of Children and Youth in Organised Armed Violence in Nigeria: Egbesu Boys, OPC and Bakassi Boys as a Case Study," in *Neither War Nor Peace: International Comparisons of Children and Youth in Organised Armed Violence*. Children and Youth in Organised Armed Violence (COAV), May 30, 2005, 256, https://www.oijj.org/sites/default/files/documentos/documental_2792_en.pdf Monty G. Marshall and Ted Robert Gurr, "Peace and Conflict 2005: A Global Survey of Armed Conflicts, Self-Determination Movements, and Democracy," Center for International Development and Conflict Management (CIDCM), University of Maryland, May 2005, 82.

35. Best and Von Kemedi, "Armed Groups and Conflict in Rivers and Plateau States, Nigeria."

36. "Report on Human Rights Issues in Nigeria: Joint British-Danish Fact-Finding Mission to Abuja and Lagos, Nigeria (19 October to 2 November 2004)," Danish Immigration Service, 2005, https://www.ecoi.net/en/file/local/1284043/470_1161611888_joint-british-danish-fact-finding-mission-to-abuja-and-lagos.pdf.

37. Global Security, "Niger Delta People's Volunteer Force, Egbesu Boys, Ijaw National Congress, Ijaw Youth Congress," April 27, 2005, https://www.globalsecurity.org/military/world/para/ijaw.htm.

38. "Report on Human Rights Issues in Nigeria"; Ibrahim, "An Empirical Survey of Children and Youth in Organised Armed Violence in Nigeria," 256.

39. For a detailed study of the Okija Shrine, see Ellis, "The Okija Shrine."

40. Dimeji Kayode-Adedeji, "Man Takes Girlfriend to 'Pastor' for Money Ritual Where She's Beheaded—Police," *Premium Times*, December 29, 2019, https://www

.premiumtimesng.com/news/more-news/370259-man-takes-girlfriend-to-pastor-for
-money-ritual-where-shes-beheaded-police.html.

41. Msuya, "Traditional 'Juju Oath' and Human Trafficking in Nigeria."

CHAPTER FIVE: BOKO HARAM AND THE NEW PHASE OF VIOLENCE

1. See, among others, Thurston, *Boko Haram*; Smith, *Boko Haram*; Comolli, *Boko Haram*.

2. Andrea Brigaglia, "Slicing Off the Tumour," 199. In some of his video releases, the current leader of the group, Abubakar Shekau, persistently protested the use of the name Boko Haram.

3. In 2018, the Islamic State West African Province (ISWAP), a breakaway faction led by Abu Mus'ab al-Barnawi, published a selective history of the Boko Haram movement with a plethora of criticisms of Shekau's Jamā 'at Ahl al-Sunna li-Da'wa wa-l-Jihād; see Aymenn Jawad Al-Tamimi, "The Islamic State West Africa Province vs. Abu Bakr Shekau: Full Text, Translation and Analysis," *Pundicity: Informed Opinion and Review* (blog), August 5, 2018, http://www.aymennjawad.org/21467/the-islamic -state-west-africa-province-vs-abu.

4. Adesoji, "The Boko Haram Uprising and Islamic Revivalism in Nigeria"; Pham, "Boko Haram's Evolving Threat"; Onuoha, *A Danger Not to Nigeria Alone*. But the gap of almost two decades between the occurrences is difficult to explain, especially as there were several opportunities in those years for similar insurgencies; and most of the identified founders would have been significantly too young to be active in the riots. Moreover, Boko Haram took theological positions contrary to the claims of prophet status and Qur'anic readings of the leader of Maitatsine. The connections between Maitatsine and Boko Haram are more likely to have been inspirational, rather than physical.

5. One of the scholars who subscribe to this line of argument is A. U. Adamu. See Adamu, "Insurgency in Nigeria."

6. Kyari, "Boko Haram Insurgency in Nigeria," 113.

7. ECOMOG is the acronym for ECOWAS Monitoring Observer Group, the peacekeeping mission Nigeria spearheaded to bring peace to Liberia during the country's civil war. It is not known why the group chose this name.

8. Atta Barkindo, "An Introduction to Boko Haram's Ideologues: From Yusuf to Shekau," Africa Research Institute, February 2, 2017, https://www .africaresearchinstitute.org/newsite/blog/introduction-boko-harams-ideologues -yusuf-shekau; A. Walker, "What Is Boko Haram?," United States Institute of Peace (USIP) Special Report, June 2012, 170; A. Murtada, "Boko Haram in Nigeria: Its Beginning, Principles, and Activities" (Kano: Bayero University, Salafi Mahaj, 2013), 9.

9. Thurston, *Boko Haram*, 98–104.

10. Jafar Mahmud Adam, "Me Yasa Suke Cewa Boko Haram Ne?," posted on You-Tube by Ibrahim Gwayo, July 26, 2012, https://www.youtube.com/watch?v =kkNDOoe2Jf8.

11. Not much was known about the circumstances of Shekau's background until Abdulbasit Kassim and Michael Nwankpa published their book *The Boko Haram Reader*, which included the Voice of America Hausa Service interview of Falmata Abubakar, who claimed to be Shekau's mother.

12. A. Nossiter, "A Jihadist's Face Taunts Nigeria from the Shadows," *New York Times*, May 18, 2014.

13. Early messages were distributed through cassettes, such that the government later made the possession of Boko Haram materials an arrestable offense. Mohammed Yusuf had only one known authored book, *Hadhihi Aqidatuna wa-Manhaj Da'watuna*, believed to have been written in 2008. Another book, *Ja al Haqq*, was written by a Boko Haram member under the name Alq'udin al-Barnawi.

14. In this sense, Boko Haram identifies with mainstream Islamic tradition, as "enjoying the good and forbidding the evil" is the core organizing principle in Islamic ethics. See Cook, *Commanding Rights and Forbidding Wrong in Islamic Thoughts*. Where Boko Haram may be said to be different is their disavowal of all forms of Western civilization.

15. I owe this point to Abdulbassit Kassim. Personal communication, June 20, 2018.

16. Junaidu, "Resistance to Western Culture in the Sakkwato Caliphate," 247.

17. Discussion with Abdulbassit Kassim, June 20, 2018.

18. Ibn Taymiyyah was a medieval Sunni Muslim theologian known for his iconoclastic views on widely accepted Sunni doctrines such as the veneration of saints and visitation to their tomb-shrines. He was one of the most influential medieval writers in contemporary Islam.

19. Kyari, "Boko Haram Insurgency in Nigeria."

20. Kassim and Nwankpa, *The Boko Haram Reader*, 174.

21. Chris Wolumati Ogbondah, and Pita Ogaba Agbese, "Terrorists and Social Media Messages: A Critical Analysis of Boko Haram's Messages and Messaging Techniques," *The Palgrave Handbook of Media and Communication Research in Africa*, 313–45, October 24, 2017, https://www.ncbi.nlm.nih.gov/pmc/articles /PMC7121539/.

22. Ogbondah and Agbese, "Terrorists and Social Media Messages."

23. A spokesperson for the group, Mallam Sanni Umaru, gave a strong condemnation of this position. See Onuoha, "Boko Haram, Nigeria's Extremist Islamic Sect."

24. Onuoha, "Boko Haram, Nigeria's Extremist Islamic Sect," 25.

25. Onuoha, "Boko Haram, Nigeria's Extremist Islamic Sect," 28.

26. Onuoha, "Boko Haram, Nigeria's Extremist Islamic Sect."

27. See the details of their debate in Kassim and Nwankpa, *The Boko Haram Reader*.

28. Kassim and Nwankpa, *The Boko Haram Reader*.

29. Lawal Danjuma, "Nigeria: Gunmen Attack Emir of Kano's Convoy—Wound Sons, Kill at Least 3," *Daily Trust*, January 19, 2013.

30. Inuwa Ibrahim, "Politicians as Terrorists," *The Insider*, no. 25, July 4, 2011.

31. I owe this point to Abdulbassit Kassim.

32. Sani Muhd Sani, "Attack on Bauchi Prison—Boko Haram Frees 721 Inmates," *Leadership Newspaper*, September 8, 2010.

33. "Army Uncovers Boko Haram Recruitment Link on Social Media," *Punch*, August 14, 2018.

34. International Crisis Group, "Curbing Violence in Nigeria (II): The Boko Haram Insurgency," April 3, 2014, https://www.crisisgroup.org/africa/west-africa/nigeria/curbing-violence-nigeria-ii-boko-haram-insurgency.

35. "Boko Haram Resurrects, Declares Total Jihad," *Vanguard*, August 14, 2009, http://www.vanguardngr.com/2009/08/boko-haram-ressurects-declares-total-jihad/.

36. Xan Rice, "Changing Face of Nigeria's Boko Haram," *Financial Times*, May 22, 2012, http://www.ft.com/cms/s/0/9d2ab750-9ac1-11e1-9c98-00144feabdc0.html#axzz4B4LYpoYr.

37. Da'wah Coordination Council of Nigeria, "The 'Boko Haram' Tragedy: Frequently Asked Questions" (Minna: DCCN, 2009), 10, http://www.scribd.com/doc/65486839/The-Boko-Haram-Tragedy-26-FAQs-by-DCCN.

38. Uduma Kalu, "How Nur, Shekau Run Boko Haram," *Vanguard*, September 3, 2011, http://www.vanguardngr.com/2011/09/how-nur-shekau-run-boko-haram/; "Nigeria 'Arrests Senior Boko Haram Official,'" *Aljazeera*, May 12, 2012, http://www.aljazeera.com/news/africa/2012/05/2012512134929196972.html; Timothy Olanrewaju, "Top Boko Haram Commander Captured," *Sun*, January 14, 2013, http://sunnewsonline.com/new/cover/top-boko-haram-commander-captured/; McGregor, "The Mysterious Death in Custody of Boko Haram Leader Habib Bama"; "Nigeria un Bomb: Video of 'Boko Haram Bomber' Released," BBC News, September 18, 2011, http://www.bbc.co.uk/news/world-africa-14964554; "The Story of Nigeria's First Suicide Bomber—Blueprint Magazine," *Sahara Reporters*, June 27, 2011.

39. Montclos, *Boko Haram*, 8.

40. Nwankpa, "The Political Economy of Securitization."

41. Ilenna Emewu and Desmond Mgboh, "Suicide Bombers; Qaqa, Boko Haram's Spokesman Open Up," *Daily Sun* (Lagos), February 9, 2012, 5.

42. Emewu and Mgboh, "Suicide Bombers."

43. Emewu and Mgboh, "Suicide Bombers."

44. "Nigeria's Boko Haram 'Got $3m Ransom' to Free Hostages," BBC News, April 27, 2013, https://www.bbc.co.uk/news/world-africa-22320077.

45. Ruth Maclean, "Boko Haram Landmines in Nigeria Killed at Least 162 in Two Years," *Guardian*, September 23, 2018.

46. Nwankpa, "The Political Economy of Securitization."

47. Cook, "Boko Haram Escalates Attacks on Christians."

48. Ahmed Mohammed, "Woman Nabbed for Attempting to Set Church Ablaze in Bauchi," *Daily Trust*, August 12, 2011.

49. Kyari, "Boko Haram Insurgency in Nigeria."

50. Video as recorded in Apard, "The Words of Boko Haram," 41. The speech was made on March 25, 2014.

51. Rock, "The Funding of Boko Haram."

52. Kieran Guilbert, "Boko Haram 'Lures, Traps' Young Nigerian Entrepreneurs with Business Loans," Reuters, April 11, 2016, http://uk.reuters.com/article/uk-nigeria-boko-haramidUKKCN0X8265.

53. Rock, "The Funding of Boko Haram."
54. Rock, "The Funding of Boko Haram."
55. "Who Is Financing Boko Haram," DW, September 2, 2014, https://www.dw.com/en /who-is-financing-boko-haram/a-17894036.
56. Utibe, Taofiq, and Idris, "Political Economy of Insurgency in Nigeria."
57. Emmanuel Aziken, AbdulSalam Muhammad, Victoria Ojeme, and Ndahi Marama, "We're on Northern Governors' Payroll: Boko Haram," Vanguard, January 24, 2012.
58. Karen Leigh, "Nigeria's Boko Haram: Al Qaeda's New Friend in Africa?," Time, August 31, 2011, http://content.time.com/time/world/article/0,8599,2091137,00.html.
59. L. Ibrahim, "Nigeria: Bank Robbery Suspects Boko Haram Members," Daily Trust, February 4, 2011.
60. Rock, "The Funding of Boko Haram."
61. P. Weber, "Who's Financing Boko Haram?," The Week Magazine, New York, May 12, 2014.
62. Rock, "The Funding of Boko Haram."
63. Kassim and Nwankpa, The Boko Haram Reader. Mubahala is the coming together of a group, if they disagree upon something, and asking God to curse those among them who are unjust.
64. Sani Tukur, "Borno's Gov. Shettima Attacks Predecessor, Sheriff, over Boko Haram," Premium Times, February 13, 2017.
65. "Boko Haram Target Types, 2009–2013," in Background Report, "Boko Haram Recent Attacks," National Consortium for the Study of Terrorism and Responses to Terrorism, May 2014, http://www.start.umd.edu/pubs/STARTBackgroundReport _BokoHaramRecentAttacks_May2014_0.pdf.
66. David Cook, "Boko Haram: A Prognosis," James Baker III Institute of Public Policy, Rice University, December 2011, 14.
67. Cook, "Boko Haram: A Prognosis."
68. Inuwa Ibrahim, "Politicians as Terrorists," The Insider, no. 25 (July 4, 2011).
69. See "Nigerian Authorities Failed to Act on Warnings about Boko Haram Raid on School," Amnesty International, May 9, 2014, https://www.amnesty.org/en/latest /press-release/2014/05/nigerian-authorities-failed-act-warnings-about-boko-haram -raid-school/.
70. Adaobi Nwaubani, "Chibok Diaries: Chronicling a Boko Haram Kidnapping," This Day, October 27, 2017.
71. Haruna Abdulkareem, "How Boko Haram Attack, Kidnap of Dapchi Schoolgirls Occurred—Residents, School Staff," Premium Times (Nigeria), March 4, 2018.
72. After most of the girls were released, there were some claims, especially coming from the opposition, that the government planned the kidnapping and quick re- lease to show how President Jonathan's incompetence made the Chibok kidnapping complicated.
73. Copy of the memo available online in Adebayo Adesanya, "Nigeria: How the Nige- rian Army Aided Dapchi Girls' Abduction," Caracal Reports, March 1, 2018, https:// www.caracalreports.com/nigeria-nigerian-army-aided-dapchi-girls-abduction/.
74. Insider Weekly, July 4, 2011.

75. *Tell*, July 4, 2011.
76. Amnesty International, "Nigeria: Trapped in the Cycle of Violence" (London: Amnesty International, 2012); Human Rights Watch, "Spiraling Violence: Boko Haram Attacks and Security Force Abuses in Nigeria," October 11, 2012, https://www.hrw.org/report/2012/10/11/spiraling-violence/boko-haram-attacks-and-security-force-abuses-nigeria.
77. "Chibok Girls: A Gaping Wound Two Years After," *This Day*, April 14, 2016.
78. "Chibok Girls: A Gaping Wound."
79. Francis, "The Rise of Boko Haram."
80. See "Boko Haram: 12 Soldiers to Die for Mutiny," *Guardian*, September 16, 2014.
81. Irabor, "Combating Boko Haram Insurgency in Nigeria," 86.
82. Buratai, "Curtailing Boko Haram Terrorism."
83. Buratai, "Curtailing Boko Haram Terrorism."
84. Buratai, "Curtailing Boko Haram Terrorism."
85. Irabor, "Combating Boko Haram Insurgency in Nigeria," 89.
86. Irabor, "Combating Boko Haram Insurgency in Nigeria," 89.
87. Tobi Soniyi, "Federal Government Begins Prosecution of 2,321 Boko Haram Suspects, *This Day*, September 21, 2018.
88. Soniyi, "Federal Government Begins Prosecution of 2,321 Boko Haram Suspects."
89. Paul Obi, "CAN Warns FG against Recruiting Repentant Boko Haram Terrorists into Army Police," *This Day*, June 20, 2018.
90. This was in the Annual Report of the UN on Children in Armed Conflict. Martins Ifijeh, "UN: How Boko Haram, Military Killed, Maimed Hundreds of Children," *This Day*, June 29, 2018.
91. Seun Opebi, "ISWAP Regrouping around Lake Chad, Army Needs Support—Ndume," *Daily Post*, November 15, 2021.
92. Okodili Ndidi, "Seven Soldiers Killed as ISWAP Rains Mortar Bombs on Maiduguri," *The Nation*, December 5, 2021.
93. Yusuf Alli, "Army Chief to Troops: Take Battle to ISWAP," *The Nation*, December 6, 2021.
94. Alli, "Army Chief to Troops."
95. "Boko Haram: Splinter Group Ansaru Emerges," *Vanguard* (Lagos), February 1, 2012.
96. Alex Johnson, "Kidnapped German Killed in Nigeria," *Epoch Times*, May 31, 2012, https://www.theepochtimes.com/kidnapped-german-killed-in-nigeria_1484892.html.
97. "Nigeria: Islamist Group Ansaru 'Kidnapped' French Man," BBC News, December 24, 2012, https://www.bbc.co.uk/news/world-africa-20833946; "French Priest Released in Cameroon After Six Weeks Hostage," *Telegraph*, December 31, 2013.
98. "7 Foreign Workers Kidnapped in Nigerian Attack," CBC News, February 17, 2013, https://www.cbc.ca/news/world/7-foreign-workers-kidnapped-in-nigerian-attack-1.1318781.
99. Olomojobi, *Frontiers of Jihad*, 304.
100. Onuoha, "Boko Haram and the Evolving Salafi Jihadist Threat."
101. Onuoha, "Boko Haram and the Evolving Salafi Jihadist Threat."
102. Onuoha, "Boko Haram and the Evolving Salafi Jihadist Threat."

CHAPTER SIX: NATIONAL POLITICS, INTERGROUP RELATIONS,
AND RELIGIOUS VIOLENCE IN NIGERIA

1. Opeloye, "Religious Factor in Nigerian Politics."
2. Opeloye, "Religious Factor in Nigerian Politics."
3. Opeloye, "Religious Factor in Nigerian Politics."
4. Dele Olojede and Soji Akinrinade, "The Trip to Fez: How Nigeria Joined OIC after 17 Years of Persistent Courtship," *Newswatch*, February 1986, 19.
5. Enwerem, *A Dangerous Awakening*.
6. Enwerem, *A Dangerous Awakening*.
7. Nicholas Omenka has written on the role of religion in explaining the Nigerian civil war. See Omenka, "Blaming the Gods."
8. Daly, "Biafra's Crisis of Faith."
9. Ajayi, *The Military and the Nigerian State*.
10. From discussions with retired army officers.
11. Obasanjo said this during a presentation he made at King's College London.
12. This revelation was made by a member of the Constituent Assembly, Omo Omoruyi, who was to become director-general of the Center for Democratic Studies. See the open letter to President Obasanjo, on March 7, 2001, titled "An Appeal to President Olusegun Obasanjo: Nigeria: Neither an Islamic nor a Christian Country," https://nigeriaworld.com/feature/publication/omoruyi/030700I.html.
13. "An Appeal to President Olusegun Obasanjo."
14. See Laitin, "The Sharia Debate and the Origins of Nigeria's Second Republic."
15. Alao, "Constitutional Guarantee of the Secularity of the State."
16. The government launched the popular "War against Indiscipline," which was to be its trademark.
17. A popular Yoruba poet who later became a radical Muslim, Olanrewaju Adepoju, recorded a song in which he attributed some of the challenges facing Nigeria during the Babangida administration to the fact that the coup was carried out while the strongman of the government was on a holy pilgrimage.
18. Akinwumi, *Hubris*, 173–75.
19. See "Nigeria: My Quarrel with IBB, by Ukiwe," *Daily Trust*, October 27, 2006.
20. Akinwumi, *Hubris*.
21. Ibrahim, "The Politics of Religion in Nigeria."
22. Ladan-Baki, "Interfaith Conflict and Political Development in Nigeria."
23. Ladan-Baki, "Interfaith Conflict and Political Development in Nigeria."
24. Maiwa, *Northern Minorities and Hausa Political Hegemony*.
25. D. Boman, "Atyap and the Struggle for Tribal Identity," *Punch* (Lagos), June 19, 1995.
26. Mikail Mumini, "Dasuki's Albatross," *Tell*, October 10 1994, 10.
27. Mumini, "Dasuki's Albatross," 11.
28. Many of the governors who introduced Sharia are now under investigation for massive corruption while in office.
29. Danbazau, *Politics and Religion in Nigeria*, vii.
30. Focus group discussions.
31. Human Rights Watch, "Jos: A City Torn Apart," December 2001.

32. Tobi Soniyi, Segun James, and Shola Oyeyipo, "Insecurity, the New Normal," *This Day*, January 8, 2018.

33. Human Rights Watch, "The Conflict in Yelwa," 2005, https://www.hrw.org/reports /2005/nigeria0505/4.htm.

34. Human Rights Watch, "The Conflict in Yelwa."

35. Abubakar Abdul-Rahman, "Yar'Adua Admits Election Flaws," *Daily Trust*, May 30, 2007.

36. Stanley Nkwocha, "Jos, Blood on the Streets Again, Abuja," *Leadership Newspaper*, December 1, 2008.

37. See Seriki Adinoyi, "Turai's Delegation Visits Jos, Shuns Governor Jang," *This Day*, December 18, 2008.

38. Between April 1991 and February 2009, Bauchi State recorded more than ten cases of religious riots that left more than 10,000 dead and 3,900 homes burned, 200 churches burned, and 20 mosques razed.

39. "Archbishop Ben Kwashi Responds to Attack on His Village," July 4, 2018, https:// www.gafcon.org/news/archbishop-ben-kwashi-responds-to-attack-on-his-village.

40. The secretary-general of the Muslim Ummah of South West Nigeria, Professor Daud Noibi, was among those who have spoken out against what he saw as a way of forcefully converting Muslims. See *This Day*, December 29, 2008, 6.

41. Adeniyi, *Power, Politics, and Death*, 116–17.

42. Adeniyi, *Power, Politics, and Death*, 106.

43. See Shola Oyeyipo, Segun James, and Jameelah Sanda, "The Politics That Shaped the Chibok Girls," *This Day*, April 18, 2016.

44. Oyeyipo et al., "The Politics That Shaped the Chibok Girls."

45. Segun Adebowale, "Jonathan's Comments on Chibok Girls, Callous, Morbid and Insensitive—APC," *The Eagle*, March 7, 2015.

46. "Chibok Girls: A Gaping Wound," *This Day*, April 14, 2016; Chiemelie Ezeobi, "Chibok Girls: A Gaping Wound Two Years After," *This Day*, April 14 2016.

47. Francis Falola, "27 Years After, Handshake between Islam and Christianity," *Sunday Punch*, February 1, 2009.

48. Quoted in "Chibok Girls: A Gaping Wound Two Years After," *This Day*, April 14, 2016.

49. Oyeyipo et al., "The Politics That Shaped the Chibok Girls."

50. Anna Cunningham, "Why Has Nigeria Failed to Rescue the Chibok Schoolgirls from Boko Haram?," CBC News, April 14, 2015, https://www.cbc.ca/news/world /nigerian-schoolgirls-boko-haram-1.3535324.

51. Bruno Uche, "Three Years of Blood Bath," *Verbatim Magazine*, June 2018, 14.

52. "Nigerian Government Paid a Ransom for the Release of Chibok Girls—Senators," *Premium Times*, February 22, 2018.

53. Emma Ujah, "Our Role in the Release of Chibok Girls, Others—Red Cross," *Vanguard*, February 23, 2018.

54. At the time of this statement, the girls had been in captivity for 663 days. See Oyeyipo et al., "The Politics That Shaped the Chibok Girls."

55. Oyeyipo et al., "The Politics That Shaped the Chibok Girls."

56. "North-East Nigeria Humanitarian Situation Update," OCHA Monthly Report, September 2017.

57. Uhia, "Boko Haram: The Military, Big Cash Cow," 85.

58. Uhia, "Boko Haram: The Military, Big Cash Cow."

59. Paden, *Muhammadu Buhari*, 171–72.

60. Alao, *Natural Resources and Conflict in Africa*.

61. "Measuring and Understanding the Impact of Terrorism," Global Terrorism Index, Institute for Economics and Peace, 2015.

62. Kanu, Ndubuise, and Kanu, *Africa at the Cross-Roads of Violence and Gender Inequality*.

63. Iyabo Lawal, "Olu Falae Kidnapped on His 77th Birthday,"*Guardian* (Lagos), September 22, 2015.

64. Ndubuisi, "A Critical Analysis of Conflicts between Herdsmen and Farmers in Nigeria."

65. Onyebuchi Ezigbo and Geore Okoh, "Taraba Governor Cries Out over Alleged Military Siege," *This Day*, April 20, 2018.

66. Uche, "Three Years of Blood Bath"; see also "Save Nigeria from Avoidable Doom, Step Aside, Catholic Bishops Tell Buhari," *This Day*, July 3, 2018.

67. "Save Nigeria from Avoidable Doom."

68. Anayochukwu Agbo, "Buhari's Big Burden," *Tell*, June 11, 2018, 21.

69. Agbo, "Buhari's Big Burden."

70. Discussion with the representative of the Fulani community in Oke-Ogun, September 2018.

71. Omololu Ogunmade, Olawale Ajimotokan, George Oboh, and David Eleke, "Thousands Pay Last Respect as Benue Buries 73 Victims of New Year Day Attack," *This Day*, January 12, 2018.

72. John Shiklam and George Okoh, "Unconfirmed Number of People Killed in Kaduna Muslim-Christian Clash," *This Day*, February 27, 2018.

73. Shiklam and Okoh, "Unconfirmed Number of People Killed in Kaduna Muslim-Christian Clash."

74. See "You Must Wield the Big Stick against Herdsmen, Soyinka Tells Buhari," *This Day*, June 28, 2018.

75. See Daji Sani, "The Adamawa Massacre," *This Day* (Lagos), January 15, 2018.

76. Okanga Agila, "Gana and the End of an Error," *Vanguard*, August 2, 2018.

77. Agbo, "Buhari's Big Burden," 21.

78. See "Fulani Herdsmen: Farmers, Hunters, Youths Amass Arms," *Punch*, May 7, 2016.

79. Onikepo Braithwaite, "Herdsmen Crisis Is Gradually Enveloping West Africa," *This Day*, February 13, 2018.

80. "I See a Link between Fulani Herdsmen and Boko Haram," *Guardian*, February 4, 2018.

81. "Bomb Attack: Bishop Oyedepo Rains Curses on Miyetti Allah and Boko Haram," posted on YouTube by Unik Empire, February 4, 2020, https://www.youtube.com/watch?v=SduF1RiOgPY.

82. Shakirah Adunola, "Oyo Islamic Community Faults Exclusion from Afenifere's Board," *Guardian* (Lagos), July 13, 2018.

83. Adunola, "Oyo Islamic Community Faults Exclusion."
84. Peter Ajayi Dada, "Nigerian Religious Leaders Condemn Attack That Kills 19 during Mass," *Catholic News Service*, April, 27, 2018, http://catholicphilly.com/2018/04/news/world-news/nigerian-religious-leaders-condemn-attack-that-kills-19-during-mass/.
85. For a detailed discussion on the impact of the Fulani Jihad on intergroup relations, see Nmah and Uchenna, "1804 Usman dan Fodio's Jihad on Inter-Group Relations in the Contemporary Nigerian State."
86. Azamazi Momoh Jimoh, "Army Faults Danjuma's Stance," *The Guardian*, March 26, 2018.
87. "Aftermath of Danjuma's Petition on Persecution Of Christians: Nigeria Writes British Parliamentary Group," *Africa News Circle: Africa and the World in Perspective*, June 2019.
88. Daji Sani, "The Adamawa Massacre," *This Day* (Lagos), January 15, 2018.
89. George Okoh, "Osinbajo: I'm Ready to Quit If Buhari Is Complicit in Benue Killings," *This Day*, May 17, 2018.
90. Okoh, "Osinbajo."
91. Onikepo Braithwaite, "As Buhari Drowns in Nepotism," *This Day*, January 16, 2018.
92. Onikepo Braithwaite, "Herdsmen Crisis Is Gradually Enveloping West Africa," *This Day*, February 13, 2018.
93. Umar Yusuf, "Yola Court Passes Death Sentence on 5 Men for Killing Herdsman," *Vanguard* (Lagos), June 13, 2018.
94. Paul Obi, "CAN Warns FG against Recruiting Repentant Boko Haram Terrorists into Army Police," *This Day*, June 20, 2018.
95. Hassan Kukah, "On Islamization of Nigeria," *The Guardian* , February 17, 2018.
96. "Stay Away from South East to Avoid Another War—Bishop Chukwuma Warns Herders," Akelicious website, February 12, 2021, https://www.akelicious.net/stay-away-from-south-east-to-avoid-another-war-bishop-chukwuma-warns-herders/.
97. *The Economy*, June 2018
98. *The Economy*, June 2018.
99. *The Economy*, June 2018.
100. See Juliet Moyo, "CAN Drags Religion in Mud for Clandestine Motives, JNI Secretary Alleges," *Independent Newspaper*, January 22, 2018.
101. See Moyo, "CAN Drags Religion in Mud for Clandestine Motives."
102. See Moyo, "CAN Drags Religion in Mud for Clandestine Motives."
103. Ejiofor Alike, "Ugwuanyi's Model for Ending Herders' Attacks," *This Day*, May 10, 2018, 10.
104. Many commentators gave specific warnings about the dangers of some of the policies pursued by the government, and a group of scholars at Harvard University again predicted the end of the Nigerian state by 2030.
105. See Oluwole Ige, "Fulanisation and Islamisation: Another Salvo from Obasanjo," *Nigeria Tribune*, May 30, 2019.
106. Femi Fani-Kayode, "Ruga and the Fulani Agenda," *Punch*, June 30, 2019.

107. *Are ona kakanfo* is the traditional title in Yorubaland for the chief warrior. Adeola Badru, "Alleged ISIS in Oke Ogun: Aseyin Calls on Gani Adams to Give Intelligence Reports against Terrorism," *Vanguard*, August 20, 2020.

108. Jacob Segun Olatunji, "DHQ Allays Fears on US Warning on Al-Qaeda's Plans to Infiltrate Southern Nigeria," *Nigerian Tribune*, August 6, 2020.

CHAPTER SEVEN: THE ECONOMICS OF RELIGIOUS VIOLENCE IN NIGERIA

1. See, for example, Collier and Hoeffler, "Greed and Grievance in Civil War."
2. Straubhaar, "An Economic Analysis of Religion and Religious Violence," 1.
3. Berger, *The Sacred Canopy.*
4. Berger, *The Sacred Canopy.*
5. Patrimonialism is the form of government, described by Max Weber, where authority flows directly from the leader.
6. Usman, "Religion and Violence in Nigeria."
7. See Oluwadare, "Boko Haram Terrorism in the Lake Chad Basin Region"; Magrin and Montclos, *Crisis and Development.*
8. Omenm, "Untold Story of Boko Haram Insurgency."
9. Ahmad Salkida, "How Boko Haram Sustains Operations through International Trade in Smoked Fish," *Premium Times*, April 26, 2020.
10. Salkida, "How Boko Haram Sustains Operations."
11. Salkida, "How Boko Haram Sustains Operations."
12. The *almajiri* factor is crucial in understanding the politics of religion in northern Nigeria. These are young students of the Qur'an.
13. Discussions held in Kaduna, November 2016.
14. Ali, "Economic Cost of Terrorism."
15. Ali, "Economic Cost of Terrorism."
16. "Economic Impact of Boko Haram in Northeast Estimated at N274.5bn," *Punch* (Lagos), August 10, 2017.
17. Tukur Buratai, "Nigeria: Economic Impact of Boko Haram in Nigeria's Northeast Now $9 Billion—Buratai," *Daily Trust.* August 11, 2017.
18. Chitra Nagarajan, "Gender Assessment of Northeast Nigeria," Managing Conflict in Northeast Nigeria, June 2017, https://www.academia.edu/35870632/Gender_Assessment_of_Northeast_Nigeria.
19. Nagarajan, "Gender Assessment of Northeast Nigeria."
20. Nagarajan, "Gender Assessment of Northeast Nigeria."
21. Nagarajan, "Gender Assessment of Northeast Nigeria."
22. Nagarajan, "Gender Assessment of Northeast Nigeria."
23. Nagarajan, "Gender Assessment of Northeast Nigeria."
24. See Chitra Nagarajan, "Conflict Analysis of Northeast Nigeria: Biu, Bursari, Gombi, Hawul, Hong, Jakusko, Jere and Kaga Local Government Areas," Feed the Future Nigeria Livelihoods Project, September 2017, https://www.academia.edu/36480218/Conflict_Analysis_of_Northeast_States_Biu_Bursari_Gombi_Hawul_Hong_Jakusko_Jere_and_Kaga_LGAs.

25. Federal Government of Nigeria, "Northeast Nigeria: Recovery and Peacebuilding Assessment," Abuja, 2015.
26. Federal Government of Nigeria, "Northeast Nigeria."
27. Nagarajan, "Gender Assessment of Northeast Nigeria."
28. Studies carried out by A. Rodogovsky, "Gender Rapid Assessment—Jere LGA, Borno State, Nigeria," Catholic Relief Services/Catholic Agency for Overseas Development (CRS/CAFOD), February 2017; "Multi-sector Initial Rapid Needs Assessment: Baga/Kukawa LGA, CRS/CAFOD, January 3, 2017.
29. Nuqe, "Boko Haram and Its Impact on the Nigerian Economy."
30. Nuqe, "Boko Haram and Its Impact on the Nigerian Economy."
31. Nagarajan, "Conflict Analysis of Northeast Nigeria."
32. Federal Government of Nigeria, "Northeast Nigeria."
33. Federal Government of Nigeria, "Northeast Nigeria."
34. Federal Government of Nigeria, "Northeast Nigeria."
35. Jason Rizzo, "A Shrinking Lake and a Rising Insurgency: Migratory Responses to Environmental Degradation and Violence in the Lake Chad Basin," in *The State of Environmental Migration*, 2015, http://labos.ulg.ac.be/hugo/wp-content/uploads/sites/38/2017/11/The-State-of-Environmental-Migration-2015-13-29.pdf.
36. Magrin and Montclos, *Crisis and Development.*
37. Rizzo, "A Shrinking Lake and a Rising Insurgency."
38. Nagarajan, "Gender Assessment of Northeast Nigeria."
39. Nagarajan, "Gender Assessment of Northeast Nigeria."
40. "Nigeria's Armsgate Scandal," World Peace Foundation and the Fletcher School, Tufts University, 2019, https://sites.tufts.edu/corruptarmsdeals/nigerias-armsgate-scandal/.
41. "Nigeria's Armsgate Scandal."
42. "Nigeria's Armsgate Scandal."
43. "Nigeria's Armsgate Scandal."
44. "Nigeria's Armsgate Scandal."
45. "$9.3m Arms Deal: Oritsejafor Opens Up," *Vanguard*, September 9, 2014.
46. Sam Eyoboka and Kingsley Omonobi, "Nigeria: FG Defends U.S. $9.3 Million Cash Seized in S-Africa, Releases Data on Transaction," *Vanguard*, September 17, 2014.
47. "Revealed: SGF, Babachir Lawal Awarded N220m Grass Removal Job for His Firm—Senate Report," *Vanguard*, December 18, 2016.
48. "Grass-Cutting Scandal: Senate Panel Indicts Suspended SGF, Recommends Prosecution," *Punch*, May 3, 2017.
49. "Grass-Cutting Scandal."
50. "Grass-Cutting Scandal."

CHAPTER EIGHT: NIGERIA'S RELIGIOUS VIOLENCE
IN THE CONTEXT OF GLOBAL POLITICS
1. Olatunbosun, "Western Nigerian Farm Settlement."
2. Akindele and Oyediran, "Federalism and Foreign Policy in Nigeria."

3. Olusanya and Akindele, "Fundamentals of Nigeria's Foreign Policy and External Economic Relations."
4. Birai, 1996, quoted in Danfulani and Buba, "Nigeria-Israeli Relations."
5. Danfulani and Buba, "Nigeria-Israeli Relations."
6. Bukarambe, cited in Danfulani and Buba, "Nigeria-Israeli Relations."
7. Enwerem, "A Dangerous Awakening," 45.
8. Enwerem, "A Dangerous Awakening."
9. *Daily Times* (Nigeria), September 12, 1959, quoted in Gambari, "The Development of Africa-Arab Relations," 229.
10. Gambari, "The Development of Africa-Arab Relations."
11. Yemisi Adeolu, "Israeli Embassy Confers Posthumous Award on Awolowo," *Today*, April 26, 2018, https://www.today.ng/news/nigeria/israeli-embassy-confers-posthumous-award-awolowo-108905.
12. Oyovbaire, "The Atlantic Ocean, Ghadaffi, Maitatsine and Rice."
13. Milligan, "Nigerian Echoes of the Israeli-Palestinian Conflict," 36.
14. Milligan, "Nigerian Echoes of the Israeli-Palestinian Conflict."
15. Milligan, "Nigerian Echoes of the Israeli-Palestinian Conflict."
16. Levey, "Israel's Exit from Africa, 1973."
17. The *New Nigerian* newspaper in the north and the *Daily Times* in the south advanced these positions, and several editorials were published by other newspapers to these effects.
18. Obasanjo successively made this declaration during OAU meetings, at the 1977 summit and the 1979 extraordinary meeting in Monrovia.
19. Professor Akinyemi indeed wrote a letter to the National Assembly in 1982 defending this position.
20. Damilola Agbalajobi, "Explainer: Factors That Foster Conflict in Nigeria's Kaduna State," *The Conversation*, February 12, 2019, http://theconversation.com/explainer-factors-that-foster-conflict-in-nigerias-kaduna-state-109899.
21. Quoted in Alao, "Islamic Radicalisation and Violent Extremism in Nigeria," 137.
22. Quoted in Alao, "Islamic Radicalisation and Violent Extremism in Nigeria," 137. El- Zakzaky was speaking during a one-day symposium, organized by the Resource Forum of the Islamic Movement in Nigeria, titled "The Creation of the Illegal State of Israel," which was held at Arewa House, Kaduna.
23. "Police Set to Sack Shi'ites," *Daily Trust*, September 11, 2009.
24. Zenn, "The Islamic Movement and Iranian Intelligence Activities."
25. "Nigeria's Khomeini, Spreading Iran's Revolution to Africa," *Daily Beast*, June 26, 2017, https://www.thedailybeast.com/nigerias-khomeini-spreading-irans-revolution-to-africa.
26. "Nigeria's Khomeini, Spreading Iran's Revolution to Africa."
27. "Iran Summons Nigerian Envoy after Shia clashes," *Aljazeera*, December 15, 2017, https://www.aljazeera.com/news/2015/12/iran-summons-nigerian-envoy-shia-clashes-151215081658668.html.
28. "Iranian President Calls Buhari, Protests Killing of Shiites," *PM News*, December 16, 2015, https://www.pmnewsnigeria.com/2015/12/16/iranian-president-calls-buhari-protests-killing-of-shiites/.

29. "Iranian President Calls Buhari."
30. Abdullateef Salau, "Iran to Build Universities to Student Flow Out of Nigeria," *Daily Trust*, February 1, 2018.
31. Monsuru Olowoopejo, "FG's Proscription of Shiites Decisive, Necessary—MURIC," *Vanguard*, July 29, 2019.
32. John Nwachukwu, "El-Zakzaky: Fani-Kayode Warns Buhari against Going into War with Iran," *Daily Post*, July 29, 2019.
33. Osakwe, "The Arab Spring and Its Implications for Nigerian National Security," 27–28.
34. International Crisis Group, "Curbing Violence in Nigeria (II)."
35. Zimet, "Boko Haram's Evolving Relationship with Al-Qaeda."
36. Zimet, "Boko Haram's Evolving Relationship with Al-Qaeda."
37. Zimet, "Boko Haram's Evolving Relationship with Al Qaeda."
38. For more on AQIM, a recent book is Venter, *Al-Qaeda in the Islamic Maghreb*.
39. Zimet, "Boko Haram's Evolving Relationship with Al-Qaeda."
40. Zimet, "Boko Haram's Evolving Relationship with Al-Qaeda."
41. Kodjo, *Mali Conflict of 2012–2013*.
42. Zenn, "Boko Haram's International Connections."
43. Ionel Zamfir, "Regional Efforts to Fight Boko Haram," European Parliament Think Tank, February 13, 2017, https://www.europarl.europa.eu/thinktank/en/document .html?reference=EPRS_ATA%282017%29599274.
44. Assanvo, Abatan, and Sawadogo, "Assessing the Multinational Joint Task Force against Boko Haram," 2.
45. Assanvo, Abatan, and Sawadogo, "Assessing the Multinational Joint Task Force against Boko Haram."
46. Jeffrey Feltman, "Security Council Briefing on the Situation in the Lake Chad Basin," United Nations, Political and Peacebuilding Affairs, July 27, 2016, https:// www.un.org/undpa/en/speeches-statements/27072016/lake-chad-basin.
47. Britain has always had a good relationship with Nigeria. Indeed, the first Commonwealth Conference to take place outside the United Kingdom was held in the African country. A Nigerian expert on Anglo-Nigerian relations describes the relationship as an entente. This special interest resulted in the formulation of an Anglo-Nigeria Defense Pact. Although pressure from students eventually resulted in its abrogation, the special interest continued, especially during the Nigerian Civil War, when Britain joined a Cold War opponent (Soviet Union) to support Nigeria's united existence. Although a few developments after the civil war battered and bruised the relationship, it remained one of the strongest in the Commonwealth.

CONCLUSION

1. See "Military Overwhelmed by Security Challenges—Governors," *Vanguard*, December 3, 2020.
2. Hassan Muaz, "ISWAP Moves N18b Annual Revenue through Nigeria's Financial System—ECOWAS body," *Sunday Punch*, December 5, 2021.

3. Muaz, "ISWAP Moves N18b Annual Revenue."
4. Muaz, "ISWAP Moves N18b Annual Revenue."
5. Garba Shehu, "Revenge Killings Worsening Security Problems in Southern Kaduna," *Vanguard*, July 21, 2020.
6. This squad particularly targeted youths with mobile phones, laptops, dreadlocks, and so on, considered to be indications of young people living in the fast lane and involved in internet fraud.
7. Isaac Taiwo, "We Either Restructure or Breakup—Pastor Adeboye," *Guardian*, October 4, 2020.
8. See "Oyedepo Backs Protesters, Says 'Lives Have No Value' under Buhari," *This Day*, October 19, 2020.
9. "See What Apostle Suleiman Says about the #EndSARS Protests . . . ," Celebration TV, October 18, 2020, https://www.youtube.com/watch?v=b8o2vFpmu3Y.
10. Ifreke Inyang, "SARS Is 'State-Aided Robbery Squad'—Pastor Tunde Bakare," *Daily Post*, October 25, 2020, https://dailypost.ng/2020/10/25/sars-is-state-aided-robbery-squad-pastor-tunde-bakare/.
11. Ajala Samuel Akindele, "#EndSARS: Adeboye, Bakare, Suleman Condemn Killing of Protesters," *Premium Times*, October 21, 2020, https://www.premiumtimesng.com/news/more-news/422181-endsars-adeboye-bakare-suleman-condemn-killing-of-protesters.html.
12. "#EndSARS: Femi Adesina Blames Churches, Mosques," *Sahara Reporters*, October 23, 2020, http://saharareporters.com/2020/10/23/endsars-femi-adesina-blames-churches-mosques.

Abd Aziz, A. R. "Terror in the Name of God: Is This Consistent with Islamic Fundamentalism?" *Seaford House Papers*, 2003.

Abdulraheem, Tajudeen. "Politics in Nigeria's Second Republic." DPhil thesis, University of Oxford, 1990.

AbdulSalam, H. A. "Islam and Public Life: An Inseparable Synergy." In *Dynamics of Revealed Knowledge and Human Sciences*, edited by Y. O. Iman, R. I. Adebayo, and A. L. Ali-Agan. Abuja: Spectrum, 2016.

Abimbola, Wande. *Ifá: An Exposition of Ifá Literary Corpus*. New York: Athelia Henrietta Press, 1997.

Abimbola, Wande. "The Place of African Traditional Religion in Contemporary Africa." In *African Traditional Religions in Contemporary Society*, edited by Jacob K. Olupona. New York: International Religious Foundation, 1991.

Abodunde, Ayodeji. *Messenger: Sydney Elton and the Making of Pentecostalism in Nigeria*. Lagos: Pierce Watershed, 2016.

Abogunrin, S. O. *Religion and Ethics in Nigeria*. Ibadan: Daystar, 1986.

Abubakar, Musa Usman. "Nigeria's Blasphemy Laws and the Competing Rights: Taming the Self-Appointed God Avengers through Judicial Process." In *Religion, Law and Security in Africa*, edited by M. C. Green, T. J. Gunn, and M. Hill. Stellenbosch: Conf-RAP, 2018.

Adam, Hussein. "Islam and Politics in Somalia." *Journal of Islamic Studies* 6, no. 2 (1995).

Adamu, A. U. "Insurgency in Nigeria: The Northern Nigeria Experience." In *Complex Emergencies in Nigeria*, edited by O. Obafemi and H. Galadima. Kuru: National Institute for Policy and Strategic Studies, 2013.

Addison, James Thayer. "Ancestor Worship in Africa." *Harvard Theological Review* 17, no. 2 (April 1924).

Adebanwi, Wale. "The Clergy, Culture and Political Conflicts in Nigeria." *African Studies Review* 53, no. 3 (2010).

Adebanwi, Wale. *Yorùbá Elites and Ethnic Politics in Nigeria: Ọbáfẹ́mi Awólówọ̀ and Corporate Agency*. New York: Cambridge University Press, 2014.

Adejumobi, Said, and Momoh Abubakar, eds. *The Political Economy of Nigeria under Military Rule: 1984–1993*. London: SAPES, 1995.

Adekunle, J. O. "The Jihads in West Africa." In *Africa: African History before 1885*, edited by Falola Toyin. Durham, NC: Carolina Academic Press, 2000.

Adeleye, Rowland. "Hausaland and Borno, 1600–1800." In *A History of West Africa*, vol. 1, edited by J. F. Ade Ajayi and Michael Crowder. London: Longman, 1974.

Adeleye, Rowland. *Power and Diplomacy in Northern Nigeria, 1804–1906: The Sokoto Caliphate and Its Enemies*. London: Longman, 1971.

Adelowo, E. D. "Mission Education and Yoruba Missions of Nigeria: A Brief History." *Religion* 10 (1986).

Adeniyi, Musa. "Evolution of Islamic Education in Nigeria." Unpublished manuscript.

Adeniyi, Olusegun. *Power, Politics and Death: A Front-Row Account of Nigeria under the Late President Yar'Adua*. Lagos: Kachifo Limited, 2011.

Adesoji, Abimbola. "Between Maitatsine and Boko Haram: Islamic Fundamentalism and the Response of the Nigerian State." *Africa Today* 57, no. 4 (September 2011).

Adesoji, Abimbola. "The Boko Haram Uprising and Islamic Revivalism in Nigeria." *Afrikaspectrum* 45, no. 2 (2010).

Adibe, J. "Boko Haram: One Sect, Conflicting Narratives." *African Renaissance* 9, no. 1 (2012).

Adinoyi, Seriki. "Turai's Delegation Visits Jos, Shuns Governor Jang." *This Day*, December 18, 2008.

Adogame, Afe. *Who Is Afraid of the Holy Ghost? Pentecostalism and Globalization in Africa and Beyond*. Trenton, NJ: Africa World Press, 2011.

Adogame, Paul. "Challenges to National and Regional Security, Boko Haram's Militant Islamic Terrorism in Nigeria." *NARC Digest, Journal of the Nigerian Army Resource Centre* 1, no. 1 (November 2018).

Agbaje, Adigun. "Travails of the Secular State: Religion, Politics and the Outlook in Nigeria's Third Republic." *Journal of Commonwealth and Comparative Politics* 28, no. 3 (1990).

Agbiboa, Daniel. "The Nigerian Burden: Religious Identity, Conflict and the Current Terrorism of Boko Haram." *Conflict, Security and Development Journal* 13, no. 1 (2013).

Agbiboa, Daniel. "The Socio-economic Dynamics of Nigeria's Boko Haram Insurgency: Fresh Insights from the Social Identity Theory." Paper presented at the Annual Bank Conference on Africa: Confronting Conflict and Fragility in Africa, Berkeley, CA, June 8–10, 2015. https://www.researchgate.net/publication/275657937.

Aghedo, I., and Osumah, O. "The Boko Haram Uprising: How Should Nigeria Respond?" *Third World Quarterly* 33, no. 5 (2012).

Ajayi, Adegboyega. *The Military and the Nigerian State, 1966–1993: A Study of the Strategies of Political Power Control*. Trenton, NJ: African World Press, 2007.

Ajayi, J. F. A. *Christian Missions in Nigeria, 1841–1891*. London: Longman, 1965.

Ajayi, J. F. A., and Michael Crowder. *A History of West Africa*, vol. 1. London: Longman, 1974.

Akanji, Okunola Rashidi, and Ojo, Matthias Olufemi Dada. "Oro Cult: The Traditional Way of Political Administration, Judiciary System and Religious Cleansing among the

Pre-colonial Yoruba Natives of Nigeria." *Journal of International Social Research* 5, no. 23 (fall 2012).

Akindele, R. A., and Oye Oyediran. "Federalism and Foreign Policy in Nigeria." *International Journal* 41, no. 3 (summer 1986).

Akinjogbin, I. A. "The Expansion of Oyo and the Rise of Dahomey, 1600–1800." In *History of West Africa*, vol. 1, edited by J. F. Ade-Ajayi and Michael Crowder. London: Longman, 1971.

Akinlotan, Idowu. "Plateau Killings and Herdsmen Sophistries." *The Nation*, July 1, 2018.

Akintoye, Adebanji. *A History of the Yoruba People*. Dakar: Amalion, 2010.

Akinwumi, Akitunde. *Hubris: A Brief Political History of the Nigerian Army*. Princeton, NJ: AMV, 2018.

Akinwumi, Olayemi, and Adesina Raji. "The Wangarawa Factor in the History of Nigerian Islam: The Example of Kano and Borgu." *Islamic Studies* 29, no. 4 (winter 1990).

Akiri, Chris. "Proposal for Pilot Ranches: Reward for Criminality?" *This Day*, July 10, 2018.

Alabi-Isama, Godwin. *The Tragedy of Victory: On-the-Spot Account of the Nigeria-Biafra War in the Atlantic Theatre*. Ibadan: Spectrum, 2013.

A'la Maududi, Sayyid Abul. *Jihad in Islam*. Privately published, September 15, 2017.

Alao, Abiodun. "Islamic Radicalisation and Political Violence in Nigeria." In *Militancy and Violence in West Africa: Religion, Politics, and Radicalisation*, edited by James Gow, Funmi Olonisakin, and Dijxhoorn Ernst. London: Routledge, 2013.

Alao, Abiodun, "Islamic Radicalisation and Violent Extremism in Nigeria." *Journal of Conflict, Security and Development* 13, no. 2 (2013).

Alao, Abiodun. *Natural Resources and Conflict in Africa: The Tragedy of Endowment*. Rochester, NY: University of Rochester Press, 2007.

Alao, Abiodun. *A New Narrative for Africa: Voice and Agency*. London: Routledge, 2020.

Alao, Akin. "Constitutional Guarantee of the Secularity of the State and Judicial Attitude to Religious Freedom in Nigeria." Unpublished manuscript.

Ali, Arshad. "Economic Cost of Terrorism: A Case Study of Pakistan." *Strategic Studies* 30, no. 1/2 (spring–summer 2010).

Ali, Yusuf O., ed. *Anatomy of Corruption in Nigeria*. Lagos: Biographer, 2016.

Allen, Tim, and Koen Vlassenroot, eds. *The Lord's Resistance Army: Myth and Reality*. London: Zed, 2010.

Alvares, Alexander C., and Ronet D. Bachman. *Violence: The Enduring Problem*. London: Sage, 2016.

Amaechi, Louisa. "The Use of Masquerade Cult and Umu-Ada Fraternity (Igbo Daughters) for Peace and Conflict Resolution in Eastern Nigeria." *American International Journal of Social Science* 7, no. 2 (June 2018).

Anifowose, Remi. *Violence and Politics in Nigeria: The Tiv and Yoruba Experience*. Enugu: Nok, 1982.

Anugwom, Edlyne. "Something Mightier: Marginalization, Occult Imaginations and the Youth Conflict in the Oil-Rich Niger Delta." *Africa Spectrum* 46, no. 3 (2011).

Apard, Élodie. "The Words of Boko Haram: Understanding Speeches by Momammed Yusaf and Abubakar Shekau." *Afrique contemporaine* 255, no. 3 (2015).

Arinze, Francis. *Christian-Muslim Relations in the Twenty-First Century*. Maryknoll, NY: Orbis, 1989.

Arinze, Francis. *Sacrifice in Ibo Religion*. Ibadan: University of Ibadan Press, 1978.

Asaju, Dapo. "Globalisation, Politicization of Religion and Religious Networking: The Case of Pentecostalism in Nigeria." In *Who Is Afraid of the Holy Ghost? Pentecostalism and Globalization in Africa and Beyond*, edited by Afe Adogame. Trenton, NJ: Africa World Press, 2011.

Asaju, Dapo. "Restoring the Religious Factor in Education and Socio-political Development of Modern Societies." In *Rethinking Higher Education and National Development*, 95. Ibadan: University Postgraduate School, 2019.

Assanvo, William, Jeannine Ella A. Abatan, and Wendyam Aristide Sawadogo. "Assessing the Multinational Joint Task Force against Boko Haram." *ISS West Africa Report*, no. 19 (September 2016).

Atanda, J. A. *The New Oyo Empire: Indirect Rule and Change in Western Nigeria, 1894–1934*. London: Longman, 1973.

Audu, Bem Japhet. "Tiv (Nigeria) Riots of 1960, 1964: The Principle of Minimum Force and Counter Insurgency." *Journal of Ethnic Minority Agitations in Nigeria since Colonial Period*, 2015.

Awolalu, J. Omosade. *Yoruba Beliefs and Sacrificial Rites*. New York: Athelia Henrietta Press, 1996.

Awolalu, Omisade. *West African Traditional Religion*. Ibadan: Onibonoje, 1979.

Awolowo, Obafemi. *Path to Nigerian Freedom*. London: Faber and Faber, 1966.

Ayandele, Emmanuel. "The Missionary Factor in Northern Nigeria, 1870–1918." *Journal of Historical Society of Nigeria* 3, no. 3 (December 1966).

Ayandele, Emmanuel. *The Missionary Impact on Modern Nigeria, 1842–1914: A Political and Social Analysis*. London: Longman, 1966.

Ayeni, Victor, and Kayode Soremekin, eds. *Nigeria's Second Republic Presidentialism, Politics and Administration in a Developing State*. Lagos: Daily Times Press, 1988.

Ayoob, M. *The Many Faces of Political Islam: Religion and Politics in the Muslim World*. Ann Arbor: University of Michigan Press, 2007.

Azeez, Gbolagade, and Abidoye Sarumi. *Ajabemokeferi the Missionary*. Ibadan: Caltop, 1992.

Badran, Margot. "Sharia Activism and Zina in Nigeria in the Era of Hudud." In *Gender and Islam in Africa: Rights, Sexuality and Law*, edited by Margot Badran. Washington, DC: Woodrow Wilson Center Press, 2011.

Bakare, Tunde. "Negotiating the New Nigeria." *Tunde Bakare* (blog), October 14, 2018. http://tundebakare.com/renegotiating-the-new-nigeria/.

Bakker, Edwin, and Leen Boer. *The Evolution of al-Qaedaism: Ideology, Terrorists and Appeal*. The Hague: Netherlands Institute of International Relations, Clingendael, 2007.

Bala, Aminu Alhaji. "Da'wah towards Alleviating Spirit Worship and Devil Possession (Bori) in Hausaland (Northern Nigeria)." *International Journal of Humanities and Social Science Invention* 4, no. 7 (July 2015).

Bala, Aminu Alhaji, and Ibrahim Shu'aibu Sa'id. "Qur'anists' Deviant Da'wah as Reflected in Their Trends of Tafsir in Northern Nigeria." *Scholars Journal of Arts, Humanities and Social Sciences,* August 2015.

Balci, Bayram. *Islam in Central Asia and the Caucasus since the Fall of the Soviet Union.* London: Hurst, 2018.

Balogun, S. A. "History of Islam up to 1800." In *Groundwork of Nigerian History,* edited by Obaro Ikime. Ibadan: Heinemann, 1980.

Basil, Ekot. *Nigeria: Ethnicity and the Dynamics of Political Transformation in Nigeria.* Sunnyvale, CA: Lap Lambert, 2011.

Batson, Daniel, Patricia Schoenrade, and W. Larry Ventis. *Religion and the Individual: A Social-Psychological Perspective.* Oxford: Oxford University Press, 1993.

Behera, Marina Ngursangzeli. *Interfaith Relations after One Hundred Years: Christian Mission among Other Faiths.* Eugene, OR: Wipf and Stock, 2011.

Bello, Abdul-Rahoof Adebayo. "Jos Crisis and Ethnic Animosity in Nigeria: A Historical Perspective." Unpublished manuscript.

Bello, Ahmadu. *My Life.* Cambridge: Cambridge University Press, 1962.

Ben Amara, Ramzi. "The Izala Movement in Nigeria: Its Split, Relationship to Sufis and Perception of Sharī'a Re-implementation." PhD thesis, University of Bayreuth, 2011.

Berger, Peter. *The Sacred Canopy.* New York: Anchor, 1990.

Bergin, Anthony. "Countering Internet Radicalisation in Southeast Asia." *Australian Strategic Policy Institute, Special Report,* no. 22 (March 2009).

Best, Shedrak Gaya, and Dimieari Von Kemedi. "Armed Groups and Conflict in Rivers and Plateau States, Nigeria." In *Armed and Aimless: Armed Groups, Guns, and Human Security in the ECOWAS Region,* edited by Nicolas Florquin and Eric G. Berman. Geneva: Small Arms Survey, May 2005.

Bezhan, Faridullah. *Women, War and Islamic Radicalisation in Maryam Mahboob's Afghanistan.* Clayton, Australia: Monash University Press, 2017.

Bienen, Henry. "Religion, Legitimacy, and Conflict in Nigeria." *Annals of the American Academy of Political and Social Science* 483, no. 1 (1986).

Block, Corrie Jonn. *The Qur'an in Christian-Muslim Dialogue: Historical and Modern Interpretations.* London: Routledge, 2014.

Borelli, Marguerite. "ASEAN Counter-terrorism Weaknesses." *Counter Terrorist Trends and Analyses* 9, no. 9 (September 2017).

Bourne, Richard. *Nigeria: A New History of a Turbulent Century.* London: Zed, 2015.

Brahimi, Alia. "Crushed in the Shadow: Why Al Qaeda Will Lose the War of Ideas." *Conflict and Terrorism* 33 (2010): 100.

Brenner, Louis, ed. *Muslim Identity and Social Change in Sub-Saharan Africa.* Bloomington: Indiana University Press, 1993.

Brigaglia, Andrea. "A Contribution to the History of the Wahhabi *Da'wa* in West Africa: The Career and the Murder of Shaykh Ja'far Mahmoud Adam (Daura, ca. 1961/1962–Kano 2007)." *Islamic Africa* 3, no. 1 (2012).

Brigaglia, Andrea. "Ja'far Mahmoud Adam, Mohammed Yusuf and Al-Muntada Islamic Trust: Reflections on the Genesis of the Boko Haram Phenomenon in Nigeria." *Annual Review of Islam in Africa,* no. 11 (2012).

Brigaglia, Andrea. "'Slicing Off the Tumour': The History of Global Jihad in Nigeria, as Narrated by the Islamic State." *Politics and Religion Journal* 12, no. 2 (2018).

Briggs, Jimmie. *Innocents Lost: When Child Soldiers Go to War*. New York: Basic Books, 2005.

Buratai, Tukur. "Curtailing Boko Haram Terrorism: The Challenges and Approaches of the Nigerian Army." *NARC Digest, Journal of the Nigerian Army Resource Centre* 1, no. 1 (November 2018).

Campbell, Bolaji. "*Eegun Ogun* War Masquerades in Ibadan in the Era of Modernization." *African Art* 48, no. 1 (spring 2015).

Caplan, Lionel, ed. *Studies in Religious Fundamentalism*. London: Macmillan, 1987.

Clarke, Peter. "Islamic Reform in Contemporary Nigeria: Methods and Aims." *Third World Quarterly* 10, no. 2 (1988).

Clarke, Peter, and Ian Linden. *Islam in Modern Nigeria: A Study of a Muslim Community in a Post-independence State, 1960-1983*. Munich: Mainz Grünewald München Kaiser, 1984.

Coleman, James. *Nigeria: Background to Nationalism*. Berkeley: University of California Press, 1958.

Collier, Paul, and Anke Hoeffler. "Greed and Grievance in Civil War." *Oxford Economic Papers* 56, no. 4 (2004).

Comolli, Virginia. *Boko Haram: Nigeria's Islamist Insurgency*. London: Hurst, 2015.

Cook, David. "Boko Haram Escalates Attacks on Christians in Northern Nigeria." *CTC Sentinel* 5, no. 4 (April 2012).

Cook, Michael. *Commanding Rights and Forbidding Wrong in Islamic Thoughts*. Cambridge: Cambridge University Press, 2000.

Coughlin, Con. *Khomeini's Ghost: The Iranian Revolution and the Rise of Militant Islam*. New York: Ecco, 2010.

Courson, Elias, and Michael Odijie. "Egbesu: An African Just War Philosophy and Practice." *Journal of African Cultural Studies*, February 2020.

Crenshaw, Martha. *Explaining Terrorism: Causes, Processes and Consequences*. London: Routledge, 2010.

Crowder, Michael. *The Story of Nigeria*. London: Faber and Faber, 1966.

Dalgaard-Nielsen, Anja. "Studying Violent Radicalization in Europe I: The Potential Contribution of Social Movement Theory." *Danish Institute for International Studies (DIIS) Working Paper* 2 (2008).

Daly, Samuel F. C. "Biafra's Crisis of Faith: The Spiritual Legacies of the Biafran War." *The Republic*, October/November 2017. https://www.republic.com.ng/octobernovember-2017/biafra.crisis-of-faith/.

Danbazau, Mallam Lawan. *Politics and Religion in Nigeria*. Kano: Tofa Commercial Press, 1991.

Danfulani, John, and Ahmed Buba. "Nigeria-Israeli Relations: From the Realm of African Solidarity to the Realm of Nigeria's National Interest." *Lapai International Journal of Politics*. Lapai, Nigeria: Ibrahim Badamasi Babangida University.

Daramola, Olu, and Adebayo Jeje. *Awǫn Àṣà ati Òrìṣà ilẹ̀ Yorùbá*. Ibadan: Onibonoje Press, 1967.

Davidson, Lawrence. *Islamic Fundamentalism: An Introduction*. London: Greenwood, 1998.

Davis, Noah R., and Abdullahi Usman Manya. *An Account of Ibrahim Zakzaky: The Shi'i Cleric of Nigeria*. Createspace, 2016.

Dennett, R. E. "The Ogboni and Other Secret Societies in Nigeria." *Journal of the Royal African Society* 16, no. 61 (October 1916).

Diamond, Larry Jay. *Class, Ethnicity, and Democracy in Nigeria: The Failure of the First Republic*. Syracuse, NY: Syracuse University Press, 1988.

Dike, K. Onwuka. "Origins of the Niger Mission 1841–1891." Paper presented at the Centenary of the Mission at Christ Church, Onitsha, on November 13, 1957.

Dowden, Richard. "Cynical Politicians, Pipedreams and How We Can Make a Difference." *The Independent* (London), June 1, 2005.

Drake, C. "The Role of Ideology in Terrorist Target-Selection." *Terrorists and Political Violence* 10, no. 2 (1998).

Dudley, B. J. *Instability and Political Order: Politics and Crisis in Nigeria*. Ibadan: Ibadan University Press, 1973.

Eitzen, S., and Zinn, M. B. "Religion." In *In Conflict and Order: Understanding Society*, edited by Stanley Eitzen, Maxine Baca Zinn, and Kelly Eitzen Smith. Boston: Pearson Allyn and Bacon, 2010.

El Fadl, Khaled Abou. *The Place of Tolerance in Islam*. Boston: Boston Review, 2002.

El-Khawas, Mohamed A. "Revolutionary Islam in North Africa: Challenges and Responses." *Africa Today* 43, no. 4 (October 1996).

Ellis, Stephen. "The Okija Shrine: Death and Life in Nigerian Politics." *Journal of African History* 49, no. 3 (November 2008).

Ellis, Stephen, and Gerrie ter Haar. "Religion and Politics in Sub-Saharan Africa." *Journal of Modern African Studies* 36, no. 2 (1998).

El-Sherif, Ashraf. *The Muslim Brotherhood and the Future of Political Islam in Egypt*. Washington: Carnegie Endowment for International Peace, 2014.

Emewu, Ilena, and Desmond Mgboh. "Suicide Bombers: Qaqa, Boko Haram's Spokesman Open Up." *Daily Sun*, February 9, 2012.

Enwerem, I. M. *A Dangerous Awakening: The Politicization of Religion in Nigeria*. Ibadan: Institut Français de Recherche en Afrique, 1995.

Esack, Farid. *Qur'an, Liberation and Pluralism: An Islamic Perspective of Interreligious Solidarity against Oppression*. Oxford: Oneworld, 1996.

Esposito, John, ed. *The Iranian Revolution: Its Global Impact*. Gainesville: University Press of Florida, 1990.

Esposito, John, ed. *The Oxford History of Islam*. New York: Oxford University Press, 1999.

Esposito, John. *Unholy War: Terror in the Name of Islam*. Oxford: Oxford University Press, 2002.

Falola, Toyin. *The History of Nigeria*. Westport, CT: Greenwood Press, 1999.

Falola, Toyin. *Violence in Nigeria: The Crisis of Religious Politics and Secular Ideologies*. Rochester, NY: University of Rochester Press, 1998.

Falola, Toyin, Roy Doron, and Okpeh Ochayi Okpeh, eds. *Warfare, Ethnicity and National Identity in Nigeria*. Trenton, NJ: Africa World Press, 2013.

Fitzgerald, Michael L., and John Borelli. *Interfaith Dialogue: A Catholic View*. Maryknoll, NY: Orbis, 2006.

Forest, James. *Confronting the Terrorism of Boko Haram in Nigeria*. Florida: JSOU Press, 2012.

Francis, David. "The Rise of Boko Haram." *Foreign Policy*, December 28, 2011. http://www.foreignpolicy.com/articles/2011/12/27/the_rise_of_boko_haram.

Frynas, Jedrzej Georg. *Oil in Nigeria: Community Rights and Corporate Dominance in Conflict*. Zurich: Lit Verlag, 2000.

Gambari, Ibrahim A. "The Development of African-Israeli Relations to the Yom Kippur War: Nigeria as a Case Study." In *Zionism and Arabism in Palestine and Israel*, edited by Elie Kedourie and Sylvia G. Haim. London: Routledge, 2015.

Gbadamosi, T. G. O. *The Growth of Islam among the Yoruba, 1841–1908*. London: Longman, 1978.

Gbadamosi, T. G. O., and J. F. Ade Ajayi. "Islam and Christianity in Nigeria." In *Groundwork of Nigerian History*, edited by Obaro Ikime. Ibadan: Heinemann, 1980.

Goddard, Hugh. *A History of Christian-Muslim Relations*. Edinburgh: Edinburgh University Press, 2000.

Gow, James, and Funmi Olonisakin. "Introduction: Militancy and Violence in West Africa." In *Militancy and Violence in West Africa: Religion, Politics and Radicalisation*, edited by James Gow, Funmi Olonisakin, and Ernst Dijxhoorn. London: Routledge, 2013.

Gregory, Kathryn. *Ansar Al-Islam*. Council on Foreign Relations, November 2008.

Griffith, Sydney H. *The Church in the Shadow of the Mosque: Christians and Muslims in the World of Islam*. Princeton, NJ: Princeton University Press, 2007.

Guichaoua, Yvan. "The Making of an Ethnic Militia: The Oodua People's Congress in Nigeria." CRISE Working Paper no. 26, November 2006.

Gumi, Abubakar. *Where I Stand*. Ibadan: Spectrum, 1992.

Hackett, Rosalind. "Rethinking the Role of Religion in the Public Sphere: Local and Global Perspectives." In *Comparative Perspectives on Shari'ah in Nigeria*, edited by Philip Ostien, Jamila Nasir, and Franz Kogelman. Ibadan: Spectrum, 2005.

Hallaq, Wael. *The Impossible State: Islam, Politics and Modernity's Moral Predicament*. New York: Columbia University Press, 2014.

Halverson, Jefferey. *Theology and Creed in Sunni Islam: The Muslim Brotherhood, Ash'arism, and Political Sunnism*. London: Palgrave, 2010.

Harasta, Jesse, and Charles Rivers, eds. *The History of the Sunni and Shia Split: Understanding the Divisions within Islam*. CreateSpace Independent Publishing Platform, 2014.

Hassan, Muhammad Haniff Bin, and Kenneth George Pereire. "An Ideological Response to Combating Terrorism—the Singapore Perspective." *Small Wars and Insurgencies* 17, no. 4 (2006).

Hirvonen, Heidi. *Christian-Muslim Dialogue: Perspectives of Four Lebanese Thinkers*. Leiden: Brill, 2012.

Hodgson, Marshall. *The Secret Order of Assassins: The Struggle of the Early Nizârî Ismâ'îlîs against the Islamic World*. Philadelphia: University of Pennsylvania Press, 2005.

Hoffman, Bruce. *Inside Terrorism*. New York: Columbia University Press, 2006.

Horsley, Richard. "The Sicarii: Ancient Jewish 'Terrorists.'" *Journal of Religion* 59, no. 4 (October 1979).

Huntington, Samuel. *The Clash of Civilization and the Remaking of World Order*. New York: Simon and Schuster, 1996. Hunwick, John. "An African Case Study of Political Islam: Nigeria." *Annals of the American Academy of Political and Social Science* 524, no. 1 (1992).

Hunwick, John. "Songhay, Borno and Hausa States, 1450–1600." In *A History of West Africa*, vol. 1, edited by Ade Ajayi and Michael Crowder. London: Longman, 1974.

Ibrahim, Inuwa. "Politicians as Terrorists." *The Insider*, no. 25 (July 4, 2011).

Ibrahim, J. "The Politics of Religion in Nigeria: The Parameters of the 1987 Crisis in Kaduna State." *Review of African Political Economy* 45/46 (1989).

Ibrahim, J. "Religion and Political Turbulence in Nigeria." *Journal of Modern African Studies* 29, no. 1 (1991).

Ibrahim, Mohammed. "An Empirical Survey of Children and Youth in Organised Armed Violence in Nigeria: Egbesu Boys, OPC, and Bakassi Boys as a Case Study." In *Neither War Nor Peace: International Comparisons of Children and Youth in Organised Armed Violence*, 2005. https://www.oijj.org/sites/default/files/documentos/documental_2792_en.pdf

Idahosa, Benson. *You Are God's Battle Axe*. Benin: Rainbow, 2010.

Idowu, Bolaji. *African Traditional Religion: A Definition*. Maryknoll, NY: Orbis, 1973.

Idowu, E. Bolaji. *Olodumare: God in Yoruba Belief*. Hoboken, NJ: Prentice Hall, 1962.

Idowu, William. "Law, Morality and the African Cultural Heritage: The Jurisprudential Significance of the Ogboni Institution." *Nordic Journal of African Studies* 14, no. 2 (2005).

Ilesanmi, Simeon. *Religious Pluralism and the Nigerian State*. Athens: Ohio University Press, 1997.

International Crisis Group. "Curbing Violence in Nigeria (II): The Boko Haram Insurgency." *Africa Report* 216 (2014).

Inuwa, S. "The Delayed Degradation of Boko Haram Terrorists: What Went Wrong?" *NARC Digest, Journal of the Nigerian Army Resource Centre* 1, no. 1 (November 2018).

Ipgrave, Michael. *Scriptures in Dialogue: Christians and Muslims Studying the Bible and the Qur'an Together*. London: Church, 2004.

Irabor, Leo. "Combating Boko Haram Insurgency in Nigeria: The Role of the Nigerian Army." *NARC Digest, Journal of the Nigerian Army Resource Centre* 1, no. 1 (November 2018).

Isichei, Elizabeth. "The Maitatsine Risings in Nigeria 1980–85: A Revolt of the Disinherited." *Journal of Religion in Africa* 17, no. 3 (October 1987).

Iwuchukwu, Marinus C., and Brian Stiltner. *Can Muslims and Christians Resolve Their Religious and Social Conflicts? Cases from Africa and the United States*. Lewiston, NY: Edwin Mellen, 2013.

Jafri, Syed Husain Muhammed. *The Origins and Early Development of Shi'a Islam*. Oxford: Oxford University Press, 2002.

Jagielski, Wojciech. *The Night Wanderers: Uganda's Children and the Lord's Resistance Army*. Translated by Antonia Lloyd-Jones. New York: Seven Stories Press, 2012.

Jimoh, Mufutau. "The Growth and Development of Islam in Epe, Lagos State." *Ilorin Journal of Religious Studies* 6, no. 2 (2016): 6.

Jones, Peter. "The Arab Spring: Opportunities and Implications." *International Journal* 67, no. 2 (spring 2012).

Juergensmeyer, Mark. *Terror in the Mind of God: The Global Rise of Religious Violence*, 3rd ed. Berkeley: University of California Press, 2003.

Junaidu, S. W. "Resistance to Western Culture in the Sakkwato Caliphate: A Lesson to Generations Yet Unborn." In *State and Society in the Sokoto Caliphate*, edited by Ahmad Mohammad Kani and Kabir Ahmed Gandi. Sokoto: Usmanu Danfodiyo University Press, 1990.

Kamolnick, Paul. *Countering Radicalization and Recruitment to Al-Qaeda: Fighting the War of Deeds*. Carlisle, PA: Strategic Studies Institute, U.S. Army War College Press, 2014.

Kanu, Ikechukwu Anthony, Ejikemeuwa J. O. Ndubuise, and Catherine Chiugo Kanu. *Africa at the Cross-Roads of Violence and Gender Inequality: The Dilemma of Continuity in the Face of Change*. Bloomington, IN: Author House, 2018.

Kassim, Abdulbasit. "Defining and Understanding the Religious Philosophy of Jihadi-Salafism and the Ideology of Boko Haram." *Politics, Religion and Ideology* 16, nos. 2–3 (2015).

Kassim, Abdulbasit, and Michael Nwankpa, eds. *The Boko Haram Reader: From Nigerian Preachers to the Islamic State*. London: Hurst, 2018.

Kastfelt, Niels. *Religion and Politics in Nigeria: A Study in Middle Belt Christianity*. London: British Academy Press, 1994.

Kastfelt, Niels. "Rumours of Maitatsine: A Note on the Political Culture in Northern Nigeria." *African Affairs* 88, no. 350 (January 1989).

Kateregga, Badru D., and David W. Shenk. *A Muslim and a Christian in Dialogue*. Harrison, VA: Herald, 2005.

Kenny, Joseph. "The Spread of Islam in Nigeria: A Historical Survey." Paper presented at Spiritan Institute of Theology, Enugu, March 2001. Online version, http://www.dhspriory.org/kenny/Sist.htm.

Khalidi, Rashid. *Sowing Crisis: The Cold War and the American Dominance in the Middle East*. Boston: Beacon, 2009.

Kirk-Greene, Anthony. *Crisis and Conflict in Nigeria: A Documentary Sourcebook, 1966–1970*. London: Oxford University Press, 1971.

Kitause, Rimamsikwe Habila, and Hilary Chukwuka Achunike. "Religion in Nigeria from 1900–2013." *Research on Humanities and Social Sciences* 3, no. 18 (2013).

Kodjo, Tchioffo. *Mali Conflict of 2012–2013: A Critical Assessment: Patterns of Local, Regional and Global Conflict and Resolution Dynamics in Post-colonial and Post-Cold War Africa*. Moldova: Lambert Academic Press, 2015.

Kukah, M. H. "Christians and Nigeria's Aborted Transition." In *The Christian Churches and the Democratisation of Africa*, edited by Paul Gifford. Leiden: Brill, 1995.

Kukah, M. H. *Religion, Politics and Power in Northern Nigeria*. Ibadan: Spectrum, 1993.

Kukah, M. H., and T. Falola. *Religious Militancy and Self-Assertion: Islam and Politics in Nigeria*. Aldershot, UK: Avebury and Ashgate, 1996.

Ladan-Baki, Ibrahim S. "Interfaith Conflict and Political Development in Nigeria: The Zangon Kataf Conflict." *Journal of Social and Administrative Sciences* 2, no. 4 (December 2015).

Laitin, David. "The Sharia Debate and the Origins of Nigeria's Second Republic." *Journal of Modern African Studies* 20, no. 3 (September 1982).

Larkin, Tim. *When Violence Is the Answer: Learning How to Do What It Takes When Your Life Is at Stake*. New York: Little, Brown, 2017.

Levey, Zach. "Israel's Exit from Africa, 1973: The Road to Diplomatic Isolation." *British Journal of Middle Eastern Studies* 35, no. 2 (August 2008).

Levitt, Matthew. *Hezbollah: The Global Footprint of Lebanon's Party of God*. London: Hurst, 2013.

Lews, Bernard. *The Assassins: A Radical Sect in Islam*. New York: Basic Books, 2002.

Loimeier, Roman. "Nigeria: The Quest for a Viable Religious Option." In *Political Islam in West Africa*, edited by William F. S. Miles. Boulder, CO: Lynne Rienner, 2007.

Lombard, Maurice. *The Golden Age of Islam*. Princeton, NJ: Markus Wiener, 2009.

Lubeck, Paul M. "Islamic Protest under Semi-industrial Capitalism: 'Yan Tatsine Explained." *Africa: Journal of the International African Institute* 55, no. 4 (1985).

Madueke, Kingsley L., and Floris F. Vermeulen. "Frontiers of Ethnic Brutality in an African City: Explaining the Spread and Recurrence of Violent Conflict in Jos, Nigeria." *Africa Spectrum* 53, no. 2 (2018).

Magrin, Géraud, and Marc-Antoine Pérouse de Montclos, eds. *Crisis and Development: The Lake Chad Region and Boko Haram*. AFD, July 2018, https://www.afd.fr/en/ressources /crisis-and-development-lake-chad-region-and-boko-haram.

Maiwa, B. *Northern Minorities and Hausa Political Hegemony*. Kaduna: Barka Press, 1996.

Makinde, A. K. "The Institution of Shari'ah in Oyo and Osun States, Nigeria, 1890–2005." PhD thesis, University of Ibadan, 2007.

Makinde, D. O. "Potentialities of the Egúngún Festival as a Tool for Tourism Development in Ogbomoso, Nigeria." *WIT Transactions on Ecology and the Environment* 148 (2011).

Malumfashi, Lawal Yusuf. "The Spread and Development of Islamic Civilisation in Northern Nigeria: Case Study of Katsina State." *International Journal of Business, Economics and Law* 9, no. 5 (April 2016).

Mantzikos, Ioannis. "Boko Haram Attacks in Nigeria and Neighbouring Countries: A Chronology of Attacks." *Perspective on Terrorism* 8, no. 6 (2014).Maskaliunaite, Asta. "Exploring the Theories of Radicalization." *International Studies Interdisciplinary Political and Cultural Journal* 17, no. 1 (2015).

Mayall, Simon. "Jihad and the Clash within Civilisation." *Seaford House Papers*, 2003.

Mbiti, John S. *African Religions, and Philosophy*. Nairobi: East African Educational Publishers, 1969.

Mbiti, John. "The Heritage of Traditional Religions." In *Kenya Churches Handbook: The Development of Kenyan Christianity, 1498–1973*, edited by David B. Barrett, George K. Mambo, Janice McLaughlin, and Malcolm J. McVeigh. Kisumu: Evangel Publishing House, 1973.

McCauley, John F. *The Logic of Ethnic and Religious Conflict in Africa*. Cambridge: Cambridge University Press, 2017.

McGlinchey, Eric. *Chaos, Violence, Dynasty: Politics and Islam in Central Asia*. Pittsburgh: University of Pittsburgh Press, 2011.

McGregor, Andrew. "The Mysterious Death in Custody of Boko Haram Leader Habib Bama." *Terrorism Monitor* 10, no. 13 (2012).

McGuire, Meredith. *Religion: The Social Context.* Belmont, CA: Wadsworth, 1992.

McHugo, John. *A Concise History of Sunnis and Shi'is.* Washington, DC: Georgetown University Press, 2018.

Means, Gordon. *Political Islam in Southeast Asia.* Boulder, CO: Lynne Rienner, 2009.

Mendelsohn, Barak. *The al-Qaeda Franchise: The Expansion of al-Qaeda and Its Consequences.* Oxford: Oxford University Press, 2016.

Milligan, Maren. "Nigerian Echoes of the Israeli-Palestinian Conflict." *ISIM Review* 21, no. 1 (spring 2008).

Milton-Edwards, Beverley, and Stephen Farrell. *Hamas: The Islamic Resistance Movement.* Cambridge: Polity, 2010.

Mohammed, Kyari. "Boko Haram Insurgency in Nigeria: An Impact Assessment." *NARC Digest, Journal of the Nigerian Army Resource Centre* 1, no. 1 (November 2018).

Mohammed, Kyari. "The Message and Methods of Boko Haram." In *Boko Haram: Islamism, Politics, Security and the State in Nigeria*, edited by Marc-Antoine Pérouse de Montclos. Leiden: African Studies Centre, 2014.

Montclos, Marc-Antoine Pérouse de. *Boko Haram: Islamism, Politics, Security and the State in Nigeria.* West African Politics and Society Series. Leiden: African Studies Centre, 2014.

Morgan, Kenneth W., ed. *Islam, the Straight Path: Islam Interpreted by Muslims.* New York: Ronald Press, 1958.

Msuya, Norah Hashim. "Traditional 'Juju Oath' and Human Trafficking in Nigeria: A Human Rights Perspective." *De Jure Law Journal* 52, no. 1 (2019).

Mustapha, Abdul Raufu, and Mukhtar Bunza. "Contemporary Islamic Sect and Groups in Northern Nigeria." In *Sect and Social Disorder: Muslim Identities and Conflict.* London: James Curry, 2014.

Nafziger, E. Wayne. *Inequality in Africa: Political Elites, Proletariat, Peasants and the Poor.* Cambridge: Cambridge University Press, 1988.

Nakash, Yitzhak. *Reaching for Power: The Shi'a in the Modern Arab World.* Princeton, NJ: Princeton University Press, 2007.

Ndubuisi, Christopher. "A Critical Analysis of Conflicts between Herdsmen and Farmers in Nigeria: Causes and Socio-religious and Political Effects on National Development." *HTS Theological Studies* 74, no. 1 (2018). https://www.ajol.info/index.php/hts/article/viewFile/177998/167368.

Neumann, Peter, ed. *Perspectives on Radicalization and Political Violence.* London: International Centre for the Study of Radicalization and Political Violence, 2008.

Neumann, Peter. *Preventing Violent Radicalization in America.* National Security Preparedness Group, Bipartisan Policy Center. https://bipartisanpolicy.org/download/?file=/wp-content/uploads/2019/03/NSPG_0.pdf.

Nielsen, Jørgen. *Christian-Muslim Frontier: Chaos, Clash, or Dialogue?* London: I. B. Tauris, 1998.

Nmah, Patrick. "Spiritual Dimension of Land Identity Crisis in Igboland of Nigeria: An Ethical Reflection." *Unizik Journal of Arts and Humanities* 12, no. 2 (2011).

Nmah, Patrick, and Uchenna Amanambu, "1804 Usman dan Fodio's Jihad on Inter-Group Relations in the Contemporary Nigerian State." *International Journal of Religion and Human Relations* 9, no 1 (June, 2017).

Nuqe, Dnein. "Boko Haram and Its Impact on the Nigerian Economy." *African Business Journal*, June 14, 2017.

Nwabueze, Ben. *Military Rule and Social Justice in Nigeria*. Ibadan: Spectrum, 1993.

Nwaka, Jacinta Chiamaka. "The Early Missionary Groups and the Contest for Igboland: A Reappraisal of Their Evangelization Strategies." *Missiology: An International Review* 40, no. 4 (October 2012).

Nwankpa, Michael. "The Political Economy of Securitization: The Case of Boko Haram, Nigeria," *The Economics for Peace and Security Journal* 10, no. 1 (April 2015).

Nwonwu, Francis, and Dirk Kotze, eds. *African Political Elites: The Search for Democracy and Good Governance*. Oxford: African Books Collective, 2008.

Obadare, Ebenezer. "The Muslim Response to the Pentecostal Surge in Nigeria: The Rise of Charismatic Islam." *Journal of Religious and Political Practice* 2, no. 1 (2016).

Obadare, Ebenezer. "Pentecostal Presidency? The Lagos-Ibadan 'Theocratic Class' and the Muslim 'Other.'" *Review of African Political Economy* 33, no. 110 (2006).

Obadare, Ebenezer. *Pentecostal Republic: Religion and the Struggle for State Power in Nigeria*. London: Zed, 2018.

Obasanjo, Olusegun. *My Command: An Account of the Nigerian Civil War, 1967–1970*. Ibadan: Heinemann, 1981.

Ogbondah, Chris Wolumati, and Pita Ogaba Agbese. "Terrorists and Social Media Messages: A Critical Analysis of Boko Haram's Messages and Messaging Techniques." *The Palgrave Handbook of Media and Communication Research in Africa*. October 24, 2017. https://www.ncbi.nlm.nih.gov/pmc/articles/PMC7121539/.

Ojo, Matthews. "The Contextual Significance of the Charismatic Movement in Independent Nigeria." *Africa* 58, no. 2 (1988).

Ojo, Matthews. "Deeper Christian Life Ministry: A Case Study of Charismatic Movement in Western Nigeria." *Journal of Religion in Africa* 18, no. 2 (1988).

Ojo, Matthews. *The End-Time Army: Charismatic Movements in Modern Nigeria*. Trenton, NJ: Africa World Press, 2006.

Okky, Feliantia. "Terrorism on the Web: The Danger of Self-Radicalisation." May 25, 2013. http://khabarsoutheastasia.com/en_GB/articles/apwi/articles/features/2013/05/25/feature-02.

Okoh, George. "Osinbajo: I Am Ready to Quit If Buhari Is Complicit in Benue Killings." *This Day*, May 17, 2018.

Olaniyan, Richard. *The Amalgamation and Its Enemies: An Interpretive History of Modern Nigeria*. Ile-Ife: Obafemi Awolowo Press, 2003.

Olatunbosun, Dupe. "Western Nigerian Farm Settlement: An Appraisal." *Journal of Developing Areas* 5, no. 3 (April 1971).

O'Leary, Stephen D., and Geln S. McGhee. *War in Heaven/Heaven on Earth: Theories of the Apocalyptic*. Oxford: Routledge, 2014.

Olomojobi, Yinka. *Frontiers of Jihad: Radical Islam in Africa*. Lagos: Safari, 2015.

Olomola, Isola. "Contradictions in Yoruba Folk Beliefs Concerning Post-life Existence: The Ado Example." *Journal des Africanistes* 58, no. 1 (1988).

Olupona, Jacob K. *African Religions: A Very Short Introduction*. Oxford: Oxford University Press, 2014.

Olupona, Jacob K. *African Spirituality: Forms, Meanings, and Expressions.* New York: Herder and Herder, 2001.

Olupona, Jacob K. *City of 201 Gods: Ilé-Ifè in Time, Space, and the Imagination.* Berkeley: University of California Press, 2011.

Olupona, Jacob K. "15 Facts of African Religions." *Interfaith Observer*, November 14, 2017. http://www.theinterfaithobserver.org/journal-articles/2017/10/30/15-facts-on-african-religions.

Olupona, Jacob K. "The Study of Yoruba Religious Tradition in Historical Perspective." *Numen* 40, no. 3 (September 1993).

Olupona, Jacob K., and T. Falola, eds. *Religion and Society in Nigeria: Historical and Sociological Perspectives.* Ibadan: Spectrum, 1991.

Olusanya, G., and Akindele, R. "The Fundamentals of Nigeria's Foreign Policy and External Economic Relations." In *Nigeria's External Relations: The First Twenty-Five Years.* Ibadan: University of Ibadan Press, 1986.

Oluwadare, Abiodun Joseph. "Boko Haram Terrorism in the Lake Chad Basin Region: Implications for Subregional Security." *Journal of International and Global Studies* 8, no. 1 (2016).Omenka, Nicholas Ibeawuchi. "Blaming the Gods: Christian Religious Propaganda in the Nigerian-Biafran War." *Journal of African History* 51, no. 3 (2010).

Omenm, Tochukwu. "Untold Story of Boko Haram Insurgency: The Lake Chad Oil and Gas Connection." *Politics and Religion* 13, no. 1 (March 2020).

Omolesky, Matthew. "Dwelling in the Fire: Boko Haram's War against the West." *American Spectator*, May 2014.

Omotoye, Rotimi Williams. "A Critical Examination of the Activities of Pentecostal Churches in National Development in Nigeria." CESNUR, n.d. https://www.cesnur.org/2010/omotoye.htm.

Onaiyekan, John. "After the Christmas Massacre, Terrorism Comes from Afar." *In the Church and in the House: International Monthly Magazine*, no. 12 (2011).

Onuoha, Freedom. "Boko Haram: Nigeria's Extremist Islamic Sect." Al Jazeera Centre for Studies, February 2009.

Onuoha, Freedom. "Boko Haram and the Evolving Salafi Jihadist Threat in Nigeria." In *Boko Haram: Islamism, Politics, Security and the State in Nigeria*, edited by Marc-Antoine Pérouse de Montclos. West African Politics and Society Series. Leiden: African Studies Centre, 2014.

Onuoha, F. *A Danger Not to Nigeria Alone: Boko Haram's Transnational Reach and Regional Responses.* Abuja: Friedrich Ebert-Staftung, 2014.

Opejobi, Seun. "Advise Your Members against Teachings of Apostle Johnson Suleman—Group Begs Mbaka, TB Joshua." *Daily Post*, January 31, 2017.

Opeloye, Muhib. "Religious Factor in Nigerian Politics: Implications for Christian-Muslim Relations in Nigeria." *Institute of Muslim Minority Affairs Journal* 10, no. 2 (1989).

Opeloye, Muhib. "The Yoruba Muslims' Cultural Identity." *Ilorin Journal of Religious Studies* 1, no. 2 (2011).

Osaghae, Eghosa. *Crippled Giant: Nigeria since Independence.* London: Hurst, 1998.

Osaghae, Eghosa. *Structural Adjustment and Ethnicity in Nigeria*. Research Report No. 98. Uppsala: Scandinavian Institute of African Studies, 1995.

Osaghae, Eghosa E., and Rotimi T. Suberu. *A History of Identities, Violence, and Stability in Nigeria*. Centre for Research on Inequality, Human Security and Ethnicity (CRISE) Working Paper no. 6. Queen Elizabeth House, Oxford University, January 2005.

Osakwe, Chukwuma. "The Arab Spring and Its Implications for Nigerian National Security." *Journal of Politics and Law* 7, no. 1 (2014): 27–28.

Osaman, Sulastri. "Jemaah Islamiyah: Of Kin and Kind." *Journal of Current Southeast Asian Affairs* 29, no. 2 (2010).

Otite, Onigu. *Ethnic Pluralism and Ethnicity in Nigeria*. Ibadan: Shaneson, 1990.

Owele, Festus. "Class of 1999 Governors: Where Are They Now?" In *Nigeria: 20 Years of Patchy Democracy: Reflections, Lessons, Opportunities*. Premium Times Special, June 2019, 33.

Oyediran, Oyeleye, ed. *Nigerian Government and Politics under Military Rule, 1966–79*. Lagos: Macmillan, 1979.

Oyeyipo, Shola, Segun James, and Jameelah Sanda. "The Politics That Shaped the Chibok Girls." *This Day*, April 18, 2016.

Oyovbaire, Sam Egite. "The Atlantic Ocean, Ghadaffi, Maitatsine and Rice: On Security and Nigeria's African Policy." *Nigeria Journal of International Studies* 4, nos. 1–2 (1980).

Paden, John. *Faith and Politics in Nigeria: Nigeria as a Pivotal State in the Muslim World*. Washington, DC: USIP, 2008.

Paden, John. *Muhammadu Buhari: The Challenge of Leadership in Nigeria*. Zaria, Huda: Hada, 2016.

Pargament, Kenneth. *The Psychology of Religion and Coping: Theory, Research, Practice*. New York: Guilford, 1997.

Parray, Tauseef Ahmad. "The Legal Methodology of 'Fiqh al-Aqalliyyat' and Its Critics: An Analytical Study." *Journal of Muslim Minority Affairs* 32, no. 1 (2012).

Parrinder, E. G. "Islam and West African Indigenous Religion." *Numen* 6, no. 2 (December 1959).

Pham, J. Peter. "Boko Haram's Evolving Threat." *African Security Review* 20 (April 2012).

Post, Jerrold M. "Terrorist Psycho-Logic: Terrorist Behavior as a Product of Psychological Forces." In *Origins of Terrorism: Psychologies, Ideologies, Theologies, States of Mind*, edited by Walter Reich. Washington, DC: Woodrow Wilson Center Press, 1998.

Pratt, Douglas. *The Challenge of Islam: Encounters in Interfaith Dialogue*. Aldershot, UK: Ashgate, 2005.

Quadri, Yasir. "All in the Name of God." Lecture, University of Ilorin, May 23, 2013.

Ramakrishna, Kumar. "'Counter-Ideological' Work in Singapore: A Preliminary Assessment." *Journal of Policing, Intelligence and Counter Terrorism* 4, no. 2 (2009).

Ranstorp, Magnus. *Understanding Violent Radicalisation: Terrorist and Jihadist Movements in Europe*. London: Routledge, 2009.

Rapoport, David. "Fear and Trembling: Terrorism in Three Religious Traditions." *American Political Science Review* 78, no. 3 (1984).

Rock, Jason. "The Funding of Boko Haram and Nigeria's Actions to Stop It." Thesis, Naval Postgraduate School, Monterey, CA.

Rufai, Saheed Ahmed. "A Foreign Faith in a Christian Domain: The Historical Development of Islam among the Igbos of Southern Nigeria." *Journal of Muslim Minority Affairs* 32, no. 3 (2012).

Sabet, Amr G. E. *Islam and the Political: Theory, Governance and International Relations.* London: Pluto, 2008.

Sabila, George. *A History of Arabic Astronomy: Planetary Theories during the Golden Age of Islam.* New York: New York University Press, 1995.

Salvatore, Armando. *The Sociology of Islam: Knowledge, Power and Civility.* Chichester, UK: John Wiley, 2016.

Schleifer, Ron. "Psychological Operations: A New Variation on an Age-Old Art: Hezbollah versus Israel." *Studies in Conflict and Terrorism* 29, no. 1 (January 2006).

Seul, Jeffrey R. "'Ours Is the Way of God': Religion, Identity and Intergroup Conflict." *Journal of Peace Research* 36, no. 5 (1999).

Sharp, Andrew M. *Orthodox Christians and Islam in the Postmodern Age.* Leiden: Brill, 2012.

Sinai, Joshua. "New Trends in Terrorism Studies: Strengths and Weaknesses." In *Mapping Terrorism Research: State of the Art, Gaps and Future Direction*, edited by Magnus Ranstorp. London: Routledge, 2007.

Singer, Peter. *Children at War.* Berkeley: University of California Press, 2006.

Smith, Jane I. *Muslims, Christians, and the Challenge of Interfaith Dialogue.* New York: Oxford University Press, 2007.

Smith, M. J. *Boko Haram: Inside Nigeria's Unholy War.* London: I. B. Tauris, 2016.

Solahudin. *The Roots of Terrorism in Indonesia: From Darul Islam to Jema'ah Islamiyah.* Translated by Dave McRae. Ithaca, NY: Cornell University Press, 2013.

Soniyi, Tobi, Segun James, and Shola Oyeyipo. "Insecurity, the New Normal." *This Day*, January 8, 2018.

Southern, R. W. *Western Views of Islam in the Middle Ages.* Cambridge, MA: Harvard University Press, 1980.

Stern, Jessica. *Terror in the Name of God: Why Religious Militants Kill.* New York: HarperCollins, 2004.

Straubhaar, Thomas. "An Economic Analysis of Religion and Religious Violence." *Trans-Atlantic Academy*, June 2015.

Stremlau, John. *The International Politics of the Nigerian Civil War, 1967–1970.* Princeton, NJ: Princeton University Press, 1977.

Tamuno, Tekena. *Peace and Violence in Nigeria: Conflict-Resolution in Society and the State.* Panel on Nigeria since Independence History Project. Ibadan: University of Ibadan Secretariat, 1991.

Taya, Shamsuddin, L. "The Political Strategies of the Moro Islamic Liberation Front for Self-Determination in the Philippines." *Intellectual Discourse* 15, no. 1 (2007).

Tchioffo, Kodjo. *Mali Conflict of 2012–2013: A Critical Assessment: Patterns of Local, Regional and Global Conflict and Resolution Dynamics in Post-colonial and Post–Cold War Africa.* Sunnyvale, CA: Lambert, 2015.

Thomas, David, ed. *The History of Christian-Muslim Relations.* Leiden: Brill, 2013.

Thomas, Douglas E. *African Traditional Religion in the Modern World.* Jefferson, NC: McFarland, 2015.

Thurston, Alexander. *Boko Haram: The History of an African Jihadist Movement*. Princeton, NJ: Princeton University Press, 2017.

Thurston, Alexander. "Nigeria's Mainstream Salafis between Boko Haram and the State." *Islamic Africa* 6, nos. 1–2 (2015). Toki, Tajudeen, Muhammad Gambari, and Muhammad Hadi. "Peace Building and Interreligious Dialogue in Nigeria." *Journal of Islam in Nigeria* 1, no. 1 (June 2015).

Tomasini, Matteo. "The Salafi Jihadist Threat in Lebanon." *Al Nakhlah: The Fletcher School Online Journal for Issues Related to Southwest Asia and Islamic Civilization*, spring 2010.

Ugarte, Eduardo, and Mark Macdonald Turner. "What Is the 'Abu Sayyaf'? How Labels Shape Reality." *Pacific Review* 24, no. 4 (2011).

Uhia, Oga Tom. "Boko Haram: The Military, Big Cash Cow." *Power Steering*, June 2018.

Umar, Muhammad S. *Islam and Colonialism: Intellectual Responses of Muslims of Northern Nigeria to British Colonial Rule*. Leiden: Koninklijke Brill NV, 2006.

Umaru, Thaddeus B. *Christian-Muslim Dialogue in Northern Nigeria: A Socio-political and Theological Consideration*. Bloomington, IN: Xlibris, 2013.

Usman, Mohammed. "Religion and Violence in Nigeria: 1980–2012." *Bangladesh e-Journal of Sociology* 10, no. 2 (July 2013).

Utibe, Titus, Fadeyi Taofiq, and Aminu Idris. "Political Economy of Insurgency in Nigeria: An Analysis of the Boko Haram Sects in the Northeast." *Research in Humanities and Social Sciences* 7, no. 11 (2017).

Uzoma, Rose C. "Religious Pluralism, Cultural Differences and Social Stability in Nigeria." *Brigham Young University Law Review*, no. 2 (summer 2004).

Vaughan, Olufemi. *Religion and the Making of Nigeria*. Durham, NC: Duke University Press, 2016.

Venter, Al. *Al-Qaeda in the Islamic Maghreb: Shadow of Terror over the Sahel, from 2007*. Barnsley, UK: Pen and Sword, 2018.

Washington, George. Letter to Edward Newenham, October 20, 1792. Washington Library, Center for Digital History. https://www.mountvernon.org/library/digitalhistory/quotes/search/?query=religion.

Weimann, Gunnar. *Islamic Criminal Law in Northern Nigeria: Politics, Religion, Judicial Practice*. Amsterdam: Amsterdam University Press, 2010.

Wheatcroft, Andrew. *Infidels: A History of the Conflict between Christendom and Islam*. New York: Random House, 2004.

Wright-Neville, David. *Dictionary of Terrorism*. Cambridge: Polity, 2010.

Yesufu, Momoh Lawani. "The Impact of Religion on a Secular State: The Nigerian Experience." *Studia Historiae Ecclesiasticae* (Pretoria) 42, no. 1 (2016).

Yinger, Milton. *The Scientific Study of Religion*. New York: Macmillan, 1970.

Zenn, Jacob. "Boko Haram's International Connections." *CTC Sentinel* 6, no. 1 (January 2013).

Zenn, Jacob. "The Islamic Movement and Iranian Intelligence Activities in Nigeria." *CTC Sentinel* 6, no. 10 (October 2013).

Bamidele, Adebayo, 96

banking, 178, 198

Baptist, 31, 35, 70, 86

Baptist High School Iwo, 70

Barra, Muhammad Abu, 125

Bauchi, 24, 33, 54, 62, 63, 79, 89, 118, 124, 129, 131, 133, 165, 199, 201, 202, 253n2, 254n48, 258n38

Bayero, Abdullahi, 29

Bayero, Ado, Emir of Kano, 123

Bayero University, 68, 252n8

b. el-Gore, Muhammad (Belgore), 26

Bello, Abubakar, 52

Bello, Ahmadu (Sultan of Sokoto), 29, 40, 154–55, 208–10, 240n38

Belmokhta, Moktar, 218

Benin City, 30

Benin: Boko Haram and, 128, 218; MNJTF and, 140, 219–21

Berger, Peter, 190

Berridge, Baroness, 180

Biafra, 90, 155, 175

Bible, 9–10, 21, 58, 71, 112; handling of, 50; Pentecostalism and, 34, 36

bin Laden, Osama, 7, 133–34, 216–17

Birni Gazagamo, 23

Bodejo, Alhaji, 176

Bohoma, 322

Boko Haram, 2, 16–17, 46, 49, 94, 113, 119–20, 129–30, 150–51, 170, 215, 223–24, 227–28, 253n14; activities, 133–37; Ahlu Sunnah and, 67; Akhwat Akwop and, 87–91, 93; Al-Qaeda and, 216; AQIM and, 216–17; Ansaru and, 145–46; birth of, 115–17; Buhari administration and, 168–69, 180; Christian-Muslim tensions and, 41; church bombings and, 80–82, 86; corruption and, 204–5; economics and, 189–200, 202–3, 205–6; elites and, 232; Fulani herdsmen and, 178; funding, 130–33, 230, 244n33; global intervention and, 208; Hausa Fulani members, 146; IEDs and, 127–28; ISIS and, 218; ISWAP and, 146–47, 227, 252n3; jihad and, 7; Jonathan administration and, 167; kidnapping, 127; Maitatsine and, 252n4; MNJTF and, 219–22; MUJAO and, 217–18; MURIC and, 75; Nigerian military response to, 140–44, 229, 236–37; Nigerian state's response to, 137–39; opposition to Muslims working in govern-

ment, 123; Oyedepo and, 83–84; recruitment, 124, 193–94; scholarship and, 237–38; structure, 125–26; suicide missions, 126–27; Western education and, 47, 121; Yar'Adua and, 166. *See also* Chibok girls; Dapchi girls; mines; Nigerian Taliban; Shekau, Abubakar; Yusuf, Mohammed

Boniface, Holy, 81, 182

Bonnke, Reinhard, 57

Borghom, 162

Bori Religion, 21

Borno, 89; Boko Haram in, 123–24, 128–29, 138, 140, 147, 178, 196–97, 199–202; Christianity and, 32; elections in, 150; Islam and, 23; terrorism in, 90

Borno State College of Legal and Islamic Studies, 119, 125

Bosnia, 7

Bring Back Our Girls campaign, 136, 167–68

British colonial rule, 26–28, 159, 175. *See also* colonialism; imperialism

Brooke, Graham, 33

Buba, Adamu, 182

Buba, Timothy, 164

Buhari, Muhammadu, 156, 163–64, 175–77, 184–85, 203, 213–14, 220–21, 234–35; administration of, 84, 87, 99, 136, 140, 142, 157, 168–70, 173, 178–81, 185, 187, 211, 231, 234; Fayose and, 85; Shi'ites and, 170–71

Bulumkutu, 48

Buratai, Lt. General Tukur Yusuf, 140, 142, 144, 196, 213, 219

Burkina Faso, 132

Calvary Bible Church, 235

Calvary Church, Idimu, 96

Cambridge University, 33

Cameroon: Boko Haram and, 126, 128–29, 132, 139, 142, 144, 192, 200, 202–3, 218–19; Kanuri language and, 124; Marwa and, 46–47, 209; MNJTF and, 220–21

capitalism, 49, 121, 123

Carlo de Genova, Father, 32

Cathedral Church of All Saints, Makurdi, 95

Cathedral Church of St Paul's Anglican Church, Oleh, 185

Catholic Church, 5, 9, 31–34

Celestial Church of Christ, 34

Chad, 142, 192, 200, 220–21; Boko Haram and, 126, 128, 218–19, 222; Kanuri language and, 124; Libyan troops in, 209. *See also* Lake Chad basin; Multinational Joint Task Force (MNJTF)

Chechnya, 7

Cherubim and Seraphim Church, 34

Chi, 21

Chibok girls, 2, 126–7, 136, 139, 148, 167–70, 219, 223

Child Right and Rehabilitation Network, 98

children, 168, 193, 198; Area Boys, 103, 250n5; captive, 221; education and, 121; Muslim, 27, 38, 154; Oro festival and, 104; Pentecostal churches and, 36; as targets of violence, 4, 16, 82, 92, 96, 143; Sharia and custody of, 39; as suicide bombers, 126; witchcraft and, 78, 96–99, 232

Chineke, 21

Christ Apostolic Church (CAC), 34, 95

Christ Chapel International, 36

Christ Embassy Church, 36

Christian Association of Nigeria (CAN), 39, 107, 168, 174, 182–84, 187, 229; Boko Haram and, 86, 143–44; Kano branch, 57

Christian Crusaders, 5

Christian Elders' Consultative Forum, 165

Christianity, 19, 22; arrival in Nigeria of, 30–33, 37, 42–43, 50; Boko Haram and, 129; colonialism and, 41, 43; conversion of Muslims to, 27, 38, 52, 57–58, 154; elections and, 9; evangelism and, 50, 120 (*see also* evangelization); indigenization of, 34; Islam and, 46, 75, 184, 208, 224, 226; Oyedepo on, 84; Pentecostal, 34, 36–37; traditional religions and, 101–2, 105–8; universities and, 68; violence and, 14–16, 76, 78, 83, 91, 94, 98–99, 101, 110, 112–13, 232 (*see also* Akhwat Akwop; Suleman, Johnson). *See also* radicalization: Christian

Christians: Bello and, 209; Boko Haram and, 120, 144, 146–47, 180; Buhari administration and, 179, 181, 187; Christian Association of Nigeria and, 183–84; colonialism and, 27, 49; Fulani herdsmen and, 172, 178, 182; Hausa Fulani, 162; indigenization and, 34; intrareligious disagreements among, 129; Islamization of, 88; Israel and, 211; Kano and, 55; media and, 72; MURIC and, 75; Muslims and, 49–50, 52, 56–57, 64, 67–69, 71, 224, 226, 228–31, 236; new, 31; non-adoption clause and, 39; Odeyepo and, 84, 179; Pentecostal, 35–36; politics and, 155–56, 160; Shi'ites and, 74; traditional religion practitioners and, 106–8; violence and, 16, 77–80, 82–83, 85–87, 92–94, 96, 98–99, 110 (*see also* Akhwat Akwop; Suleman, Johnson); Yoruba, 30, 179; Yusuf on, 120

Chukwu, 21

Chukwuma, Archbishop Emmanuel, 182

Church Missionary Society, 31, 35, 180

Church of Christ in Nigeria, 129, 165

Church of God Mission, 36

Church of the Lord, 34

civil war, 11–12, 115, 155, 180, 240n39, 257n7, 264n47

Civilian Joint Task Force (JTF), 81, 126, 128, 138, 142, 145

Clapperton, Hugh, 25

Cole, Reverend M. S., 37

Colonial Office London, 1, 28

colonialism, 11, 26–27, 40–43, 46, 49, 75, 105, 231. *See also* imperialism

Committee on Dialogue and Peaceful Resolution on Security Challenges in the North, 138

Concerned Citizens of Kano, 93

constitution (Nigerian), 38–39, 43, 121, 123, 130; Sharia and, 72, 139, 156–57

Constitution Drafting Committee, 156

Cook, David, 129,

corruption, 13, 47, 60, 150, 161, 204, 229, 244n20, 257n28; in arms procurement, 203; Buhari administration and, 168; Shagari administration and, 191; Special Anti-robbery Squad (SARS) and, 233

coups, 11–12, 155–56, 180, 240n38, 257n17

COVID-19 pandemic, 233; relief, 235, 237; supplies, 236

Cross River State, 96, 157

Crowther, Samuel Ajayi, 31–33, 38

Da'wah, 58, 125, 241n10, 245n37, 254n37

Da'wah Coordination Council of Nigeria, 125, 254n37

Dabalemi, Dunama, 22

Daesh, 146, 218, 223

Daley-Oladele, Favour, 111

Ijebu, 24, 31, 33
Ikirun, 24
Ilesanmi, Simeon, 39–41
Ilorin, 25, 26, 64, 65, 235
imperialism, 65; British, 27; Western, 6
improvised explosive devices (IEDs), 127–28, 139, 197–98, 222. *See also* mines
independence (Nigerian), 5, 12, 16–17, 38, 105, 150, 208, 224, 226, 231
indigenous religions, 20–21, 24, 26, 30, 41, 108, 110
Inisa, 66, 245n61
Institute for Economics and Peace, 174, 239n2, 259n61
Intercontinental Bank, 132
Inter-Governmental Action Group Against Money Laundering, 230
intergroup relations, 9, 11–12, 17, 43, 45, 80, 84, 90, 108, 160, 168, 226, 231; Fulani Jihad and, 260n85; herdsmen issue and, 173; in the Middle Belt, 179; MURIC and, 186; politics of, 102, 151; postindependence, 187; violence and, 112, 153–54, 230
internally displaced persons (IDPs), 194–95, 200, 205, 220
International Crisis Group, 149, 216, 254n34, 264n34
Iorapuu, Father Moses, 179
Ipokia, 107
Iran, 88, 224, 232; elections in, 9; El-Zakzaky and, 72, 212–13; Muslim Brothers and, 61; Shi'ites and, 60, 214, 227. *See also* Islamic Movement of Nigeria (IMN); Khomeini, Ayatollah
Iranian revolution (1978–1979), 46, 49, 72, 210, 212–13
Iraq, 3, 186, 214, 222; ISIS and, 148, 215; US activities in, 51, 56. *See also* Islamic State in Iraq and the Levant (ISIL)
Ishaku, Dairus, 174
Islam, 16, 19, 22–25, 30, 52, 65–67, 224, 240n28, 245n41; British colonialism and, 27–28; Christianity and, 42–43, 57–58; Christian violence and, 79, 83; conversion to, 154–55, 209; Fulani herdsmen and, 176, 178; in Hausaland, 21; political, 5–6; radical, 7, 49, 58, 70, 117, 210, 217; revivalist, 239n17; rivalry with Christianity, 208, 226; Sunni, 118; traditional religions and, 32, 37, 106, 108, 110, 112, 232; unity in, 64; violence and, 8–9, 14–15, 41, 43, 45–46, 75, 78,

98; Wahabi strain of, 55; Western education and, 47; in Yorubaland, 25–26. *See also* Islamic sects; Sharia; Shi'ites; Sunnis
Islamic Movement of Nigeria (IMN), 60–61, 71–75, 212–13, 245n46. *See also* El-Zakzaky; Muslim Brothers
Islamic movements, 46, 65–66
Islamic revival, 6–7, 49, 210, 239n17
Islamic sects, 28, 45–46, 62–63. *See also* Qadriyya; Tijaniyya
Islamic State in Iraq and Syria (ISIS/Daesh), 128, 146–48, 150, 185–86, 215, 218, 223, 229, 232. *See also* Al-Baghdadi; Abu Bakr
Islamic State in Iraq and the Levant (ISIL), 146, 214
Islamic State West Africa Province (ISWAP), 136–37, 143–50, 186, 194, 218, 227, 229–30, 252n3. *See also* Boko Haram
Islamization, 24–25, 61, 121, 157, 180, 182; Bello's policies of, 40; Fulanization and, 231; in Kano, 23
Israel, 208–12; Islamic Movement of Nigeria (IMN) and, 73; Palestinians and, 51, 70; Sunnis and, 133
Itauma, Sam, 98
Iwo, 24, 38, 58, 70, 107, 245n40, 251n27
Iyalawo, 22
Izala (Jamācat Izālatil Bidca wa Iqāmatus Sunnah), 58–59, 75, 165; Lawan and, 125; Yusuf and, 118, 122

Ja'afar, Abu, 91
Ja'amatu Tajidmul Islamia (Movement of Islamic revival), 6, 61
Jackson, General Mike, 223
jahanama, 67
jahiliyya, 50, 61, 73
Jamā 'at Ahl al-Sunna li-Da'wa wa-l-Jihād. *See* Boko Haram
Jama'atu Ansarul Muslimina fi Biladi Sudan, 91, 92, 249n38
Jama'atul Ansaru Muslimina fi Biladis Sudan (Vanguard for the Protection of Muslims in Black Africa), 145
Jama'atu Nasil Islam (JNI), 58, 62–63, 74, 161, 183–84, 229
Jama'tu Ahlis Sunna Lidda'awati wal-Jihad (JAS), 148–49. *See also* Boko Haram; Islamic State West Africa Province (ISWAP)

Printed in the USA
CPSIA information can be obtained
at www.ICGtesting.com
LVHW081007120124
768765LV00002B/42

9 781478 018162